Peterson's GRE®/GMAT® Math Review

7th Edition

PETERSON'S
Publishing

About Peterson's Publishing

To succeed on your lifelong educational journey, you will need accurate, dependable, and practical tools and resources. That is why Peterson's is everywhere education happens. Because whenever and however you need education content delivered, you can rely on Peterson's to provide the information, know-how, and guidance to help you reach your goals. Tools to match the right students with the right school. It's here. Personalized resources and expert guidance. It's here. Comprehensive and dependable education content—delivered whenever and however you need it. It's all here.

For more information, contact Peterson's Publishing, 2000 Lenox Drive, Lawrenceville, NJ 08648; 800-338-3282 Ext. 54229; or find us online at www.petersonspublishing.com.

Bernadette Webster, Director of Publishing; Mark D. Snider, Editor; Ray Golaszewski, Publishing Operations Manager; Linda M. Williams, Composition Manager; An American BookWorks Corporation Project: Contributing Writers: Joan Marie Rosebush, Mark Allen McCombs

ISBN-13: 978-0-7689-3431-1
ISBN-10: 0-7689-3431-1

Printed in the United States of America

10 9 8 7 6 5 4 3 2 1   13 12 11

Seventh Edition

By printing this book on recycled paper (40% post-consumer waste) 63 trees were saved.

Petersonspublishing.com/publishingupdates

Check out our Web site at www.petersonspublishing.com/publishingupdates to see if there is any new information regarding the test and any revisions or corrections to the content of this book. We've made sure the information in this book is accurate and up-to-date; however, the test format or content may have changed since the time of publication.

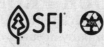

OTHER RECOMMENDED TITLES

Peterson's Master the GRE®

Peterson's Master the GMAT®

Contents

Contents

PART III: THREE MATH PRACTICE TESTS

SPECIAL ADVERTISING SECTION

Preface

Beginning in August 2011, the Quantitative Reasoning section of the GRE will include a number of new math question types. *Peterson's GRE®/GMAT® Math Review* explains these new question types and provides a variety of ways to help you solve the GRE® revised General Test math problems and improve your math skills in general.

After June 2012, the GMAT will also be going through some changes, but as of now there are no changes to the Quantitative section of the test. Therefore, our review of the GMAT question types is accurate for both the current and Next Generation GMAT® exams.

Both GRE and GMAT Quantitative sections are designed to assess your basic mathematical skills and understanding of elementary mathematical concepts, as well as your ability to reason quantitatively using mathematical models and graphic data to represent real-world problems. By reviewing each section of *Peterson's GRE/GMAT Math Review*, you will come that much closer to scoring high on your exam.

PART I provides an introduction to the question types in the GRE and the GMAT exams. Review these question types first before moving on to the next four chapters.

PART II contains four chapters, each dedicated to a different quantitative topic: arithmetic, algebra, geometry, and data interpretation. The first part of each chapter contains essential math review of the relevant chapter topic with exercises and answer explanations. At the end of each chapter there are practice tests that include examples of math questions set up with directions like those you would encounter on the actual exams.

After studying these chapters, you can take the three math practice tests in **PART III** that cover quantitative questions from both the GRE and the GMAT. At the back of the practice tests, you will find detailed explanations to help you check your work and review your answers. These tests will help you strengthen your math skills and prepare for the real exams.

Please note that although Peterson's does its best to conform to actual GRE and GMAT exam formats, there are limits to what can be demonstrated on paper. You may notice slight differences in question presentation if you are taking the computer-based exams. However, rest assured that all question types and content are accurate and up-to-date.

As you make your way through this guide, pay special attention to boxed information, which includes *important notes* and warnings about potential mistakes that you should *be careful* not to make. The boxes are there to help you focus on important tips that will help you reach your goal of a high score on the GRE or GMAT exam.

At the end of this book, don't miss the special section of ads placed by Peterson's preferred clients. Their financial support helps make it possible for Peterson's Publishing to continue to provide you with the highest-quality test-prep, educational exploration, and career-preparation resources you need to succeed on your educational journey.

And don't forget to join the GRE and GMAT conversation on Facebook® at www.facebook.com/petersons publishing and receive additional test-prep advice. Peterson's resources are available to help you do your best on these important exams—and others in your future.

At Peterson's we publish a full line of books—test prep, career preparation, financial aid, and education exploration. Peterson's publications can be found at high school guidance offices, college libraries and career centers, and your local bookstore and library. Peterson's books are now also available as eBooks.

We welcome any comments or suggestions you may have about this publication. Your feedback will help us make educational dreams possible for you—and others like you.

GRE and GMAT Quantitative Section Basics

CHAPTER 1

Introduction to Quantitative Questions on the GRE and GMAT

This book is specifically designed to familiarize you with the exact format and style of each of the Quantitative Reasoning question types found on the GRE and GMAT. Each chapter will help you master the mathematical concepts and skills needed to be successful on these tests. More importantly, each chapter also includes a comprehensive collection of examples, practice problems, and practice tests based on actual GRE and GMAT test questions. Every question is accompanied by a step-by-step explanation of both the correct answer and the most effective problem-solving strategies to employ.

A WORD ABOUT GRE QUESTIONS

As of August 1, 2011, there are important new changes to the GRE test. There is increased maneuverability and functionality in the computer-based version. Test-takers can now edit and change their work, and even skip questions within a section to return to before timing out of that section. In other words, the GRE revised General Test is not so computer adaptive, and thus, more closely resembles a paper test in which you can go back and forth within sections and "erase" and change answers. However, the Quantitative Reasoning section is section-level adaptive, that is, the questions for the second Quantitative reasoning and Verbal Reasoning sections are based on how well you perform on the first sections of questions.

GRE Answer Option Differences

All multiple-choice questions in the GRE computer-based test will have answer options preceded by either blank ovals or blank squares depending on the question type. You will use your mouse to select one or more of these options. The paper-and-pencil test will follow the same format of answer choices, but use letters instead of ovals or squares for answer choices.

For your convenience in answering questions and checking answers in this book, we use (A), (B), (C), etc. By using letters with parentheses, you will find it easy to check your answers against the answer key and explanation sections.

Numeric entry questions need to be typed in using a keyboard and mouse in the computer-based test. For this guide and the paper-and-pencil exam, you will have to handwrite all of your answers.

The GRE Calculator

Those taking the computer version of the GRE will have an on-screen calculator to use. It will allow you to add, subtract, multiply, divide, and find square roots. Those taking the paper-and-pencil test outside the United States will be given a calculator at the test site. Don't bring your own because you won't be allowed to use it.

The GRE On-Screen Calculator

The GRE revised General Test provides you with an on-screen calculator. You may use the calculator at any point during the Quantitative Reasoning sections, but you may find it particularly useful with the numeric entry questions. Before we talk about how you may use the calculator, let's discuss when you should and should not use it.

In general, you *should use* the on-screen calculator if you need to perform difficult calculations. However, most calculations on the GRE are not that complicated, so most of the time you will not need the calculator. In particular, you *should not use* it in the following cases:

- when the required calculations are simple to perform mentally or on scratch paper.
- when you need to give the answer as a fraction rather than a decimal (either in numeric entry questions or in multiple-choice ones).
- when estimating will suffice (for instance, in certain quantitative comparison or data interpretation questions).

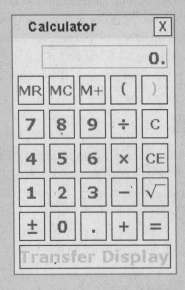

The following are a few notes on using the calculator. Learn them before test day to relieve some of the stress you may experience on that day.

- Unlike some other calculators, this one follows the order of operations. So, for instance, if you type in sequence "1", "+", "3", "×", "5", "=" the GRE calculator will yield "16" as the answer because it will perform the multiplication of 3 by 5 first and then add 1 to the result. If, however, you need to compute $(1+3)\times 5$ instead, then you must type the following sequence: "(", "1", "+", "3", ")", "×", "5", "=". Alternatively, you may type "1", "+", "3", "=", "×", "5", "=". However, it is easy to make mistakes if you try to perform a lengthy combination of operations as a single sequence on the calculator. It may be better to perform each individual computation on its own, use your scratch paper to note intermediate results, and then perform new computations on these results. In the above example, calculate $1+3$ first, note the result ("4") on your scratch paper, clear the calculator display by pressing the "C" button, and finally calculate 4×5.

IMPORTANT NOTE: You are NOT allowed to bring in or use a calculator on the Quantitative section of the GMAT exam.

QUANTITATIVE QUESTION TYPES

GRE Quantitative Reasoning Question Types

The GRE Quantitative Reasoning test has four types of questions:

- Multiple-Choice Questions—Select One Answer Choice
- Multiple-Choice Questions—Select One or More Answer Choices
- Quantitative Comparison Questions
- Numeric Entry Questions

The official GRE Web site (http://www.ets.org/gre) states the following:

"Each question appears either independently as a discrete question or as part of a set of questions called a *Data Interpretation set*. All of the questions in a Data Interpretation set are based on the same data presented in tables, graphs, or other displays of data. You are allowed to use a basic calculator on the GRE Quantitative Reasoning measure. For the computer-based test, the calculator is provided on-screen. For the paper-based test, a hand-held calculator is provided at the test center."

GMAT Quantitative Reasoning Question Types

The GMAT Quantitative Reasoning test has two types of multiple-choice questions:

- Problem Solving Questions
- Data Sufficiency Questions

The official GMAT Web site (http://www.mba.com/mba/thegmat) states the following:

"*Problem-Solving* questions are designed to test basic mathematical skills, understanding of elementary mathematical concepts, and the ability to reason quantitatively and solve quantitative problems.

Data-Sufficiency questions are designed to measure your ability to analyze a quantitative problem, recognize which information is relevant, and determine at what point there is sufficient information to solve a problem."

GRE and GMAT Sample Questions

The following sample questions illustrate the format and style of each type of Quantitative Reasoning question found on the GRE and GMAT.

GRE Multiple-Choice Questions—Select One Answer Choice

This type of question requires you to select the best single answer choice from a list of 5 possible answers.

BE CAREFUL: Many of the incorrect choices correspond to the most common mistakes made when working through the given problem.

---

1. Find the 11th term in the sequence $\dfrac{15625}{3}, \dfrac{6250}{3}, \dfrac{2500}{3}, \dfrac{1000}{3}, \ldots$

   (A) $\dfrac{2048}{9375}$

   (B) $\dfrac{1024}{1875}$

   (C) $\dfrac{512}{375}$

   (D) $\dfrac{635}{3}$

   (E) $\dfrac{2048}{3}$

This question tests your ability to recognize a *geometric sequence*. Note that we can determine the common ratio of consecutive terms of the given sequence by calculating $\left(\dfrac{6250}{3}\right) \div \left(\dfrac{15625}{3}\right) = \left(\dfrac{6250}{3}\right)\left(\dfrac{3}{15625}\right) = \dfrac{2}{5}$. We can now use the fact that the 11th term in a geometric sequence with common ratio $\dfrac{2}{5}$ and 1st term $\dfrac{15625}{3}$ is given by the formula:

$$11\text{th term} = (\text{first term})(\text{common ratio})^{10} = \left(\dfrac{15625}{3}\right)\left(\dfrac{2}{5}\right)^{10} = \dfrac{(5)^6(1024)}{(3)(5)^{10}} = \dfrac{1024}{(3)(5)^4} = \dfrac{1024}{1875}.$$

The correct answer is (B).

GRE Multiple-Choice Questions—Select One or More Answer Choices

This type of question requires you to select *all applicable answer choices* from a list of 3 to 8 possible answers. This means that it is possible for more than one of the answer choices to be correct.

2. Let $x \,\boxed{\Omega}\, y$ be defined to mean $\dfrac{x^2 - 7x + 10}{y^3 + 1}$. If $x \,\boxed{\Omega}\, y = 0$, then $x =$
   (A) -2
   (B) 2
   (C) -5
   (D) 5
   (E) -10 or 10

This question is an example of a *strange function* problem. In this type of problem, you will always be given a description of a specific rule for combining two or more values. The rule is typically denoted by a symbol that you haven't seen used before. In this problem, the symbol $\boxed{\Omega}$ represents a rule to combine a given pair of values. In particular, $x \boxed{\Omega} y$ tells us to combine the first value, x, with the second value, y, by using the formula $\dfrac{x^2 - 7x + 10}{y^3 + 1}$.

For example, if $x = 1$ and $y = 3$, we have $1 \boxed{\Omega} 3 = \dfrac{(1)^2 - 7(1) + 10}{(3)^3 + 1} = \dfrac{1 - 7 + 10}{27 + 1} = \dfrac{4}{28} = \dfrac{1}{7}$.

Similarly, if $x = 3$ and $y = 1$, we have $3 \boxed{\Omega} 1 = \dfrac{(3)^2 - 7(3) + 10}{(1)^3 + 1} = \dfrac{9 - 21 + 10}{1 + 1} = \dfrac{-2}{2} = -1$.

In order to answer the given question, we must determine which numerical value(s) of x will solve the equation $x \boxed{\Omega} y = 0$.

Note that $x \boxed{\Omega} y = 0$ requires that $\dfrac{x^2 - 7x + 10}{y^3 + 1} = 0$. In order to solve this equation for x, we need to remember that the only way a fraction can possibly equal zero is if the numerator equals zero. This means we have the equation $x^2 - 7x + 10 = 0$. We can solve this equation by using factoring techniques as follows.

$$x^2 - 7x + 10 = 0$$
$$(x - 2)(x - 5) = 0$$
$$x = 2, x = 5$$

Therefore, $x = 2$ and $x = 5$ yield the result $x \boxed{\Omega} y = 0$. **The correct answers are (B) and (D).**

GRE Quantitative Comparison Questions

This type of question describes 2 different quantities and requires you to use basic mathematical concepts to compare the relative sizes of the quantities being described.

Directions: For Question 3, compare Quantity A and Quantity B, using additional information centered above the two quantities if such information is given, and select one of the following four answer choices:

    (A) Quantity A is greater.

    (B) Quantity B is greater.

    (C) The two quantities are equal.

    (D) The relationship cannot be determined from the information given.

A symbol that appears more than once in a question has the same meaning throughout the question.

Given the line with equation $8x - 11y + 3 = 0$

3.

Quantity A	Quantity B
The slope of a line that is parallel to the given line	The slope of a line that is perpendicular to the given line

    (A) Quantity A is greater.

    (B) Quantity B is greater.

    (C) The two quantities are equal.

    (D) The relationship cannot be determined from the information given.

This question tests your knowledge of linear equations and slopes. Note that the given linear equation can be rewritten into "slope y-intercept form" as follows.

$$8x - 11y + 3 = 0$$
$$-11y = -8x - 3$$
$$y = \frac{-8}{-11}x - \frac{3}{-11}$$
$$y = \frac{8}{11}x + \frac{3}{11}$$

Thus, the given line has a slope equal to $\frac{8}{11}$. This means that every line parallel to this line must also have slope equal to $\frac{8}{11}$. On the other hand, every line that is perpendicular to the given line must have slope $-\frac{11}{8}$. Since $\frac{8}{11} > -\frac{11}{8}$, Quantity A is greater. **The correct answer is (A).**

GRE Numeric Entry Questions

This type of question is basically a multiple-choice question without any answer choices. You must solve the problem and then enter your numerical answer according to the given instructions.

Directions: For Question 4, enter your answer as an integer or as a decimal if there is a single answer box OR as a fraction if there are two separate boxes—one for the numerator and one for the denominator.

To enter an integer or a decimal, write the number in the answer box provided. On the computer-based test you can either type the number in the answer box using the keyboard or use the Transfer Display button on the calculator. Also, note the following directions for the computer-based test:

- You can click on the answer box and then type the number. You can use the backspace key to erase a number.
- Type a hyphen for a negative sign. Type a hyphen again, and it will disappear. For a decimal point, type a period.
- The Transfer Display button on the calculator will move the calculator display to the answer box.
- Equivalent forms of the correct answer, such as 2.5 and 2.50, are all correct.
- Enter the exact answer unless the question asks you to round your answer.

4. When both drainpipes are open, a water tank empties in 45 minutes. If only the first pipe is open, the tank drains in 60 minutes. How many hours will it take for the tank to drain if only the second pipe is open?

 hours

This question is an example of a "work" algebraic word problem. Perhaps the most efficient solution strategy is to assign variables to the important quantities in the problem. Ultimately, we need to determine the time it takes for the second drainpipe working alone to empty the tank. So let's use the variable x to represent the number of hours needed for the second pipe to drain the tank. The given information tells us that the first pipe has a drain time of 1 hour (i.e.,

60 minutes). We are also told the combined drain time for both pipes working together is 0.75 hour (i.e., 45 minutes). We can use a table to help us organize all of this information as follows.

	Drain time (hours)	Drain rate
Pipe 1	1	$\dfrac{1 \text{ tank}}{1 \text{ hour}}$
Pipe 2	x	$\dfrac{1 \text{ tank}}{x \text{ hours}}$
Pipe 1 + Pipe 2	0.75	$\dfrac{1 \text{ tank}}{0.75 \text{ hours}}$

If we add the individual drain rates for Pipe 1 and Pipe 2, we get the combined drain rate. So we have the equation $\dfrac{1}{1} + \dfrac{1}{x} = \dfrac{1}{0.75}$. We now need to solve this equation for x.

$$\frac{1}{1} + \frac{1}{x} = \frac{1}{0.75}$$
$$\frac{x+1}{x} = \frac{1}{0.75}$$
$$(0.75)(x+1) = (1)(x)$$
$$0.75x + 0.75 = x$$
$$0.75 = x - 0.75x$$
$$0.75 = 0.25x$$
$$\frac{0.75}{0.25} = x$$
$$3 = x$$

Therefore, we conclude that it will take 3 hours for Pipe 2 to drain the tank by itself. **The correct answer is 3 hours.**

GMAT Problem-Solving Questions

This type of question requires you to select the best single answer choice from a list of 5 possible answers.

GMAT PROBLEM-SOLVING QUESTIONS

Please note the following for GMAT Problem-Solving questions:

Numbers: All numbers used are real numbers.

Figures: A figure accompanying a Problem Solving question is intended to provide information useful in solving the problem. Figures are drawn as accurately as possible EXCEPT when it is stated in a specific problem that its figure is not drawn to scale. Straight lines may sometimes appear jagged. All figures lie on a plane unless otherwise indicated.

Directions: For Question 5, solve the problem and indicate the best of the answer choices given.

5. Roger has a pair of dice. Each die has 6 sides, numbered 1 through 6. One die is "rigged" so that it always lands on 3. On the other die, each side is equally likely to occur. If the dice are rolled together, what is the probability that the roll will produce a sum of 8 or more?

(A) $\dfrac{2}{3}$

(B) $\dfrac{1}{6}$

(C) $\dfrac{5}{6}$

(D) $\dfrac{1}{2}$

(E) $\dfrac{1}{3}$

This question tests your knowledge of basic probability concepts. Note that the desired outcome requires a roll such that the two numbers displayed yield a sum that is greater than or equal to 8. We are told that one die will always land on 3. Thus, since the other die is equally likely to land on any of its six sides, the possible sums are $3 + 1, 3 + 2, 3 + 3, 3 + 4, 3 + 5,$ and $3 + 6$. Of these six possibilities, only the last two yield a sum that is greater than or equal to 8. Therefore, the desired outcome

has probability given by $\dfrac{\text{total number of desired outcomes possible}}{\text{total number of outcomes possible}} = \dfrac{2}{6} = \dfrac{1}{3}$. **The correct answer is (E).**

GMAT Data Sufficiency Questions

This type of question requires you to determine whether you have enough given information to answer a specific question being posed by the problem. The given information will be in the form of two separate statements. You must decide between the following scenarios:

(i) *exactly one* of the statements *alone* is enough to answer the question

(ii) *both* statements *together* are *required* to answer the question

(iii) the statements *neither alone nor together* are enough to answer the question

---

GMAT DATA SUFFICIENCY QUESTIONS

Please note the following for GMAT Data Sufficiency questions:

Numbers: All numbers used are real numbers.

Figures: A figure accompanying a Data Sufficiency problem will conform to the information given in the question, but will not necessarily conform to the additional information in statements (1) and (2). Lines shown as straight can be assumed to be straight and lines that appear jagged can also be assumed to be straight. You may assume that positions of points, angles, regions, etc., exist in the order shown and that angle measures are greater than zero. All figures lie in a plane unless otherwise indicated.

Note: In Data Sufficiency problems that ask you for the value of a quantity, the data given in the statements are sufficient only when it is possible to determine exactly one numerical value for the quantity.

Directions: Question 6 consists of a question and two statements, labeled (1) and (2), in which certain data is given. You have to decide whether the data given in the statements is sufficient for answering the question. Using the data given in the statements plus your knowledge of mathematics and everyday facts (such as the number of days in July and the meaning of "counterclockwise"), you must indicate whether

(A) Statement (1) ALONE is sufficient, but statement (2) is not sufficient.

(B) Statement (2) ALONE is sufficient, but statement (1) is not sufficient.

(C) BOTH statements TOGETHER are sufficient, but NEITHER statement ALONE is sufficient.

(D) EACH statement ALONE is sufficient.

(E) Statements (1) and (2) TOGETHER are NOT sufficient.

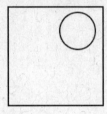

6. A point is selected at random from the interior of the square shown in the diagram above. What is the probability that the point is also within the interior of the circle?

(1) The perimeter of the square is 80.
(2) The circumference of the circle is 10.

(A) Statement (1) ALONE is sufficient, but statement (2) is not sufficient.

(B) Statement (2) ALONE is sufficient, but statement (1) is not sufficient.

(C) BOTH statements TOGETHER are sufficient, but NEITHER statement ALONE is sufficient.

(D) EACH statement ALONE is sufficient.

(E) Statements (1) and (2) TOGETHER are NOT sufficient.

This question tests your knowledge of the concept of geometric probability. In order to determine the probability of a randomly selected point being inside the circle, we must compare the area of the circle to the area of the square. Specifically, we need to determine the value of the ratio given by $\dfrac{\text{circle area}}{\text{square area}}$.

Calculating the area of the circle requires that we know the circle's radius. Similarly, calculating the area of the square requires that we know the square's side length. If statement (1) is true, we can determine the square's side length since the perimeter is four times the side length. Thus, given that the perimeter = 80, we conclude that the side length must = 20. However, statement (1) does not enable us to determine a specific value for the circle's radius. The most we can say is that the radius must be less than 10, or else the circle wouldn't fit inside the square. Therefore, statement (1) ALONE is not sufficient.

If statement (2) is true, we can determine the circle's radius since the circumference is given by the formula: circumference $= 2\pi(\text{radius})$. Thus, given that the circumference = 10, we conclude that the radius must $= \dfrac{10}{2\pi} = \dfrac{5}{\pi}$. However, statement (2) does not enable us to determine a specific value for the square's side length. The most we can say is that the side length must be greater than $\dfrac{10}{\pi}$, or else the circle wouldn't fit inside the square. Therefore, statement (2) ALONE is not sufficient. We can now see that if we know BOTH statements TOGETHER are true, then we have enough information to determine the exact value of the desired probability. **The correct answer is (C).**

PART II

GRE and GMAT Quantitative Review

CHAPTER 2

Arithmetic Review

The arithmetic questions on the GRE and GMAT are designed to test your knowledge of the following basic concepts:

- Basic properties of numbers

- The real number line

- Decimal place values and operations

- Simplifying and combining fractions

- Factors, multiples, and divisibility

- Prime numbers and prime factorization

- Percent, fractions, and decimals

- Ratios and proportions

- Basic properties of sets

- Arithmetic word problems involving proportion, percent, and percent of change

The arithmetic problems on the GRE and GMAT can be placed in two different categories. The first category consists of *operations and numerical skills problems*. In these problems, you are asked to work with numbers of various types, such as integers, fractions, decimals, percents, and ratios. These problems will not ask you to simply perform computations. You will be asked to deal with concepts such as properties and types of integers, divisibility, factorization, prime numbers, remainders and odd and even integers, arithmetic operations, exponents and radicals, and concepts such as estimation, percent, ratio, rate, absolute value, the number line, decimal representation, and sequences of numbers.

The second category consists of *arithmetic word problems*. In these problems, you will need to be able to work with percents, proportions, and fractions.

In the first part of this chapter, we are going to take a look at all of the definitions and properties of numbers and operations that you will need to know for the operations and numerical skills problems. While you may already be familiar with much of what is in this chapter, you should refresh your memory by reading all of the definitions and properties. After this, we will show you how to solve GRE- and GMAT-type questions that use these definitions and properties.

We will then discuss effective strategies for solving the types of arithmetic word problems that frequently occur on the GRE and GMAT.

NUMBERS AND OPERATIONS

Let's begin by taking a look at the following multiple-choice question.

1. If x is a positive integer, with $x > 1$, which of the following correctly lists the numbers x, x^2, x^3, and $\dfrac{1}{x}$ in order from smallest to largest?

(A) $x, x^2, x^3, \dfrac{1}{x}$

(B) $\dfrac{1}{x}, x, x^2, x^3$

(C) $x^3, x^2, x, \dfrac{1}{x}$

(D) $\dfrac{1}{x}, x^3, x^2, x$

(E) The order cannot be determined.

In order to answer this question, the first thing you need to know is what a positive integer is. You may recall that positive integers are simply the counting numbers, that is, 1, 2, 3, 4, 5, 6, and so on. Also, recall that the symbol ">" means greater than, so that we are being told that x is a positive integer greater than 1.

Recall also that x^2 is simply a shorthand notation for $x \times x$. Similarly, x^3 denotes $x \times x \times x$. Knowing this, we can begin to put the four quantities in order. First of all, since $x > 1$, x^2 is bigger than x, and x^3 is bigger than x^2. Therefore, we know that x, x^2, and x^3 occur in that order from smallest to biggest.

Consider next the number $\dfrac{1}{x}$. Since $x > 1$, the number $\dfrac{1}{x}$ is less than 1. Thus, the correct order, from smallest to biggest, is $\dfrac{1}{x}, x, x^2, x^3$, and therefore the correct answer is choice (B). One way to illustrate this explanation is to try a specific x value bigger than 1. For example, for x equal to 2, we have $\dfrac{1}{x} = \dfrac{1}{2}$, $x = 2$, $x^2 = 4$, $x^3 = 8$. **The correct answer is (B).**

Let's consider a slightly different version of this problem.

2. If $0 < x < 1$, which of the following correctly lists the numbers x, x^2, x^3, and $\dfrac{1}{x}$ in order from smallest to largest?

(A) $x, x^2, x^3, \dfrac{1}{x}$

(B) $\dfrac{1}{x}, x, x^2, x^3$

(C) $x^3, x^2, x, \dfrac{1}{x}$

(D) $\dfrac{1}{x}, x^3, x^2, x$

(E) The order cannot be determined.

Note that the only difference between problem 1 and problem 2 is the fact that x represents a different kind of number in each problem. In this second problem, we are told that $0 < x < 1$. The statement $0 < x < 1$ means that x is a number between 0 and 1. Let's consider sizes.

To begin, note that in this case, $x^2 < x$, when you multiply a number that is between 0 and 1 by itself, it gets smaller. For example, note that $\frac{1}{2} \times \frac{1}{2} = \frac{1}{4}$. The number x^3 is smaller still. Therefore, we know that x^2, x, and x^3 occur in order from smallest to biggest.

Consider next the number $\frac{1}{x}$. Since $0 < x < 1$, the denominator (the number on the bottom) of this fraction is smaller than the numerator (the number on top). Therefore, the value of the fraction $\frac{1}{x}$ is greater than 1, which makes it greater than x, x^2, and x^3. Another way to think about this is to notice that if we divide each term in the expression $0 < x < 1$ by x, we have $\frac{0}{x} < \frac{x}{x} < \frac{1}{x}$, which means that $0 < 1 < \frac{1}{x}$. Thus, the correct order, from smallest to biggest, is $x^3, x^2, x, \frac{1}{x}$. **The correct answer is (C).**

Let's consider one more, very similar, version of this problem.

3. If x is a positive real number, which of the following correctly lists the numbers x, x^2, x^3, and $\frac{1}{x}$ in order from smallest to largest?

   (A) $x, x^2, x^3, \frac{1}{x}$

   (B) $\frac{1}{x}, x, x^2, x^3$

   (C) $x^3, x^2, x, \frac{1}{x}$

   (D) $\frac{1}{x}, x^3, x^2, x$

   (E) The order cannot be determined.

Begin by noticing that the only difference between this problem and the others is that we are now told that x is a positive *real* number. Does this make a difference? It certainly does. The real numbers include all of the integers, but also all of the fractions, as well as all of the irrational numbers. Therefore, x could possibly be 2, in which case the correct order would be $\frac{1}{x}, x, x^2, x^3$. Also, however, x could possibly be $\frac{1}{2}$, in which case the order would be $x^3, x^2, x, \frac{1}{x}$. Since either of these values for x is possible, we really cannot be certain as to the correct order. Thus, for this third problem, the order is unknown.

The correct answer is (E).

You can see that being able to determine the correct answers to the three questions above hinges on knowing what is meant by the words "integer" and "real number." In the same way, on other GRE and GMAT questions, you will need to know what is meant by words like "prime," "divisible," "least common multiple," and "factor." You will also need to know how to do different things with specific sets of numbers. The following pages contain definitions and examples of these and other important words. In addition, there are problems for you to try that use these terms.

Equality and Inequality Symbols

Equality and inequality symbols are used on the GRE and GMAT as a way of telling you when certain numbers are equal to, not equal to, larger than, or smaller than other numbers. You are certainly already familiar with the equal sign. If a test question, for example, tells you that "$a = 7$," you know that a is equal to 7. In the same way, if you see the statement "$a \neq 7$," you know that a may be any number *except* 7.

The symbol "$<$" means "less than," and the statement "$b < 9$" tells you that the value of b is less than 9. The symbol "$>$" means "greater than," so "$c > 12$" tells you that c is bigger than 12.

There are also symbols that combine these inequality symbols with the equal sign. The statement "$d \geq 5$" tells you that d is either equal to 5 or larger. In the same way, the notation "$e \leq 21$" tells you that e is either equal to 21 or smaller.

Finally, as we have seen above, the notation "$2 < f < 6$" tells you that f lies somewhere between 2 and 6. Since the statement $2 < f < 6$ uses the symbol "$<$", the value of f lies somewhere between 2 and 6, but cannot be 2 or 6. In the statement $2 \leq f \leq 6$, the value of f lies between 2 or 6 but could be 2 or 6. Similarly, the statement $2 \leq f < 6$ tells us that f lies between 2 and 6, and that f could be 2 but can't be 6.

Frequently, GRE and GMAT problems use equality or inequality signs to indicate the possible values of quantities. Pay very careful attention to all equality or inequality statements. As we saw in the problems above, the same question could have two different answers depending upon whether the value of a quantity, for example, is between 0 and 1 or is larger than 1.

Positive and Negative Numbers

Recall that numbers that have a negative sign in front of them are called *negative numbers*. For example, numbers such as $-27, -435.42,$ and $-\frac{5}{9}$ are negative numbers. Non-zero numbers that are preceded by a plus sign, or are preceded by no sign at all, are called *positive numbers*. The numbers $+19.85, 457,$ and $\frac{5}{9}$ are positive. Note that the number 0 is neither positive nor negative.

The notation "$g > 0$" is a shorthand way of telling you that g represents a positive number. Similarly, the notation "$h < 0$" is a shorthand way of saying that h is negative. The statement $i \geq 0$ tells you that i is *non-negative*. In other words, i is either 0 or positive, Similarly, $j \leq 0$ tells you that j is either negative or 0.

Set of Integers

The numbers ..., $-5, -4, -3, -2, -1, 0, 1, 2, 3, 4, 5,$ ... comprise the *set of integers*. As you can see, integers are whole numbers and can be positive, negative, or 0.

Note that every integer consists of a certain number of *digits*. For example, the integer 12,345 is known as a 5-digit integer. The "ones," or "units," digit is 5, the "tens" digit is 4, the "hundreds" digit is 3, the "thousands" digit is 2, and the "ten thousands" digit is 1. Another way of expressing this is to say:

$$12{,}345 = \underbrace{1 \times 10{,}000}_{ten\ thousands} + \underbrace{2 \times 1000}_{thousands} + \underbrace{3 \times 100}_{hundreds} + \underbrace{4 \times 10}_{tens} + \underbrace{5 \times 1}_{ones}$$

Even and Odd Integers

The *even integers* are the numbers ..., $-8, -6, -4, -2, 0, 2, 4, 6, 8,$ ... while the *odd integers* are the integers ..., $-7, -5, -3, -1, 1, 3, 5, 7, ...$

Even and odd integers can be either positive, negative, or 0. Sometimes, it will be useful to think about odd and even integers in this way: even integers can be evenly divided by 2, and odd integers cannot. That is, when you divide an even integer by 2 there is no remainder, but when an odd integer is divided by 2, there will be a remainder of 1. This means that 0 is an even integer since it is divisible by 2.

There is a common type of GRE and GMAT question that asks you to combine even and odd integers using arithmetic operations and to determine whether the result will be even or odd. In order to help you answer these questions, it is useful to be familiar with the rules given below for adding, subtracting, and multiplying even and odd integers.

Addition of Odd and Even Integers

Even + Even = Even

Odd + Odd = Even

Odd + Even = Odd

Subtraction of Odd and Even Integers

Even − Even = Even

Odd − Odd = Even

Odd − Even = Odd

Even − Odd = Odd

Multiplication of Odd and Even Integers

Even × Even = Even

Odd × Odd = Odd

Even × Odd = Even

You can check that all of these properties are true by trying them with actual odd and even integers. Also note that if you multiply more than two integers together, the product will be even if one or more of the integers are even. The only way that the product of a group of integers can be odd is if every single one of the integers is odd.

Consecutive Integers

Consecutive integers are integers that differ by 1. For example, the integers 5, 6, 7, 8, 9, and 10 are consecutive integers. Sometimes, GRE and GMAT word problems refer to *consecutive even integers*, which are integers such as 6, 8, 10, 12, and 14. A group of *consecutive odd integers* would be 17, 19, 21, 23, and 25. Thus, consecutive even integers differ by 2, as do consecutive odd integers.

Multiples and Factors

The *multiples* of an integer are numbers that are obtained by multiplying that integer by other integers. For example, some of the multiples of 6 are 12, 18, 24, and 30, since 12 = 6 × 2, 18 = 6 × 3, 24 = 6 × 4, and 30 = 6 × 5. A *factor* of a given integer is a number that divides evenly into that integer. For example, the factors of 12 are 1, 2, 3, 4, 6, and 12, since these numbers divide evenly into 12.

There are two other terms that sometimes appear on the GRE and GMAT. The first is the *least common multiple* of two integers. As the name implies, the least common multiple of two integers is the smallest number that is a multiple of both of the integers. For example, the least common multiple of 10 and 15 is 30. One way to determine the least common multiple of two integers is to make a list of the multiples of each, and look for the smallest number that occurs on both lists. For example, in the case of 10, the multiples would be 10, 20, 30, 40, 50, etc. For 15, we would have 15, 30, 45, 60, etc. We can see that the least common multiple is 30.

The other term is the *greatest common factor,* also known as the *greatest common divisor*, of two integers. As this name implies, the greatest common factor of two integers is the largest number that divides evenly into both. For example, what would be the greatest common factor of 36 and 48? Note that 6 divides evenly into both numbers, but so does 12, and no integer bigger than 12 divides evenly into both 36 and 48. Therefore, in this case, the greatest common factor is 12.

Divisibility

Note that the integer 5 can be divided evenly into the integer 35. As we have seen, in this situation we can say that 35 *is divisible by* 5. A number is divisible by a second number if dividing the first by the second yields a remainder of 0.

One way to tell whether a particular integer is divisible by another is to simply perform the division and see if there is a remainder (i.e., a decimal part) or not. For example, you could determine that 687 is not divisible by 7 since when you divide 687 by 7, you get 98.1428. The decimal part 0.1428 indicates that dividing 687 by 7 yields a non-zero remainder.

In addition to testing divisibility, there are certain so-called *divisibility tests* that can be used to tell whether one number is divisible by another without actually doing the division. These divisibility tests are useful to know, as they will help you in certain problems that do not lend themselves to calculator use.

The following table summarizes the divisibility tests that you should know, and it gives some examples.

Integer	Divisibility Test	Examples
2	An integer is divisible by 2 if its ones digit is even.	The integers 6,542 and −6,458 are divisible by 2 because their ones digits are even.
3	An integer is divisible by 3 if the sum of its digits is divisible by 3.	The integer 5,916 is divisible by 3 since $5 + 9 + 1 + 6 = 21$, and 21 is divisible by 3.
4	An integer is divisible by 4 if its last two digits form an integer that is divisible by 4.	The integer 321,512 is divisible by 4 since 12 is divisible by 4.
5	An integer is divisible by 5 if its last digit is either 5 or 0.	The integers 1,765 and 6,570 are divisible by 5. The first integer ends in 5 and the second integer ends in 0.
6	An integer is divisible by 6 if it is divisible by both 2 and 3, in other words, if it is even and the sum of its digits is divisible by 3.	The integer 8,094 is divisible by 6 since it is even and the sum of its digits is 21, which is divisible by 3.
9	An integer is divisible by 9 if the sum of its digits is divisible by 9.	The integer 6,831 is divisible by 9 since the sum of its digits is $6 + 8 + 3 + 1 = 18$, which is divisible by 9.
10	An integer is divisible by 10 if its last digit is 0.	The integer 546,500 is divisible by 10 since its last digit is 0.
100	An integer is divisible by 100 if its last two digits are both 0.	The integer 534,400 is divisible by 100 since its last two digits are 0.

Prime Numbers

A *prime number* is a positive integer that is greater than 1 and is only divisible by itself and by 1. For example, 17 is prime since its only divisors are 1 and 17. On the other hand, the number 14 is not prime, since, in addition to 1 and 14, it has divisors 2 and 7. Note that, by definition, the number 1 is not considered to be a prime number. Thus, the smallest prime number is 2. Moreover, 2 *is the only even prime number*.

GRE and GMAT questions involving prime numbers are fairly common. For this reason, it is worthwhile for you know the first ten or so prime numbers. The first ten prime numbers are: 2, 3, 5, 7, 11, 13, 17, 19, 23, and 29.

Prime Factorization

Any integer that is not prime can be written as a product of prime numbers in one and only one way. This product is known as the *prime factorization* of the integer. In order to factor an integer into primes, we take the integer and write it as a product of two smaller integers. If either or both of these smaller integers is not prime, write it as a product of smaller integers. Keep going until there are only prime numbers in the product. Note that sometimes you will have a choice as to how to factor a number. For example, if you are trying to factor 30 into primes, you can begin by writing $30 = 2 \times 15$ or $30 = 5 \times 6$. Regardless of the choices that you make, you will always end up with the same prime factorization.

Suppose we began by writing $30 = 2 \times 15$. The factor 2 is prime, but 15 is not. Therefore, we must break 15 down into $15 = 3 \times 5$. Thus, the prime factorization of 30 is $2 \times 3 \times 5$. We say that 30 has three distinct prime factors: 2, 3, and 5.

Consider the prime factorization of 48. Note that $48 = 6 \times 8$. The integer 6 can be further broken down into 2×3, while 8 can be broken down into $2 \times 2 \times 2$. Thus, the prime factorization of 48 is $2 \times 2 \times 2 \times 2 \times 3$; i.e., $48 = 2^4 \times 3$. The number 48 has two distinct prime factors, 2 and 3. The factor 2 appears four times, and the factor 3 appears only once.

Rational, Irrational, and Real Numbers

We have already defined several sets of numbers, including the integers, the positive integers, and the negative integers. Several other types of numbers are used on the GRE and GMAT.

A number is called a *rational* number if it can be written in the form $\frac{a}{b}$, where a and b are integers and b is not equal to 0.

Note that all integers are rational numbers since, for example, the integer 7 can be written in the form $\frac{7}{1}$. In addition, all fractions, such as $\frac{2}{3}$, $-\frac{5}{8}$, $\frac{19}{3}$, are rational numbers. Decimals and percents are rational numbers as well. For example, $50\% = \frac{1}{2}$, and $0.3 = \frac{3}{10}$.

Numbers that are not rational are called *irrational numbers*. The most common irrational numbers that you will see on the GRE and GMAT are square roots, such as $\sqrt{5}$ or $-\sqrt{17}$, and the number that is represented by the Greek letter π, which we will discuss in Chapter 4: Geometry Review.

When the sets of rational numbers and irrational numbers are combined, we obtain a set of numbers called the *real numbers*. All numbers that appear on the GRE and GMAT are real numbers.

Unless the problem specifies otherwise, remember that an arbitrary number is not necessarily an integer. It might be a fraction, a decimal, a square root, or any other type of real number. If a problem speaks of a "number between 4 and 6," do not make the mistake of concluding that the number must be 5. It might be $4\frac{2}{3}$, 5.3, $\sqrt{21}$, or any other number between 4 and 6.

Sets of Numbers

In mathematics, a *set* is a collection of objects. The objects in a particular set are called the *members,* or the *elements,* of the set. Sets are typically represented by capital letters, and their members are written within braces, "{" and "}". For example, we indicate that set A contains the members 2, 4, and 6 by writing $A = \{2, 4, 6\}$.

A set that has an infinite number of elements can be indicated by writing dots within the braces. For example, the set of negative integers can be indicated by writing $\{-1, -2, -3, -4, -5....\}$, and the set of positive even integers can be written as $\{2, 4, 6, 8, 10, ...\}$. A set that has no members at all, called the *empty set*, can be indicated by writing { }, or using the symbol $\varnothing$.

The *union* of two sets A and B is the set of all elements that are in either A or B. The union of A and B is indicated in the following way: $A \cup B$. For example, if $A = \{2, 4, 6, 8\}$ and $B = \{3, 6, 9, 12\}$, then $A \cup B = \{2, 3, 4, 6, 8, 9, 12\}$. Note that if an element, such as 6, is in both sets A and B, it does not have to be written twice when forming the union.

The *intersection* of two sets A and B is the set of all elements that are in both A and B. The intersection of A and B is indicated in the following way: $A \cap B$. For example, if $A = \{2, 4, 6, 8\}$ and $B = \{3, 6, 9, 12\}$, then $A \cap B = \{6\}$. If two sets S and T do not share any common elements, we say that they are *disjoint*, and we write $S \cap T = \varnothing$. For example, given $S = \{2, 4, 6, 8\}$, and $T = \{1, 3, 5\}$, we have $S \cap T = \varnothing$.

The following problems illustrate some of the ways in which the above properties and definitions are used on the GRE and GMAT.

1. What is the largest prime divisor of 128?
   (A) 2
   (B) 3
   (C) 8
   (D) 13
   (E) 64

Be careful to read this problem closely. Although 64 is the largest answer choice that divides 128, it is not a *prime* divisor since $64 = 2 \times 32$. In fact, the only prime number choices are 2, 3, and 13. Of these choices, only 2 is a divisor of 128. Thus, the largest prime factor of 128 is 2. **The correct answer is (A).**

2. If the four-digit number 7,4P2 is divisible by 9, what is the value of P?
   (A) 2
   (B) 3
   (C) 4
   (D) 5
   (E) 6

You could solve this problem by trial and error. However, it is probably a bit faster to use the divisibility test for 9 instead. Remember that a number is divisible by 9 if the sum of its digits is divisible by 9. We know that $0 \leq P \leq 9$, since a digit must be either 0, 1, 2, 3, 4, 5, 6, 7, 8, or 9. Also, the sum of the given digits is $7 + 4 + P + 2 = 13 + P$. Note that if $P = 5$, the sum would be 18, which is divisible by 9. Therefore, the value of P must be 5. **The correct answer is (D).**

3. If $q + 33$ is an odd integer, then the value of q could be which one of the following?
   (A) −33
   (B) −17
   (C) 3
   (D) 17
   (E) 24

Again, this problem can be solved by using trial and error, but it is faster to use the properties of odds and evens discussed earlier. Note that 33 is odd, and recall that an odd number plus an even number is odd. Therefore, the answer to this question must be an even number, and 24 is the only one listed. **The correct answer is (E).**

4. If p is a prime number such that $p > 2$, which of the following must be true?

   I. p^3 is odd

   II. $12p$ is even

   III. $9p$ is odd

   (A) I only

   (B) II only

   (C) III only

   (D) I and III only

   (E) I, II, and III

The key to this problem is to remember that any prime number bigger than 2 must be odd. Thus, options I and III must be true, because the product of odd numbers is odd. Further, option II must be true because the product of an odd and an even is always even. Thus, all three statements are true. **The correct answer is (E).**

5. If A is the set of all positive even integers, and B is the set of all even integers that are multiples of 5, which of the following best describes $A \cap B$?

   (A) The set of all integers that are multiples of 10.

   (B) The set of all positive integers that are multiples of 10.

   (C) The set of all positive integers that are multiples of 2.

   (D) The set of all positive odd integers.

   (E) The set of all integers that are multiples of 2.

The set $B = \{\pm 5, \pm 10, \pm 15, \pm 20, \ldots\}$. For a number to be in set A, it has to be even and positive. For a number to be in both sets A and B, therefore, it has to be even, positive, and in set B. You can see that the positive numbers that are even and in set B are the numbers 10, 20, 30, 40, etc., that is, the positive multiples of 10. **The correct answer is (B).**

EXERCISES: NUMBERS AND OPERATIONS

Directions: Select the answer choice that best answers the question.

1. The number a is equal to the product of two different prime numbers, each of which is between 1 and 10. What is the largest possible value of a?

    (A) 35

    (B) 42

    (C) 49

    (D) 56

    (E) 63

2. When the positive integer N is divided by 7, the remainder is 3. If $N < 15$, what is the remainder when N is divided by 8?

    (A) 1

    (B) 2

    (C) 4

    (D) 5

    (E) 6

3. When a is divided by 5, the remainder is 4. When b is divided by 5, the remainder is 3. What is the remainder when $a + b$ is divided by 5?

    (A) 0

    (B) 1

    (C) 2

    (D) 3

    (E) 4

4. If f and g are integers, and $f = 6$ and $g > 7$, which of the following must be true?

    I. fg is odd
    II. $fg > 47$
    III. fg is even

    (A) I only

    (B) II only

    (C) III only

    (D) I and II only

    (E) II and III only

5. If $5k + 7$ represents an odd integer, which of the following represents the next *largest* odd integer?

    (A) $5k + 8$

    (B) $6k + 7$

    (C) $6k + 8$

    (D) $5k + 9$

    (E) $7k + 7$

6. If 668 is divided by 11, the remainder is equal to r. If 668 is divided by 22, the remainder is equal to R. What is the value of $\dfrac{r}{R}$?

(A) $\dfrac{1}{8}$

(B) $\dfrac{1}{4}$

(C) 1

(D) 4

(E) 8

ANSWER KEY AND EXPLANATIONS

1. A	3. C	5. D
2. B	4. E	6. C

1. **The correct answer is (A).** In order to answer this question, you need to find the two largest prime numbers that are less than 10. Since 9 and 8 are not prime, the largest prime number less than 10 is 7. The next largest prime is 5, and so the maximum product is $5 \times 7 = 35$. Be certain to read every word carefully. The problem states that *the two prime numbers must be different*. If you missed the word "different," you might select choice (C), since $7 \times 7 = 49$.

2. **The correct answer is (B).** The quickest way to attack this divisibility problem is to choose an actual number that is less than 15, which, when divided by 7, gives a remainder of 3. An efficient way to do this is to add the divisor and the remainder. Since 7 and 3 adds up to 10, 10 will be a number that, when divided by 7, has a remainder of 3. Using $N = 10$, we divide by the number 8, which yields a remainder of 2.

   Note that divisibility problems with variables can often be quickly solved by selecting appropriate numbers to stand for the variables. The problem can also be answered by thinking about remainders and division. Note that if we divide a number by 8 (which is 1 bigger than 7), we will get a remainder that is 1 smaller than the remainder we get if we divide by 7. The general principle can be stated this way: if we divide by a number that is "1 bigger," we get a remainder that is "1 smaller."

3. **The correct answer is (C).** This is another question that can be solved by selecting numbers to stand for a and b. For example, if $a = 9$, the remainder will be 4 when a is divided by 5. Similarly, if $b = 8$, the remainder will be 3 when b is divided by 5. Since, in this case, $a + b = 8 + 9 = 17$, we can divide 17 by 5 to determine the answer. When 17 is divided by 5, the remainder is 2.

4. **The correct answer is (E).** Let's begin by seeing if we can determine if fg is odd or even. We know that f is even, and therefore, regardless of whether g is odd or even, fg must be even. This means that option III is true and I is false. Even if you can go no further, you can now choose between choices (C) and (E). Next, note that the smallest value that g can possibly have is 8. Thus, the smallest possible value for fg is $6 \times 8 = 48$. This means that option II is true, as well.

5. **The correct answer is (D).** Perhaps the quickest approach is to note that the "next largest odd integer" is 2 more than the current number, and $(5k + 7) + 2 = 5k + 9$. Thus, choice (D) must be the answer. A more time-consuming way to solve this problem is to select a value for k, and then substitute that value into all of the answer choices.

6. **The correct answer is (C).** If you divide 668 by 11, you get 60.7, so 11 can go into 668 a total of 60 times, with a remainder. Since $11 \times 60 = 660$, the remainder is $668 - 660 = 8$. In the same way, if you divide 668 by 22, you obtain 30.4, so 22 goes into 668 a total of 30 times, with a remainder. Since $22 \times 30 = 660$, the remainder is also 8. This means the ratio of the remainders is 1.

COMPUTATIONS WITH FRACTIONS, DECIMALS, AND PERCENTS

There are a few computational skills relating to fractions, decimals, and percents that you need to know in order to be able to answer the word problems and certain other types of questions that you will see. These skills are reviewed in this section.

Computations with Fractions

A fraction is essentially a way of indicating a division. For example, the fraction $\frac{4}{9}$ represents the division of the number 4, which is known as the *numerator*, by the number 9, which is called the *denominator*. In certain problems, an efficient strategy is to convert the given fractions to decimal form. Consider the following sample question.

1. Which of the following fractions is the largest?

   (A) $\frac{1}{4}$

   (B) $\frac{2}{7}$

   (C) $\frac{3}{8}$

   (D) $\frac{2}{5}$

   (E) $\frac{5}{14}$

Although you could solve this problem by determining the *least common denominator* for all of the given fractions, a much quicker strategy is to write each fraction as a decimal and compare the decimals. Some of the decimal equivalents you are probably already familiar with, for example, $\frac{1}{4} = 0.25$, $\frac{3}{8} = 0.375$, and $\frac{2}{5} = 0.4$. Divide the numerator by the denominator and express the other fractions as decimals, written to 3 decimal places: $\frac{2}{7}$ yields 0.285, and $\frac{5}{14}$ yields 0.347. **The correct answer is (D).**

In this problem, we were able to simplify the problem by converting the fractions to decimal form. However, in other problems, we will need to be able to work with numbers expressed as fractions. So, in the next section, let's review the computational skills that you need to remember.

Simplifying Fractions

A fraction has been reduced to *simplest form* if its numerator and denominator do not have any common factors other than 1. For example, the fraction $\frac{10}{21}$ is in simplest form since the numbers 10 and 21 have no common factors other than 1. To see this, note that the numerator and denominator factor into primes as $\frac{2 \times 5}{3 \times 7}$.

On the other hand, the fraction $\frac{28}{35}$ can be simplified. Factoring the numerator and denominator into primes gives us $\frac{2 \times 2 \times 7}{5 \times 7}$. The common factor of 7 can be divided out, leaving us with the simplified fraction $\frac{4}{5}$.

Only simplified fractions appear as the answer choices to multiple-choice questions. Therefore, if your answer to a GRE and GMAT question is a fraction, you must simplify the fraction before you will be able to find it in the multiple-choice answers. If you are solving a problem and obtain the answer $\frac{20}{25}$, don't worry when you don't see it in the multiple-choice answers. The fraction needs to be simplified. Divide the top and bottom by 5, obtaining $\frac{4}{5}$, and look for that as the answer.

Adding and Subtracting Fractions

Before you can add or subtract two or more fractions, they must have the same denominator. Once they have a *common denominator*, simply add or subtract the numerators and retain the common denominator. For example, $\frac{5}{12} + \frac{1}{12} = \frac{6}{12} = \frac{1}{2}$. Similarly, $\frac{6}{7} - \frac{1}{7} = \frac{5}{7}$.

If you need to add or subtract fractions that do not have a common denominator, the fractions must be rewritten as equivalent fractions that do have a common denominator. This is accomplished by rewriting either or both of the fractions in *higher terms*. To write a fraction in higher terms, multiply the numerator and denominator of the fraction by the same number. This multiplier should be chosen so that the individual rewritten fractions end up with the same denominator. For example, $\frac{3}{7} + \frac{1}{5} = \frac{5}{5}\left(\frac{3}{7}\right) + \frac{7}{7}\left(\frac{1}{5}\right) = \frac{15}{35} + \frac{7}{35} = \frac{22}{35}$.

Note that 22 and 35 do not have any common factors, so $\frac{22}{35}$ is in simplified form.

Subtraction is handled in the same way, as this example shows: $\frac{4}{5} - \frac{1}{3} = \frac{3}{3}\left(\frac{4}{5}\right) - \frac{5}{5}\left(\frac{1}{3}\right) = \frac{12}{15} - \frac{5}{15} = \frac{7}{15}$.

Note that, as a final step in the subtraction, the resulting fraction was written in simplest form.

Multiplying and Dividing Fractions

Adding and subtracting fractions is a bit more tedious than multiplying and dividing them. There is no need to obtain common denominators before multiplying or dividing. To multiply fractions, simply multiply the numerators and denominators, and, if possible, simplify the result. This procedure is illustrated in the example: $\frac{5}{6} \times \frac{3}{10} = \frac{5 \times 3}{6 \times 10} = \frac{15}{60} = \frac{1}{4}$. In the last step, the fraction was simplified by dividing the numerator and denominator by 15. Note that you can also cancel the common factors in the numerator and denominator before multiplying, i.e., $\frac{5}{6} \times \frac{3}{10} = \frac{5}{3 \times 2} \times \frac{3}{5 \times 2} = \frac{1}{2 \times 2} = \frac{1}{4}$.

The technique for dividing two fractions involves changing the division into a multiplication problem, and then performing the multiplication. To change a division problem to a multiplication problem, you need to replace the second fraction by its *reciprocal*. The reciprocal of a fraction is the fraction that is obtained when the numerator and denominator are switched. For example, to perform the division $\frac{3}{8} \div \frac{5}{2}$, change the division to multiplication as follows: $\frac{3}{8} \div \frac{5}{2} = \frac{3}{8} \times \frac{2}{5} = \frac{3 \times 2}{8 \times 5} = \frac{6}{40} = \frac{3}{20}$.

Improper Fractions and Mixed Numbers

So far, in every fraction that we have seen, the numerator has been smaller than the denominator. Such fractions are called *proper fractions,* and their value is less than 1. On the other hand, a fraction like $\frac{31}{10}$, in which the numerator is larger than the denominator, is called an *improper fraction*, and it is larger than 1.

One way to determine the size of the improper fraction $\frac{31}{10}$ is to express it as a *mixed number*. A mixed number is an integer together with a proper fraction. To do this, divide the numerator by the denominator, and put the remainder over the denominator. In the case of $\frac{31}{10}$, 10 divides into 31 three times, with a remainder of 1. Therefore, $\frac{31}{10} = 3\frac{1}{10}$.

To reverse this process, and write the mixed number as an improper fraction, multiply the denominator by the integer part of the mixed number, add this to the original numerator, and place it over the original denominator. Therefore, $3\frac{1}{10} = \frac{(10 \times 3)+1}{10} = \frac{31}{10}$.

Complex Fractions

Occasionally, GRE and GMAT questions involve a rather complicated type of fraction called a *complex fraction*. A complex fraction is a fraction whose numerator or denominator (or both) are also fractions. The best way to work with such fractions is to simplify them, which means to rewrite them as a simplified fraction. The following two examples show how this is done. In the first example, we have a fraction whose numerator and denominator are both fractions. To simplify, remember that a fraction represents a division, and follow the rules for dividing fractions.

$$\frac{\frac{5}{8}}{\frac{11}{4}} = \frac{5}{8} \div \frac{11}{4} = \frac{5}{8} \times \frac{4}{11} = \frac{20}{88} = \frac{5}{22}$$

Sometimes, you need to work with complex fractions that contain additions or subtractions in their numerators or denominators. For example, consider the complex fraction $\frac{7+\frac{1}{5}}{\frac{2}{9}}$. The quickest way to simplify this is to find the least common denominator of all of the terms in the complex fraction and to multiply *every* term by this number. In this case, the least common denominator would be 45. Thus, you should multiply every term by 45, as shown below:

$$\frac{7+\frac{1}{5}}{\frac{2}{9}} = \frac{7(45)+\frac{1}{5}(45)}{\frac{2}{9}(45)} = \frac{315+9}{2(5)} = \frac{324}{10} = \frac{162}{5}$$

NOTE: In any question that contains complex fractions, begin by changing the complex fraction to a proper fraction, improper fraction, or mixed number before attempting to solve the problem.

Ratios

A *ratio* is simply a comparison of two different numbers. A ratio can be written in three different ways. For example, if the senior class has 37 boys and 29 girls, the "boy to girl ratio" is 37 to 29, which can also be written as 37:29. It is, however, usually best to write the ratio as a fraction, $\frac{37}{29}$. Note that the order in which the numbers in the ratio are written is important. The "boy to girl" ratio is $\frac{37}{29}$, but the "girl to boy" ratio is $\frac{29}{37}$.

Decimals

A fraction that has a denominator that is either 10 or a power of 10 is called a *decimal fraction*, or simply a *decimal*. You are already familiar with the shorthand notation used to express decimal fractions:

$\frac{7}{10} = 0.7$ $\qquad \frac{37}{100} = 0.37$ $\qquad \frac{59}{1,000} = 0.059$ $\qquad \frac{4,139}{10,000} = 0.4139$

As noted in the previous section, when a problem involves fractions, it is sometimes easier to change each fraction into a decimal.

Comparing Decimals

The simplest way to compare a group of decimal numbers is to add zeros to the end of each decimal number, until all of the numbers have the same number of digits to the right of the decimal point. Then, ignore the decimal point, and directly compare the resulting numbers.

Suppose you need to put the decimals 0.73, 0.737, and 0.7314 in order from smallest to largest. The number 0.7314 contains four digits to the right of the decimal point, and this is more digits than any of the other numbers. Therefore, add zeros to each of the other numbers until they also have four digits to the right of the decimal point. The numbers become 0.7300, 0.7370, and 0.7314. From this, we can see that 0.737 is the largest of the numbers, followed by 0.7314. Lastly, 0.7300 is the smallest.

The Meaning of Percent

A *percent* is nothing more than a fraction whose denominator is 100. As a matter of fact, the word "percent" means "per hundred" or "out of one hundred." It is easy to write any percent as either a fraction or a decimal. For example, $59\% = \dfrac{59}{100}$ = 0.59.

A useful skill is the ability to express a fraction, a decimal, or a percent as one of the other types of numbers. We have already discussed how to perform most of these conversions, and the following table summarizes the results.

Fraction, Decimal, and Percent Conversions

To Convert a Fraction to a Decimal	Divide the numerator by the denominator.	$\dfrac{3}{8} = 0.375$
To Convert a Decimal to a Fraction	Form a fraction whose numerator is the decimal (without the decimal point) and whose denominator is a 1 followed by the same number of zeros as there are digits in the numerator. Simplify if possible.	$0.45 = \dfrac{45}{100} = \dfrac{9}{20}$ $0.875 = \dfrac{875}{1,000} = \dfrac{7}{8}$
To Convert a Fraction to a Percent	Divide the numerator by the denominator, and move the decimal point two places to the right.	$\dfrac{3}{4} = 0.75 = 75\%$
To Convert a Decimal to a Percent	Move the decimal point two places to the right.	$0.123 = 12.3\%$
To Convert a Percent to a Fraction	Place the percent over 100. Simplify if possible.	$94\% = \dfrac{94}{100} = \dfrac{47}{50}$
To Convert a Percent to a Decimal	Move the decimal point two places to the left.	$55\% = 0.55$

The following problems illustrate how some of the previous properties are used in GRE and GMAT questions.

1. Which of the following five numbers is greater than 5.724?

    (A) 5.72

    (B) 5.7203

    (C) 5.089

    (D) 5.726

    (E) 5.7239

Since each of the numbers begins with integer part "5," the correct answer is the number with a digit bigger than 4 located 3 places to the right of the decimal. Thus, 5.726 is larger than 5.724. **The correct answer is (D).**

2. Which of the following is equal to $a + 900\%$ of a?

    (A) $0.19a$

    (B) $1.9a$

    (C) $10a$

    (D) $91a$

    (E) $901a$

The correct answer is (C). The key to solving this problem lies in determining how to express 900% of a. The first thing to note is that $900\% = \dfrac{900}{100} = 9$. Also, remember that in mathematics, the word "of" is typically associated with multiplication. In other words, the phrase "900% of a" simply means $9 \times a$, or $9a$. Therefore, "$a + 900\%$ of a" $= a + 9a = 10a$. **The correct answer is (C).**

3. Dividing the number y by $\left(\dfrac{3}{8} \div \dfrac{3}{8} \right)$ would be the same as

    (A) multiplying y by $\dfrac{64}{9}$.

    (B) multiplying y by $\dfrac{3}{8}$.

    (C) multiplying y by 1.

    (D) dividing y by $\dfrac{3}{8}$.

    (E) dividing y by $\dfrac{64}{9}$.

Perhaps the easiest way to solve this problem is to begin by finding the value of $\left(\dfrac{3}{8} \div \dfrac{3}{8} \right)$. Remember that, in order to divide two fractions, you need to invert the second fraction and multiply. Thus, $\left(\dfrac{3}{8} \div \dfrac{3}{8} \right)$ is the same as $\left(\dfrac{3}{8} \times \dfrac{8}{3} \right) = 1$. Therefore, we are dividing y by 1, which is the same as multiplying it by 1. **The correct answer is (C).**

4. The positive difference between f and $\frac{1}{3}$ is the same as the positive difference between $\frac{1}{9}$ and $\frac{1}{6}$. What is the value of f if $f > \frac{1}{3}$?

(A) $\frac{2}{9}$

(B) $\frac{5}{18}$

(C) $\frac{1}{3}$

(D) $\frac{7}{18}$

(E) $\frac{4}{9}$

We need to begin by finding the positive difference between $\frac{1}{9}$ and $\frac{1}{6}$.

$\frac{1}{6} - \frac{1}{9} = \frac{3}{18} - \frac{2}{18} = \frac{1}{18}$. We are looking for the value of f such that $f - \frac{1}{3} = \frac{1}{18}$. Adding $\frac{1}{3}$ to both sides of this expression yields $f - \frac{1}{3} + \frac{1}{3} = \frac{1}{18} + \frac{1}{3}$, which means $f = \frac{1}{18} + \frac{1}{3} = \frac{1}{18} + \frac{6}{18} = \frac{7}{18}$. **The correct answer is (D).**

EXERCISES: COMPUTATIONS WITH FRACTIONS, DECIMALS, AND PERCENTS

Directions: Select the answer choice that best answers the question.

1. If $x = \dfrac{1}{6}$ and $y = \dfrac{1}{12}$, what is the value of $\dfrac{x}{y} - \dfrac{y}{x}$?

   (A) 0

   (B) $1\dfrac{1}{2}$

   (C) 3

   (D) 4

   (E) $\dfrac{71}{72}$

2. In which of the following numbers is the digit 4 in the hundredths place?

   (A) 4,000.0

   (B) 400.0

   (C) 0.4

   (D) 0.04

   (E) 0.004

3. If the fractions $\dfrac{3}{q}$ and $\dfrac{18}{p}$ are equal, then which of the following must be true?

   (A) q and p are equal.

   (B) q is 6 times as big as p.

   (C) p is 6 times as big as q.

   (D) p is 3 times as big as q.

   (E) q is 3 times as big as p.

4. Two positive integers have a ratio of 9 to 8. Which of the following statements about these two integers has to be true?

   (A) The sum of the two integers is 17.

   (B) The sum of the two integers is even.

   (C) The sum of the two integers is odd.

   (D) The product of the two integers is odd.

   (E) The product of the two integers is even.

5. If Herb estimates that he can complete his homework in 3 hours, what fraction of his homework can he complete in 40 minutes?

(A) $\dfrac{3}{40}$

(B) $\dfrac{1}{12}$

(C) $\dfrac{1}{9}$

(D) $\dfrac{1}{6}$

(E) $\dfrac{2}{9}$

ANSWER KEY AND EXPLANATIONS

1. B	2. D	3. C	4. E	5. E

1. **The correct answer is (B).** Perhaps the most straightforward solution strategy is to evaluate $\dfrac{x}{y}$ and $\dfrac{y}{x}$ using the technique discussed in the complex fraction section, and then perform the subtraction.

$$\frac{x}{y} = \frac{\frac{1}{6}}{\frac{1}{12}} = \frac{1}{6} \times \frac{12}{1} = \frac{12}{6} = 2$$

$$\frac{y}{x} = \frac{\frac{1}{12}}{\frac{1}{6}} = \frac{1}{12} \times \frac{6}{1} = \frac{6}{12} = \frac{1}{2}$$

Therefore, $\dfrac{x}{y} - \dfrac{y}{x} = 2 - \dfrac{1}{2} = 1\dfrac{1}{2}$.

2. **The correct answer is (D).** This problem tests your understanding of place value. But let's use this problem to emphasize something else, as well. On the GRE and GMAT, you must be certain to take your time to *read* each problem slowly and carefully. Make certain you answer the correct question. What a difference two letters make! If you rush, and read this problem as "In which of the following numbers is the digit 4 in the *hundred*s place?", you will be led to pick choice (B). The problem says *hundredths*, not *hundreds*, and the correct answer is choice (D), which has the digit 4 positioned two digits to the right of the decimal point, that is, in the hundredths place.

3. **The correct answer is (C).** Perhaps the quickest way to solve this problem is to use the least common denominator of the given fractions $\dfrac{3}{q}$ and $\dfrac{18}{p}$. We know that the least common denominator is $p \times q$. Moreover, we are told that these fractions are equal to one another. So we have the expression $\dfrac{3}{q} = \dfrac{18}{p}$. Multiplying both sides by $p \times q$ yields $p \times q \times \dfrac{3}{q} = p \times q \times \dfrac{18}{p}$. Simplifying both sides yields $3 \times p = q \times 18$. Finally, dividing both sides by 3 yields $p = q \times 6$.

4. **The correct answer is (E).** We can attack this problem by remembering that the statement "Two positive integers have a ratio of 9 to 8" can be expressed using variables as follows: $\dfrac{p}{q} = \dfrac{9}{8}$ for some positive integers p and q. As we did in Question 3, we can use the least common denominator, $8 \times q$, to rewrite this expression as $8 \times q \times \dfrac{p}{q} = 8 \times q \times \dfrac{9}{8}$.

Simplifying both sides yields $8 \times p = 9 \times q$. Note that, since $8 \times p$ must be an even integer, we know that $9 \times q$ must also be even. This means that q must be even. So choice (E) must be true, since $p \times q = even$ requires $p \times even = even$. And this is always true, no matter whether p is even or odd. Also note that p can be either even or odd. Note that choice (A) requires p to be odd, since $p + q = 17$ means that $p + even = odd$, which can only be true if p is odd. Choice (B) requires p to be even, since $p + q = even$ means that $p + even = even$, which can only be true if p is even. Choice (C) requires p to be odd, since $p + q = odd$ means that $p + even = odd$, which can only be true if p is odd. Choice (D) is impossible since $p \times q = odd$ requires $p \times even = odd$, which is impossible.

5. **The correct answer is (E).** Once again, we see that one word can make such a difference on the GRE and GMAT. Be careful. Geometry test questions often involve a subtle unit change. Note that the problem begins by talking about hours and ends up by talking about minutes. If you are not careful, and don't notice this, it is easy to think that you need to form some fraction using the numbers 3 and 40. This might lead you into selecting choice (A).

However, if you notice the change in units, the problem becomes less tedious to solve. Just change the two numbers so that they have the same units—it is easiest to write 3 hours as 180 minutes. Thus, you are asked to express "40 out of 180" as a fraction. This is $\frac{40}{180} = \frac{2}{9}$. So, this problem is testing nothing more than your ability to read carefully and to reduce fractions.

ARITHMETIC WORD PROBLEMS

At the start of this chapter, we discussed the fact that the GRE and GMAT exams contain relatively few problems that only consist of arithmetic computations. However, you will likely have quite a few arithmetic word problems. As you go about solving these problems, you are going to have to work with fractions, decimals, and percents, using computational techniques that we discussed above. In addition, you must also know the techniques for solving the different types of arithmetic word problems on the test. There are three types of arithmetic word problems that frequently occur on the GRE and GMAT: *proportion problems*, *percent problems,* and *fraction problems*.

Proportion Word Problems

Let's begin this section by taking a look at three sample proportion problems.

Sample Word Problem #1: If tomatoes sell at 4 for 80 cents, what would 13 tomatoes cost at the same rate?

Sample Word Problem #2: If Susan makes $40 for 8 hours of work, how much would she earn for 10 hours of work, at the same rate?

Sample Word Problem #3: A recipe that will serve five people requires 2 cups of sugar. How many cups of sugar would be required to make enough to serve fifteen people?

At first reading, these problems probably seem to be quite different. After all, the first problem involves buying tomatoes, the second is about getting paid for work, and the third relates to cooking. However, from a mathematical standpoint, these problems are almost identical.

Each problem involves a relationship between certain items. For example, the first problem involves a relationship between *tomatoes* and *cents*. The second problem establishes a relationship between *dollars* and *hours*. The third problem involves a relationship between *people* and *cups* of sugar.

All three problems begin by telling you how many of one item is associated with a certain number of the other item. In the first problem, we are told that we can associate 4 *tomatoes* with 80 *cents*. The second problem links 40 *dollars* with 8 *hours*. In the third problem, we are relating five *people* to 2 *cups* of sugar.

The third number in each of the four problems is in the same units as one of the first two numbers. For example, in the first problem, we are told that we can associate 4 *tomatoes* with 80 cents. We then are asked for the cost of 13 *tomatoes*. In the same way, after we are told, in the second problem, that 40 dollars are earned by working 8 *hours*, we are asked how much money would be earned by working 10 *hours*. The third problem is similar in structure.

If we look past the surface details, we can see that each of the three problems has the same fundamental structure. To begin, each problem involves two items, which we can call *Item 1* and *Item 2*. We are initially told that a given amount of Item 1 is associated with a given amount of Item 2. We are then asked how much of a *different* amount of Item 1 should be associated with Item 2. Note that the first two problems tell us that the items vary "at the same rate," and variation at the same rate is implied in the recipe problem.

Such problems are called *proportion* problems, and we say that the two items in each problem vary proportionately to each other. In order to find the answer to each of these problems, you need to write and solve a proportion.

A proportion is really just another name for two fractions, i.e., ratios, set equal to each other. For example, $\frac{1}{3} = \frac{2}{6}$ is a proportion. As you can see, this proportion contains four numbers, and you know them all. For the sample problems, we are going to write a proportion in which we know three of the numbers and need to find the fourth one.

In order to see how to find the missing value in a proportion, let's look at the sample proportion $\frac{5}{8} = \frac{20}{N}$, and try to find the value of N that makes the two fractions equal. In order to do this, begin by "cross-multiplying." That is, you simply multiply the two numbers along one of the diagonals of the proportion, and set the product equal to the product of the two numbers along the other diagonal. In this case, you will get:

Thus, we get $5 \times N = 20 \times 8$, which means that $5 \times N = 160$.

Since 5 times N is equal to 160, N must be equal to 160 divided by 5, i.e., $N = \frac{160}{5} = 32$.

Let's solve the sample problems. The first step in solving a proportion problem is to determine which two units we are comparing.

In problem 1, we are comparing tomatoes to cents. So, we must write a proportion comparing tomatoes to cents. When we do this, the key is to remember that *it does not matter whether we put tomatoes or cents in the numerator of our fraction. However, whatever we decide to put in the numerator of the first fraction must also be put in the numerator of the second fraction.*

For example, suppose we decide to put tomatoes in the numerator and cents in the denominator. Then, letting N once again represent the unknown, we see that $\frac{\text{Tomatoes}}{\text{Cents}}$ yields the proportion $\frac{4}{80} = \frac{13}{N}$.

Next, we cross-multiply to get $80 \times 13 = 4 \times N$, so that $1{,}040 = 4 \times N$, which means $N = 260$. Thus, the correct answer is 260 cents, or \$2.60.

To solve the second problem, we can write the following proportion:

$\frac{\$}{\text{Hours}}$ yields the proportion $\frac{40}{8} = \frac{N}{10}$.

After cross-multiplying, we obtain $400 = 8 \times N$, which means $N = 50$.

As for the third problem, we write the following proportion:

$\frac{\text{People}}{\text{Cups}}$ yields the proportion $\frac{5}{2} = \frac{15}{N}$.

The cross-multiplication gives us $30 = 5 \times N$, which means $N = 6$.

NOTE: Remember that the procedure for correctly solving a proportion problem involves three steps. First, read the problem carefully to determine the two units that are being compared. Then, set up a proportion in which one of the units is in the numerator and the other is in the denominator. Finally, solve the proportion to find the value of the missing number.

Consider the following examples.

1. A paint can holds 40 ounces of paint. If it takes 13 ounces of paint for two complete doors, how many complete doors can be painted with a full can of paint?

   (A) 6
   (B) 7
   (C) 8
   (D) 9
   (E) 10

Begin by noting that we are comparing ounces to doors. We know that 13 ounces are needed to paint two doors, and we need to determine how many doors we can paint with 40 ounces. Set up a proportion in the usual way:

$\dfrac{\text{Ounces}}{\text{Doors}}$ yields the proportion $\dfrac{13}{2} = \dfrac{40}{N}$

Cross-multiplying yields:

$40 \times 2 = 13 \times N$

$80 = 13 \times N$

$N = \dfrac{80}{13} = 6\dfrac{2}{13}$

Note that the problem asks how many *complete* doors we can paint. This means we should not include the fractional part in our answer. We can only paint 6 complete doors, and we will have a little paint left over. **The correct answer is (A).**

2. A dog runs at a constant speed of 6 feet per second. At this rate, how far would the dog run in $\dfrac{4}{5}$ of a minute?

   (A) 96 feet
   (B) 144 feet
   (C) 240 feet
   (D) 288 feet
   (E) 384 feet

This proportion problem is a little more complicated. Note that in the first sentence, we are comparing feet to seconds. Then, in the second sentence, we are comparing feet to minutes. We have already commented how important it is to look for changes of units within problems. When you find one in a proportion problem, you must convert to a common unit. Usually, it is best to convert everything to the smaller unit.

Thus, let's change $\dfrac{4}{5}$ of a minute to seconds. Since each minute is 60 seconds, we have that $\dfrac{4}{5}$ of a minute is $\dfrac{4}{5} \times 60 = 48$ seconds. We can set up a proportion to solve the problem.

$\dfrac{\text{Feet}}{\text{Seconds}}$ yields the proportion $\dfrac{6}{1} = \dfrac{N}{48}$

Cross-multiplying yields:

$48 \times 6 = 1 \times N$

$288 = 1 \times N$, so $N = 288$ feet

The correct answer is (D).

> **BE CAREFUL:** When solving a proportion problem, note the units that are mentioned in the problem. Look for "unit changes," such as minutes to hours, and, if there are any such changes, set up the problem so as to take them into account.

3. Dan can clean 5 carpets in 6 hours. At this rate, how long would it take him to clean 7 carpets?
   (A) 7 hours 40 minutes
   (B) 8 hours and 4 minutes
   (C) 8 hours and 24 minutes
   (D) 8 hours and 36 minutes
   (E) 8 hours and 40 minutes

This problem is straightforward to set up, but you must be careful to correctly express your answer. We are comparing carpets to hours, so we set up our proportion as shown below:

$$\frac{5 \text{ carpets}}{6 \text{ hours}} = \frac{7 \text{ carpets}}{N \text{ hours}}$$

When we cross-multiply, we get $5 \times N = 7 \times 6$, which means that $5 \times N = 42$.

Therefore, $N = 42 \div 5 = 8.4$ hours. **The correct answer is (C).**

Note that all of the answers are expressed in terms of hours and minutes, so we need to change our answer into hours and minutes. In order to determine how many minutes are in 0.4 hours, remember that there are 60 minutes in an hour, so there are $0.4 \times 60 = 24$ minutes in 0.4 hours. Thus, the total time required is 8 hours and 24 minutes. A very common mistake is to conclude that 8.4 hours is equal to 8 hours and 4 minutes or 8 hours and 40 minutes.

Percent Word Problems

Every GRE and GMAT test contains a variety of *percent word problems*. For example, you may be asked to solve problems involving markups, markdowns, commissions, discounts, interest, percents of change, and so on.

Instead of examining how to solve every different possible type of percent problem, we are going to begin by taking a look at the things that all percent problems have in common. While different types of percent word problems may appear to be different from each other, *all* percent problems have certain similarities, and recognizing these similarities makes them much easier to solve.

To begin, every percent problem involves three specific quantities. An appropriate name for the first of these quantities is the *whole*. The whole represents the total upon which the problem is based. In a given problem, the whole might be Matthew's total weekly pay, the total number of cans of juice sold at a grocery store, or the total amount of rainfall in a particular city.

The second quantity that occurs in every percent problem can be termed the *part*. The part is a piece of the whole. For example, if the whole is Matthew's total weekly pay, the part might be the part of that money that he uses to pay his rent. If the whole is the total number of cans of juice sold at a grocery store, the part might be the number of those cans that contain a specific brand of juice. If the whole is the amount of rainfall in a particular city, the part might be the amount of rain that fell on the weekend.

Lastly, the third quantity is the *percent*. The percent expresses how much the part is of the whole. For example, if Matthew's weekly pay is $250 (the *whole*), and he spends $100 (the *part*) on rent, then he spends $\frac{100}{250} = 0.4 = 40\%$ of his pay on rent.

> **NOTE:** In almost every percent problem, you will be told the value of two of these three quantities, and then be asked to find the third quantity. For example, you might be told the whole and the part and be asked to find the percent. All in all, there really are only three different types of percent problems: finding the whole, finding the part, and finding the percent.

When you need to solve a percent word problem, the best way to begin is by identifying which two of the three quantities you are given. Then, you will know which quantity you are trying to find, and this will tell you how to proceed.

Consider the three sample problems below.

Sample Word Problem #1: Matthew's weekly salary is $250. If he spends 40% of his weekly salary on rent, how much does he spend each week on rent?

Sample Word Problem #2: Matthew's weekly salary is $250, and he spends $100 a week on rent. What percent of his weekly salary does he spend on rent?

Sample Word Problem #3: Matthew spends $100, or 40% of his weekly salary, on rent. What is his total weekly salary?

Note that each one of these problems has the same context, but that the given information varies from problem to problem. In the first problem, we are given the whole, $250, and the percent, 40%, and asked to find the part. In the second problem, we are given the whole, $250, and the part, $100, and asked to find the percent. In the final problem, we are given the part, $100, and the percent, 40%, and are asked to find the whole.

All three of these problems can be solved by using an appropriate version of the basic percent formula. The basic percent formula can be expressed in the words: "*Part* is equal to *Percent* times *Whole*." If we let P represent the part, % represent the percent, and W represent the whole, then the basic percent formula can be written as: $P = \% \times W$.

In Sample Word Problem #1, we are asked to find the part. The basic percent formula tells you to simply multiply the percent by the whole to find the part. By manipulating this formula, it can be rewritten in two other equivalent forms that can be used to solve the other two problems. Namely, $\% = \dfrac{P}{W}$, and $W = \dfrac{P}{\%}$. Thus, to find the percent, divide the part by the whole. To find the whole, divide the part by the percent.

Let's use these formulas to solve the three sample problems given above.

Sample Word Problem #1: Matthew's weekly salary is $250. If he spends 40% of his weekly salary on rent, how much does he spend each week on rent?

In this problem, the *whole* is 250 and the *percent* is 40%. We are asked to find the *part* of Matthew's salary that he spends on rent. In order to find the answer, simply use the appropriate version of the percent formula, which in this case is $P = \% \times W$:

$P = 40\% \times \$250 = 0.40 \times \$250 = \$100.$

As you see, when solving percent problems that ask you to find the part, it is usually easier to perform the computation if you change the percent to a decimal and then perform multiplication.

Sample Word Problem #2: Matthew's weekly salary is $250, and he spends $100 a week on rent. What percent of his weekly salary does he spend on rent?

In this version of the problem, $250 is the whole and $100 is the part. To find the percent, simply substitute the given values for the part and for the whole into the appropriate version of the percent formula, which is $\% = \dfrac{P}{W}$:

$\% = \dfrac{P}{W} = \dfrac{\$100}{\$250} = 0.4 = 40\%$

> **BE CAREFUL:** Remember that when you are solving this type of percent problem, you must take the decimal answer and write it as a percent. In this problem, the correct answer is *not* 0.40%. The correct answer is 40%.

Sample Word Problem #3: Matthew spends $100, or 40% of his weekly salary, on rent. What is his total weekly salary?

In this problem, the part is $100 and the percent is 40%. To find the whole, simply use the version of the percent formula that says $W = \dfrac{P}{\%}$:

$$W = \frac{P}{\%} = \frac{\$100}{40\%} = \frac{\$100}{0.4} = \$250$$

> **BE CAREFUL:** When solving this type of problem, remember to write the percent as a decimal before performing the division.

> **NOTE:** Almost all GRE and GMAT percent problems can be solved by using the appropriate form of the basic percent formula: $P = \% \times W$. To find the part, simply substitute into the formula: $P = \% \times W$. To find the percent, use: $\% = \dfrac{P}{W}$, and to find the whole, use: $W = \dfrac{P}{\%}$.

The following percent word problems are based on actual GRE and GMAT questions. See if you can use the above formulas to determine the solutions. Remember to read each problem carefully. Make sure that you have matching units, and make sure that you answer the question being asked.

1. In a student council election, Ted received 18 out of 120 votes. What percent of the students did not vote for Ted?
   - **(A)** 8%
   - **(B)** 12%
   - **(C)** 15%
   - **(D)** 85%
   - **(E)** 92%

In this problem, selecting choice (C) is a common mistake. Once again, answering this question correctly hinges on carefully reading each word. If you miss the word "not" in the second sentence, you will end up selecting choice (C). The computation to solve the problem can be done in two different ways. One way is to begin by determining the percent of students who voted for Ted. Here, the part would be 18 and the whole would be 120, so the percent is $18 \div 120 = 0.15 = 15\%$. The percent of the students who did not vote for Ted would be $100\% - 15\% = 85\%$. You also could get the answer by realizing that $120 - 18 = 102$ students did not vote for Ted. Thus, $102 \div 120 = 0.85 = 85\%$ of the students did not vote for Ted. **The correct answer is (D).**

2. At Union College, there are 4,000 juniors and 5,000 seniors. If 25% of the juniors and 60% of the seniors went to the championship football game, approximately what percent of the junior and senior class, taken together, went to the championship football game?
   - **(A)** 28.6%
   - **(B)** 42.5%
   - **(C)** 44.4%
   - **(D)** 54.2%
   - **(E)** 85.0%

In order to solve this problem, we need to perform three rather straightforward percent computations. To begin, in the junior class, $4{,}000 \times 25\% = 4{,}000 \times 0.25 = 1{,}000$ students went to the game. In the senior class, $5{,}000 \times 60\% = 5{,}000 \times 0.60 = 3{,}000$ students went to the game. Therefore, the total number of students who went to the game would be $1{,}000 + 3{,}000 = 4{,}000$, out of a total junior and senior size of $4{,}000 + 5{,}000 = 9{,}000$. Thus, the overall percent of juniors and seniors who went to the game would be $4{,}000 \div 9{,}000 = 44.4\%$.

Students commonly make the following errors when solving this problem. If you add the two percents in the problem together, you will get $25\% + 60\% = 85\%$, which is choice (E). If you compute the average of the given percents, you will get $\dfrac{25\% + 60\%}{2} = \dfrac{85\%}{2} = 42.5\%$ which is choice (B). The reason you cannot average the two percents is that there are different numbers of students in the junior and senior classes, so their percentages are "weighted" differently. Much more will be said about this when we talk about "weighted averages" in Chapter 3: Algebra Review. **The correct answer is (C).**

3. What percent of 30 is 48?

    (A) 37.5%

    (B) 60%

    (C) 62.5%

    (D) 140%

    (E) 160%

This problem is asking you to find a percent. So, the key is to correctly identify the part and the whole right at the beginning. While it is relatively easy to tell the part from the whole in a word problem with a context, in this problem you are just given the two numbers. Note that, if you decide that the part is 30 and the percent is 48, you will arrive at choice (C): $30 \div 48 = 0.625 = 62.5\%$. On the other hand, if you conclude that the part is 48 and the whole is 30, you will be led to answer choice (E): $48 \div 30 = 1.6 = 160\%$. So how do you distinguish the part from the whole?

To help you determine which is which, remember that the basic percent formula that we are using to solve all of these problems is *percent* × *whole* = *part*, which, in words, can be stated as "percent of whole is part." Note that the word "of" precedes the whole and the word "is" precedes the part. In our problem, the word "of" precedes the 30 and the word "is" precedes the 48. This tells us that the whole is 30 and the part is 48. To find the percent, divide the part by the whole. The correct answer is $48 \div 30 = 1.6 = 160\%$. The reason that the correct answer is larger than 100% is that the part is bigger than the whole in this problem. **The correct answer is (E).**

4. A snack food manufacturer discovers that 0.12 percent of the bags of pretzels that they fill are underweight. On the average, how many bags of pretzels would have to be filled in order to end up with 3 bags that are underweight?

    (A) 4,000

    (B) 2,500

    (C) 400

    (D) 250

    (E) 25

Let's start by looking at something that causes many students to compute the wrong answer to this problem. The percent in this problem is 0.12 percent. What is this percent written as a decimal? Be careful—it is not 0.12. Actually, 0.12 percent is equal to $0.12\% = 0.0012$. Note that choices (B), (D), and (E) differ from each other by factors of 10. The problem is set up so that if you mistakenly write the percent as 0.12, or make any other error in decimal point placement, the answer you obtain will be there.

We are given the *percent*, and we also have the number 3, which represents the *part* of the bags that are underweight. To find the whole, we merely divide the part by the percent: $3 \div 0.12\% = 3 \div 0.0012 = 2{,}500$. If you make the mistake discussed above, you will get 25 as your answer, and if you divide in the wrong order, you will likely select choices (A) or (C). **The correct answer is (B).**

Percent of Change Word Problems

There is a special type of percent problem, known as a *percent of change* problem, which often appears on the GRE and GMAT. Percent of change problems really are just special cases of the percent problems already discussed, and can be solved using the basic percent formula. However, it is actually a bit easier to use special forms of the percent formulas to solve these problems.

In a percent of change problem, the starting value of a particular quantity (its *original value)* changes by a certain amount (the *increase* or the *decrease*) and ends up having a different value (the *new value)*. One common type of question gives you the original value and the new value and asks you to find the *percent of change*. For example, a store might originally have 40 employees (thus 40 is the original value), and hire 10 new employees (an increase of 10), resulting in a store with 50 employees (thus, 50 is the new value). The question would be to find the percent of increase, that is, the percent by which the number of employees has increased.

In the previous section, we discussed the fact that every percent problem involves three quantities: the percent, the part, and the whole. Percent of change problems are no exception. All you need to know in order to be able to solve any percent of change problem is the following: in a percent of change problem, the original value is the whole, the amount of change is the part, and the percent of change is the percent.

Consider the following sample problems.

Sample Word Problem #1: A store originally has 40 employees and hires 10 new employees. What is the percent of increase in the number of employees?

In this problem, we are asked to find the percent of increase. Recall the formula we used previously to find a percent: $\% = \dfrac{P}{W}$. Since, in a percent of change problem, the amount of change is the part, and the original value is the whole, we modify the formula as follows: % of change $= \dfrac{\text{change}}{\text{original}}$.

> **NOTE:** To solve any problem that asks you to find a percent of change, you can use the formula % of change $= \dfrac{\text{change}}{\text{original}}$.

Since the original value is 40, and the change is 10, we can determine the percent of change as follows:

% of change $= \dfrac{\text{change}}{\text{original}} = \dfrac{10}{40} = 0.25 = 25\%$

Sample Word Problem #2: From one year to the next, the number of students in the freshman class decreases from 550 to 440. What is the percent of decrease in the number of students?

Unlike the previous problem, this problem does not tell us the change, that is, the amount of the decrease in the size of the class. To find the amount of decrease, however, we just need to subtract the new value from the original value: 550 − 440 = 110.

After this, we can continue as in Sample Word Problem #1: % of change $= \dfrac{\text{change}}{\text{original}} = \dfrac{110}{550} = 0.20 = 20\%$.

Another version of the percent of change problem gives you the original value and the percent of change (either a *percent of increase* or a *percent of decrease*) and asks you to find the new value. The next example shows you how to solve such problems.

Sample Word Problem #3: Shawn has a part-time job and earns $64.00 a week. If he is given a 12% raise, what is his new weekly salary?

In this problem, the original value is $64, and the percent of change is 12%. To solve this problem, we begin by finding the amount of change, that is, the amount of the salary increase. The amount of increase is the part, and we can find it by modifying the "Percent × Whole = Part" formula into its special "percent of change" version: "Percent of Change × Original Value = Change." Specifically, in this problem, Percent of Change × Original Value = 12% × 64.00 = 0.12 × $64 = $7.68.

Once you know that the amount of the raise is $7.68, you simply need to add it to the original value to find the new value. Since the change is an increase of $7.68, the new value will be $64.00 + $7.68 = $71.68.

NOTE: To solve a problem that asks you to find the new value, begin by determining the amount of change. Then, if the change is an increase, add it to the original value, and if the change is a decrease, subtract it from the original value.

The problems below give you some practice with percent of change problems.

1. Dan borrowed $3,000 from his father. They agreed that Dan would pay back the money after one year, along with 6% interest. How much money will Dan need in total to pay back his father?
   (A) $180
   (B) $1,800
   (C) $3,018
   (D) $3,180
   (E) $3,360

This problem is asking you to find the new value after a percent of increase. To begin, find the amount of the increase, that is, the amount of interest that Dan needs to pay his father.

$$\text{increase} = \text{percent of change} \times \text{original value} = 6\% \times \$3,000 = 0.06 \times \$3,000 = \$180.$$

Now add the interest of $180 to the original value of $3,000 to get the total amount owed of $3,180. **The correct answer is (D).**

BE CAREFUL: A common mistake is choosing choice (A), the amount of interest, but not the total owed. Similarly, if you make a decimal place error, you might end up with choice (C).

---

2. During a sale, the price of a pair of shoes is reduced by 18%. If the shoes originally cost $80, how much is the sale price?
   (A) $14.40
   (B) $62.00
   (C) $64.80
   (D) $65.60
   (E) $66.20

This problem asks you to find the new value after a percent of decrease. Be careful not to select choice (A), which represents the amount of the discount: $80 × 0.18 = $14.40. Also, avoid choice (B), which represents the price of the shoes reduced by $18, not by 18%. Instead, take the amount of the discount, $14.40, and subtract it from $80 to get the sale price: $80 − $14.40 = $65.60.

Note that a slightly quicker way to solve the problem is to use the fact that if 18% is removed from the regular price, 82% is left. Therefore, the answer would be $80 × 0.82 = $65.60. **The correct answer is (D).**

3. Before going shopping, Hazel had $300. When she returned, she had $240 left. What percent of her money did she spend?

  (A) 20%

  (B) 25%

  (C) 25%

  (D) 30%

  (E) 60%

This question tests whether you know how to find a percent of change. Begin by computing the change in the amount of money that she had, which is $300 − $240 = $60. To find the percent of change, you must divide the change (which is $60) by the original value (which is $300). Thus, $60 ÷ $300 = 0.20 = 20% yields choice (A). If you mistakenly divide the change by the new value, you will be led to choice (C). If you compute the change of $60 and stop there, you might mistakenly pick choice (E). **The correct answer is (A).**

Word Problems Involving Fractions

Once you have mastered the problem-solving techniques that have already been discussed in this chapter, this section will be less intimidating. Most of the problems are similar to ones we have already learned how to solve.

Fraction word problems that appear on the GRE and GMAT tend to call upon your ability to perform computations on fractions, as well as your ability to solve percent problems. Unlike the problems that we solved at the beginning of the section, however, this time you need to carefully read a word problem in order to determine the operations that need to be performed. Once you determine what needs to be done, these problems are identical to problems that we have already solved.

The sample GRE and GMAT questions below illustrate both types of fraction word problems.

1. If the cost of a bottle of iced tea is $\frac{2}{3}$ of the cost of a bottle of lemonade, and a bottle of lemonade costs 90 cents, what is the total cost of four bottles of iced tea and two bottles of lemonade?

  (A) $1.50

  (B) $2.40

  (C) $3.00

  (D) $4.20

  (E) $12.60

Make sure you read this problem carefully so that you can identify the important components. First of all, we are told that a bottle of lemonade costs 90 cents, and that a bottle of iced tea costs $\frac{2}{3}$ of this. Since $\frac{2}{3}$ of 90 cents is $\frac{2}{3}$ × 90 cents = 60 cents, a bottle of iced tea costs 60 cents. Next, four bottles of iced tea would cost 4 × 60 cents = $2.40, and, if we add on $1.80 for two bottles of lemonade, we get a total cost of $4.20. The various wrong answers relate to the mistakes that you might make if you do not read the problem carefully and make common errors. For example, you would get choice (A) if you add up the cost of only *one* bottle of iced tea and only *one* bottle of lemonade. **The correct answer is (D).**

2. Rachel did $\frac{2}{5}$ of her homework on Saturday and then $\frac{1}{3}$ of the rest of her homework on Sunday morning. What part of her homework remains to be completed?

(A) $\frac{1}{5}$

(B) $\frac{4}{15}$

(C) $\frac{2}{5}$

(D) $\frac{1}{2}$

(E) $\frac{11}{15}$

Once again, reading the problem carefully is crucial. There are two key phrases here. The first key phrase is the fact that she did "$\frac{1}{3}$ of the *rest* of her homework on Sunday morning." If you read this problem too quickly, and conclude that she did "$\frac{1}{3}$ of her homework" on Sunday morning, you would compute that she did $\frac{2}{5} + \frac{1}{3} = \frac{11}{15}$ of her homework.

The second key phrase is "remains to be completed." The problem does not ask what part of her homework *was* actually completed, but instead asks what part *remains* to be completed. If you misread the problem and answer with the part of her homework that she completed, you would be led to choice (E). If you correctly read "remains to be completed," but misread the first key phrase, you would get choice (B).

If she does $\frac{2}{5}$ of her homework on Saturday, that leaves $\frac{3}{5}$ of her work to still be done. We are told that, on Sunday morning, she does $\frac{1}{3}$ of that remaining $\frac{3}{5}$. If you remember that the word "of" when preceded by a percent or a fraction is an indication to multiply, we see that on Sunday morning, she does $\frac{1}{3} \times \frac{3}{5} = \frac{1}{5}$ of her homework. She has now done $\frac{2}{5} + \frac{1}{5} = \frac{3}{5}$ of her work, leaving her with an additional $\frac{2}{5}$ to complete. **The correct answer is (C).**

3. Alex spent $\frac{1}{5}$ of his money on clothes, and then $\frac{1}{4}$ of what was left on a movie ticket. If he started with $40, how much money did he have left after buying the clothes and seeing the movie?

(A) $16

(B) $18

(C) $22

(D) $24

(E) $30

This problem is very similar to the previous one, with an additional step. Once again, *make sure you answer the question being asked*. You are told that he spent $\frac{1}{4}$ of *what was left* on a movie ticket. After spending $\frac{1}{5}$ of his money on clothes, he has $\frac{4}{5}$ of the money left. For the movie, he uses $\frac{1}{4}$ of the remaining $\frac{4}{5}$, which is an additional $\frac{1}{4} \times \frac{4}{5} = \frac{1}{5}$ of his money.

Therefore, he has now used $\frac{1}{5} + \frac{1}{5} = \frac{2}{5}$ of his money, which leaves him $\frac{3}{5}$ of his money. Thus, the problem becomes a standard fraction word problem. He started with \$40, and has $\frac{3}{5}$ of that left. In this problem, $\frac{3}{5}$ is the fraction, \$40 is the whole, and we need to find the part. Note that $\frac{3}{5} \times \$40 = 0.60 \times \$40 = \$24$. A common error is to compute money spent = $\frac{1}{5} \times \$40 + \frac{1}{4} \times \$40 = \$8 + \$10 = \$18$. Thus money left = \$40 − \$18 = \$22, which is choice (C). **The correct answer is (D).**

EXERCISES: ARITHMETIC WORD PROBLEMS

Directions: Select the answer choice that best answers the question.

1. If x is 50% of y, then y is what percent of x?
   (A) 20%
   (B) 40%
   (C) 120%
   (D) 125%
   (E) 200%

2. A gas tank containing 3 gallons is $\frac{1}{8}$ full. How many additional gallons of gas are needed to fill the tank?
   (A) 15 gallons
   (B) 16 gallons
   (C) 18 gallons
   (D) 21 gallons
   (E) 24 gallons

3. If $\frac{13}{19} = \frac{a}{13}$, then what is the value of a?
   (A) $\frac{1}{19}$
   (B) $\frac{19}{169}$
   (C) 19
   (D) $\frac{169}{19}$
   (E) 169

4. A long piece of metal tubing that weighs 32 pounds is cut into two pieces. If one of the pieces is 12 feet long and weighs 8 pounds, what was the total length of the pipe before it was cut?
   (A) 24 feet
   (B) 30 feet
   (C) 36 feet
   (D) 40 feet
   (E) 48 feet

5. An athletic footwear store is having a "going out of business" sale. At the start of the first week of the sale, all pairs of shoes are marked down 25%. All pairs of shoes that are not sold by the beginning of the second week are marked down an additional 20%. Finally, all pair of shoes that haven't been sold by the start of the third week are marked down an additional 15%. If the original price of a pair of shoes is S, which of the following represents the price of the shoes after the markdown at the start of the third week?

   (A) $0.40S$

   (B) $0.49S$

   (C) $0.51S$

   (D) $0.55S$

   (E) $0.60S$

6. Dennis goes to the mall with four friends. The amount of money that Dennis brings with him is equal to 25% of the total amount of money that the rest of his friends bring with them. The amount of money that Dennis has is equal to what percent of the entire amount of money that Dennis and all four of his friends have?

   (A) 6.25%

   (B) 12%

   (C) 20%

   (D) 25%

   (E) 50%

ANSWER KEY AND EXPLANATIONS

1. E	3. D	5. C
2. D	4. E	6. C

1. **The correct answer is (E).** Usually, percent problems that contain only letters and no actual numbers are much easier to solve if you substitute actual numbers for the letters. So, let's say that y is 100. In this case, x is 50% of 100, or 50. We need to determine what percent 100 is out of 50. In this case, 100 would be the part, and 50 would be the whole. Thus, we compute $100 \div 50 = 2.0 = 200\%$.

2. **The correct answer is (D).** Read the problem carefully so that you will be sure to answer the question being asked.

   Let's first find the capacity of the tank. We have the fraction, $\frac{1}{8}$, and the part, 3, and the whole is the part divided by the fraction, or, $\frac{3}{\frac{1}{8}} = 3 \times \frac{8}{1} = \frac{24}{1} = 24$. Based on this work, a common mistake is to select choice (E) as the answer. Note that the problem asks for the number of *additional* gallons needed to fill the tank. Since the tank already has 3 gallons in it, it would take $24 - 3 = 21$ gallons to fill the tank.

3. **The correct answer is (D).** This is a proportion problem in which we are already given the proportion and simply asked to find the value of a. Our first step is to cross-multiply to get $13 \times 13 = 19 \times a$. Then, $169 = 19 \times a$, which means $a = \frac{169}{19}$.

   Be careful. In this problem, all of the incorrect answers have been carefully selected to represent all of the possible mistakes that you could make when solving a proportion involving two 13's and a 19.

4. **The correct answer is (E).** There are several different proportions that you could set up to help you solve this problem. Perhaps the easiest way to proceed would be to compare the weight of the 12-foot-long cut piece to that of the original *uncut* piece.

   $$\frac{8 \text{ pounds}}{12 \text{ feet}} = \frac{32 \text{ pounds}}{N \text{ feet}}$$

   Cross-multiplying yields:

   $32 \times 12 = 8 \times N$

   $384 = 8 \times N$

   $N = 384 \div 8 = 48$ feet

   Another strategy is to set up a proportion that compares one piece of the cut tube to the other.

   $$\frac{8 \text{ pounds}}{12 \text{ feet}} = \frac{24 \text{ pounds}}{x \text{ feet}}$$

   Cross-multiplying yields:

   $24 \times 12 = 8 \times N$

   $288 = 8 \times N$

   $N = 288 \div 8 = 36$ feet

Be careful. We haven't yet answered the original question. We need to consider that one piece is 12 feet and the other is 36 feet long in order to determine that the total is 48 feet.

5. **The correct answer is (C).** The most common error in a problem involving this "successive discount" problem is to simply add the discounts together. Adding discounts of 25%, 20%, and 15% yields a total discount of 60%, and a final price of 40% of S, or $0.40S$. However, you need to remember that after the first discount, the second discount is taken off of the already reduced price, and so on. Therefore, you cannot add the discounts together. Another way to see this is to consider the example in which a store offers successive discounts of 50%, 40%, and 30%. Adding the discounts results in a total discount of 120%, which would mean that the *store paid customers to buy the product*.

As mentioned earlier, it is often easier to work with a real number in a percent problem, instead of a variable like the "S" that you are given here. In percent problems the easiest number to work with is almost always 100. Assume, therefore, that the original price of an item is $100. If such an item is marked down 25%, this means that $25 has been taken off, and the price becomes $75. A 20% discount on $75 is worth $0.20 \times 75 = \$15$, so the item is now worth $60. Finally, 15% discount on $60 is $0.15 \times 60 = \$9.00$, and when this is subtracted from $60, we get $51 as the final price. Since the item originally cost $100, it has been discounted to 51% of its original value. If the original price was S, the final sale price would be $0.51S$.

6. **The correct answer is (C).** This would be considered a "hard" GRE and GMAT question. An effective solution strategy is to select a convenient specific number value to work with. Suppose, for example, that Dennis has $10. Since this is equal to 25%, i.e., $\frac{1}{4}$, of the amount of money that the rest of his friends have, then the rest of his friends must have $40. The total money is $10 + $40 = $50. Since we are assuming that Dennis has $10, we can now compute $\frac{\$10}{\$50} = 0.2 = 20\%$. Thus, we conclude that Dennis has 20% of the total money.

ARITHMETIC PRACTICE TEST

GRE Multiple-Choice Questions—Select One Answer Choice

Directions: For Questions 1–5, select a single answer choice.

1. On a business trip, Roy drove 750 miles. How many fifths of a mile did he drive?

   (A) 150

   (B) 370

   (C) 1,500

   (D) 3,750

   (E) 37,500

Disc Package	Price
A	$9.00 for 4
B	$13.40 for 6
C	$4.05 for 2
D	$22.40 for 10
E	$6.75 for 2

2. Glenn needs to buy some recordable compact discs to use with his computer. Based on the data in the table, which package of discs is the least expensive per disc?

   (A) A

   (B) B

   (C) C

   (D) D

   (E) E

3. If x is divided by 13, the remainder is 8. What is the remainder if $5x$ is divided by 13?

   (A) 1

   (B) 3

   (C) 5

   (D) 7

   (E) 9

4. On a chemistry test with 80 questions, Stephen answered 64 questions correctly. What percent of the total number of questions did Stephen answer incorrectly?

   (A) 15%

   (B) 20%

   (C) 25%

   (D) 75%

   (E) 80%

5. If $y = 3x$, what is the value of 40% of x + 20% of y in terms of x?
   (A) $0.80x$
   (B) $0.90x$
   (C) x
   (D) $1.10x$
   (E) $1.20x$

GRE Multiple-Choice Questions—Select One or More Answer Choices

Directions: For Questions 6–8, select one or more answer choices according to the specific question directions. If the question does not specify how many answer choices to select, select all that apply.

- The correct answer may be just one of the choices or may be as many as all of the choices, depending on the question.
- No credit is given unless you select all of the correct choices and no others.

If the question specifies how many answer choices to select, select exactly that number of choices.

6. Which of the following integers are multiples of both 3 and 4?

   Indicate all such integers.
   (A) 8
   (B) 9
   (C) 12
   (D) 24
   (E) 36
   (F) 40

7. Each employee of a certain company is in either Department X or Department Y, and there are more than three times as many employees in Department X as in Department Y. The average (arithmetic mean) salary is $30,000 for the employees in Department X and is $42,000 for the employees in Department Y. Which of the following amounts could be the average salary for all of the employees in the company?

   Indicate all such amounts.
   (A) $30,000
   (B) $31,000
   (C) $32,000
   (D) $33,000

8. Which of the given integers can be written as a difference of two perfect squares?

   Indicate all such integers.
   (A) 1
   (B) 3
   (C) 5
   (D) 7
   (E) 9
   (F) 11

GRE Quantitative Comparison Questions

Directions: For Questions 9–12, compare Quantity A and Quantity B, using additional information centered above the two quantities if such information is given, and select one of the following four answer choices:

(A) Quantity A is greater.

(B) Quantity B is greater.

(C) The two quantities are equal.

(D) The relationship cannot be determined from the information given.

A symbol that appears more than once in a question has the same meaning throughout the question.

Given the positive real number x.

9.　　　　Quantity A　　　　　　　　　　Quantity B

　　　　　　x　　　　　　　　　　　　　x^2

(A) Quantity A is greater.
(B) Quantity B is greater.
(C) The two quantities are equal.
(D) The relationship cannot be determined from the information given.

Given the positive integer n.

10.　　　　Quantity A　　　　　　　　　　Quantity B

　　　　$\dfrac{2^{n+1} - 2^n}{2}$　　　　　　　　　2^{n-1}

(A) Quantity A is greater.
(B) Quantity B is greater.
(C) The two quantities are equal.
(D) The relationship cannot be determined from the information given.

Given the real number $x > 5$.

11.　　　　Quantity A　　　　　　　　　　Quantity B

　　　　$\dfrac{x^2 - 25}{x - 5}$　　　　　　　　　$\dfrac{x^2 - 25}{5 - x}$

(A) Quantity A is greater.
(B) Quantity B is greater.
(C) The two quantities are equal.
(D) The relationship cannot be determined from the information given.

Given the real number x.

12.

Quantity A	Quantity B

$$12x - 5 \qquad\qquad x^2 + 36$$

(A) Quantity A is greater.

(B) Quantity B is greater.

(C) The two quantities are equal.

(D) The relationship cannot be determined from the information given.

GRE Numeric Entry Questions

Directions: For Questions 13–18, enter your answer as an integer or as a decimal if there is a single answer box OR as a fraction if there are two separate boxes—one for the numerator and one for the denominator.

To enter an integer or a decimal, write the number in the answer box provided. On the computer-based test you can either type the number in the answer box using the keyboard or use the Transfer Display button on the calculator. Also, note the following directions for the computer-based test:

- You can click on the answer box and then type the number. You can use the backspace key to erase a number.
- Type a hyphen for a negative sign. Type a hyphen again, and it will disappear. For a decimal point, type a period.
- The Transfer Display button on the calculator will move the calculator display to the answer box.
- Equivalent forms of the correct answer, such as 2.5 and 2.50, are all correct.
- Enter the exact answer unless the question asks you to round your answer.

13. On a soccer team with 11 players in the field, the ratio of defenders to forwards is $\frac{4}{3}$. What is the ratio of forwards to total number of players?

    Give your answer as a fraction.

14. Oranges sell for $7.95 for 5 pounds. What is the cost of 3 pounds of oranges?

    $

15. A piece of wood is cut into 6 pieces, each of which is 2 feet 4 inches long. How long, in feet, was the piece of wood before it was cut?

     feet

16. The Lorenzo's poodle was put on a diet. After 8 weeks, he weighed 28 pounds, which was 70% of his weight prior to being put on the diet. What was the dog's weight before the diet?

17. A tennis ball is dropped from a height of 12 yards. Every time that the ball hits the ground, it bounces back to $\frac{2}{5}$ of its previous height. After the ball hits the ground for the second time, how high does it bounce?

$$\boxed{} \text{ yards}$$

18. The value of a $5,500 investment increases by 12%. What is the value of the investment after the increase?

$$\$\boxed{}$$

GMAT Problem-Solving Questions

Directions: For Questions 19–22, solve the problems and indicate the best of the answer choices given.

19. Which number is divisible by 4, 5, 6, and 7?
    (A) 210
    (B) 120
    (C) 240
    (D) 160
    (E) 420

20. What is the sum of the prime numbers between $\frac{1}{3}$ and $11\frac{3}{4}$?
    (A) 26
    (B) 29
    (C) 27
    (D) 28
    (E) 30

21. In one box of candy, 45% is chocolate. In another box of candy, twice the size of the first one, 35% is chocolate. Both boxes are emptied into the same bowl. What percentage of the candy in the bowl is not chocolate?

    (A) $61\frac{2}{3}\%$
    (B) $38\frac{1}{3}\%$
    (C) 40%
    (D) $41\frac{2}{3}\%$
    (E) 60%

22. If $\dfrac{w}{n-w} = \dfrac{7}{13}$, what does $\dfrac{n}{w}$ equal?

    (A) $\dfrac{7}{20}$

    (B) $\dfrac{20}{7}$

    (C) $\dfrac{6}{7}$

    (D) $\dfrac{7}{6}$

    (E) $\dfrac{27}{20}$

GMAT Data Sufficiency Questions

Directions: Questions 23–26 consist of a question and two statements, labeled (1) and (2), in which certain data is given. You have to decide whether the data given in the statements is sufficient for answering the question. Using the data given in the statements plus your knowledge of mathematics and everyday facts (such as the number of days in July and the meaning of "counterclockwise"), you must indicate whether

   (A) Statement (1) ALONE is sufficient, but statement (2) is not sufficient.

   (B) Statement (2) ALONE is sufficient, but statement (1) is not sufficient.

   (C) BOTH statements TOGETHER are sufficient, but NEITHER statement ALONE is sufficient.

   (D) EACH statement ALONE is sufficient.

   (E) Statements (1) and (2) TOGETHER are NOT sufficient.

23. Given that J, K, L, M, and N are consecutive integers, when is $J \times K \times L < 12$?

    (1) J is odd.

    (2) $J \leq 2$

    (A) Statement (1) ALONE is sufficient, but statement (2) is not sufficient.

    (B) Statement (2) ALONE is sufficient, but statement (1) is not sufficient.

    (C) BOTH statements TOGETHER are sufficient, but NEITHER statement ALONE is sufficient.

    (D) EACH statement ALONE is sufficient.

    (E) Statements (1) and (2) TOGETHER are NOT sufficient.

24. How far can Julie travel in her car on $48 of gas?

    (1) Julie's car gets 32 miles per gallon.

    (2) The gas cost $3.03 per gallon.

    (A) Statement (1) ALONE is sufficient, but statement (2) is not sufficient.

    (B) Statement (2) ALONE is sufficient, but statement (1) is not sufficient.

    (C) BOTH statements TOGETHER are sufficient, but NEITHER statement ALONE is sufficient.

    (D) EACH statement ALONE is sufficient.

    (E) Statements (1) and (2) TOGETHER are NOT sufficient.

25. Given $x^2 - y^2$, what is the value of $3y$?

(1) $x = 0$

(2) $y > 1$

(A) Statement (1) ALONE is sufficient, but statement (2) is not sufficient.

(B) Statement (2) ALONE is sufficient, but statement (1) is not sufficient.

(C) BOTH statements TOGETHER are sufficient, but NEITHER statement ALONE is sufficient.

(D) EACH statement ALONE is sufficient.

(E) Statements (1) and (2) TOGETHER are NOT sufficient.

26. If y is an integer, is it an odd number?

(1) $y^3 \geq 0$

(2) y is either an odd number or a negative number

(A) Statement (1) ALONE is sufficient, but statement (2) is not sufficient.

(B) Statement (2) ALONE is sufficient, but statement (1) is not sufficient.

(C) BOTH statements TOGETHER are sufficient, but NEITHER statement ALONE is sufficient.

(D) EACH statement ALONE is sufficient.

(E) Statements (1) and (2) TOGETHER are NOT sufficient.

ANSWER KEY AND EXPLANATIONS

1. D	7. B, C	12. B	17. 1.92	22. B
2. C	8. A, B, C, D,	13. $\dfrac{3}{11}$	18. 6,160	23. B
3. A	E, F		19. E	24. C
4. B	9. D	14. 4.77	20. D	25. E
5. C	10. C	15. 14	21. A	26. C
6. C, D, E	11. A	16. 40		

1. **The correct answer is (D).** Since every mile contains 5 fifths of a mile, 750 miles must contain 750×5 fifths $= 3,750$ fifths. Be careful not to *divide* 750 by 5, which yields the incorrect answer 150.

2. **The correct answer is (C).** In this question, you need to determine which of five proportions is the largest. The easiest way to determine which proportion is the largest is to simply perform the division indicated by each proportion, and then compare the values. By dividing, you can determine that $9.00 for 4 is the same as $2.25 for 1. In the same way, $13.40 for 6 is the same as $2.23 per 1, $4.05 for 2 is the same as $2.03 per 1, $22.40 for 10 is the same as $2.24 per 1, and $6.75 for 2 is the same as $3.38 per 1. Thus, Package C is the least expensive per disc.

3. **The correct answer is (A).** As we have seen, a straightforward way to solve this type of problem is by picking a number for x and working with that value instead of x. All we need is a number which, when divided by 13, gives us a remainder of 9. The quickest way to find such a number is to just add 13 and 9 together to get 21. Let's say x is equal to 21. Note that 5×21 is 105, and when 105 is divided by 13, the remainder will be 1.

4. **The correct answer is (B).** Here we have another question that requires careful reading. We are told that Stephen answered 64 out of 80 questions correctly, and we need to determine the percent of questions that he answered *incorrectly*. He answered $80 - 64 = 16$ questions incorrectly, and 16 out of 80 is given by $16 \div 80 = 0.20 = 20\%$.

5. **The correct answer is (C).** Begin by writing the percents as decimals, so that we are being asked to find $0.40x + 0.20y$. Next, since $y = 3x$, replace the y in the expression with $3x$.

    Thus, we have $0.40x + 0.20y = 0.40x + 0.20(3x) = 0.40x + 0.60x = 1.0x = x$.

6. **The correct answers are (C), (D), and (E).** Since there are only 6 answer choices listed, perhaps the quickest way to solve this problem is to divide each number in the list by 12. Note that any number divisible by both 3 and 4 must also be divisible by 12, since 3 and 4 do not share a common factor. The only listed numbers divisible by 12 are 12, choice (C), 24, choice (D), and 36, choice (E).

7. **The correct answers are (B) and (C).** One strategy for answering this kind of question is to find the least and/or greatest possible value. We know that the average salary must be between $30,000 and $42,000, since these are the smallest and largest salary values in the list. Since you are told that there are more employees with the lower average salary, the average salary of all employees must be less than the average of $30,000 and $42,000, which is $36,000. If there were exactly three times as many employees in Department X as in Department Y, then the average salary for all employees would be, to the nearest dollar, the following weighted mean, $\dfrac{(3)(30,000)+(1)(42,000)}{3+1} = 33,000$ dollars, where the weight for $30,000 is 3 and the weight for $42,000 is 1. Since there are *more* than three times as many employees in Department X as in Department Y, the actual average salary must be even closer to $33,000 because the weight for $33,000 is greater than 3.

This means that $33,000 is the greatest possible average. Among the choices given, the possible values of the average are therefore $31,000 and $32,000. Thus, the correct answer consists of choices (B) ($31,000) and (C) ($32,000).

Intuitively, you might expect that any amount between $30,000 and $33,000 is a possible value of the average salary. To see that $31,000 is possible, in the weighted mean above, use the respective weights 5 and 1 instead of 3 and 1. To see that $33,000 is possible, use the respective weights 10 and 3.

8. **The correct answers are (A), (B), (C), (D), (E), and (F).** The solution to this problem uses the fact that *every odd integer can be written as a difference of 2 perfect squares*. For the numbers listed as answer choices, we have: $1 = 1 - 0$; $3 = 4 - 1$; $5 = 9 - 4$; $7 = 16 - 9$; $9 = 25 - 16$; $11 = 36 - 25$ .... To see the pattern, note that we can generate a list of odd integers by using the expression $2n + 1$, with $n = 0, 1, 2, 3, ...$ We can then use the fact that $(n+1)^2 - n^2 = n^2 + 2n + 1 - n^2 = 2n + 1$.

9. **The correct answer is (D).** If x is a positive whole number, then we know that $x^2 > x$. However, the key to this problem is to notice that x can represent *any positive real number*, and not just a whole number. For example, if $x = \dfrac{1}{2}$, then $x^2 = \left(\dfrac{1}{2}\right)^2 = \dfrac{1}{4}$, which means that, in this case $x^2 < x$. Thus, the relationship cannot be determined from the information given.

10. **The correct answer is (C).** A useful strategy in this type of comparison problem is to try to simplify one of the given expressions. In this problem, properties of factoring and exponents tell us that $\dfrac{2^{n+1} - 2^n}{2} = \dfrac{(2^n)(2^1 - 1)}{2} = \dfrac{(2^n)(1)}{2} = 2^{n-1}$. Thus, the given quantities are equal.

11. **The correct answer is (A).** As in the previous problem, simplifying one of the expressions can help us determine the correct answer. In this problem, we can factor the numerator to see that $\dfrac{x^2 - 25}{x - 5} = \dfrac{(x+5)(x-5)}{x - 5} = x + 5$, as long as $x \neq 5$. Since we are told that $x > 5$, this simplification is valid. Similarly, $\dfrac{x^2 - 25}{5 - x} = \dfrac{(x+5)(x-5)}{5 - x} = \left(\dfrac{x-5}{5-x}\right)(x+5) = (-1)(x+5)$, since the expression $5 - x = -(-5 + x) = -(x - 5)$. Because $x > 5$, we know that $x + 5$ is positive, which means that $-(x + 5)$ is negative. Therefore, Quantity A is greater.

12. **The correct answer is (B).** An effective strategy for solving this problem is to compare the two given expressions using properties of algebra. That is, we consider the expression $12x - 5 \boxed{?} x^2 + 36$. The choices for the $\boxed{?}$ are the symbols $>, <, \geq, \leq,$ and $=$. Note that in every case, we can use basic arithmetic to rearrange the terms in the original expression without changing the value of the expression. For example, we can subtract $12x$ from each side as follows:

$12x - 5 \boxed{?} x^2 + 36$ yields $-5 \boxed{?} x^2 + 36 - 12x$

We now rearrange the right hand side to get $-5 \boxed{?} x^2 - 12x + 36$.

Note that the right hand side can now be factored as $-5 \boxed{?} (x - 6)^2$.

Since $(x - 6)^2$ is always greater than or equal to 0, we conclude that $-5 < (x - 6)^2$. Thus, the correct form of the original expression is $12x - 5 < x^2 + 36$. Therefore, Quantity B is greater.

13. **The correct answer is $\frac{3}{11}$.** The ratio is 3 forwards to 11 players.

14. **The correct answer is $4.77.** This problem can be solved by setting up and solving a proportion.

$$\frac{\$7.95}{5 \text{ pounds}} = \frac{N}{3 \text{ pounds}}$$

Cross-multiplying yields:

$$\$7.95 \times 3 \text{ pounds} = N \times 5 \text{ pounds}$$
$$\$23.85 = N \times 5 \text{ pounds}$$
$$N = \$4.77$$

15. **The correct answer is 14 feet.** To solve this problem, all that we need to do is multiply 2 feet 4 inches by each of the 6 pieces. One way to organize our work is to consider the product given by $6 \times (2 \text{ feet} + 4 \text{ inches}) = 6 \times (2 \text{ feet}) + 6 \times (4 \text{ inches}) = 12 \text{ feet} + 24 \text{ inches}$. Since 24 inches = 2 feet, our final answer is $14 + 2 = 14$ feet.

16. **The correct answer is 40.** In this percent word problem, the part is 28 and the percent is 70%. You are asked to find the whole, which represents the dog's total weight before the diet.

$$W = \frac{P}{\%} = \frac{28}{70\%} = \frac{28}{0.70} = 40$$

Therefore, the dog originally weighed 40 pounds.

17. **The correct answer is 1.92 yards.** This problem tests whether you know how to multiply fractions and whole numbers. After the ball hits the ground for the first time, it bounces to a height of $12 \times \frac{2}{5} = \frac{24}{5}$ yards. After another bounce, it reaches a height of $\frac{24}{5} \times \frac{2}{5} = \frac{48}{25}$ yards. Since $\frac{2}{5} = 0.4$, we have $12 \times 0.4 \times 0.4 = 1.92$ yards.

18. **The correct answer is $6,160.** The amount by which the investment increases is given by $\$5,500 \times 12\% = \$5,500 \times 0.12 = \$660$. Thus the new value of the investment is $\$5,500 + \$660 = \$6,160$.

19. **The correct answer is (E).** The quickest way to solve this problem is to note that any number divisible by 4, 5, 6, and 7 must be divisible by $3 \times 4 \times 5 \times 7 = 420$.

20. **The correct answer is (D).** Note that the prime numbers between $\frac{1}{3}$ and $11\frac{3}{4}$ are 2, 3, 5, 7, and 11. Thus, we get the sum $2 + 3 + 5 + 7 + 11 = 28$. Perhaps the two most common mistakes in this problem are forgetting that 1 *is not* prime and that 2 *is* prime.

21. **The correct answer is (A).** An effective strategy to use here is to choose convenient specific values for the total number of pieces of candy in each box. Also, be careful to notice that you are being asked a question about the *non-chocolate* pieces. For example, if the first box contains 100 pieces, 45% of which are chocolate, then there are $45\% \times 100 = 0.45 \times 100 = 45$ chocolates and 55 *non-chocolates*. Since the second box contains twice as many pieces as the first, we have a total of 200 pieces in the second box, of which 35% are chocolate. Thus, the second box contains $35\% \times 200 = 0.35 \times 200 = 70$ chocolates, and, therefore, 130 *non-chocolates*. This means that, once the boxes are emptied into the bowl, we have a total of $100 + 200 = 300$ pieces, of which $55 + 130 = 185$ are not chocolate. Therefore, the percentage of candy in the bowl that is *not* chocolate is $\frac{185}{300} = 61\frac{2}{3}\%$.

22. **The correct answer is (B).** This problem requires you to solve a given proportion. Notice that the given proportion $\frac{w}{n-w} = \frac{7}{13}$ can be rewritten by inverting both sides to get $\frac{n-w}{w} = \frac{13}{7}$. We can now break apart the fraction of the left side of the equation as follows:

$$\frac{n-w}{w} = \frac{13}{7}$$

$$\frac{n}{w} - \frac{w}{w} = \frac{13}{7}$$

$$\frac{n}{w} - 1 = \frac{13}{7}$$

Adding 1 to both sides yields $\frac{n}{w} = \frac{13}{7} + 1 = \frac{13}{7} + \frac{7}{7} = \frac{20}{7}$.

23. **The correct answer is (B).** Note that if $J = 3$, then statement (1) is true, but $J \times K \times L = 3 \times 4 \times 5 = 60$, which is greater than 12. So statement (1) ALONE is not sufficient. If $J = 2$, then statement (2) is true. If $J = 2$ means that $K = 3$, and $L = 4$. And $J \times K \times L = 2 \times 3 \times 4 = 24$, which is greater than 12. So statement (2) ALONE is not sufficient. But if we combine the given information from both statements we see that J has to be 1, since 1 is the only odd number less than 2. $J \times K \times L = 1 \times 2 \times 3 = 6$, which is less than 12. So, BOTH statements TOGETHER are sufficient, but NEITHER statement ALONE is sufficient.

24. **The correct answer is (C).** Note that statement (1) gives us data with units of "miles per gallon," and statement (2) gives us data with units of "dollars per gallon." We need to answer a question with units of "miles." In order to convert miles per gallon to miles, we must know the total number of gallons so that we can calculate $\frac{\text{miles}}{\text{gallon}} \times \text{gallons} = \text{miles}$. However, the original question only tells us how many dollars were spent. Thus, statement (1) ALONE is not sufficient. Moreover, using statement (2) ALONE with the given information only allows us to calculate $\frac{\text{dollars}}{\left(\frac{\text{dollars}}{\text{gallon}}\right)} = \text{dollars} \times \frac{\text{gallons}}{\text{dollar}} = \text{gallons}$. Thus, statement (2) ALONE is not sufficient. But if we combine the given information with the data from BOTH statements (1) and (2) TOGETHER, we have $\$48 \times \frac{1 \text{ gallon}}{\$3.00} \times \frac{32 \text{ miles}}{\text{gallon}} = \frac{48 \times 32}{3} = 512 \text{ miles}$.

25. **The correct answer is (E).** If statement (1) is true, then all we can conclude is that $x = 0$, which means that $x^2 - y^2 = 0 - y^2 = y^2$. So statement (1) ALONE is not sufficient. Similarly, if statement (2) is true, then all we can conclude is that $y^2 > 1$. So statement (2) ALONE is not sufficient. Moreover, even if statements (1) and (2) are BOTH true, we still don't have enough information to determine a specific value for y, and therefore, we cannot determine the value of $3y$. Thus, statements (1) and (2) TOGETHER are NOT sufficient.

26. **The correct answer is (C).** If statement (1) is true, then y can be even, odd, or zero. So statement (1) ALONE is not sufficient. Note that if $y = -2$, then statement (2) is true, but y is not odd. So statement (2) ALONE is not sufficient. However, if statements (1) and (2) are BOTH true, then we know that $y^3 \geq 0$ forces y to be non-negative, since y^3 will be negative whenever y is negative. Since statement (2) says that y must be negative or odd, if y is not negative, then it must be odd. Thus, BOTH statements TOGETHER are sufficient, but NEITHER statement ALONE is sufficient.

CHAPTER 3

Algebra Review

The algebra questions on the GRE and GMAT are designed to test your knowledge of the following basic concepts:

- Properties of exponents, roots, and radicals

- Combining algebraic expressions using addition, subtraction, multiplication, and division

- Factoring algebraic expressions

- Linear equations with one variable

- Linear equations with two variables

- Solving algebraic inequalities

- Factorable quadratic equations with one variable

- Absolute value equations

- Radical equations

- Strange function problems

- Algebraic word problems involving ratios, percent, mixtures, weighted averages, and rate of travel

Many of the math questions on the GRE and GMAT tests involve algebra in some way. At the start of Chapter 2: Arithmetic Review, we discussed the fact that the arithmetic problems on the GRE and GMAT could be placed in two different categories—*operations and numerical skills problems* and *arithmetic word problems*. Similarly, there are two main types of algebra problems on the GRE and GMAT. First of all, there will be problems that test your knowledge of algebraic techniques. In these problems, you will be asked to compute or to manipulate algebraic expressions and equations involving exponents, positive and negative numbers, polynomials, and so on. In addition, you will need to use algebraic techniques to solve many of the word problems that appear on the test.

The new GRE and GMAT tests contain more algebra topics than ever before. For the first time, you will need to know how to work with things like functions, negative and rational exponents, and absolute values.

ALGEBRAIC COMPUTATIONS

We will begin by reviewing algebraic computations, and then move on to other topics.

Consider the following multiple-choice question.

1. If $x^2 = y^2$, which of the following *must* be true?

    I. $x = y$
    II. $x^3 = y^3$
    III. $x^4 = y^4$

    (A) I only
    (B) II only
    (C) III only
    (D) I and II only
    (E) I, II, and III

Recall that x^2, which is read "x squared," is simply mathematical shorthand for $x \times x$.

In this problem, we are given two quantities, x and y, which, when squared, are equal. It is tempting to reason that if $x^2 = y^2$, then it follows that $x = y$. In other words, it is tempting to conclude that if x and y square to the same number, then x and y must have been the same to begin with. If this is true, then not only does $x = y$, but $x^3 = y^3$, and $x^4 = y^4$. The answer must be choice (E).

However, this reasoning is incorrect. What if x was equal to 4, but y was equal to –4? Then x^2 would be equal to 4^2, or 16. But, $y^2 = (-4)^2 = -4 \times -4 = 16$ also. Thus, $x^2 = y^2$, but x and y are not equal. So option I is not necessarily true. Still using $x = 4$ and $y = -4$, we have $x^3 = 64$ and $y^3 = -64$, so option II is not necessarily true either. In fact, the only statement that *has* to be true is option III, since squaring both sides of the equation $x^2 = y^2$ yields $x^4 = y^4$. The answer, therefore, is not choice (E), but choice (C). **The correct answer is (C).**

This example illustrates that it is crucial to know how to work with "signed," that is, positive and negative numbers, and to know the properties of exponents. The fundamental rules for these concepts, and many other critical concepts, are reviewed in this chapter.

Adding and Subtracting Signed Numbers

In order to add or subtract signed numbers, you need to consider two different situations: the numbers have the same signs or the numbers have different signs.

To add two numbers whose signs are the same, start by ignoring the signs and add the numbers in the usual way. The sign of the answer will be the common sign of the two numbers. For example, to add $(-6) + (-7)$, begin by ignoring the signs, and add 6 and 7 to get 13. Then, since both numbers are negative, the answer would be –13.

To add two numbers whose signs are different, start by ignoring the signs, and subtract the smaller number from the larger. The sign of the correct answer is the sign of the number with the larger size. For example, to add $(-4) + (+7)$, begin by computing $7 - 4 = 3$. Then, since 7 is of larger size than 4, and the sign attached to the 7 is "+," the answer would be +3. In the same way, $(+4) + (-7) = -3$, since the number of larger size is 7, and the 7 has a negative sign attached to it.

The rule for subtracting signed numbers can be stated as follows: change the sign of the second number and add. The three examples below will help make this clear:

$$(-8) - (+3) = (-8) + (-3) = -11$$

$$(+7) - (-8) = (+7) + (+8) = +15$$

$$(-5) - (-4) = (-5) + (+4) = -1$$

In order to add three or more signed numbers you can proceed in two different ways. One option is to keep a running total, adding the numbers two at a time until finished. The other option would be to add the positive and negative numbers separately, and then combine the resulting sums.

As an example, let's add $(+7) + (-6) + (+3) + (-8)$. If you decide to keep a running total, you would think $(+7) + (-6)$ is $+1$; $+1$ and $+3$ is $+4$; and finally $+4$ and -8 is -4. If you decide to add the positive and negative numbers separately, add $+7$ and $+3$ to get $+10$, and then add -6 and -8 to get -14. Finish by combining $+10$ and -14 to get -4.

As a final comment, if your computation involves subtraction as well as addition, change all of the subtractions to additions. Then, use one of the techniques discussed earlier.

GRE CALCULATOR

Since the provided onscreen calculator has a "+/−" key, you can use it to do your computations for you. Simply enter the numerical part of each number and use the "+/−" key to tell the calculator if the entry is positive or negative. So, for example, to perform the above computation, you would press the following calculator keys in the following order: $7 + 6 +/- = + 3 = + 8 +/- = -4$.

As you can see, this will also give you the answer -4.

Multiplying and Dividing Signed Numbers

Multiplication and division with signed numbers is, in most cases, easier than addition and subtraction. The fastest way to proceed is to begin by ignoring the signs, and multiply or divide as usual. Then, count the number of negative signs in the problem. If the number of negative signs is even, the correct answer is positive; if the number of negative signs is odd, the correct answer is negative. Consider the following examples.

$12 \times (-5) = -60$ (there is one negative sign, which means the correct answer is negative)

$(-8) \times (-3) = +24$ (there are two negative signs, which means the correct answer is positive)

The above rules can be used to help you find the value of more complex expressions. For example, if you need to find the value of $\dfrac{(+18)(-8)}{(-6)(-4)}$, begin by ignoring the negative signs and simply evaluate the fraction. When you do this, you end up with the number 6. Next, count the total number of negative signs. Since the computation, when taken as a whole, contains three negative signs, and since three is odd, the correct answer is negative. Thus, the final answer is -6.

Positive Integer Exponents

When a number is multiplied by itself a number of times, there is a useful shorthand involving "exponents," which can be used to indicate the product. For example, instead of writing $9 \times 9 \times 9 \times 9 \times 9$, you can simply write 9^5, which is read "9 to the fifth."

Similarly, the expression 2^6 represents $2 \times 2 \times 2 \times 2 \times 2 \times 2 = 64$.

You may also remember that any number raised to the first power is defined to be equal to the number itself. Thus, for example, $7^1 = 7$ and $x^1 = x$.

Much more will be said about exponents in the next section, where we will discuss the properties of exponents and the meaning of negative and fractional exponents.

The Order of Operations

When you need to perform a series of arithmetic computations on the GRE and GMAT, it is important that you perform them in the correct order or else you may get the wrong answer. As a simple example, consider the computation $3 + 4 \times 5$. If you evaluate this by performing the addition first, you will get $3 + 4 \times 5 = 7 \times 5 = 35$. On the other hand, if you do the multiplication first, you will get $3 + 20 = 23$. In order for everyone to get the same result when they perform the same computation, there needs to be a rule regarding the order in which the computations should be performed.

You may remember the acronym **PEMDAS** from school. This acronym gives you a quick way to remember the 4-step procedure for performing computations correctly. Begin by performing any computations in **P**arentheses. Secondly, evaluate any **E**xponents. For the third step, perform any **M**ultiplications and **D**ivisions in the order they appear in the problem, moving from left to right. In the final step, perform any **A**dditions and **S**ubtractions in order, from left to right. Thus, to evaluate $2^3 - 3(7 - 3)^2$, begin by performing the computation in parentheses. Since $7 - 3 = 4$, the expression becomes $2^3 - 3(4)^2$. Evaluate the two exponents, leading to $8 - 3(16)$. Avoid the temptation to subtract 3 from 8, and instead multiply $3(16) = 48$. To finish the problem, simply subtract $8 - 48 = -40$.

The following problems will help you to understand how the properties of signed numbers are used on the GRE and GMAT.

1. If $a < 0$, which of the following *must* be true?
   (A) $a \times a \times a \times a = a + a + a + a$
   (B) $a \times a \times a \times a > a + a + a + a$
   (C) $a \times a \times a \times a < a + a + a + a$
   (D) $a \times a \times a > a + a + a$
   (E) $a \times a \times a < a + a + a$

Let's begin by considering the first three answer choices, which ask us if we can determine the relationship between a^4 and $4a$. We are told that x is negative, and so a^4 represents a negative number to the fourth power, which would be positive. On the other hand, $4a$ represents a negative number multiplied by 4, which is negative. Since any positive number is larger than any negative number, choice (B) *must* be true.

Let's consider choices (D) and (E), which ask us to compare a^3 to $3a$. Note that a^3 and $3a$ are both negative, so the size relationship is actually going to depend on the value of x. For example, if $a = -1$, $a^3 = -1$ and $3a = -3$, so a^3 is larger. On the other hand, if $a = -2$, $a^3 = -8$ and $3a = -6$, so $3a$ is bigger. Therefore, it is only choice (B) that *must* be true. **The correct answer is (B).**

> **NOTE:** When comparing numerical expressions, always remember that *any* positive number is bigger than *any* negative number.

2. If $x = 3$ and $y = -6$, what is the value of $4x - 6y$?

(A) -48

(B) -36

(C) -24

(D) 36

(E) 48

This type of problem is called a "numerical evaluation problem." You are given the values of x and y and asked to evaluate an expression containing x and y. All you need to do is substitute the values of x and y into the expression, and apply the rules for signed numbers and the order of operations. Thus, $4x - 6y = 4(3) - 6(-6)$.

Begin by performing the multiplications: $4(3) - 6(-6) = 12 - (-36)$.

Finish by subtracting. Remember to change the subtraction sign to addition, and change the sign of the second number: $12 - (-36) = 12 + (+36) = 48$.

Let's take a look at two of the common wrong answers and examine some common errors. First of all, if you perform the operations in order, from left to right, you will evaluate the problem as follows.

$4x - 6y = 4(3) - 6(-6) = 12 - 6(-6) = 6(-6) = -36$. Another common error is to miss one of the minus signs in the second product, and end up with $4x - 6y = 4(3) - 6(-6) = 12 - 6(-6) = 12 - 36 = -24$. This answer is also wrong. Note that both of these common wrong answers are available choices for you. **The correct answer is (E).**

Adding and Subtracting Algebraic Terms

Recall that a *variable* is a letter that is used to stand for an unknown number. Algebraic *terms* are formed by multiplying and dividing variables and numbers. For example, $-5abc$, $12xy^3$, and $15p^2b^3$ are terms.

Two terms are called *like* terms if their variable factors are the same, that is, if they only differ in their *coefficients* (the numbers in front). Therefore, $-52abc$ and $42abc$ are like terms, but $7abc$ and $14bcd$ are not.

To add or subtract like terms, simply add or subtract their coefficients, and put the result in front of the common variable factor. Thus, for example, $-52abc + 42abc = -10abc$.

As another example, $12a^5 - 9a^5 + 5a^5 = 8a^5$.

Unlike terms cannot be combined. So, if you are solving an algebra problem and end up with the expression $5a + 12b$, this will be the final answer. There is no way to combine $5a$ and $12b$ into a single term.

> **BE CAREFUL:** Suppose you end up with $y^2 + y^3$ as the answer to a problem. These 2 terms cannot be combined to get y^5. Sometimes, y^5 will even appear as a multiple-choice answer just to encourage you to make this error.

Multiplying and Dividing Algebraic Terms

We have just seen that only like terms can be added or subtracted. Multiplication and division, however, can be performed on both like and unlike terms. As an example, to multiply $(9a^5)(3b^3)$, simply multiply the coefficients, and place the variable factors at the end. Thus, $(9a^5)(3b^3) = 27a^5b^3$.

Division is performed in an analogous way. The technique is illustrated in the following problem:

$$\frac{-15a^5b^7}{5c^2d^8} = \frac{-3a^5b^7}{c^2d^8}$$

Properties of Exponents

When you are multiplying two expressions that contain the same variable factor, you can use the properties of exponents to simplify the result. Suppose, for example, you needed to perform the multiplication $(a^2)(a^3)$. This problem can be solved by rewriting it as follows: $(a^2)(a^3) = (a \times a) \times (a \times a \times a) = a^5$.

This problem is an example of the first of the *Properties of Exponents*. You may have seen the rule written in this way: $a^m \times a^n = a^{m+n}$. In words, "To multiply two powers with the same base, keep the common base and add the exponents."

A somewhat more complex example of the same concept is shown below:

$$(5a^4b^2)(-4a^2b^3c^5)(3a^3c^8) = (5)(-4)(3)(a^{4+2+3})(b^{2+3})(c^{5+8}) = -60a^9b^5c^{13}$$

In order to quickly perform this computation, you can follow these steps. To begin, determine whether the answer will be positive or negative. Since the product only contains one negative sign, the answer will be negative. Then, multiply the coefficients. Then, take a, b, and c, and add the exponents.

The second of the Properties of Exponents tells us how to divide an expression containing terms with exponents. Consider, for example, the division problem $\dfrac{c^7}{c^4}$. Note that in this problem, you essentially have seven c's multiplied together on the top of a fraction, and four c's multiplied together on the bottom. As long as c is not equal to 0, four of the c's on the top will cancel four of the c's on the bottom. This will leave you with three c's on the top. Algebraically, we say, $\dfrac{c^7}{c^4} = c^{7-4} = c^3$.

Thus, to divide powers with the same base, you keep the same base and subtract the exponents.

So far, we have seen two Properties of Exponents. Let's consider one additional property. What happens when we take a number raised to a power and raise it to a power? For example, what would be the value of $\left(a^3\right)^2$? This expression is easier to evaluate if we break it into pieces. Raising a quantity to the second power means that we are multiplying it by itself two times. Therefore, $\left(a^3\right)^2 = (a^3)(a^3) = a^{3+3} = a^6$.

As this problem demonstrates, to raise a power of a given base to another power, keep the base and multiply the exponents.

SUMMARY OF THE PROPERTIES OF EXPONENTS

The properties of exponents can be summarized in the following way: To multiply two powers with the same base, keep the base and add the exponents; to divide two powers with the same base, keep the base and subtract the exponents; and finally, to raise a power of a given base to another power, keep the base and multiply the exponents. These properties can be written as shown below:

(i) $a^n \times a^m = a^{m+n}$

(ii) $\dfrac{a^n}{a^m} = a^{n-m}$

(iii) $\left(a^m\right)^n = a^{m \times n}$

The common intuition that squaring a number makes it bigger and cubing it makes it bigger still is only true for numbers bigger than 1. If $x = 1$, then x^2, x^3, and so on, are all equal. And, if $0 < x < 1$, squaring x will make it smaller, and cubing x will make it smaller still.

In the same way, the intuition that taking the square root of a number makes it smaller is only true for numbers bigger than 1. The square root of 1 is equal to 1, and the square root of a number between 0 and 1 is bigger than the number itself. For example, $\sqrt{\dfrac{1}{4}} = \dfrac{1}{2}$.

Negative and Rational Exponents

In the previous section, we developed and discussed the rules for computing with positive integer exponents. On the GRE and GMAT, you will also need to understand and be able to work with exponents that are 0, negative, and rational.

Let's reconsider the rule for dividing mathematical expressions containing exponents. Recall that we previously stated the rule as $\dfrac{a^n}{a^m} = a^{n-m}$, so that, for example, $\dfrac{8^9}{8^5} = 8^{9-5} = 8^4$. However, in every example we looked at in the previous section, the exponent of the expression in the numerator was larger than the exponent of the expression in the denominator. What would happen if the exponents were the same?

As an example, what would $\dfrac{8^9}{8^9}$ be equal to? Since the numerator is the same as the denominator, $\dfrac{8^9}{8^9}$ is equal to 1. Note that if we applied the rule for the division of exponents to the expression $\dfrac{8^9}{8^9}$, we would get $\dfrac{8^9}{8^9} = 8^{9-9} = 8^0$. The expression 8^0 may seem strange. After all, what does it mean to multiply 8 by itself "0 times"? However, it turns out that it is very convenient to define 8^0 to be equal to 1. If we do this, the previously mentioned rule for the division of exponents makes sense not only when the exponent of the number in the numerator is larger than that in the denominator, but also when the exponents are equal.

Therefore, mathematicians make a convenient definition, and state that $8^0 = 1$. In fact, any non-zero number raised to the "0 power" is defined to be equal to 1. This definition greatly simplifies computations with exponents.

> **NOTE:** Remember that any non-zero expression that is raised to the "0 power" is equal to 1. So if, for example, you see an expression like $\left(6^3 - 5\sqrt{7} + 21^{49}\right)^0$ on your test, don't waste any time evaluating it. The messy expression in the parentheses is raised to the "0 power," and so the entire expression is equal to 1.

What if the exponent of the expression in the denominator is larger than the exponent of the number in the numerator? For example, what is the value of $\dfrac{8^5}{8^7}$?

Let's begin by evaluating this expression by using the rules for the simplification of fractions. The numerator of the expression consists of five 8's multiplied together. The denominator has seven 8's multiplied together. We can divide the five 8's on the top into five of the 8's on the bottom. This will leave us with a 1 on the top and 8^2 on the bottom, as shown below:

$$\frac{8^5}{8^7} = \frac{8\times8\times8\times8\times8}{8\times8\times8\times8\times8\times8\times8} = \frac{8\times8\times8\times8\times8}{8\times8\times8\times8\times8\times8\times8} = \frac{1}{8^2}$$

Note what happens when we apply the rule for the division of exponents to the expression $\dfrac{8^5}{8^7}$? Subtracting the exponents in the usual way yields $\dfrac{8^5}{8^7} = 8^{5-7} = 8^{-2}$.

This example leads to a convenient definition. We define 8^{-2} to represent the fraction $\frac{1}{8^2}$. With this definition, the rule for the division of exponents will hold no matter what the relative sizes of the exponents in the numerator and denominator are.

> **NOTE:** The easiest way to think about negative exponents is that the negative sign is a "code" that tells you that the base of the exponent needs to be *reciprocated*. A number in the numerator actually belongs in the denominator, and a number in the denominator actually belongs in the numerator.

Carefully study the following examples to make certain that you understand this idea.

$$5^{-2} = \frac{1}{5^2} = \frac{1}{25}$$

$$\left(\frac{1}{3}\right)^{-3} = \left(\frac{3}{1}\right)^3 = 3^3 = 27$$

$$\left(\frac{3}{2}\right)^{-2} = \left(\frac{2}{3}\right)^2 = \frac{2^2}{3^2} = \frac{4}{9}$$

We now have given meaning to both positive and negative integer exponents. It is also useful to give meaning to fractional exponents.

Let's begin by considering what value it might make sense to associate with the expression $2^{1/2}$. Note that, if the first property of exponents is to hold, it must follow that $2^{1/2} \times 2^{1/2} = 2^{1/2+1/2} = 2^1$. Therefore, $2^{1/2}$ must be the number with the property that, when it is multiplied by itself, the result is 2. The number that has this property is $\sqrt{2}$. Thus, if we define $2^{1/2}$ to be $\sqrt{2}$, the first property of exponents still makes sense.

In general, $x^{1/n}$ is defined to represent the nth root of x, that is, $\sqrt[n]{x}$. For example, then, $27^{1/3} = \sqrt[3]{27} = 3$, and $16^{1/4} = \sqrt[4]{16} = 2$.

What would be the interpretation of an expression like $27^{2/3}$? If the third property of exponents is to be true, then it follows that $27^{2/3} = \left(27^{1/3}\right)^2$. This enables us to make sense of fractional exponents. The numerator of the exponent represents the power to which the number is to be raised, and the denominator represents the root of the number to be taken. As another example, to evaluate $9^{3/2}$, we would need to take the square root of 9 and then cube the result. In other words, $9^{3/2} = \left(\sqrt{9}\right)^3 = 3^3 = 27$.

> **NOTE:** Previously we said that the easiest way to think of a negative sign in an exponent is that it is a code that tells you to reciprocate the base. In the same way, think of the numerator of a fractional exponent as a code that tells you the power that the base is to be raised to, and the denominator of the fraction as the root to be taken.

According to the strategy above, for example, if a number x was raised to the $-\frac{4}{5}$ power, we would know that we needed to reciprocate x, take the fifth root, and raise it to the fourth power.

Below are a few additional examples of working with rational exponents.

$$25^{3/2} = \left(\sqrt{25}\right)^3 = 5^3 = 125$$

$$27^{-4/3} = \left(\frac{1}{27}\right)^{4/3} = \left(\sqrt[3]{\frac{1}{27}}\right)^4 = \left(\frac{1}{3}\right)^4 = \frac{1}{81}$$

$$\left(\frac{16}{49}\right)^{-3/2} = \left(\frac{49}{16}\right)^{3/2} = \left(\sqrt{\frac{49}{16}}\right)^3 = \left(\frac{7}{4}\right)^3 = \frac{343}{64}$$

Multiplying and Dividing Polynomials

A *monomial* is an algebraic expression containing only one term. An algebraic expression that contains two terms is called a *binomial*, and an algebraic expression that contains three terms is called a *trinomial*. In general, any algebraic expression with two or more terms is called a *polynomial*.

To multiply a monomial by a binomial, it is necessary to distribute the monomial factor to the two terms in the binomial. For example, $5y(2y - 6) = (5y)(2y) - (5y)(6) = 10y^2 - 30y$.

How would you multiply a binomial by a binomial? You may remember that the acronym **FOIL** can be used to help you remember what to do. **FOIL** is short for "Firsts, Outers, Inners, Lasts." To multiply a binomial by a binomial, simply multiply the two first terms, then the two outermost terms, then the two innermost terms, then the two last terms. This will result in four terms. Should any of these terms be like terms, they should be combined so as to arrive at the final answer. Consider the example, $(x + 7)(x - 3) = (x)(x) - 3(x) + 7(x) + 7(-3) = x^2 - 3x + 7x - 21 = x^2 + 4x - 21$.

Finally, to divide a binomial (or any sort of polynomial) by a monomial, break up the quotient into separate pieces, and perform the resulting divisions.

As an example, consider $\dfrac{15x^5y^7 + 24x^3y^5}{3x^2y^3} = \dfrac{15x^5y^7}{3x^2y^3} + \dfrac{24x^3y^5}{3x^2y^3} = 5x^3y^4 + 8xy^2$.

The following examples illustrate how these properties can be used on GRE and GMAT test questions.

1. If $3.2a + 3.5b = 3.2(a + b)$, which of the following must be true?
   (A) $a = 0$
   (B) $b = 0$
   (C) $a = b$
   (D) $a = b + 0.3$
   (E) $b = a + 0.3$

Begin by performing the multiplication on the expression on the right-hand side. Since $3.2(a + b) = 3.2a + 3.2b$, the given information in the problem tells us that $3.2a + 3.5b = 3.2a + 3.2b$.

Note that we really cannot conclude anything about the value of a. This is because, regardless of the value of a, the $3.2a$ term on the left is going to be equal to the $3.2a$ term on the right. Note also, however, that it must be true that $3.5b = 3.2b$. The only way that this can possibly be true is if $b = 0$. Therefore, we can conclude nothing about the value of a, but we do know that the value of $b = 0$. **The correct answer is (B).**

2. If $x^2 + y^2 = (x - y)^2$, which of the following *must* be true?

   (A) $x + y = 0$

   (B) $x - y = 0$

   (C) $x = 0$

   (D) $y = 0$

   (E) $xy = 0$

Let's begin by performing the multiplication that appears on the right-hand side of the expression. In order to do this, note that $(x - y)^2 = (x - y)(x - y)$. We can perform this multiplication by using the **FOIL** method: $(x - y)(x - y) = x^2 - xy - xy + y^2 = x^2 - 2xy + y^2$.

Essentially, the problem statement is telling us that $x^2 - 2xy + y^2$ is equal to $x^2 + y^2$, which can only be true if $2xy$ is equal to 0.

Under what circumstances is $2xy$ equal to 0? Note that $2xy$ equal to 0 if *either* x or y is equal to 0. With this knowledge, let's look at the answer choices. Remember, all we know is that either x or y is equal to 0. We can eliminate choices (A) and (B), as there is no reason that either $x + y$ must be 0 or $x - y$ must be 0. We can also eliminate choices (C) and (D) since, while we know that either x or y is 0, we don't actually know which one is equal to 0. All that is left is choice (E), which says that $xy = 0$. This statement is true if either x or y is equal to 0. **The correct answer is (E).**

Factoring

In the previous section, we saw how to multiply a monomial by a binomial (by using the distributive property), and how to multiply a binomial by a binomial (by using the **FOIL** method). For example, we now know that $x(x - 7) = x^2 - 7x$ and $(x + 5)(x + 7) = x^2 + 12x + 35$.

The process of "factoring" a polynomial refers to reversing the multiplication processes that are shown above. That is, factoring refers to taking the product of two or more factors and breaking it down into its original factors. For example, if you were asked to factor $x^2 - 7x$, you would need to break it back down into $x(x - 7)$. Similarly, if you were asked to factor $x^2 + 12x + 35$, you would need to break it back down into $(x + 5)(x + 7)$.

The GRE and GMAT tests probably won't contain problems that simply give you a polynomial and ask you to factor it. However, there are some circumstances that *do* occur on the GRE and GMAT that will require factoring. Perhaps the most common situation is one in which you are solving a problem and find the answer, but it doesn't match any of the five answer choices. In this case, before concluding that you have made a mistake, it is worthwhile to try to rewrite the expression in another form. Thus, if you get $y^2 + 5y$ as your answer and it is not among the answer choices, perhaps $y(y + 5)$ will be.

Another circumstance relates to problems involving "quadratic equations." The technique for solving such equations involves factoring and will be reviewed later in the chapter. From time to time you will also see a problem in which knowledge of factoring will help you out. Consider, for example, the problem below:

1. If $(a + b) = 12$, and $(a - b) = 20$, then what is the value of $a^2 - b^2$?

   (A) 8

   (B) 16

   (C) 120

   (D) 240

   (E) 256

The fastest way to find the correct answer is to remember that $a^2 - b^2$ can be factored into $(a + b)(a - b)$. So we have $a^2 - b^2 = (a + b)(a - b) = (12)(20) = 240$. **The correct answer is (D).**

Let's spend a while reviewing factoring. For starters, let's see how to reverse the distributive property and factor out the "largest common factor." Consider the expression $12x^2 - 6x$. The largest common factor of the two terms in this expression is $6x$. In order to "factor out" the $6x$, write the common factor outside of a pair of parentheses, and then divide this common factor into each of the terms of the polynomial and write the resulting terms inside the parentheses.

$$12x^2 - 6x = 6x\left(\frac{12x^2}{6x} - \frac{6x}{6x}\right) = 6x(2x - 1)$$

> **NOTE:** Remember that you can check that you have factored correctly by multiplying the factors you obtained and making certain that you get the original expression. For example, does $9x^2 - 12x = 3x(3x - 4)$? To check, use the distributive property on $3x(3x - 4)$ and you will see that you get $9x^2 - 12x$.

As another example, consider the expression $6x^2y^3 - 3x^4y^6 + 9x^3y^2$. The greatest common factor is $3x^2y^2$, so the factored expression would be $3x^2y^2(2y - x^2y^4 + 3x)$. This answer can be checked by multiplying $3x^2y^2$ by $2y - x^2y^4 + 3x$ to obtain the result $6x^2y^3 - 3x^4y^6 + 9x^3y^2$.

Let's take a look at how to reverse the process of multiplying two binomials. Consider a problem that requires you to factor the expression $x^2 + 12x + 35$. The factoring process relies on a bit of trial and error. Begin by writing two sets of parentheses. The idea is to position the appropriate factors within the parentheses so that when we multiply the quantities in the two parentheses together, we will get the expression $x^2 + 12x + 35$.

The first conclusion to make is that, within each set of parentheses, the first entries must be x's, since we must generate a product of x^2 as our first term.

Thus, as a first step, we can write $x^2 + 12x + 35 = (x \quad)(x \quad)$.

Next, note that both signs have to be positive in order to generate the positive signs in the product. Therefore, $x^2 + 12x + 35 = (x + \quad)(x + \quad)$.

Note that the two missing entries must multiply to the number 35. There are only two integer possibilities. Either the two missing entries are 35 and 1, or they are 7 and 5. Which one is correct? Here is where the trial and error enters the procedure. The correct factorization is the one that produces the correct middle term of $12x$. If you multiply $(x + 35)(x + 1)$ the result is $x^2 + 36x + 35$, which is incorrect. On the other hand, $(x + 7)(x + 5) = x^2 + 12x + 35$, so $(x + 7)(x + 5)$ is the correct factorization.

Let's consider another example. How would you factor $x^2 - 7x - 18$? One again, the two first entries need to be x's, and the signs need to be different so as to be able to generate the product -18. Thus, begin by writing $(x + \quad)(x - \quad)$.

Note that the two missing numbers must be correctly chosen so as to multiply to -18. There are several possibilities, such as $+18$ and -1, -18 and $+1$, $+6$ and -3, -6 and $+3$. However, the only pair that generates the correct middle coefficient of -7 is -9 and $+2$. The correct factorization is $(x + 2)(x - 9)$.

Finally, there is one additional type of factoring, which is really a special case of the factoring we did above. It is known as *factoring the difference of two squares*, and it is the process that enables you to factor expressions such as $x^2 - 16$ or $25a^2 - 9b^2$. Let's start by seeing how to factor $x^2 - 16$.

Begin by making two sets of parentheses. Enter a plus sign within one set of parentheses, and a minus sign within the other. The two first entries must be the same and must multiply to x^2, and the two last terms must be the same and multiply out to 4. Thus, the factorization is $x^2 - 16 = (x + 4)(x - 4)$.

In the same way, to factor $25a^2 - 9b^2$, make two sets of parentheses, and enter a plus sign in one and a minus sign in the other. Again, the two first entries must be the same, so they have to be $5a$. Similarly, the two last entries must be $3b$. Thus, $25a^2 - 9b^2 = (5a + 3b)(5a - 3b)$.

There are three very common factorizations that are regularly used in GRE and GMAT questions and should be memorized:

(i) $\quad x^2 - y^2 = (x + y)(x - y)$

(ii) $\quad x^2 - 2xy + y^2 = (x - y)(x - y) = (x - y)^2$

(iii) $\quad x^2 + 2xy + y^2 = (x + y)(x + y) = (x + y)^2$

> **BE CAREFUL:** A common factoring error is to try to factor a *sum of two perfect squares*. For example, it is tempting to factor the expression $x^2 + 25$ as $x^2 + 25 = (x + 5)(x + 5)$. However, using **FOIL** to multiply out the right-hand side yields $x^2 + 10x + 25$. In fact, the *sum* of two perfect squares DOES NOT factor when working with real numbers.

Algebraic Fractions

Algebraic fractions are fractions that contain variables, for example, $\dfrac{x^2 - 16}{x^2 - x - 12}$. In general, computing with algebraic fractions is very similar to working with regular arithmetic fractions. Just as some arithmetic fractions can be simplified, some algebraic fractions can also be simplified. In order to determine whether a particular fraction can be simplified, you need to factor both the numerator and denominator. If there are any common factors, they can be canceled. For example, to simplify the fraction above, note that $\dfrac{x^2 - 16}{x^2 - x - 12} = \dfrac{(x - 4)(x + 4)}{(x + 3)(x - 4)}$.

The common factors of $x - 4$ can be divided out, giving you the simplified fraction $\dfrac{x + 4}{x + 3}$.

> **BE CAREFUL:** Be certain *not* to cancel common terms before rewriting the expressions in factored form. For example, if you have the fraction $\dfrac{p + 11}{2q + 11}$, you cannot cancel the 11's to get $\dfrac{p}{2q}$. The fraction $\dfrac{p + 11}{2q + 11}$ is already simplified. In the same way, the fraction $\dfrac{a^2 + 15}{a + 3}$ is already in its most simplified form. You cannot divide the a into the a^2, and you cannot divide the 3 into the 15.

Adding, subtracting, multiplying, and dividing algebraic fraction is also very similar to performing these operations on arithmetic fractions. Follow the steps in the two problems below, and you will see the similarities.

$$\frac{y + 3}{6y + 21} + \frac{y + 4}{6y + 21} = \frac{2y + 7}{6y + 21} = \frac{2y + 7}{3(2y + 7)} = \frac{1}{3}$$

$$\frac{x^2 + 7x + 12}{8x} \div \frac{x + 4}{16x} = \frac{x^2 + 7x + 12}{8x} \times \frac{16x}{x + 4} = \frac{(x + 3)(x + 4)}{8x} \times \frac{16x}{x + 4} = 2(x + 3)$$

Square Roots

Note that the "square root of 36" is the positive number that when multiplied times itself yields 36.

Since $6 \times 6 = 36$, the value of $\sqrt{36}$ is 6.

As you will see in Chapter 4: Geometry Review, square roots sometimes appear in problems involving the Pythagorean theorem. Furthermore, sometimes you might see algebraic problems that ask you to manipulate an expression that contains a square root, or be asked to solve an equation that involves square roots.

Numbers such as 0, 1, 4, 9, 16, 25, 36, 49, 64, 81, and 100 are called *perfect squares*, since their square roots are integers. For example, $\sqrt{64} = 8$, $\sqrt{81} = 9$, and $\sqrt{49} = 7$.

The square roots of numbers that are not perfect squares can sometimes be simplified. To simplify a square root, express the number under the square root sign as a product of two numbers, one of which is a perfect square. Then, take the square root of the perfect square, and place it in front of the square root of the remaining number. For example, $\sqrt{18} = \sqrt{2 \times 9} = \sqrt{9} \times \sqrt{2} = 3\sqrt{2}$.

As another example, consider the simplification of $\sqrt{72}$. Since $72 = 36 \times 2$, we can simplify as follows:

$$\sqrt{72} = \sqrt{36} \times \sqrt{2} = 6\sqrt{2}$$

> **NOTE:** Only simplified square roots appear as the solutions to GRE and GMAT multiple-choice questions. If you solve a problem and obtain a square root answer but do not see the square root among the answer choices, see if the square root can be reduced. Perhaps your reduced answer will be among the choices. For example, if you get an answer of $\sqrt{98}$, you will not find this answer among the choices. However, you might find $\sqrt{98} = \sqrt{49 \times 2} = \sqrt{49} \times \sqrt{2} = 7\sqrt{2}$.

Square roots are added and subtracted in the same way like and unlike terms are. Two square root expressions with the same number under the square root sign, such as $5\sqrt{7}$ and $11\sqrt{7}$, are called *like radicals*. Like radicals can be added and subtracted by adding or subtracting their coefficients. For example, $5\sqrt{13} + 12\sqrt{13} = 17\sqrt{13}$, and $19\sqrt{13} - 4\sqrt{13} = 15\sqrt{13}$.

In general, unlike radicals, such as $\sqrt{11}$ and $\sqrt{5}$, cannot be combined.

Let's take a look at how to multiply and divide square roots. The product of two square roots is equal to the square root of the product: $\sqrt{18} \times \sqrt{4} = \sqrt{18 \times 4} = \sqrt{72} = 6\sqrt{2}$.

The quotient of two square roots is equal to the square root of the quotient:

$\dfrac{\sqrt{120}}{\sqrt{3}} = \sqrt{\dfrac{120}{3}} = \sqrt{40} = \sqrt{4 \times 10} = 2\sqrt{10}$.

Here are some sample GRE and GMAT problems involving exponents, signed numbers, factoring, and roots.

1. If $(7^4)^{-5} = 7^n$, what is the value of n?
    - (A) −20
    - (B) −9
    - (C) −1
    - (D) 9
    - (E) 15

In this problem, you need to correctly apply the third property of exponents. Remember that $\left(a^m\right)^n = a^{mn}$. Thus, $\left(7^4\right)^{-5} = 7^{(4) \times (-5)} = 7^{-20}$. Therefore, the value of n is −20. **The correct answer is (A).**

2. If p and q are positive integers with $p \geq 2$ and $q > p$, which of the following fractions must be smaller than $\dfrac{q}{p}$?

  I. $\dfrac{q-1}{p}$

  II. $\dfrac{q}{p-1}$

  III. $\dfrac{q-1}{p-1}$

  (A) I only
  (B) III only
  (C) II and III only
  (D) I and III only
  (E) I, II, and III

This problem is more manageable if you take it a step at a time. First, look at the fraction $\dfrac{q-1}{p}$ as compared to $\dfrac{q}{p}$. These fractions have the same denominators, but the numerator of $\dfrac{q-1}{p}$ is smaller, which means this fraction is smaller. So, we can conclude that $\dfrac{q-1}{p}$ is smaller than $\dfrac{q}{p}$. Thus, the fraction given in option I is smaller.

Let's consider the fraction $\dfrac{q}{p-1}$ as compared to $\dfrac{q}{p}$. These fractions have the same numerators, but the denominator of $\dfrac{q}{p-1}$ is smaller, which makes $\dfrac{q}{p-1}$ larger than $\dfrac{q}{p}$. Thus, the fraction given in option II is larger.

It is the final choice, option III, that is a bit problematic. Note, however, that even if you do no more work, you have cut the correct answer down to two possibilities, choices (A) or (D). Perhaps the best way to deal with the fraction $\dfrac{q-1}{p-1}$ is to try a few examples. Let's say, first of all, that p is 2 and q is 3. Then $\dfrac{q}{p} = \dfrac{3}{2}$. On the other hand, $\dfrac{q-1}{p-1} = \dfrac{2}{1}$, which is larger than $\dfrac{3}{2}$. What would happen if p were 3 and q were 4? Then $\dfrac{q}{p} = \dfrac{4}{3}$. On the other hand, $\dfrac{q-1}{p-1} = \dfrac{3}{2}$, which is larger than $\dfrac{4}{3}$. Another substitution or two should be enough to convince you that $\dfrac{q-1}{p-1}$ is always bigger. **The correct answer is (A).**

3. If $p^2 - q^2 = 70$, and $p + q = 5$, then what is the value of $p - q$?
  (A) 14
  (B) 21
  (C) 65
  (D) 75
  (E) 350

Earlier in this chapter, it was suggested that you memorize three factorization formulas. One of them is $p^2 - q^2 = (p + q)(p - q)$. This formula is fairly common on the GRE and GMAT, and it will help you here. If we take the formula and substitute the information we are given in the problem, we get $70 = 5(p - q)$. So $p - q$ must equal 14. **The correct answer is (A).**

4. If x is a positive number, which of the following is equal to $8x$?

(A) $\sqrt{64x}$

(B) $\sqrt{8x^2}$

(C) $\sqrt{16x^2}$

(D) $2\sqrt{2x}$

(E) $4\sqrt{4x^2}$

Be careful. Since all of the answers involve square roots, it's tempting to square $8x$, obtaining $64x^2$, and put it under a square root sign, obtaining $\sqrt{64x^2}$. Unfortunately, this isn't one of the choices. This can only mean that one of the answer choices must be equivalent to $\sqrt{64x^2}$. So we need to simplify the five answer choices until we determine the correct choice. Note that choice (E) simplifies as follows. Since $\sqrt{4x^2} = 2x$, we have $4\sqrt{4x^2} = 4(2x) = 8x$. **The correct answer is (E).**

EXERCISES: ALGEBRAIC COMPUTATIONS

Directions: Select the answer choice that best answers the question.

1. If $(11^3)^{-4} = \left(\dfrac{1}{11}\right)^q$, what is the value of q?
   (A) -12
   (B) -1
   (C) 1
   (D) 7
   (E) 12

2. Which of the following is equal to $\left(\dfrac{125}{8}\right)^{-2/3}$?

   (A) $-\dfrac{25}{4}$

   (B) $-\dfrac{4}{25}$

   (C) $\dfrac{4}{25}$

   (D) $\dfrac{25}{4}$

   (E) $\dfrac{625}{16}$

3. If $2x^2 + kx - 21 = (2x + 7)(x - 3)$, what is the value of k?
   (A) -6
   (B) -1
   (C) 1
   (D) 7
   (E) 13

4. If $y^9 = 19$, and $y^8 = \dfrac{5}{x}$, what is the value of y in terms of x?

   (A) $\dfrac{x}{95}$

   (B) $\dfrac{95}{x}$

   (C) $\dfrac{19x}{5}$

   (D) $\dfrac{5}{19x}$

   (E) $19 - \dfrac{5}{x}$

5. If $x^4y^3 < 0$, which of the following cannot be true?
   (A) $x > 0$
   (B) $x < 0$
   (C) $xy < 0$
   (D) $xy > 0$
   (E) $y > 0$

6. What is the value of $a^2 - b^2$ if $a - b = 6$, and $a + b = 7$?
   (A) 1
   (B) 42
   (C) 43
   (D) 52
   (E) 84

ANSWER KEY AND EXPLANATIONS

1. E	3. C	5. E
2. C	4. C	6. B

1. **The correct answer is (E).** This problem tests your knowledge of the properties of exponents discussed in this chapter. Using the third property of exponents, $(11^3)^{-4} = 11^{-12} = \left(\frac{1}{11}\right)^{12}$. Therefore, $q = 12$.

2. **The correct answer is (C).** This problem also tests your knowledge of the meaning of rational exponents. Using the definitions from this chapter, you can compute $\left(\frac{125}{8}\right)^{-2/3} = \left(\frac{8}{125}\right)^{2/3} = \left(\frac{\sqrt[3]{8}}{\sqrt[3]{125}}\right)^2 = \left(\frac{2}{5}\right)^2 = \frac{4}{25}$

3. **The correct answer is (C).** This problem tests your knowledge of factoring and multiplication. To solve this problem, perform the multiplication in the expression $(2x + 7)(x - 3)$. $2x^2 + 7x - 6x - 21 = 2x^2 + x - 21$, which means that $k = 1$.

4. **The correct answer is (C).** The challenging part of this problem is determining how to combine the two equations so as to get an expression for y. One mistake to avoid is trying to subtract the second equation from the first. If you make the mistake of thinking $y^9 - y^8 = y$, then you will be led to incorrect answer choice (E). If you remember the properties of exponents, you will realize that $\frac{y^9}{y^8} = y$. If you plug in the values for y^9 and y^8 accordingly you will get $\frac{y^9}{y^8} = \frac{19}{\frac{5}{x}} = \frac{19x}{5}$. Note how the properties of complex fractions discussed in Chapter 2: Arithmetic Review are used in this problem as well.

5. **The correct answer is (E).** Before we examine any of the multiple-choice answers, let's see what we can conclude from the inequality $x^4y^3 < 0$. The first thing to note is that neither x nor y is 0, since the product is negative. Another conclusion is that x^4 is positive, since the fourth power of any non-zero number is positive. However, there is no way to tell if x itself is positive or negative. The final conclusion is that, since x^4 is positive, y^3 must be negative since their product is negative. The only way y^3 can be negative is if y is negative.

Let's look at the answer choices, remembering that we know y is negative, and that we don't know anything about a (except that it is not zero). Very quickly, we can eliminate the first four answers, since whether they are true or not hinges on whether x is positive or negative. In fact, the only thing we are certain of is that $y < 0$, so the correct answer is choice (E).

6. **The correct answer is (B).** There are two ways to do this problem. One method is to find the common solution of the two equations, perhaps by using the addition method. We haven't yet discussed this technique, but you may remember that we can add the two equations together, which allows us to eliminate the variable b.

$a - b = 6$
$\underline{a + b = 7}$
$2a = 13$, which means that $a = \frac{13}{2}$.

If we substitute the value of a into either of the equations, we find that $b = \frac{1}{2}$.

We need to find the value of $a^2 - b^2$.

$$a^2 - b^2 = \left(\frac{13}{2}\right)^2 - \left(\frac{1}{2}\right)^2 = \frac{169}{4} - \frac{1}{4} = \frac{168}{4} = 42$$

A much quicker strategy is to use factoring. Remember, one of the useful factoring formulas is $a^2 - b^2 = (a - b)(a + b)$. And, if you know this, you can solve the problem very quickly.

That is, $a^2 - b^2 = (6)(7) = 42$.

MANIPULATING EQUATIONS

Let's begin this section by looking at a sample GRE and GMAT question involving an equation.

1. If $2x + y = 12$, what is the value of $6x + 3y$?
   - (A) 24
   - (B) 36
   - (C) 48
   - (D) 64
   - (E) It cannot be determined.

In order to be able to handle these types of GRE and GMAT questions, the most important skill that you need to develop is the ability to *manipulate equations*. Not to actually *solve* equations, although that is a part of it, but to *manipulate* them. Manipulating an equation refers to the skill of quickly rewriting it in a variety of equivalent forms. Often, finding the correct way to rewrite an equation is the key to solving the problem.

Note that we can use the problem's given information to find the value of $6x + 3y$, even without knowing the values of x and y. At the start of the problem, we were told that $2x + y = 12$. How about if we were to take both sides of this equation and multiply them by 3? The result would be $6x + 3y = 36$. **The correct answer is (B).**

> **NOTE:** Very often on the GRE and GMAT, when you are given some information about two variables and asked to evaluate some algebraic expression involving these variables, there is a way to evaluate the expression without finding the values of the individual variables. In order to be able to quickly perform the computations required to solve such problems, it is important to be able to manipulate equations quickly.

Consider the following example.

2. If $31a - 11 = 7b$, what is the value of $\dfrac{31a - 11}{7}$ in terms of b?

   - (A) $\dfrac{b}{14}$

   - (B) $\dfrac{b}{7}$

   - (C) b
   - (D) $7b$
   - (E) $14b$

Note that dividing both sides of the given equation by 7 yields $\dfrac{31a - 11}{7} = b$. **The correct answer is (C).**

Performing Manipulations on First-Degree Equations in One Unknown

There are three different types of equations that you need to be able to solve and manipulate on the GRE and GMAT. The first, and by far the most common, is what is known as a *first-degree equation in one unknown*. Such an equation contains only one unknown (although it may appear several times within the equation), and that variable is of the "first degree," that is, it is raised to the first power (not squared, or cubed, etc.). An example of such an equation would be $7x + 12 = 3x - 16$.

In order to "solve" an equation, we need to determine the numerical value (or values) of the given variable that will make the equation a true statement.

> **IMPORTANT FACT:** We can manipulate a given equation using arithmetic (i.e., addition, subtraction, multiplication, and division), provided we perform the same operations on both sides of the equation.

In practice, we can use the following basic rules:

- If you wish to remove a quantity that is added to one side of an equation, subtract it from the other side of the equation.
- If you wish to remove a quantity that is subtracted from one side of an equation, add it to the other side of the equation.
- If you wish to remove a quantity that is multiplied on one side of an equation, divide by it on the other side of the equation.
- If you wish to remove a quantity that is divided on one side of an equation, multiply by it on the other side of the equation.

For Example:

To solve $x + 12 = 18$, change the "addition of 12" on the left-hand side to a "subtraction of 12" on the right-hand side, so $x = 18 - 12 = 6$.

To solve $x - 8 = 9$, change the "subtraction of 8" on the left-hand side to an addition of 8 on the right-hand side, so $x = 9 + 8 = 17$.

To solve $6x = 42$, change the "multiplication by 6" on the left-hand side to a division by 6 on the right-hand side, to get $x = \dfrac{42}{6} = 7$.

To solve $\dfrac{x}{5} = 6$, change the "division by 5" on the left-hand side to a multiplication by 5 on the right-hand side, to get $x = 6 \times 5 = 30$.

This technique can also be used to work with equations whose solution requires more than one step. For example, in order to solve $5x - 4 = 21$, first get rid of the subtraction of 4 on the left by adding 4 to the right. This leaves you with the equation $5x = 25$. Then, get rid of the multiplication by 5 on the left by dividing by 5 on the right. This gives you $x = \dfrac{25}{5} = 5$.

Becoming skilled at solving equations by quickly moving quantities from one side to the other will save you a lot of time and effort when you take your test. Equation manipulation is one of the most crucial skills on the GRE and GMAT.

The following are some problems that you can use to practice your equation manipulation skills.

1. If $y - 13 = 5 - 2y$, then $y =$
   - **(A)** 3
   - **(B)** 6
   - **(C)** 9
   - **(D)** 18
   - **(E)** 54

To solve the equation, you can begin by changing the subtraction by $2y$ on the right to an addition of $2y$ on the left. This will give you $3y - 13 = 5$. Then, change the subtraction of 13 on the left to an addition of 13 on the right. You will now have $3y = 18$. Finally, change the multiplication by 3 on the left to a division by 3 on the right. This will give you $y = 6$. **The correct answer is (B).**

Another way to get the correct answer is to substitute the answer choices into the equation. Even though this is an acceptable way to do the problem, it is typically a more time-consuming strategy.

2. If $\dfrac{(Z+16)-(40-60)}{4}=14$, what is the value of Z?

    (A) 5

    (B) 10

    (C) 20

    (D) 36

    (E) 56

The correct answer is (C). It is always a good strategy to try to simplify the expressions in the given equation whenever possible. In this problem, we can rewrite the numerator as follows:

$$\frac{(Z+16)-(40-60)}{4}=\frac{Z+16-40+60}{4}=\frac{Z+36}{4}$$

Thus, the equation becomes $\dfrac{Z+36}{4}=14$.

The next step should be to get rid of the division by 4 on the left by multiplying by 4 on the right. If you do this, the equation will become $Z + 36 = 56$. Finally, the solution to $Z + 36 = 56$ is $Z = 20$.

Typically, the incorrect answer choices are carefully chosen to reflect the most common mistakes. Note, for example, what happens if you cancel incorrectly in the equation $\dfrac{Z+36}{4}=14$ by dividing the 4 into the 36. If you do this, you will get the equation $Z + 9 = 14$, or $Z = 5$, which is choice (A).

3. If $\dfrac{13}{23}\times a=\dfrac{9}{16}\times\dfrac{13}{23}$, then what is the value of a?

    (A) $\dfrac{9}{16}$

    (B) $\dfrac{16}{9}$

    (C) 9

    (D) 16

    (E) 23

This is an example of a problem that can be solved more quickly by noticing that both sides of the equation include a common factor, in this case $\dfrac{13}{23}$. This means that we can simplify the equation by dividing both sides by $\dfrac{13}{23}$, so that we have $a=\dfrac{9}{16}$. Thus, we only need one step to solve the equation. **The correct answer is (A).**

4. If $\dfrac{3}{8}y=\dfrac{6}{16}y$, what is the value of y?

    (A) 0

    (B) 1

    (C) 2

    (D) 3

    (E) It cannot be determined.

Occasionally, there are problems on the GRE and GMAT that have answers that cannot be determined. This means that you need to be very careful when trying to solve an equation by the substitution method. In this problem, notice that replacing y in the equation with each of the choices 0, 1, 2, and 3 solves the equation. In fact, reducing the fraction on the right side of the equation reveals that $\frac{3}{8}y = \frac{3}{8}y$, *which is true for every possible value of y*. **The correct answer is (E).**

NOTE: When a multiple-choice question has "It cannot be determined." as one of the answer choices, be very careful when using substitution to try to solve the problem. It is possible that every answer that you substitute will solve the problem.

Performing Manipulations on First-Degree Literal Equations

An equation that contains more than one variable is known as a *literal* equation. For example, $xy + z = t$ is a literal equation. This equation contains four variables, x, y, z, and t. It is not possible to "solve" this equation and find the actual values of these variables. However, it is possible to rewrite the equation in a number of different ways. In its present form, the equation is said to be "solved" for t, since the variable t appears by itself on one side of the equation only, and all other terms appear on the other side.

If you were asked to solve this equation for z, you would need to rewrite the equation in such a way that z appeared by itself on one side of the equation only, and the other variables appeared on the other side. Solving for z is quite straightforward. You simply need to treat all of the other variables as if they were constants and apply the rules for manipulating equations discussed in the previous section. Thus, starting with $xy + z = t$, simply remove the term xy from the left by subtracting it from the right. The equation solved for z would be $z = t - xy$.

Suppose you were asked to solve the equation $xy + z = t$ for x. It takes two steps to do this. Starting with $xy + z = t$, begin by moving z from the left by subtracting it from the right. This would give you $xy = t - z$. Remove the y from the left by dividing the right by y. This gives you $x = \frac{t - z}{y}$, and you have successfully solved the equation for x.

Questions on the GRE and GMAT often involve variations on the standard literal equation problem. Examine the following sample problems.

1. If $5p = xy^2$, which of the following is equal to $5px$?

    (A) xy

    (B) y^2

    (C) $(xy)^2$

    (D) x^2y

    (E) $\frac{5p}{y^2}$

Recall that we are allowed to "do the same thing" to both sides of an equation at any time. Perhaps the quickest way to solve this problem is to multiply both sides by x. This would give us the $5px$ we want. In fact, starting with $5p = xy^2$, if we multiply both sides by x, the result is $5px = xy^2(x)$. This means that $5px = x^2y^2$. Thus, $5px = (xy)^2$. **The correct answer is (C).**

2. If $p = \dfrac{q^4}{r^2}$, what is the value of $\dfrac{1}{q^4}$?

(A) $\dfrac{p}{r^2}$

(B) $\dfrac{r^2}{p}$

(C) pr^2

(D) 1

(E) $\dfrac{1}{pr^2}$

In this problem, we are given a literal equation and asked to solve it for $\dfrac{1}{q^4}$. Note that the expression q^4 appears on the top of the fraction on the right. An efficient way to solve this problem is to rewrite the equation by inverting both sides to get $\dfrac{1}{p} = \dfrac{r^2}{q^4}$. We can now divide both sides by r^2 to get $\dfrac{1}{r^2 p} = \dfrac{1}{q^4}$. **The correct answer is (E).**

Working with Systems of Equations

At the start of this section, we saw that a *first-degree equation* with two variables, such as $2x + y = 12$, has an infinite number of solutions. For example, $x = 3$, $y = 6$ is a solution of this equation. So is $x = 6$, $y = 0$, as is $x = 0$, $y = 12$.

Therefore, if you have a single *first-degree equation* with two variables, it is impossible to find a unique solution. Consider, however, having two such equations. Each of these equations has an infinite number of solutions. However, typically, if you have two *first-degree equations in two unknowns,* there is only one solution that they have in common. Finding this common solution is an important algebraic skill.

Consider again, for example, the equation, $2x + y = 12$, and the equation $3x - y = 8$. There are two primary techniques that can be used to find the common solution. The first is called the *addition method.* As shown below, if you write the two equations on top of each other and add both sides together, the variable y cancels out of the equation:

$2x + y = 12$

$\underline{3x - y = 8}$

$\quad 5x = 20,\qquad$ which means that $x = 4$.

We can now substitute $x = 4$ into either of the two original equations to determine the value of y. For example, if we put $x = 4$ into the first equation, we compute $2(4) + y = 12$ or $8 + y = 12$, so $y = 4$. The common solution would be $x = 4$ and $y = 4$. To make certain you have computed correctly, you should check the values $x = 4$ and $y = 4$ in the second equation to make certain that they solve it as well.

Since $3(4) - 4 = 12 - 4 = 8$, the solution checks.

Note that the above two equations were set up very nicely—when you added them together, one of the variables canceled out. If the equations are not already set up so that when you add them together one of the variables cancels out, then you need to change one of the equations (or possibly both of the equations) so that when you add them together, one of the variables will cancel out. By multiplying one equation or the other by the appropriate number, you can cause this to happen. For example, consider the following two equations.

$3a - 10b = 0$

$\quad a + 5b = 18$

If we multiply every term in the second equation by 2, we will be able to add the two equations together and eliminate a variable.

$3a - 10b = 0$

$2a + 10b = 36$

$5a = 36$, which means that $a = \dfrac{36}{5}$.

We can now substitute $a = \dfrac{36}{5}$ into either of the two original equations to determine the value of b.

Using $a + 5b = 18$, we have $\dfrac{36}{5} + 5b = 18$, which means that $5b = 18 - \dfrac{36}{5} = \dfrac{54}{5}$. Thus, $b = \dfrac{54}{25}$.

Sometimes, particularly when one equation is already solved for one of the variables, it is quicker to use the *substitution method* to find the common solution. For example, consider the following equation pair:

$6x + 2y = 28$

$y = x + 2$

Here, we can substitute the value for y given in the second equation into the first equation to obtain:

$6x + 2(x + 2) = 28$, which means that $6x + 2x + 4 = 28$. Combining the like terms yields $8x + 4 = 28$.

Thus, $8x = 24$, which means that $x = 3$. Therefore, if $x = 3$, $y = x + 2 = 5$.

Consider the following examples.

1. If $8y = 7$ and $16y - 3x = 11$, what is the value of x?
   (A) -1
   (B) $\dfrac{11}{16}$
   (C) $\dfrac{7}{8}$
   (D) 1
   (E) $\dfrac{8}{7}$

Don't get nervous when you see that the first equation doesn't contain the variable x. Not having x in one of the equations actually makes the problem easier. Solving the first equation for y we obtain $y = \dfrac{7}{8}$. Substitute this value for y in the other equation. **The correct answer is (D).**

$16y - 3x = 11$

$16\left(\dfrac{7}{8}\right) - 3x = 11$

$14 - 3x = 11$

$-3x = -3$

$x = 1$

> **BE CAREFUL:** Note that the value of y is choice (C), but you were asked to find the value of x.

2. If the sum of two numbers is 40 and their difference is 14, what is their product?
   - **(A)** 338
   - **(B)** 351
   - **(C)** 560
   - **(D)** 702
   - **(E)** 756

This problem is really an algebraic word problem, and word problems will be discussed in more detail later in the chapter. However, you can handle this problem, as long as you remember that *sum* refers to addition, *difference* refers to subtraction, and *product* refers to multiplication. **The correct answer is (B).**

If we let x represent the larger of the two numbers and y represent the smaller number, then the problem statement tells us that $x + y = 40$ and $x - y = 14$. We can solve for x and y using the addition method.

$$x + y = 40$$
$$\underline{x - y = 14}$$
$$2x = 54, \quad \text{which means that } x = 27.$$

This tells us that y must be 13. Therefore, the product xy is equal to $27 \times 13 = 351$.

Working with Quadratic Equations in One Unknown

Another type of equation that you will encounter on the GRE and GMAT tests is called a *quadratic equation in one unknown*. In this section, you will practice using techniques especially designed for solving such equations. Unlike the first-degree equation in one unknown, which has at most one solution, quadratic equations in one unknown may have as many as two different solutions.

By definition, a quadratic equation in one unknown is an equation containing one variable that appears raised to the second power, and possibly to the first power as well. In other words, a quadratic equation is an equation that can be written in the form $ax^2 + bx + c = 0$, where a, b, and c are constants, and $a \neq 0$. This form of the quadratic equation is called its *standard form*.

> **NOTE:** You may recall that not every quadratic equation could be factored. Perhaps you have even seen some methods for solving quadratic equations that do not factor, such as *completing the square* or using the *quadratic formula*. You do not need to know these other techniques for the GRE and GMAT. Every quadratic equation that you see will be factorable.

In order to solve a quadratic equation by factoring, we begin by making sure the given equation is in standard form. In other words, we need to move all non-zero terms to one side so that only 0 remains on the other side.

Consider the quadratic equation: $5x^2 = 21 - 32x$.

Begin by manipulating the equation into standard form by moving the two terms on the right-hand side to the left-hand side.

$$5x^2 + 32x - 21 = 0$$
$$(5x - 3)(x + 7) = 0$$
$$x = \frac{3}{5}, x = -7$$

As another example, consider the quadratic equation $4x^2 = 9$. The standard form for this equation is $4x^2 - 9 = 0$. The left-hand side is a difference of two squares and can be factored as shown below.

$$4x^2 - 9 = 0$$
$$(2x + 3)(2x - 3) = 0$$
$$x = -\frac{3}{2}, x = \frac{3}{2}$$

Here are some sample problems involving quadratic equations.

1. What are all of the values of a for which $a^2 = 7a$?

   (A) 0

   (B) 7

   (C) 0, 7

   (D) 0, –7

   (E) 0, 7, –7

Be very careful with this problem. If you try to use the substitution technique, and you substitute choice (A) first, you will find that $a = 0$ *does* solve the equation. However, the problem asks for *all* of the values that solve the equation, and, as discussed above, quadratic equations may have two solutions. If you continue your trial and error, you will discover that 7 also works, but that –7 does not. **The correct answer is (C).**

If you wish to solve the problem using algebra, begin by expressing the equation in standard form as $a^2 - 7a = 0$. If you factor, you will obtain $a(a - 7) = 0$. Setting each factor equal to 0 gives you $a = 0$, and $a = 7$.

NOTE: Remember that quadratic equations often have two solutions. Thus, if you wish to substitute the answer choices to try to find the solution, make certain to try all of the answer choices so you will find all of the solutions.

---

2. If $(x + 5)^2 = (x - 5)^2$, then what is the value of x?

   (A) –25

   (B) –5

   (C) 0

   (D) 5

   (E) 25

If you square both sides, you obtain $x^2 + 10x + 25 = x^2 - 10x + 25$. Subtracting off the x^2 terms and the 25 terms, you end up with the equation $10x = -10x$. Combining like terms changes this equation to $20x = 0$, which is only true if $x = 0$. **The correct answer is (C).**

Solving Square Root Equations

A *square root equation* is an equation that contains a variable under a square root. Let's consider some examples of the procedure for solving such equations.

We'll begin by looking at the equation $\sqrt{3x+15}+2=8$.

The first step in solving an equation involving a variable under a square root is to *isolate the radical*, which simply means to get the square root by itself on one side of the equation. In this case, we need to subtract 2 from each side to get $\sqrt{3x+15}=6$.

IMPORTANT NOTE: A fundamental principle in equation solving is that, whenever necessary, you can perform the same operation on both sides of an equation. In order to solve this equation, we need to perform an operation we have not yet employed—we need to square both sides. This operation enables us to eliminate the radical sign, as shown below.

$$\sqrt{3x+15}=6$$
$$\left(\sqrt{3x+15}\right)^2=6^2$$
$$3x+15=36$$
$$3x=21$$
$$x=7$$

We can check that this is the correct solution by substituting 7 into the original equation as shown below.

$$\sqrt{3(7)+15}+2\overset{?}{=}8$$
$$\sqrt{3(7)+15}\overset{?}{=}6$$
$$\sqrt{21+15}\overset{?}{=}6$$
$$\sqrt{36}\overset{?}{=}6$$

Since this last statement is true, we have found the correct solution.

Let's apply the same steps on the equation $\sqrt{3x}+10=1$. As before, we will begin by isolating the radical.

$$\sqrt{3x}+10=1$$
$$\sqrt{3x}=-9$$
$$\left(\sqrt{3x}\right)^2=(-9)^2$$
$$3x=81$$
$$x=27$$

Thus, using the same technique as before, we have determined that the solution is $x = 27$. Just to be certain, let's check the solution in the original equation.

$$\sqrt{3(27)} + 10 \overset{?}{=} 1$$

$$\sqrt{81} + 10 \overset{?}{=} 1$$

$$9 + 10 \overset{?}{=} 1$$

$$19 \overset{?}{=} 1$$

Since the last line is not true, the solution we obtained, $x = 27$, does not solve the original equation. Yet, if you recheck the computation, you will see that we didn't make any computational errors. So, what is going on?

This equation illustrates the fact that sometimes the solution that we obtain by using this procedure will solve the "squared equation," that is, the equation obtained by squaring both sides, but will not solve the original equation. Such a solution is called an *extraneous* solution. In fact, the equation $\sqrt{3x} + 10 = 1$ does not have any solutions. This concept is summarized in the box below.

> **BE CAREFUL:** Sometimes, the procedure of squaring both sides of a radical equation will lead to *extraneous* solutions, that is, solutions that do not solve the original equation. Therefore, when you are solving such equations, you *must* check your solution to make certain that it does solve the original equation.

Solving Absolute Value Equations

Recall that the *absolute value* of a number technically represents the distance that the number is away from 0 on the number line. Therefore, the absolute value of 7 is equal to 7, and the absolute value of –7 is also equal to 7. Intuitively, then, the absolute value of a number can be thought of as the number without regard to its sign.

The absolute value of a number k can be symbolized by writing it between two vertical lines:

$|k|$. Using this notation, we can say that $|7| = 7$, and that $|-7| = 7$. Before we take a look at equations that involve absolute values, take a look at the sample computations with absolute values below to make certain that you understand the concept.

$|-5-4| = |-9| = 9$

$-|-12| = -(12) = -12$

$-|-5 - (+13)| = -|-18| = -(18) = -18$

$|-7| - |11| - |-5||-3| = 7 - 11 - (5)(3) = 7 - 11 - 15 = -19.$

Note that equations that contain absolute values typically have more than one solution. For example, the equation $|x| = 17$ has two solutions, i.e., $x = 17$ and $x = -17$.

Suppose you needed to solve the equation $|y| + 3 = 12$. Begin by moving the 3 to the right-hand side, so as to obtain $|y| = 9$. Note that this equation will be true for $y = 9$ or $y = -9$, so once again there are two solutions.

Let's now consider an absolute value equation that is a bit more challenging.

$|3x + 2| = 14$

Perhaps the most efficient way to proceed is to recognize that the equation will be true for the values of x for which $3x + 2 = 14$ and $3x + 2 = -14$. Solving these two equations separately will give the two solutions to the equation.

$$3x + 2 = 14 \quad \text{or} \quad 3x + 2 = -14$$

$$3x = 12 \quad \text{or} \quad 3x = -16$$

$$x = 4 \quad \text{or} \quad x = -\frac{16}{3}$$

Therefore, there are two solutions to this equation, $x = 4$ and $x = -\frac{16}{3}$. You can check that both of these answers solve the equation by substituting them back into the original equation.

Remember that absolute value equations often have two solutions. Therefore, if you are substituting answers to find the solution, be certain to try all answer choices so as to not miss one of the solutions.

Solving Equations Involving Algebraic Fractions

An *algebraic fraction* is a fraction that contains variables in its numerator or its denominator or both. There is more than one technique that can be used to solve such equations, but the quickest way is usually to find the least common denominator (LCD) of all of the fractions in the equation, and then to multiply all of the terms in the equation by this LCD. This will eliminate the fractions and leave you with an equation that can be solved using the methods already discussed in this chapter. The best way to learn this technique is to work your way through a few specific examples.

Solve the following equation for x: $\frac{3x}{5} + \frac{2}{3} = 4$.

The LCD of the two fractions in the equation is $3 \times 5 = 15$, so *all* terms in the equation must be multiplied by 15.

$$15\left(\frac{3x}{5}\right) + 15\left(\frac{2}{3}\right) = 15(4)$$

$$3(3x) + 5(2) = 60$$

$$9x + 10 = 60$$

$$9x = 50$$

$$x = \frac{50}{9}$$

Note that you can check this solution by substituting $\frac{50}{9}$ into the original equation.

Let's look at an equation that contains the variable in the denominator.

Solve the following equation for y ($y \neq 0$): $\frac{1}{2} - \frac{1}{3} = \frac{1}{y}$.

To begin, note that the problem statement tells you that $y \neq 0$. This fact is included within the problem statement as a way of letting you know that the equation does not contain a division by 0.

In this equation, the LCD is $2 \times 3 \times y = 6y$, and so every term must be multiplied by $6y$.

$$\frac{1}{2} - \frac{1}{3} = \frac{1}{y}$$

$$6y\left(\frac{1}{2}\right) - 6y\left(\frac{1}{3}\right) = 6y\left(\frac{1}{y}\right)$$

$$3y - 2y = 6$$

$$y = 6$$

It is straightforward to check that $y = 6$ solves the equation. Note how much simpler it is to solve the equation once you have multiplied by the LCD.

Finally, let's consider one additional equation of this type.

Solve the following equation for z ($z \neq -1$): $\dfrac{3z}{z+1} + \dfrac{3}{z+1} = 1$

In this equation, the LCD is $z + 1$, so this is what we must multiply each term by.

$$\frac{3z}{z+1} + \frac{3}{z+1} = 1$$

$$(z+1)\left(\frac{3z}{z+1}\right) + (z+1)\left(\frac{3}{z+1}\right) = (1)(z+1)$$

$$3z + 3 = z + 1$$

$$2z = -2$$

$$z = -1$$

Note, however, that the original equation yields a 0 in the denominator when $z = -1$. Thus, we say that this equation has no solution.

Equations involving algebraic fractions become much easier to solve if you begin by multiplying all terms of the equation by the LCD of all of the fractions in the equation.

BE CAREFUL: If the original equation includes a denominator that contains a variable, you must check your answers to make sure that they don't cause a denominator to equal 0.

Here are some sample GRE and GMAT questions.

1. Solve the following equation for p: $5 = |2 - 4p|$

   (A) $p = \dfrac{3}{4}, \dfrac{7}{4}$

   (B) $p = -\dfrac{3}{4}, \dfrac{7}{4}$

   (C) $p = \dfrac{3}{4}, -\dfrac{7}{4}$

   (D) $p = -\dfrac{3}{4}, -\dfrac{7}{4}$

   (E) $p = -\dfrac{3}{4}$

The equation is true when $2 - 4p = 5$ and when $2 - 4p = -5$.

$$2 - 4p = 5 \quad \text{or} \quad 2 - 4p = -5$$

$$-4p = 3 \quad \text{or} \quad -4p = -7$$

$$p = -\frac{3}{4} \quad \text{or} \quad p = \frac{7}{4}$$

The correct answer is (B).

2. If $\dfrac{1 - 3y}{5} + 6 = \dfrac{3y + 4}{2}$, what is the value of y?

   (A) -5

   (B) -2

   (C) $-\dfrac{4}{7}$

   (D) 2

   (E) 5

The LCD of the two denominators of the equation is $2 \times 5 = 10$. Therefore, you need to multiply every term in the equation by 10.

$$10\left(\frac{1 - 3y}{5}\right) + 10(6) = 10\left(\frac{3y + 4}{2}\right)$$

$$2(1 - 3y) + 60 = 5(3y + 4)$$

$$2 - 6y + 60 = 15y + 20$$

$$62 - 6y = 15y + 20$$

$$42 = 21y$$

$$2 = y$$

The correct answer is (D).

BE CAREFUL: One of the most common mistakes made in solving equations involving algebraic fractions is to neglect to multiply *all* of the terms in the equation by the LCD. A common mistake in solving the above problem is neglecting to multiply the constant term of 6 by the LCD of 10. If you make this mistake, you will get the incorrect answer $-\dfrac{4}{7}$, which is choice (C).

---

3. Solve the following equation for x: $\sqrt{2x} + 20 = 12$

   (A) $x = -32$

   (B) $x = -8$

   (C) $x = 8$

   (D) $x = 32$

   (E) There are no solutions.

To solve the equation, we need to begin by "isolating the radical," in other words, rewriting the equation as $\sqrt{2x} = -8$. Next, we square both sides, as shown below.

$$\left(\sqrt{2x}\right)^2 = (-8)^2$$
$$2x = 64$$
$$x = 32$$

It is tempting to select choice (D), but remember that *all solutions to radical equations must be checked*.

$$\sqrt{2(32)} + 20 \overset{?}{=} 12$$
$$\sqrt{64} + 20 \overset{?}{=} 12$$
$$8 + 20 \overset{?}{=} 12$$
$$28 \overset{?}{=} 12$$

Since the last statement is false, the solution $x = 32$ is an extraneous solution. Thus, the equation actually has no solutions. **The correct answer is (E).**

Solving Inequalities

An equation is a mathematical statement that contains an equal sign. On the other hand, an inequality is a mathematical statement that contains an inequality sign. Recall that the inequality signs are ">" which means "greater than," "<" which means "less than," "≥" which means "greater than or equal to," and "≤" which means "less than or equal to."

The procedure for solving an inequality is identical to the procedure for solving an equation, with one crucial difference. During the process of solving an inequality, whenever you divide or multiply both sides by a *negative* number, you must "reverse" the inequality sign. This means, that if the sign originally was "<", it will become ">" after dividing or multiplying by a negative number. Similarly, if the sign was "≤", it will become "≥".

Consider the following problem.

Solve for x: $\dfrac{-5x}{9} \leq -15$

The best first step to solve this equation would be to multiply both sides by 9. Since 9 is a positive number, the inequality sign remains as it is.

$-5x \leq -15(9)$

$-5x \leq -135$

The next step is to divide both sides by -5 and since this number is negative, the inequality sign must be reversed.

$\dfrac{-5x}{-5} \geq \dfrac{-135}{-5}$

This becomes $x \geq 27$, which is the solution to the inequality. The value of x, therefore, can be 27 or any number larger.

Here are some sample GRE and GMAT questions involving inequalities.

1. Given $4y \leq 84 \leq 5y$, how many different possible integers values for y are there?
   (A) one
   (B) two
   (C) three
   (D) four
   (E) five

The key to this problem is being able to interpret the "compound inequality" given in the problem statement: $4y \leq 84 \leq 5y$. This inequality is telling us that 84 is somewhere between the value of $4y$ and $5y$. In other words, we are being told that both $4y \leq 84$ and $84 \leq 5y$ must be true.

In order to determine the biggest value y can have, solve the inequality $4y \leq 84$. If we divide both sides by 4, we determine that $y \leq 21$. Therefore, y can be no larger than 21. To determine the smallest value that y can have, solve $84 \leq 5y$. Dividing both sides by 5 gives us the inequality $16.8 \leq y$, which means that the smallest y can be is 17. Since y must be an integer, the possible values for y are 17, 18, 19, 20, and 21. There are five possible values for y. **The correct answer is (E).**

2. If $q > 6$, which of the following is *not* true?

   (A) $-q < -6$

   (B) $q + 5 > 11$

   (C) $2q > 12$

   (D) $q - 4 < 2$

   (E) $\dfrac{q}{2} > 3$

One way to solve this problem is to solve each of the answer choice inequalities for q. Note that multiplying both sides of choice (A) by -1 yields $q > 6$, since multiplying by a negative reverses the inequality. Subtracting 5 from both sides of choice (B) yields $q > 6$. Dividing both sides of choice (C) by 2 yields $q > 6$. However, adding 4 to both sides of choice (D) yields $q < 6$. **The correct answer is (D).**

EXERCISES: MANIPULATING EQUATIONS

Directions: Select the answer choice that best answers the question.

1. If $5x - 15 = 20$, what is the value of $5x + 15$?
   (A) 40
   (B) 45
   (C) 50
   (D) 55
   (E) 60

2. If $a = -b$, what is the value of $a + b$?
   (A) −1
   (B) 0
   (C) 1
   (D) 2
   (E) It cannot be determined.

3. If x and y are positive integers and $x^2 + y^2 = 13$, what is the value of xy?
   (A) 5
   (B) 6
   (C) 8
   (D) 10
   (E) 36

4. $12 = 3 \times 44 \times K$, then $K =$
   (A) $\dfrac{1}{12}$
   (B) $\dfrac{1}{11}$
   (C) $\dfrac{1}{10}$
   (D) 11
   (E) 12

5. If $\dfrac{1}{2} - \dfrac{3}{b} = \dfrac{5}{b}$, what is the value of b?
   (A) −14
   (B) 6
   (C) 10
   (D) 14
   (E) 16

6. If $x = 7y$, and $y = 9z$, what is the value of x in terms of z?

(A) $\dfrac{1}{63}z$

(B) $\dfrac{1}{7}z$

(C) $7z$

(D) $63z$

(E) $126z$

ANSWER KEY AND EXPLANATIONS

1. C	3. B	5. E
2. B	4. B	6. D

1. **The correct answer is (C).** Perhaps the quickest way to solve this problem is to notice that adding 30 to both sides of the original equation yields $5x - 15 + 30 = 20 + 30$, which means $5x + 15 = 50$.

2. **The correct answer is (B).** Once again, a quick way to solve this problem is to manipulate the given equation using basic algebra. In this case, adding b to both sides yields $a + b = -b + b$, which means that $a + b = 0$.

3. **The correct answer is (B).** One effective strategy for solving this problem is to consider the smallest and largest possible values that x and y can have. We are told that x and y are positive integers. This means that $x \geq 1$ and $y \geq 1$. Moreover, since $4^2 = 16 > 13$, we know that $x < 4$ and $y < 4$. So, we have $1 \leq x < 4$ and $1 \leq y < 4$. Note also that the answer choices factor as follows: $5 = 5 \times 1$, $6 = 6 \times 1 = 3 \times 2$, $8 = 8 \times 1 = 4 \times 2$, $10 = 10 \times 1 = 5 \times 2$, and $36 = 36 \times 1 = 18 \times 2 = 12 \times 3 = 9 \times 4 = 6 \times 6$. The only factors in this list that are within the required range are 1, 2, and 3. Note that $2^2 + 3^2 = 4 + 9 = 13$. Thus, either $x = 2$, and $y = 3$, or $x = 3$, and $y = 2$. In either case, we have $xy = 6$.

4. **The correct answer is (B).** The first step in dealing with this equation would be to multiply 3 by 44, obtaining 132, so that the equation can be rewritten as $12 = 132 \times K$. Let's take a moment to look at the answers. First of all, since we are looking for a number that can be multiplied by 132 to give us 12, it should be clear that K has to be one of the fractional answers, choices (A), (B), or (C). Note that choice (B) yields $132 \times \dfrac{1}{11} = \dfrac{132}{11} = 12$.

5. **The correct answer is (E).** The LCD of the fractions in the equation is $2b$, so each term needs to be multiplied by $2b$.

$$2b\left(\frac{1}{2}\right) - 2b\left(\frac{3}{b}\right) = 2b\left(\frac{5}{b}\right)$$
$$b - 6 = 10$$
$$b = 16$$

6. **The correct answer is (D).** Perhaps the quickest way to solve this problem is to use the method of substitution as follows. The second equation tells us that $y = 9z$. So we can replace the y in the first equation with $9z$ to get $x = 7y = 7(9z) = 63z$. We now have x written exclusively in terms of z.

ALGEBRAIC WORD PROBLEMS

Algebra students frequently comment, "I can handle everything except the word problems." There is no doubt that solving word problems is one of the most difficult algebraic skills. The key to building your confidence when faced with word problems is to strengthen your ability to identify the fundamental relationships that define the problem. This section is designed to help you practice the types of algebraic word problems that typically appear on the GRE and GMAT.

Let's begin by taking a look at the question below. This would be considered a very difficult GRE and GMAT algebraic word problem.

1. When two numbers are added together, the result is 20 more than the difference between the two numbers. The product of two numbers is 720. Which of the following is the smaller of the two numbers?
   (A) 10
   (B) 20
   (C) 24
   (D) 72
   (E) 144

At first glance, this problem may seem rather intimidating. Setting up this problem algebraically will involve two equations, one of which will contain a multiplication of variables. Multiplied variables often lead to quadratic equations, which have to be solved by factoring.

Before you start to feel overwhelmed, let's think about what the problem says. In the second sentence, we are told that the product of two numbers is 720. We need to determine which of the five answer choices is the smaller of the two numbers.

Note that you can immediately eliminate choices (D) and (E) since they are too big. If, as in choice (D), 72 were one of the numbers, the other would have to be $720 \div 72 = 10$. If the two numbers were 72 and 10, then 72 would be the *larger*, not the smaller, of the numbers. In the same way choice (E), 144, would be paired with 5, and 5 would be the smaller number.

If choice (A) were correct, the two numbers would be 10 and 72, since $10 \times 72 = 720$. If choice (B) were correct, the two numbers would be 20 and 36. Finally, if choice (C) is correct, the two numbers would be 24 and 30. All we need to do is find the pair whose sum and difference differ by 20.

In the case of choice (C), 30 and 24, the sum is 54 and the difference is 6, and these two numbers do not differ by 20. In choice (B), 20 and 36, the sum is 56 and the difference is 16; again, no good. In the case of choice (A), 72 and 10, the sum is 82 and the difference is 62. 82 and 62 differ by 20. **The correct answer is (A).**

You could also use variables to solve this problem. Suppose we call the two unknowns x and y. Let the larger be x, and the smaller be y. Then, we know that $xy = 720$, and $x + y = 20 + (x - y)$.

Note that we can simplify the second equation. When we remove the parentheses, we obtain the equation $x + y = 20 + x - y$.

Note that, upon simplification, the x's cancel out, and we are left with $y = 20 - y$, or $2y = 20$, so y must be 10. That is the smaller of the two numbers, and so that is the answer.

In most algebraic word problems you are asked to find the value of an unknown that satisfies a certain condition. The key is to express the condition as an algebraic equation by changing the words and phrases into mathematical symbols. This is usually fairly straightforward. Translate the condition step by step until you end up with an equation that you can solve.

The information in the table below helps you to do this. The table contains the most common words and phrases that appear in algebraic word problems, along with their algebraic meanings.

Algebraic Meaning	Word or Phrase
$x = 11$	x is equal to 11, x is 11, x is the same as 11
$x + 13$	the sum of x and 13, x plus 13, 13 more than x, 13 added to x, x increased by 13
$x - 7$	7 less than x, x minus 7, x decreased by 7, x less 7, the difference of x and 7
$9x$	9 times x, x multiplied by 9, the product of x and 9
$\frac{1}{4}x$ $0.25x$	one quarter of x 25 percent of x
$\frac{x}{5}$	x divided by 5, the quotient of x and 5, 5 divided into x

Let's use this table as an aid in solving the following problems.

2. If $\frac{1}{6}$ of a number is 2 less than $\frac{1}{5}$ of the number, what is the number?

(A) 15

(B) 30

(C) 45

(D) 60

(E) 120

We can let x represent the unknown in the problem. As the table above indicates, a fraction *of* a number is an indication of multiplication. Also, *less than* indicates subtraction, and *is* means equals. Thus, we are quickly led to the equation $\frac{1}{6}x = \frac{1}{5}x - 2$.

As we saw earlier in this chapter, the quickest way to solve an equation involving fractions is to eliminate the fractions by multiplying all terms in the equation by their LCD. The LCD in this case is $5 \times 6 = 30$. Therefore, $30\left(\frac{1}{6}x\right) = 30\left(\frac{1}{5}x\right) - (30)2$. Simplifying yields $5x = 6x - 60$, which means that $x = 60$. **The correct answer is (D).**

3. If Bob is currently B years old, and Sue is 7 years younger than Bob, how many years old will Sue be in 13 years?

(A) $B + 6$

(B) $B - 6$

(C) $B + 20$

(D) $B - 20$

(E) $6B$

If Bob is B years old, then, right now, Sue would be $B - 7$ years old. In 13 years, Sue will be $(B - 7) + 13 = B + 6$. **The correct answer is (A).**

4. If the sum of three consecutive even integers is 66, what is the largest of the three integers?

(A) 16

(B) 18

(C) 20

(D) 22

(E) 24

This problem is an example of what is known as a consecutive integer problem. *Consecutive integers* can be expressed algebraically as $N, N+1, N+2$, and so on. This problem, however, involves consecutive *even* integers. Consecutive even integers are even integers that *differ by* 2, such as 4, 6, and 8. Algebraically, consecutive even integers can be expressed as $N, N+2, N+4$. By the way, since consecutive *odd* integers also differ by 2, they can be algebraically expressed in the same way.

The equation to solve this problem is $N + N + 2 + N + 4 = 66$.

$3N + 6 = 66$

$3N = 60$

$N = 20$

Be careful. Do not select choice (C) at this point. $N = 20$ is the smallest of the even integers. The next integer would be 22, and the largest is 24. **The correct answer is (E).**

5. On a Saturday morning, Peter bicycles from his home to the park at an average speed of 10 miles per hour. He then returns home along the same route, traveling at an average speed of 15 miles per hour. If Peter's total travel time was 5 hours, how many miles did he travel from his home to the park?

(A) 15 miles

(B) $17\frac{1}{2}$ miles

(C) 20 miles

(D) 30 miles

(E) 60 miles

This problem is an example of what is known as a motion problem. Motion problems frequently appear on the GRE and GMAT, and you need to know a special formula in order to find the answer. This formula is $d = rt$, which stands for distance = rate × time. In this problem, Peter takes a round trip. Every motion problem that involves a round trip is essentially the same. If we let d_{away} stand for the distance Peter travels away from home and d_{back} stand for the distance he travels coming back, it must be true that $d_{away} = d_{back}$. **The correct answer is (D).**

According to the motion formula above, it must be true that $d_{away} = r_{away} \times t_{away}$, and $d_{back} = r_{back} \times t_{back}$. Since $d_{away} = d_{back}$ we can write $r_{away} \times t_{away} = r_{back} \times t_{back}$.

NOTE: This is the formula that is used to solve "round-trip problems." This equation involves four quantities, and, in order to solve it, we are going to have to reduce it down to one unknown quantity. Which of the quantities do we already know? We are told that $r_{away} = 10$, and that $r_{back} = 15$. Therefore, the equation can be rewritten as $10 \times t_{away} = 15 \times t_{back}$.

We do not know how long Peter spent on the trip out or back, but we do know that his total travel time was 5 hours. So, let's say that the time traveling away was equal to t hours. In this case, the time traveling back must be equal to the total time less the time traveling away, or, $5 - t$. Substituting all of this into the above equation gives us $10 \times t = 15 \times (5 - t)$.

$10t = 75 - 15t$

$25t = 75$

$t = 3$

Thus, it took 3 hours to travel to the park, and $5 - 3 = 2$ hours to travel back. So, how far away was the park? We know that $d = rt$, and on the way to the park, $r = 10$, and $t = 3$. Therefore, $d = 10 \times 3 = 30$ miles. To check, let's make certain that he went the same distance on the way back. On the way back, $r = 15$, $t = 2$, and $d = 15 \times 2 = 30$, just as it should.

> **BE CAREFUL:** Make sure that you answer the correct question. A common mistake is to choose the total distance traveled, which would be 60 miles.

6. A piece of wood 120 inches long is cut so that one piece is 34 inches longer than the other. What is the length of the shorter of the two pieces?
   - (A) 34
   - (B) 38
   - (C) 43
   - (D) 77
   - (E) 83

This problem has two unknowns—the length of the shorter piece and the length of the longer piece. If we let the length of the shorter piece be S and the length of the longer piece be L, then the information given in the problem enables us to write the following two equations: $L + S = 120$ and $L - S = 34$. We can use the addition method to solve for the unknowns.

$L + S = 120$

$\underline{L - S = 34}$

$2L = 154$

Note that, if $2L = 154$, then $L = 77$, and $S = 120 - 77 = 43$. Therefore, the length of the shorter piece is 43 inches. **The correct answer is (C).**

> **BE CAREFUL:** A very common error in word problems with two unknowns is to select the answer that represents the value of the "other" unknown—the one they did not ask for. Note that if you accidentally select the length of the longer piece, you will be led to choice (E) instead of choice (C). This type of error is easier to make if you let the two variables be represented by x and y, since it is easy to forget what x stands for. Naming the variables L and S for "long" and "short" helps to avoid this error.

STRANGE FUNCTIONS

Consider the following sample problem.

1. If a is a positive integer, then $\psi_a = \dfrac{a}{2}$ if a is even, and $\psi_a = 3a$ if a is odd. What is the value of $\dfrac{\psi_5}{\psi_6}$?

   (A) $\dfrac{1}{5}$

   (B) $\dfrac{5}{6}$

   (C) $2\dfrac{1}{2}$

   (D) 5

   (E) 10

This problem is an example of a type of GRE and GMAT question that we'll call a *Strange Function* question. In this problem, you are presented with a new mathematical symbol and a definition of what the symbol means. Solving the problem requires you to understand the definition well enough to be able to perform a computation using it. The definition of ψ is given in the problem: If a is a positive integer, then $\psi_a = \dfrac{a}{2}$ if a is even, and $\psi_a = 3a$ if a is odd.

This particular *Strange Function* question gives you a rule that is different for odd and even integers. According to the definition, for example, $\psi_8 = \dfrac{8}{2} = 4$ since 8 is even. On the other hand, $\psi_9 = 3(9) = 27$ since 9 is odd. Since 5 is odd, $\psi_5 = 3(5) = 15$. And, since 6 is even, the value of $\psi_6 = \dfrac{6}{2} = 3$.

Therefore, $\dfrac{\psi_5}{\psi_6} = \dfrac{15}{3} = 5$. **The correct answer is (D).**

Consider the following examples.

2. If $\{y\}$ is defined by the equation $\{y\} = 3\sqrt{2y}$, which of the following is equal to 24?
   (A) $\{4\}$
   (B) $\{12\}$
   (C) $\{16\}$
   (D) $\{32\}$
   (E) $\{64\}$

This problem takes the typical *Strange Function* problem and turns it around. Instead of asking you to evaluate an expression, such as $\{12\}$, you are asked which of five specific strange values is equal to 24. The problem can be solved directly by solving the equation $3\sqrt{2y} = 24$. If you divide both sides by 3, the equation becomes $\sqrt{2y} = 8$. For this to be true, $2y$ has to equal 64, which means y must be 32. **The correct answer is (D).**

3. Let $\left\langle \begin{matrix} a \\ b \end{matrix} \right\rangle\left\langle \begin{matrix} c \\ d \end{matrix} \right\rangle$ be defined to mean $ac - bd$. If $\left\langle \begin{matrix} x \\ 3 \end{matrix} \right\rangle\left\langle \begin{matrix} x \\ 8 \end{matrix} \right\rangle = 12$, then $x =$

   (A) -36

   (B) -6

   (C) 6

   (D) -6 or 6

   (E) -36 or 36

Let's begin by understanding the rule that is given in the problem. You are told that $\left\langle \begin{matrix} a \\ b \end{matrix} \right\rangle\left\langle \begin{matrix} c \\ d \end{matrix} \right\rangle$ is equal to $ac - bd$. Essentially, this means that to evaluate $\left\langle \begin{matrix} a \\ b \end{matrix} \right\rangle\left\langle \begin{matrix} c \\ d \end{matrix} \right\rangle$ you simply find the product of the two numbers on the top, and subtract from it the product of the two numbers on the bottom.

Using this definition, $\left\langle \begin{matrix} x \\ 3 \end{matrix} \right\rangle\left\langle \begin{matrix} x \\ 8 \end{matrix} \right\rangle$ is equal to $x^2 - 24$. Thus, we know that $x^2 - 24 = 12$. By solving this equation, we can find the value of x. Moving the 24 to the right gives us the equation $x^2 = 36$. **The correct answer is (D).**

BE CAREFUL: A common mistake is to conclude that $x = 6$. The value of x could also be -6, since $(-6)^2 = 36$ as well. Thus, there are two answers, 6 or -6.

EXERCISES: ALGEBRAIC WORD PROBLEMS AND STRANGE FUNCTIONS

Directions: Select the answer choice that best answers the question.

1. For all real numbers a and b, let ψ be defined by $a \; \psi \; b = (a + b)^2$. What is the value of $(x \; \psi \; y) - (x \; \psi \; (-y))$?
   - **(A)** 0
   - **(B)** $4xy$
   - **(C)** $2x^2 + 2y^2$
   - **(D)** $2x^2 - 2y^2$
   - **(E)** $-4xy$

2. The number H is doubled, and the result is decreased by 12. This result is then multiplied by 13 to obtain a final value. Which of the expressions below represents the final value?
   - **(A)** $13(2H - 12)$
   - **(B)** $13(12 - 2H)$
   - **(C)** $2H - (12)(13)$
   - **(D)** $13(2 + H - 12)$
   - **(E)** $13(12 - 2 + H)$

3. Brian has a job delivering newspapers in his neighborhood. Every week, he collects $4.50 from each of his customers to pay for the current week's newspapers. If, during a particular week, he collects $114, which includes $15 in tips, how many customers did he collect money from?
   - **(A)** 22
   - **(B)** 25
   - **(C)** 26
   - **(D)** 28
   - **(E)** 29

4. The sum of three consecutive odd integers is -21. What is the smallest of the integers?
   - **(A)** -5
   - **(B)** -6
   - **(C)** -7
   - **(D)** -8
   - **(E)** -9

5. Two trains leave the same station at the same time and travel in opposite directions. The average speed of Train A is 62 miles per hour, and the average speed of Train B is 74 miles per hour. After how many hours will the trains be 476 miles apart?
   - **(A)** 2
   - **(B)** $2\frac{1}{2}$
   - **(C)** 3
   - **(D)** $3\frac{1}{2}$
   - **(E)** 4

ANSWER KEY AND EXPLANATIONS

1. B	2. A	3. A	4. E	5. D

1. **The correct answer is (B).** To begin, since $a \, \psi \, b = (a + b)^2$, it follows that $x \, \psi \, y = (x + y)^2 = x^2 + 2xy + y^2$. Similarly, $x \, \psi \, (-y) = (x + (-y))^2 = x^2 - 2xy + y^2$. Finally, $(x \, \psi \, y) - (x \, \psi \, (-y)) = (x^2 + 2xy + y^2) - (x^2 - 2xy + y^2) = x^2 + 2xy + y^2 - x^2 + 2xy - y^2 = 4xy$.

2. **The correct answer is (A).** The result of doubling H is $2H$. Decreasing this by 12 will give you $2H - 12$, and multiplying the result by 13 gives you $13(2H - 12)$, which is choice (A).

3. **The correct answer is (A).** Let x represent the number of customers Brian collected money from. Since each customer paid him $4.50, he collected a total of $4.50x$ from his customers. In addition to this, he collects $15 in tips, so the total amount of money he has is $4.50x + 15. Since this amount is equal to $114, we simply need to solve the equation $4.5x + 15 = 114$ to find the solution to the equation.

$$4.5x + 15 = 114$$
$$4.5x = 99$$
$$x = 22$$

Thus, Brian had 22 customers.

4. **The correct answer is (E).** As we saw previously in this chapter, the three consecutive odd integers can be named N, $N + 2$, and $N + 4$. Since these integers add up to -21, we can write:

$$N + N + 2 + N + 4 = -21$$
$$3N + 6 = -21$$
$$3N = -27$$
$$N = -9$$

Therefore, $N + 2 = -9 + 2 = -7$, and $N + 4 = -9 + 4 = -5$.

Thus, the three numbers are -5, -7, and -9. The problem asks for the smallest of these numbers, which is -9. Be careful to not make the error of selecting -5 as the answer since $-9 < -5$.

5. **The correct answer is (D).** The problem asks us to determine how long it will take for the two trains to be 476 miles apart. Since the trains are traveling away from each other in the opposite direction, they will be 476 miles apart when the total distance the two trains have traveled is 476 miles.

Let d_C represent the total distance between the two trains. Further, let d_A represent the distance that Train A has traveled and d_B represent the distance that Train B has traveled. Then, $d_C = d_A + d_B$.

We need to determine how long it will take for d_C to equal 476. Therefore, we need to work with the equation $476 = d_A + d_B$.

Recall that $d = rt$. Therefore, we can rewrite the above equation as $476 = r_A d_A + r_B d_B$.

We are told that $r_A = 62$ and $r_B = 74$. Further, while we don't know what t_A and t_B are, we do know that they are the same since the trains leave the station at the same time. Let $t = t_A = t_B$. Then, the above equation becomes $476 = 62t + 74t$, which means that $476 = 136t$. We can solve for t by dividing both sides by 136 to get $t = 3.5$. Thus, it takes $3\frac{1}{2}$ hours for the trains to be 476 miles apart.

ALGEBRA PRACTICE TEST

GRE Multiple-Choice Questions—Select One Answer Choice

Directions: For Questions 1–5, select a single answer choice.

1. If $5x + 7 = 12y$, then $\dfrac{5x + 7}{12} =$

   (A) $\dfrac{y}{12}$

   (B) $\dfrac{y}{6}$

   (C) y

   (D) $6y$

   (E) $12y$

2. If $x + y = 12$ and $y + 7 = 13$, what is the value of xy?

   (A) -36

   (B) -6

   (C) 0

   (D) 6

   (E) 36

3. If Z is equal to the sum of 6, 8, 10 and w, what is the value of w if $w = \dfrac{1}{4}Z$?

   (A) 4

   (B) 8

   (C) 16

   (D) 32

   (E) 64

4. If $7x - 3y = 12$, what is the value of $21x - 9y$?

   (A) 12

   (B) 24

   (C) 36

   (D) 48

   (E) It cannot be determined.

5. $(a^{-4}b^3c^{-2})^{-5} =$

    (A) $\dfrac{1}{a^9b^2c^7}$

    (B) $\dfrac{a^9c^7}{b^2}$

    (C) $\dfrac{a^{20}}{b^{15}c^{10}}$

    (D) $\dfrac{a^{20}c^{10}}{b^{15}}$

    (E) $\dfrac{b^{15}}{a^{20}c^{10}}$

GRE Multiple-Choice Questions—Select One or More Answer Choices

Directions: For Questions 6–8, select one or more answer choices according to the specific question directions. If the question does not specify how many answer choices to select, select all that apply.

- The correct answer may be just one of the choices or may be as many as all of the choices, depending on the question.
- No credit is given unless you select all of the correct choices and no others.
- If the question specifies how many answer choices to select, select exactly that number of choices.

6. Which of the given quadratic equations have only positive integer roots?

    (A) $x^2 - 11x + 24 = 0$

    (B) $x^2 + 11x + 24 = 0$

    (C) $x^2 + 100 = 0$

    (D) $x^2 - 2x + 1 = 0$

7. If the sum of three consecutive odd integers is 51, which of the following is greater than the largest of the three integers?

    (A) 15

    (B) 17

    (C) 21

    (D) 23

8. If x is a real number greater than 5, which expression is not in simplest form?

(A) $\dfrac{x^2 + 25}{x - 5}$

(B) $\dfrac{6 + 7x}{2}$

(C) $\dfrac{x^2 + 25}{x + 5}$

(D) $\dfrac{6 + 7x}{7}$

(E) $\dfrac{x^2 - 25}{x - 5}$

(F) $\dfrac{6 + 14x}{7}$

GRE Quantitative Comparison Questions

Directions: For Questions 9–11, compare Quantity A and Quantity B, using additional information centered above the two quantities if such information is given, and select one of the following four answer choices:

(A) Quantity A is greater.

(B) Quantity B is greater.

(C) The two quantities are equal.

(D) The relationship cannot be determined from the information given.

A symbol that appears more than once in a question has the same meaning throughout the question.

Jane is older than Hector.

9.
Quantity A	Quantity B
Hector's age	Half of Jane's age

(A) Quantity A is greater.

(B) Quantity B is greater.

(C) The two quantities are equal.

(D) The relationship cannot be determined from the information given.

A farmer has two plots of land that are equal in area. The first plot is divided into 20 parcels with m acres in each parcel, and the second plot is divided into 12 parcels with n acres in each parcel.

10.

Quantity A	Quantity B
m	n

(A) Quantity A is greater.

(B) Quantity B is greater.

(C) The two quantities are equal.

(D) The relationship cannot be determined from the information given.

Given that x and y are real numbers such that $x \neq y$.

11.

Quantity A	Quantity B
$|x - y|$	$|y - x|$

(A) Quantity A is greater.

(B) Quantity B is greater.

(C) The two quantities are equal.

(D) The relationship cannot be determined from the information given.

GRE Numeric Entry Questions

Directions: For Questions 12–14, enter your answer as an integer or as a decimal if there is a single answer box OR as a fraction if there are two separate boxes—one for the numerator and one for the denominator.

To enter an integer or a decimal, write the number in the answer box provided. On the computer-based test you can either type the number in the answer box using the keyboard or use the Transfer Display button on the calculator. Also, note the following directions for the computer-based test:

- You can click on the answer box and then type the number. You can use the backspace key to erase a number.

- Type a hyphen for a negative sign. Type a hyphen again, and it will disappear. For a decimal point, type a period.

- The Transfer Display button on the calculator will move the calculator display to the answer box.

- Equivalent forms of the correct answer, such as 2.5 and 2.50, are all correct.

- Enter the exact answer unless the question asks you to round your answer.

12. In a certain year, Minnesota produced $\frac{3}{4}$ and Michigan produced $\frac{1}{5}$ of all the iron ore produced in the United States. If all the other states combined produced 15 million tons that year, how many million tons did Minnesota produce that year?

☐ million tons

13. To produce embroidered golf shirts, a company charges x dollars to make the design, $\frac{2x}{3}$ dollars for each of the first 20 shirts, and $\frac{x}{5}$ dollars for each shirt in excess of 20 shirts. If $245 is the total charge to make a design and 30 shirts, what is the value of x?

$ ☐

14. The cost, in dollars, of manufacturing x cell phones is $6,720 + 90x$. The amount received when selling these x cell phones is $150x$ dollars. What is the least number of cell phones that must be manufactured and sold so that the amount received is at least equal to the manufacturing cost?

GMAT Problem-Solving Questions

Directions: For Questions 15–18, solve the problems and indicate the best of the answer choices given.

15. Jack and Kevin play in a basketball game. If the ratio of points scored by Jack to points scored by Kevin is 4 to 3, which of the following could NOT be the total number of points scored by the two boys?

    (A) 7

    (B) 14

    (C) 16

    (D) 28

    (E) 35

16. The members of the Glee Club sell greeting cards in their neighborhood to raise money to go to the state competition. The profit on each box of cards that they sell is $3. One Friday, each member of the Club sold 8 boxes. In addition, on that day, the Club was given an extra $25 from the faculty. If their total profit for the day was $313, how many members are in the Glee Club?

    (A) 8

    (B) 10

    (C) 12

    (D) 14

    (E) 15

17. The number p is 5 less than 3 times the number q. The sum of the number p and twice the number q is 13. Which of the following pairs of equations could be used to solve for the values of p and q?

    (A) $p = 3q - 5$
    $2(p + q) = 13$

    (B) $p = 3q - 5$
    $2pq = 13$

    (C) $p = 5 - 3q$
    $2(p + q) = 13$

    (D) $p = 5 - 3q$
    $p + 2q = 13$

    (E) $p = 3q - 5$
    $p + 2q = 13$

18. Two planes start from Detroit at the same time and fly in opposite directions. The first plane averages 55 miles per hour faster than the second plane. After 4 hours. the planes are 1,700 miles apart. What is the average speed of the faster plane?

(A) 185 mph

(B) 190 mph

(C) 220 mph

(D) 240 mph

(E) 265 mph

GMAT Data Sufficiency Questions

Directions: Questions 19–21 consist of a question and two statements, labeled (1) and (2), in which certain data is given. You have to decide whether the data given in the statements is sufficient for answering the question. Using the data given in the statements plus your knowledge of mathematics and everyday facts (such as the number of days in July and the meaning of "counterclockwise"), you must indicate whether

(A) Statement (1) ALONE is sufficient, but statement (2) is not sufficient.

(B) Statement (2) ALONE is sufficient, but statement (1) is not sufficient.

(C) BOTH statements TOGETHER are sufficient, but NEITHER statement ALONE is sufficient.

(D) EACH statement ALONE is sufficient.

(E) Statements (1) and (2) TOGETHER are NOT sufficient.

19. Given real numbers x and y. Is $xy > 0$?

(1) $x^2 + y^2 = 0$

(2) $x^2 + y^2 = (x+y)^2$

(A) Statement (1) ALONE is sufficient, but statement (2) is not sufficient.

(B) Statement (2) ALONE is sufficient, but statement (1) is not sufficient.

(C) BOTH statements TOGETHER are sufficient, but NEITHER statement ALONE is sufficient.

(D) EACH statement ALONE is sufficient.

(E) Statements (1) and (2) TOGETHER are NOT sufficient.

20. Lucy and Ethel share a lottery jackpot. What is the total value of the jackpot?

(1) Lucy's share is $\dfrac{2}{3}$ of the total jackpot.

(2) Ethel's share is $500,000.

(A) Statement (1) ALONE is sufficient, but statement (2) is not sufficient.

(B) Statement (2) ALONE is sufficient, but statement (1) is not sufficient.

(C) BOTH statements TOGETHER are sufficient, but NEITHER statement ALONE is sufficient.

(D) EACH statement ALONE is sufficient.

(E) Statements (1) and (2) TOGETHER are NOT sufficient.

21. What is the ratio of M to N?

(1) M is 5 more than N tripled.
(2) $5N + 11M = 0$

(A) Statement (1) ALONE is sufficient, but statement (2) is not sufficient.

(B) Statement (2) ALONE is sufficient, but statement (1) is not sufficient.

(C) BOTH statements TOGETHER are sufficient, but NEITHER statement ALONE is sufficient.

(D) EACH statement ALONE is sufficient.

(E) Statements (1) and (2) TOGETHER are NOT sufficient.

ANSWER KEY AND EXPLANATIONS

1. C	6. A, D	10. B	14. 112	18. D
2. E	7. C, D	11. C	15. C	19. D
3. B	8. E	12. 225	16. C	20. C
4. C	9. D	13. 15	17. E	21. B
5. D				

1. **The correct answer is (C).** The quickest way to solve this problem is to note that we can manipulate the given equation by dividing both sides by 12 as follows:

$$5x + 7 = 12y \text{ yields } \frac{5x + 7}{12} = y$$

2. **The correct answer is (E).** We can solve this problem by using the substitution method. Note that the equation $y + 7 = 13$ means that $y = 6$. Plugging $y = 6$ into the first equation yields $x + 6 = 12$, which means that $x = 6$. So $xy = 36$.

3. **The correct answer is (B).** This problem tests your ability to translate a given statement into an appropriate equation using variables. The first part of the statement yields the equation $Z = 6 + 8 + 10 + w$. The second part of the statement provides the equation $w = \frac{1}{4}Z$. We are being asked to find the value of w that makes both equations true. Once again, we can use the substitution method. Since we are trying to find a value for w, it will be most efficient to replace Z with $6 + 8 + 10 + w$ in the second equation so that we get $w = \frac{1}{4}(6 + 8 + 10 + w) = \frac{1}{4}(24 + w)$. We now solve for w as follows:

$$w = \frac{1}{4}(24 + w)$$
$$4w = 24 + w$$
$$3w = 24$$
$$w = 8$$

4. **The correct answer is (C).** Once again, we can solve the problem by manipulating the given equation in an appropriate way. In this case, multiplying both sides of the equation by 3 yields $(3)(7x - 3y) = (3)(12)$. So, we have $21x - 9y = 36$.

5. **The correct answer is (D).** This problem requires you to know the basic properties of exponents presented in this chapter. In particular, we know that raising an exponent to another power means that we need to multiply the exponents together. Thus, $\left(a^{-4}b^{3}c^{-2}\right)^{-5} = a^{(-4)(-5)}b^{(3)(-5)}c^{(-2)(-5)} = a^{20}b^{-15}c^{10}$. We now need to remember that a negative exponent in the numerator moves that part of the expression to the denominator. So. we have $a^{20}b^{-15}c^{10} = \frac{a^{20}c^{10}}{b^{15}}$.

6. **The correct answers are (A) and (D).** This problem tests your ability to solve a quadratic equation by factoring. Note that choice (A) has factored form $(x - 3)(x - 8) = 0$, which yields the roots 3 and 8. So this choice is correct. Choice (B) has factored form $(x + 3)(x + 8) = 0$, which yields the roots –3 and –8. So this choice is not correct. Choice (C) cannot be factored since it is the sum of two squares, which means the equation does not have any integer roots. So this

choice is not correct. Finally, choice (D) has factored form $(x-1)(x-1)=0$, which yields the root 1. So this choice is correct.

7. **The correct answers are (C) and (D).** Note that we can express the three consecutive odd integers as n, $n+2$, and $n+4$. Since the sum of these integers equals 51, we have the equation $n+n+2+n+4=51$. Combining terms yields $3n+6=51$. Solving for n yields $3n=45$, which means $n=15$. Thus, the largest of the three consecutive odd integers is 19, which means only choices (C) and (D) are correct.

8. **The correct answer is (E).** This problem tests your factoring skills. The only answer choice that contains a common factor in the numerator and denominator is choice (E), since $\dfrac{x^2-25}{x-5}=\dfrac{(x+5)(x-5)}{x-5}=x+5$.

9. **The correct answer is (D).** Perhaps the quickest way to solve this problem is to examine some specific cases. For example, if Jane is 50 years and Hector is 1 year old, Quantity B is greater than Quantity A. If Jane is 50 years old and Hector is 49 years old, then Quantity A is greater than Quantity B. If Jane is 50 years old and Hector is 25 years old, then Quantity A is equal to Quantity B. Thus, the relationship cannot be determined from the information given.

10. **The correct answer is (B).** In this problem you need to be able to compare the sizes of fractions. Suppose the area of each plot equals A acres. This means the size of each parcel in the first plot is given by $m=\dfrac{A}{20}$ acres. Similarly, the size of each parcel in the second plot is given by $n=\dfrac{A}{12}$ acres. Since these two fractions have the same numerator, the largest value is given by the fraction with the smallest denominator. Thus, $n>m$.

11. **The correct answer is (C).** This problem tests your understanding of expressions involving absolute value. Note that reversing the order of subtraction between two non-zero numbers changes the sign of the outcome. For example, $3-2=1$, and $2-3=-1$. But applying the absolute value to a non-zero number always yields a positive number. Thus, $|x-y|=|y-x|$.

12. **The correct answer is 225 million tons.** Perhaps the most efficient way to solve this problem is to build a one-variable equation that describes the total amount of iron ore produced. If we let x represent the total amount of iron ore produced, we can translate the given information as follows.

"Minnesota produced $\dfrac{3}{4}$ of all iron ore" translates as $\dfrac{3}{4}x$.

"Michigan produced $\dfrac{1}{5}$ of all iron ore" translates as $\dfrac{1}{5}x$.

We also know that the total amount of iron ore produced is the sum of the Minnesota amount plus the Michigan amount plus the amount produced by all other states combined. Thus, we have the equation $\dfrac{3}{4}x+\dfrac{1}{5}x+15=x$. Solving this equation for x yields:

$$15=x-\frac{3}{4}x-\frac{1}{5}x$$
$$15=\frac{20x}{20}-\frac{15x}{20}-\frac{4x}{20}$$
$$15=\frac{x}{20}$$
$$300=x$$

So, the total amount of iron ore produced is 300 million tons. However, be careful to make sure that you answer the question being asked. In this case, we need to determine the amount of iron ore produced by Minnesota. So we compute $\left(\frac{3}{4}\right)(300) = 225$ million tons.

13. **The correct answer is \$15.** This problem also tests your ability to construct and solve an appropriate one-variable equation. We can represent the total charge for the shirt order as the sum of the design cost plus the cost of the first 20 shirts plus the cost of the next 10 shirts. That is, we have the equation:

$$\text{total cost} = \underbrace{x}_{\text{design cost}} + \underbrace{\left(\frac{2x}{3}\right)(20)}_{\text{cost of 1st 20 shirts}} + \underbrace{\left(\frac{x}{5}\right)(10)}_{\text{cost of next 10 shirts}}$$

We know that the total cost of the order is \$245. Thus, we need to solve for x in the equation $245 = x + \left(\frac{2x}{3}\right)(20) + \left(\frac{x}{5}\right)(10)$.

$$245 = x + \frac{40x}{3} + \frac{10x}{5}$$
$$245 = \frac{15x}{15} + \frac{200x}{15} + \frac{30x}{15}$$
$$245 = \frac{245x}{15}$$
$$(245)(15) = 245x$$
$$15 = x$$

14. **The correct answer is 112.** Once again, we need to construct and solve an appropriate one-variable equation. In this problem, the given information provides a head start to the solution since we already have variable expressions for the manufacturing cost, $6,720 + 90x$, and the amount received, $150x$, each given in terms of the number of cell phones produced. To answer the question, we should first determine the value of x for which these two expressions are equal. Solving the equation $150x = 6,720 + 90x$ yields $150x - 90x = 6,720$, which means that $60x = 6,720$. Thus, we have the solution $x = \frac{6,720}{60} = 112$. Therefore, at least 112 cell phones must be manufactured.

15. **The correct answer is (C).** One effective strategy for solving this problem is to make a list of possible ratios that compare Jack's point total to Kevin's point total. Consider the list $\frac{4}{3}, \frac{8}{6}, \frac{12}{9}, \frac{16}{12}, \frac{20}{15}$, and so on. Note that we can generate the list by successively adding 4 to the numerator and 3 to the denominator. Note also that in each case, the total number of points scored by the two boys is given by the sum of the numerator and denominator for that ratio. Thus, our list yields totals of 7, 14, 21, 28, and 35. The only answer choice not on our list is choice (C).

16. **The correct answer is (C).** Since we need to determine how many members are in the Glee Club, let's use the given information to construct a one-variable equation in which x represents the number of club members. We are told that each member sold 8 boxes of greeting cards, and that each box earns a profit of \$3. Thus, the profit earned from card sales is given by $\underbrace{(8)}_{\text{boxes per member}} \times \underbrace{(3)}_{\text{profit per box}} \times \underbrace{(x)}_{\text{\# of members}} = 24x$.

The total profit earned is given by the profit from card sales plus the additional \$25 from the faculty. Thus, we have the equation $313 = 24x + 25$. Solving for x yields $288 - 24x$, which means that $x = \frac{288}{24} = 12$ members.

17. **The correct answer is (E).** This problem tests your ability to translate statements into equations. Let's work one piece at a time. "The number p is 5 less than 3 times the number q" translates into the equation $p = 3q - 5$. "The sum of the number p and twice the number q is 13" translates into the equation $p + 2q = 13$. We can see immediately that choice (E) matches our pair of equations.

18. **The correct answer is (D).** This problem requires you to remember how to use the formula (rate) × (time) = distance. One effective strategy is to construct an equation in which the variable x represents the faster plane's speed. We know that each plane flies for a total of 4 hours, so the faster plane travels a distance of $(4)(x)$ miles. The slower plane also flies 4 hours, but its speed is 55 miles per hour less than the faster plane. Thus, the slower plane travels a distance of $(4)(x - 55)$ miles. Since the planes are 1,700 miles apart after flying 4 hours, the distance traveled by the first plane plus the distance traveled by the second plane must equal 1,700. So we have the equation $4x + 4(x - 55) = 1,700$. Solving for x yields $4x + 4x - 220 = 1,700$.

$8x - 220 = 1,700$

$8x = 1,920$, which means that $x = \dfrac{1,920}{8} = 240$ miles per hour.

19. **The correct answer is (D).** If statement (1) is true, then both x and y must equal 0, since the only way the sum of two non-zero numbers can equal zero is if one of them is negative. But neither x^2 nor y^2 can be negative. So we can conclude that xy is not greater than 0. Thus, statement (1) alone is sufficient. If statement (2) is true, we have $x^2 + y^2 = (x + y)^2$. Multiplying out the right-hand side yields $x^2 + y^2 = x^2 + 2xy + y^2$, which simplifies to $0 = 2xy$. But this can only be true if $x = 0$ or $y = 0$. In either case, we know that xy is not greater than 0. Thus, statement (2) alone is sufficient. Therefore, EACH statement ALONE is sufficient.

20. **The correct answer is (C).** An effective strategy for solving this problem is to let the variable x equal the total value of the jackpot, and then interpret statements (1) and (2) in terms of x. Note that Lucy's share plus Ethel's share must add up to the value x. If statement (1) is true, we can express Lucy's share as $\dfrac{2}{3}x$ and Ethel's share as $\dfrac{1}{3}x$. However, the equation $\dfrac{2}{3}x + \dfrac{1}{3}x = x$ will be true for every real number x. So, statement (1) alone is not sufficient. If statement (2) is true, we can express Lucy's share as $x - 500,000$. However, the equation $x - 500,000 + 500,000 = x$ will be true for every real number x. So, statement (2) alone is not sufficient. If statements (1) and (2) are true, then we can use Ethel's information to construct the equation $\dfrac{1}{3}x = 500,000$, which means $x = 1,500,000$. Thus, BOTH statements TOGETHER are sufficient, but NEITHER statement ALONE is sufficient.

21. **The correct answer is (B).** We need to determine a numerical value for the ratio $\dfrac{M}{N}$. If statement (1) is true, then we know that $M = 3N + 5$. But this equation has more than one solution. For example, $N = 1$, $M = 8$, solves the equation, which yields $\dfrac{M}{N} = \dfrac{8}{1} = 8$. Note also that $N = 2$, $M = 11$ solves the equation, which yields $\dfrac{M}{N} = \dfrac{11}{2} = 5\dfrac{1}{2}$. Thus, statement (1) is not sufficient to determine the value of $\dfrac{M}{N}$. If statement (2) is true, then we know that $5N + 11M = 0$. This equation can be rewritten as $11M = -5N$, which means that $\dfrac{M}{N} = -\dfrac{5}{11}$. So statement (2) is sufficient. Thus, statement (2) ALONE is sufficient, but statement (1) is not sufficient.

CHAPTER 4

Geometry Review

The geometry questions on the GRE and GMAT are designed to test your knowledge of the following basic concepts:

- Degrees

- Lines

- Angles

- Squares and rectangles

- Triangles, including equilateral, isosceles, right, obtuse, acute, 45-45-90, and 30-60-90

- Pythagorean theorem

- Circles, including radius, diameter, circumference, and arcs

- Coordinate system, including *y*-intercept and slope

- Solid geometry, including volume, diagonals, and total surface area

You will not be required to write proofs. Rather, you will need to apply these concepts in a variety of problem-solving contexts.

GEOMETRIC DEFINITIONS AND NOTATION

Before working on practice problems, we need to review some basic geometric definitions and notation.

Points and Lines

A *point* is defined as having no size, only position. On the GRE and GMAT, a point is typically represented by a dot and named by using a capital letter. The graphic below depicts point *A*.

$$\cdot A$$

A *line* is a continuous set of points. It only has one dimension, length, and has no width. Lines can be named in several ways. Sometimes, a letter is placed next to a drawing of the line, and the line is named using this letter. For example, the following figure is a picture of line *l*.

l

Lines are also commonly named by putting a double-headed arrow over any two of the points on the line. For example, the figure below is a picture of line $\overleftrightarrow{AB}$.

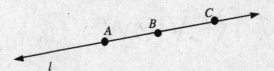

Note that, since the point C is also on this line, the line could just as well have been called line $\overleftrightarrow{AC}$

or line $\overleftrightarrow{BC}$. Also note that it is standard to put arrowheads on the ends of lines to indicate that the line "keeps going" in both directions forever.

A *line segment* is the portion of line between two of its points, which are called the *endpoints* of the line segment. A line segment is named by placing a bar over its endpoints. For example, the figure below depicts line segment $\overline{PQ}$.

Note that, while $\overleftrightarrow{AB}$ and $\overleftrightarrow{AC}$ refer to the same line, $\overline{AB}$ and $\overline{AC}$ refer to different line segments. Line segment $\overline{AB}$ runs between points A and B, while line segment $\overline{AC}$ runs between points A and C.

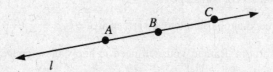

Unlike a line, which is of infinite length, a line segment is of finite length. The length of a line segment is indicated by writing its two endpoints next to each other. For example, based on the figure below, $EF = 12$.

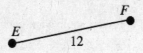

If two line segments have the same length, they are said to be *congruent*. There is a special symbol for congruence, which may be used on the GRE and GMAT. The symbol is $\cong$. Thus, if $\overline{BC}$ and $\overline{EF}$ have the same length, that is, if $BC = EF$, we write $\overline{BC} \cong \overline{EF}$.

A *ray* is a portion of a line, beginning at one point on the line, called the *endpoint, and* extending infinitely in one direction. A ray is indicated by writing the endpoint of the ray next to another point on the ray and placing a one-headed arrow over it. For example, the figure below depicts $\overrightarrow{AB}$.

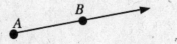

Angles

Angles are formed when two lines or two line segments intersect. The point of intersection is called the *vertex* of the angle, and the two lines (or line segments) are called the *sides* of the angle. Sometimes, an angle is named by referring to the vertex. The symbol that represents an angle is $\angle$. The figure below, for example, depicts $\angle P$.

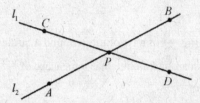

On the GRE and GMAT, angles can be named in several different ways. In some figures, a letter or a number will be placed inside the angle near the vertex, and this letter or number will be used to name the angle. The figure below shows two angles, $\angle 5$ and $\angle k$.

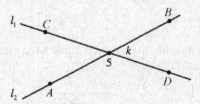

This notation can be confusing when the figure is more complicated, however. In the figure below, for example, it would not be clear which of three possible angles we meant if we wrote $\angle Q$.

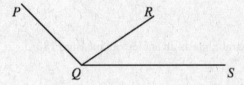

To avoid this ambiguity we can identify an angle by naming a point on one side, then naming the vertex, and then naming a point on the other side. The entire "big" angle in the picture would be called $\angle PQS$, while the other two angles would be called $\angle PQR$, and $\angle RQS$.

You may recall that angles are measured in *degrees*, and that degrees are indicated by the symbol °. By definition, the amount of rotation needed to make one complete revolution around a circle is 360°.

Every angle, then, can be measured as a fraction of one complete revolution around a circle, that is, as a fraction of 360°. For example, an angle formed by making $\frac{1}{6}$ of a revolution around a circle has a measure of $\frac{1}{6} \times 360° = 60°$.

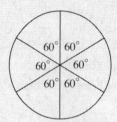

In the same way, an angle formed by making $\frac{1}{12}$ of a revolution around a circle has a measure of $\frac{1}{12} \times 360° = 30°$, and an angle formed by making $\frac{2}{3}$ of a revolution around a circle has a measure of $\frac{2}{3} \times 360° = 240°$.

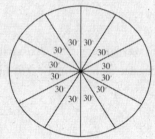
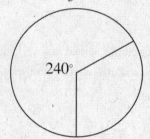

Note that an angle formed by making $\frac{1}{2}$ of a revolution around a circle has a measure of $\frac{1}{2} \times 360° = 180°$. Moreover, such an angle forms a straight line.

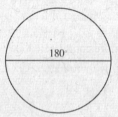

Thus, in a sense, you can think of a straight line as an angle with measure 180°.

An angle formed by making $\frac{1}{4}$ of a revolution around a circle has a measure of $\frac{1}{4} \times 360° = 90°$. Such an angle is called a *right angle*. As shown in the following figure, a right angle is depicted by placing the symbol ⌐ within the angle.

We have already seen that congruent line segments are line segments that have the same length. In the same way, if two angles have the same measure, they are said to be *congruent*. For example, if $\angle A$ and $\angle B$ both measure 55°, we write $\angle A \cong \angle B$.

Let's review a few geometric vocabulary terms relating to angles.

Angles can be placed in categories according to their size. Angles that have a measure of less than 90° are called *acute angles*. An angle of 90°, as we have already seen, is called a *right angle*. An angle that has a measure greater than 90° but less than 180° is called an *obtuse angle*. Finally, an angle of 180°, sometimes called a *straight angle,* is actually the same as a straight line.

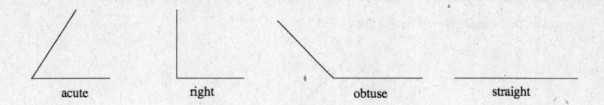

acute   right   obtuse   straight

BE CAREFUL: When looking at geometric figures on the GRE and GMAT, be careful not to make the mistake of assuming that an angle is of a certain size just because it *looks like* it is that size. For example, you cannot assume that an angle must be a right angle just because it looks like a right angle in a figure. You do not really know for certain that an angle is a right angle unless it is marked as a right angle with the symbol ⌐, or you perform a computation that demonstrates that it must have measure 90°.

Two angles are said to be *complementary* if the sum of their measures is 90°. For example, a 50° angle and a 40° angle are complementary. Similarly, the *complement* of a 10° angle is an 80° angle. In the following figure, ∠ABC and ∠CBD are complementary.

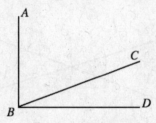

Two angles are said to be *supplementary* if the sum of their measures is 180°. For example, a 50° angle and a 130° angle are supplementary. In the figure below, ∠ABC and ∠CBD are supplementary.

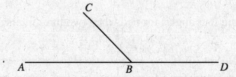

The Measurement of Angles

One of the most common types of geometry problems that you will see on the GRE and GMAT asks you to determine the measurement of an angle in a geometric figure. These *measurement of angles* problems are based on a number of important key properties.

Straight Lines and Supplementary Angles

Recall that a *straight angle* (i.e., a straight line) measures 180°.

Key Property #1: Whenever a straight line is partitioned into two angles, the angles are supplementary.

In the figure below, for example, it must be true that $x° + y° = 180°$.

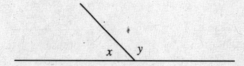

The reason that this property is so important is that if a straight line is partitioned into two angles and you know the measure of one of those angles, you can quickly find the measure of the other angle by subtracting from 180. For example, in the figure below, $a° = 120°$, since $180° − 60° = 120°$.

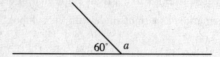

Vertical Angles

As the figure below shows, whenever two lines intersect, four angles are formed.

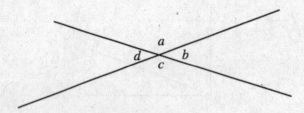

The pairs of angles that are opposite each other are called *vertical angles,* and the pairs of angles that are next to each other are called *adjacent* angles. In the figure above, angles *a* and *c* are vertical angles, as are angles *d* and *b*. Also, for example, angle *a* is adjacent to angles *b* and *d*.

There is a special relationship between the four angles formed when two lines intersect.

Key Property #2: When two lines intersect to form four angles, vertical angles are congruent, and adjacent angles are supplementary.

In the figure above, $a° = c°$ and $b° = d°$. In addition, $a° + b° = 180°$, and so on.

Thus, if you know the measure of any *one* of the four angles formed by intersecting lines, you can find measures of the other three. Consider the graphic below.

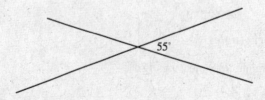

In this figure, one of the angles is labeled as 55°. Therefore, the angle opposite it is also 55°. The other two angles are supplementary to the 55° angle and must therefore have measure 180° − 55° = 125°. The figure below shows the figure with the measures of all four angles indicated.

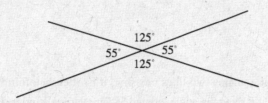

Let's take a look at some sample GRE and GMAT questions that involve these first two key properties:

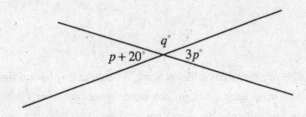

1. In the figure above, what is the value of q?
   (A) 10
   (B) 30
   (C) 60
   (D) 120
   (E) 150

On the GRE and GMAT, geometry problems are very often used as contexts in which to ask algebra questions. In this problem, Key Property #2 tells us that vertical angles are congruent. Thus, we know that $3p = p + 20$. Solving this equation yields $p = 10$.

Note that if $p = 10$, then $3p = 3(10) = 30$. We further know (also from Key Property #2) that $3p + q = 180$. Since $3p = 30$, it follows that $30 + q = 180$. Solving for q yields $30 + q = 180$, which means that $q = 150$. **The correct answer is (E).**

BE CAREFUL: Remember that incorrect multiple-choice answers on the GRE and GMAT are frequently the most common mistakes made when working the problems. One of the most common mistakes to make in a geometry problem is to answer the wrong question. Note that, for example, at the beginning of the problem above, we determined that $p = 10$. Choice (A) is 10, but the problem does not ask for the value of p. Next, we determined that $3p = 30$, which is the value given in choice (B). However, the problem does not ask for the value of $3p$.

If an angle is *bisected,* it means that it has been cut into two congruent halves. For example, if a 40° angle is bisected, the result is two 20° angles.

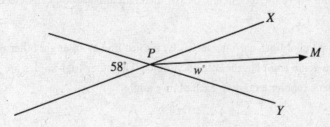

2. In the figure above, if ray $\overrightarrow{PM}$ bisects $\angle XPY$, then $w =$

(A) 17

(B) 25

(C) 29

(D) 32

(E) 34

Whenever you are given a figure that contains two lines crossing, it is often helpful to look for pairs of involved vertical angles. In this case, we can see that $\angle XPY$ and the angle labeled 58° are vertical angles. By Key Property #2, this means that $\angle XPY$ also measures 58°. Since $\overrightarrow{PM}$ bisects this angle, the angle labeled $w°$ must be half of 58°, which is 29°. **The correct answer is (C).**

Parallel Lines

The next key property relates to what are known as *parallel* lines. Whenever you have a figure that contains two lines, there are two possibilities—either the lines cross each other, or they never cross each other. Two lines that never cross each other are said to be parallel to each other. For example, the figure below shows two lines that are parallel to one another.

The symbol for parallel lines is ‖. For the figure above, we write $l_1 \parallel l_2$.

Let's consider what happens when a third line intersects the two parallel lines. As the figure below shows, when this happens, eight angles are formed.

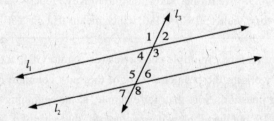

Note, first of all, that four of the angles appear to be *acute*, and four appear to be *obtuse*. It can be demonstrated that all four of the acute angles are congruent, and all four of the obtuse angles are also congruent. Further, each acute angle is supplementary to each obtuse angle. Thus, whenever you have a figure with two parallel lines cut by another line, eight angles are formed. If you are given the number of degrees in any one of the eight angles, you can determine the number of degrees in the other seven.

Key Property #3: When two parallel lines are intersected by a third line at an angle other than 90°, then eight angles are formed. Four of the angles are acute and congruent to each other. The other four angles are obtuse and congruent to each other. Finally, each acute angle is supplementary to each obtuse angle.

For example, in the figure, suppose you are told that $m\angle 7$ measures 55°. This means that the other three acute angles, $m\angle 2$, $m\angle 4$, and $m\angle 6$, are also equal to 55°. In addition, all of the other angles are supplementary to a 55° angle, that is, they all have measures of $180° - 55° = 125°$.

SPECIAL CASE: If the line that intersects the parallel lines intersects them at a right angle, all eight angles formed are right angles. Thus, they are all congruent.

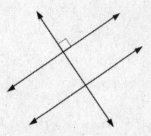

A particularly convenient way to think about Key Property #3 is as follows: When two parallel lines are cut by another line, eight angles are formed. In this situation, any two acute angles are the same size, any two obtuse angles are the same size, and any acute angle is supplementary to any obtuse angle.

Let's try some problems that use this key property.

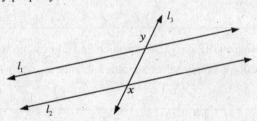

1. In the figure above, l_1 is parallel to l_2. Which one of the following relationships *must* be true?

   (A) $x + y = 180$

   (B) $2x = y$

   (C) $6x = 3(x + y)$

   (D) $2y = x$

   (E) $6x = 4x + y$

Consider the angles labeled x and y in the figure. Note that both of these angles are obtuse. Therefore, $x = y$. If x and y have the same value, then $3(x + y) = 3(x + x) = 6x$. **The correct answer is (C).**

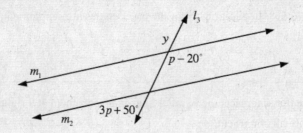

2. In the figure above, lines m_1 and m_2 are parallel. What is the value of p?

(A) 32

(B) $34\frac{1}{2}$

(C) 35

(D) $37\frac{1}{2}$

(E) 39

Since lines m_1 and m_2 are parallel, the two labeled angles must be supplementary. Therefore, we have $(3p + 50°) + (p - 20°) = 180°$, which means that $4p + 30° = 180°$. Solving for p yields $4p = 150°$, which means that $p = 37\frac{1}{2}$. **The correct answer is (D).**

BE CAREFUL: If you are solving a GRE or GMAT question and you end up with an answer that doesn't match any of the multiple-choice answers, don't simply select a multiple-choice answer which "looks close" to the answer you found.

Triangles

Recall that a triangle is a figure with three line segments as sides and three angles. One of the fundamental properties of all triangles is that, no matter what the triangle looks like, the measures of its three angles always add up to 180. For example, in the figure below, $p° + q° + r° = 180°$.

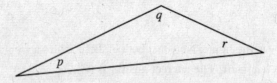

Key Property #4: The sum of the measures of the three angles in a triangle is always 180°.

NOTE: The fact that the three angles of a triangle add up to 180° is probably the most common "measurement of angles" fact on the GRE and GMAT.

In many triangles, the three sides have different lengths. However, there is a special type of triangle called an *isosceles* triangle in which two of the sides have the same length. An isosceles triangle can be drawn as shown below, with the two sides that have the same length marked with little "tic" marks.

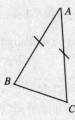

For example, in the figure above, $AB = AC$, so we write $\overline{AB} \cong \overline{AC}$.

An important fact about isosceles triangles is that the angles opposite the two equal sides must have the same measure. This is shown in the figure below.

The reason this result is so important is that if you are given the measures of any one of the angles in an isosceles triangle, you can find the measures of the other two. Consider these two examples.

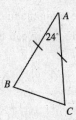 

In the first triangle, we are told that the measure of the angle opposite the non-congruent side is 24°. Based on this, the other two angles in the triangle must add up to $180° - 24° = 156°$. And, since these two angles are equal, each must measure $156° \div 2 = 78°$.

In the second triangle, we are given the measure of an angle opposite one of the congruent sides. Therefore, the angle opposite the other congruent side must also be 78°. And, if a triangle has two 78° angles, the remaining angle must be $180° - 78° - 78° = 24°$.

There is a special type of triangle called an *equilateral* triangle that has all three sides the same length. In such a triangle, all three angles must also have the same measure. Since all three angles must add up to 180°, each angle in an equilateral triangle must equal $180° \div 3 = 60°$.

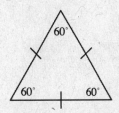

A good way to summarize these results is given below.

- If you are given a triangle in which all three sides have different lengths, then you need to know the measures of two of the angles in order to find the third.

- If you are given an isosceles triangle, you need to know the measure of one angle in order to find the other two.

- If you have an equilateral triangle, you do not need to be told anything in order to find the measures of all three angles—they are all 60°.

The property that there are 180° in a triangle can be used to determine the number of degrees in "line segment" figures with four sides, five sides, or more. For example, consider the four-sided figure below.

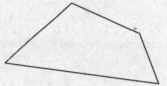

As shown below, this figure can be divided into two triangles.

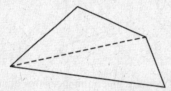

Since every triangle contains 180°, the sum of the measures of the four angles in the four-sided figure above contains 180° + 180° = 360°. In general, all four-sided figures—as long as the sides are straight and don't cross each other except at their endpoints—contain 360°. In the same way, since the five-sided following figure can be partitioned into three triangles, it, and all five sided figures, contain 3 × 180° = 540°.

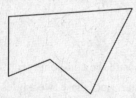
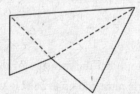

> **NOTE:** If you need to determine the sum of the measures of the angles in any geometric figure with straight lines sides, try partitioning the figure into triangles. Then, count 180° for each of the triangles in your figure.

The following problems illustrate how the given information in a single problem can be varied to create an angle measurement question. While these problems are all different, they all hinge on the four key properties that we have already discussed.

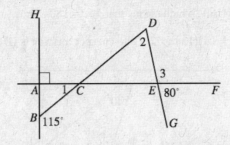

1. In the figure above, m∠1 + m∠2 + m∠3 =
   (A) 100°
   (B) 120°
   (C) 180°
   (D) 200°
   (E) It cannot be determined.

This problem is more manageable if we work in stages. Note first that angle ABC is supplementary to an angle with measure 115°. Thus, $\angle ABC$ has measure $180° - 115° = 65°$. The figure also tells us that ABC is a right triangle, which means that $m\angle 1 = 180° - 90° - 65° = 25°$. We can now conclude that $\angle DCE$ also has measure 25° since it is a vertical angle to $m\angle 1$. Similarly, $\angle DCE$ has measure 80° since it is a vertical angle to $\angle FEG$. Since the angles of triangle DCE must sum to 180°, we have $m\angle 2 = 180° - 80° - 25° = 75°$. Finally, since $m\angle 3$ is supplementary to an angle with measure 80°, we know that $m\angle 3 = 180° - 80° = 100°$. Therefore, $m\angle 1 + m\angle 2 + m\angle 3 = 25° + 75° + 100° = 200°$. **The correct answer is (D).**

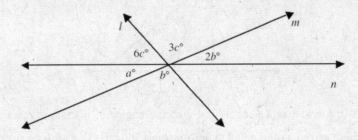

2. In the figure above, what is the value of a?
   (A) 30
   (B) 45
   (C) 60
   (D) 72
   (E) 90

First note that, by vertical angles, $b = 3c$, which means that $2b = 6c$. Thus, we can relabel the figure as follows.

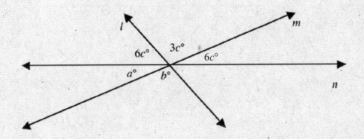

We can now conclude that $6c + 3c + 6c = 180$, which means that $15c = 180$. Thus, $c = \dfrac{180}{15} = 12$. The figure also shows that $a = 6c$ by vertical angles. Therefore, $a = (6)(12) = 72$. **The correct answer is (D).**

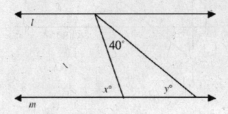

3. From the figure above, which of the following *must* be true?

    I. $x + y = 90$

    II. $y = 40 + x$

    III. $x = 40 + y$

    (A) I only

    (B) II only

    (C) III only

    (D) I and II only

    (E) I and III only

Let's relabel the figure to help us identify the relationships among the angles.

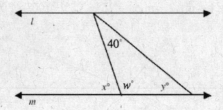

By supplementary angles, we know that $x + w = 180$. Since the angles of a triangle must sum to 180, we also have $40 + y + w = 180$. Setting these two equations equal to one another yields $x + w = 40 + y + w$.

Subtracting w from both sides yields $x = 40 + y$. Thus, only option III is true. **The correct answer is (C).**

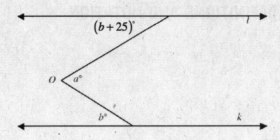

4. From the figure above, lines *l* and *k* are parallel. Which of the following *must* be true?

(A) $b < a$

(B) $b = a$

(C) $b \leq a$

(D) $b > a$

(E) $b \geq a$

This is a more challenging problem. Note that it sometime helps to add an extra line to the given figure. In this case, let's draw a line through point *O* that is parallel to both line *l* and line *k*.

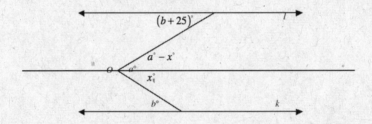

We now have a pair of alternate interior angles. Namely, $x^\circ = b^\circ$, and $b^\circ = a^\circ - x^\circ$. Substituting the first equation into the second yields $b^\circ = a^\circ - b^\circ$, which means that $2b^\circ = a^\circ$. Thus, $b^\circ = \frac{1}{2}a^\circ$, i.e., $b < a$. **The correct answer is (A).**

EXERCISES: GEOMETRIC DEFINITIONS AND NOTATION

Directions: Select the answer choice that best answers the question.

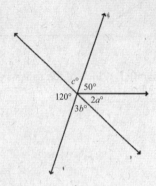

1. In the figure above, what is the value of $a + b$?

   (A) 35

   (B) 55

   (C) 60

   (D) 70

   (E) 130

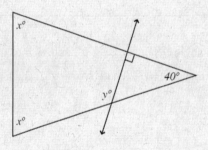

2. Based on the figure above, which of the following relationships *must* be true?

   (A) $x = y$

   (B) $2x = y$

   (C) $2x > y$

   (D) $2x < y$

   (E) $x = 2y$

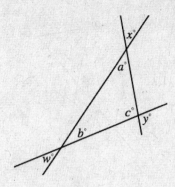

3. In the figure above, $x + y + w =$

(A) 360

(B) 120

(C) 240

(D) 180

(E) It cannot be determined.

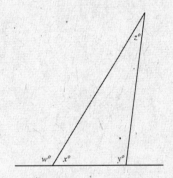

4. In the figure above, if $w = 110$, what is the value of $y + z$?

(A) 55

(B) 70

(C) 100

(D) 110

(E) 120

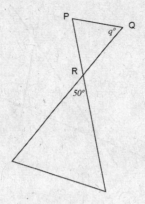

5. In the figure above, if $PR = QR$, then $q =$

    (A) 45

    (B) 50

    (C) 55

    (D) 65

    (E) 75

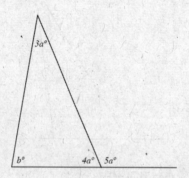

6. In the figure above, what is the value of b?

    (A) 20

    (B) 25

    (C) 30

    (D) 35

    (E) 40

ANSWER KEY AND EXPLANATIONS

1. B	3. D	5. D
2. C	4. D	6. E

1. **The correct answer is (B).** Notice that the angle formed by adding the 50° angle and the $2a°$ angle is vertical to the 120° angle. By Key Property #1, then, $50 + 2a = 120$. This means that $2a = 70$, i.e., $a = 35$. Next, by Key Property #2, the angle labeled $3b°$ is supplementary to the 120° angle. Thus, $3b + 120 = 180$, or $3b = 60$, so $b = 20$. Thus, $a + b = 35 + 20 = 55$.

2. **The correct answer is (C).** Let's begin by determining the value of a. Looking at the large triangle, we have one angle of 40° and two angles of $x°$. Since the three angles must add up to 180, we must have $x + x = 140$, which means the value of $x = 70$.

   In order to find value of y, we can consider the smaller triangle on the right side of the figure. We know one of the angles is 90° and another is 40°, so the remaining angle must be 50°. Note that the angle labeled $y°$ is supplementary to the angle that we have just determined is 50°. Therefore, it must be 130°. Finally, the value of $2x$ is 140, so the value of $2x$ is larger than y. None of the other relationships holds.

3. **The correct answer is (D).** We know that $a + b + c = 180$, since the angles of a triangle sum to 180. Note that x, y, and w correspond to vertical angles a, c, and b, respectively. Since pairs of vertical angles are congruent, we have $x + y + w = 180$.

4. **The correct answer is (D).** Note that, if $d = 110$, then we know that $x = 70$. Thus, since there are 180° in a triangle, $x + y + z$ must equal 180. Therefore, $70 + y + z = 180$, or $y + z = 180 - 70 = 110$.

5. **The correct answer is (D).** This problem uses two of the Key Properties. To begin, the angle vertical to the angle labeled 50° must also be 50°. Now, the angle at Q is $q°$, and since this triangle is isosceles, the angle at P is also $q°$. Finally, since there are 180° in a triangle, we have $q + q + 50 = 180$, which means that $2q = 130$. Thus, $q = 65$.

6. **The correct answer is (E).** By Key Property #1, the two angles named $4a$ and $5a$ here are supplementary, so $4a + 5a = 180$. Solving this equation yields $9a = 180$, which means that $a = 20$.

   Note that, if $a = 20$, then $4a = 80$ and $3a = 60$. Thus, two of the angles in the triangle are 80° and 60°, and since these add up to 140°, the remaining angle must be 40°.

PROPERTIES OF GEOMETRIC FIGURES

This next category of geometry problems requires you to know certain characteristics of geometric figures. In this section, we will begin by taking a look at additional important properties of triangles, then we take a look at the key properties of figures with more than three sides. After this, we will examine the key properties of circles.

Properties of Triangles

We have already seen how triangles can be classified by the lengths of their sides, e.g., *isosceles* and *equilateral* triangles. Triangles can also be classified by the size of their angles.

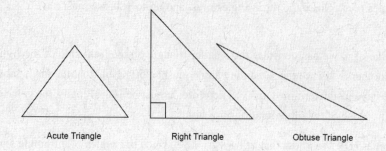

Acute Triangle   Right Triangle   Obtuse Triangle

An *acute* triangle is a triangle that contains three acute angles. If a triangle has a right angle, it is called a *right* triangle. Finally, if a triangle has an obtuse angle (note that it can only have one, since it can only have 180° total), it is called an *obtuse* triangle.

Geometric Figures

Key Property #1: In any triangle, the largest angle is opposite the longest side, and the smallest angle is opposite the shortest side.

This property is often called the *Hinge theorem*, since it illustrates the intuitive notion that the farther a door is open, the bigger the angle its hinges form. In other words, in a triangle that has three sides of different lengths, the longest side is opposite the largest angle, the second longest side is opposite the second largest angle, and the shortest side is opposite the smallest angle.

We have already discussed what happens if a triangle has two sides that are the same length, namely, the angles opposite the congruent sides have the same measures. Moreover, if all three sides of a triangle are of the same length, then the three angles all measure 60°.

The following problems show how this key property can help you on the GRE and GMAT.

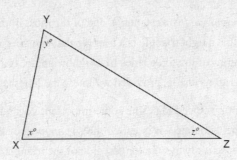

1. In triangle *XYZ* above, if *YZ* > *XZ*, which of the following must be true?

   (A) $x > z$

   (B) $x = y$

   (C) $z > y$

   (D) $x > y$

   (E) $z > x$

This problem can be solved by remembering Key Property #1. If *YZ* > *XZ*, then the angle opposite $\overline{YZ}$ must be larger than the angle opposite $\overline{XZ}$. Since the angle opposite $\overline{YZ}$ measures $x°$, and the angle opposite $\overline{XZ}$ measures $y°$, it must be true that $x > y$.

Let's take a look at the other answer choices. To begin, choices (A), (C) and (E) involve the angle labeled $z°$, so they cannot be correct, since we know nothing about this angle. Also, note that choice (B) contradicts the inequality $x > y$. **The correct answer is (D).**

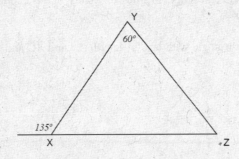

2. Based on the figure above, which of the following relationships must be true?

   (A) $XY > XZ > YZ$

   (B) $XZ > XY > YZ$

   (C) $YZ > XY > XZ$

   (D) $YZ > XZ > XY$

   (E) $XZ > YZ > XY$

The first thing to note in this problem is that the angle supplementary to the angle labeled 135° must be equal to 45°. Now, since there are 180° in a triangle, the angle at vertex *Z* must be equal to $180° - 60° - 45° = 75°$. Thus, $\overline{XY}$ is opposite the biggest angle and is thus the longest side. Also, $\overline{XZ}$ is opposite the second largest angle, so it must be the second longest side. It follows that $\overline{YZ}$ is the shortest side. **The correct answer is (A).**

The Pythagorean Theorem

The next key property is called the *Pythagorean theorem*, and is one of the most important facts you need to know for GRE and GMAT geometry problems. Recall that a right triangle is a triangle that contains a right angle. The Pythagorean theorem is actually a formula that relates the lengths of the three sides of a right triangle. Using the Pythagorean theorem allows us to determine the length of one side of a right triangle, provided we know the lengths of the other two sides.

Before we state the Pythagorean theorem, we need to define some important vocabulary terms. The side of a right triangle that is opposite the right angle has a special name—it is called the *hypotenuse* of the triangle. Since the 90° angle is the largest angle in the triangle, the hypotenuse is always the longest side of the triangle. The other two sides of the triangle are called its *legs*.

Consider the triangle below, which has sides of length AB, BC, and AC.

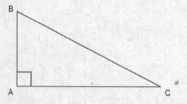

In this triangle, the side of length BC is opposite the right angle, and is therefore the hypotenuse. The sides of length AB and AC are the legs. The Pythagorean theorem tells us the following:

> The sum of the squares of the lengths of the legs of the triangle is equal to the square of the length of the hypotenuse. For this triangle, the Pythagorean theorem yields the equation $(AB)^2 + (AC)^2 = (BC)^2$.

Remember that, for example, AB represents the length of side $\overline{AB}$. Thus, in this geometric context, $(AB)^2$ means the square of the length of side AB.

The Pythagorean Theorem: In a right triangle with legs of length AB and AC and hypotenuse of length BC, it is always true that $(AB)^2 + (AC)^2 = (BC)^2$.

Consider the following two examples:

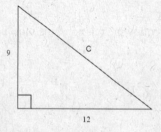

In this triangle, we are given the lengths of the legs. To determine the length of the hypotenuse, we compute $9^2 + 12^2 = C^2$. Thus, $81 + 144 = C^2$, which means that $225 = C^2$. Therefore, $C = \sqrt{225} = 15$.

You must be careful when using the Pythagorean theorem. Note that, in the figure below, it is the length of one of the legs that is missing.

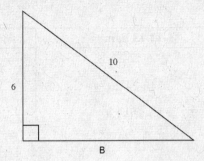

Therefore, to find the missing length, we can compute $6^2 + B^2 = 10^2$. Thus, $36 + B^2 = 100$, which means that $B^2 = 64$. Therefore, $B = \sqrt{64} = 8$.

The Pythagorean theorem is used very frequently on the GRE and GMAT. Thus, whenever you see a right angle or a right triangle in a geometry problem, it will often be helpful to use the Pythagorean theorem to solve the problem.

BE CAREFUL: A common mistake when applying the Pythagorean theorem is to automatically use the equation $a^2 + b^2 = c^2$. However, this equation is valid only for right triangles whose legs are labeled a and b, and whose hypotenuse is labeled c. To avoid this mistake, remind yourself that the theorem yields the equation $\left(leg\right)^2 + \left(leg\right)^2 = \left(hypotenuse\right)^2$. For example, in the next triangle, we have the equation $c^2 + b^2 = a^2$.

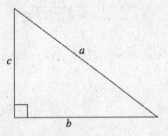

Note that, in the two problems we solved earlier, the missing lengths turned out to be whole numbers. This is because, in both cases, the length of the missing side ended up being expressed as the square root of a perfect square. However, this does not always have to happen. In most real-world situations, in fact, the length of the missing side is much more likely to end up as the square root of a non-perfect square number.

There are a few commonly encountered sets of three whole numbers that represent the sides of a right triangle. Such triples are called *Pythagorean triples*. We have already seen two sets of Pythagorean triples, i.e., 6, 8, 10, and 9, 12, 15. In order to keep the answers to Pythagorean theorem problems more manageable, such triples are used regularly on the GRE and GMAT.

The Pythagorean triples occur in what are called "families." The most common family is the 3-4-5 family. Note that $3^2 + 4^2 = 5^2$. Thus, if a right triangle has legs of length 3 and 4, the hypotenuse will be of length 5. Multiples of 3-4-5 also solve the Pythagorean theorem. For example, if we double all of the numbers, we get 6-6-10. If we triple 3-4-5, we obtain 9-12-15. Other common members of this family include 30-40-50, 60-80-100, and 300-400-500.

Another common family of triples is the 5-12-13 family. Note that $5^2 + 12^2 = 13^2$, since $25 + 144 = 169$. Other triples from this family that might appear on the test include 10-24-26, and 50-120-130. One additional triple family that you sometimes see on the test is based on 8-15-17. Note that $8^2 + 15^2 = 17^2$.

Common Pythagorean Triples

3-4-5 Family	5-12-13 Family	8-15-17 Family
3-4-5	5-12-13	8-15-17
6-8-10	10-24-26	
9-12-15	50-120-130	
12-16-20		
30-40-50		
60-80-100		
300-400-500		

Let's consider some problems that require the use of the Pythagorean theorem.

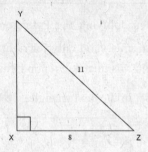

1. Which of the following is the closest to the length of side $\overline{XY}$ in the triangle above?

(A) 3

(B) 5.5

(C) 6.5

(D) 7

(E) 7.5

Note that this problem doesn't involve one of the triples that we have learned, but it still requires knowing the Pythagorean theorem. Since the triangle in the figure is a right triangle with a hypotenuse of 11, it must be true that $(XY)^2 + 8^2 = 11^2$, which means that $(XY)^2 = 121 - 64 = 57$. Thus, $XY = \sqrt{57}$. You can figure out that $\sqrt{57}$ is about 7.5. **The correct answer is (E).**

> **NOTE:** Remember that the Pythagorean theorem states that $(leg)^2 + (leg)^2 = (hypotenuse)^2$, and not $(leg) + (leg) = (hypotenuse)$. In other words, the sum of the *squares* of the lengths of the legs of the triangle is equal to the *square* of the hypotenuse.

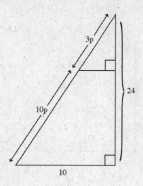

2. In the figure above, what is the value of p?

(A) $\dfrac{1}{2}$

(B) 1

(C) 2

(D) 13

(E) 26

Perhaps the quickest way to solve this problem is to notice that the legs of the right triangle are members of the 5-12-13 family of Pythagorean triples, i.e., 10-24-26. Thus, the hypotenuse must have length 26. According to the figure, the length of the hypotenuse is $10p + 3p = 13p$, which yields the equation $13p = 26$. Therefore, the value of p must be 2. **The correct answer is (C).**

Let's look at a Pythagorean theorem problem that doesn't include a figure.

3. An airplane starts at point A and flies due south for 60 miles to point B. It then turns and flies due east for an additional 80 miles to point C. How far is point A from point C?

(A) 20

(B) 70

(C) 100

(D) 120

(E) 140

HINT: In any geometry problem that does not contain a figure, it is often very helpful to draw and label a figure to help you see the important relationships in the problem.

A helpful figure of the problem is shown below:

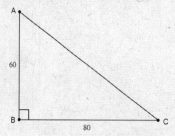

Once you have labeled your figure, you will be able to see that this problem contains a member of the 3-4-5 family of Pythagorean triples. In this case, the legs have been multiplied by 20. Thus, the hypotenuse must equal $5 \times 20 = 100$. **The correct answer is (C).**

Special Right Triangles

Note that there are two special types of right triangles for which you only need to be given the length of one of the sides of the triangle in order to find the other two. These two special triangles are called the 30-60-90 triangle and the 45-45-90 triangle. A 30-60-90 triangle is a triangle whose angles measure $30°, 60°,$ and $90°$. Similarly, a 45-45-90 triangle is a triangle whose angles measure $45°, 45°,$ and $90°$.

In general, if you are given a right triangle, you need to know the lengths of *two* of the sides to compute the third by means of the Pythagorean theorem. If, however, the triangle happens to have angles of $30°$-$60°$-$90°$ or $45°$-$45°$-$90°$, you only need to know the length of *one* of the sides of the triangle to find the lengths of the other two.

The first figure below shows the relative sizes of the sides opposite the $30°, 60°,$ and $90°$ angles in a 30-60-90 triangle. The second figure shows the relative sizes of the sides opposite the $45°$ and $90°$ angles in a 45-45-90 triangle.

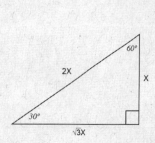 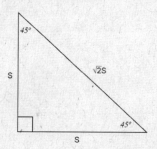

Let's look at some examples of how this information can be used. Suppose you were told that in a 30-60-90 triangle, the length of the side opposite the $30°$ angle is 11. This means that the hypotenuse is $11 \times 2 = 22$, and the side opposite the $60°$ angle is $11\sqrt{3}$.

Suppose, instead, that the hypotenuse is 14? This means that the side opposite the $30°$ angle would be $14 \div 2 = 7$, and the side opposite the $60°$ angle would be $7\sqrt{3}$.

Finally, suppose that the side opposite the $60°$ angle is $17\sqrt{3}$. In this case, to find the side opposite the $30°$ angle, we have to divide by $\sqrt{3}$. Thus, the side opposite the $30°$ side is 17, and the side opposite the hypotenuse is $17 \times 2 = 34$.

As you will see in the next section of this chapter, the special triangle relationships tend to be especially useful in area and perimeter problems. However, some geometry problems simply ask you to use the properties. Consider the example shown below.

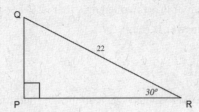

1. In triangle PQR above, what is the length of side $\overline{PR}$?
    (A) 11
    (B) $11\sqrt{3}$
    (C) 14
    (D) $14\sqrt{3}$
    (E) $22\sqrt{3}$

Note that the triangle is a 30-60-90 triangle. We are told that one of the angles is 30°, and another of the angles is marked so as to indicate that it is 90°. Since all of the angles in a triangle must add up to 180°, the remaining angle must equal 60°. Also note that the hypotenuse is 22. Thus, the side opposite the 30° angle is 11. However, this is not the side that we want. The side opposite the 60° angle must be $11\sqrt{3}$. **The correct answer is (B).**

In the 45-45-90 triangle, the figure gives us the following result. If we are given the length of the side opposite the 45° angle, we can get the length of the side opposite the 90° angle by multiplying the 45° length by $\sqrt{2}$. Similarly, if we are given the length of the hypotenuse, we can get the length of the two 45° sides by dividing by $\sqrt{2}$.

For example, if the length of the side opposite the 45° angle is 16, the length of the side opposite the 90° angle is $16\sqrt{2}$. If, instead, the length of the side opposite the 90° angle is $19\sqrt{2}$, then the sides opposite the 45° angles are both 19.

The following problem below illustrates how, sometimes, you might need to use both the 30-60-90 and the 45-45-90 property in the same problem.

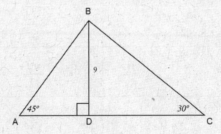

2. In the figure above, what is the length of side $\overline{AC}$?
    (A) 9
    (B) $9\sqrt{3}$
    (C) 18
    (D) $8\sqrt{3}$
    (E) $9 + 9\sqrt{3}$

This figure consists of two triangles that share a common side. Let's first look at the triangle to the right. Here, we can see that the side opposite the 30° angle is of length 9. So the side opposite the 60° angle has length $9\sqrt{3}$. As for the other triangle, it is a 45-45-90 triangle, with one of the 45° sides equal to 9. In this case, the side opposite the other 45° angle is also 9. The length we are asked to find is the sum of these two lengths, that is, $9 + 9\sqrt{3}$. Be careful. We *cannot* simplify this by adding the 9's to get $18\sqrt{3}$. **The correct answer is (E).**

Trigonometry and the GRE and GMAT

This section reviews some basic facts from Trigonometry as it applies to right triangles.

Consider the given right triangle.

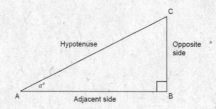

Relative to $\angle A$, which measures $a°$, side $\overline{AB}$ is called the *adjacent* side; side $\overline{BC}$ is called the *opposite* side, and side $\overline{AC}$ is called the *hypotenuse*. The *trigonometric ratios* "sine," "cosine." and "tangent" of $\angle A$ are defined as follows:

Sine of $a° = \sin a° = \dfrac{\text{Opposite}}{\text{Hypotenuse}}$

Cosine of $a° = \cos a° = \dfrac{\text{Adjacent}}{\text{Hypotenuse}}$

Tangent of $a° = \tan a° = \dfrac{\text{Opposite}}{\text{Adjacent}}$

In general you would need a "table of trigonometric values" or a scientific calculator to determine the values of these ratios for various angles. The values for angles of 30°, 45°, and 60° are summarized in the table below.

TRIGONOMETRIC RATIOS FOR 30°, 45°, AND 60°			
Angle $a°$	Sine $a°$	Cosine $a°$	Tangent $a°$
30°	$\dfrac{1}{2}$	$\dfrac{\sqrt{3}}{2}$	$\dfrac{\sqrt{3}}{3}$
45°	$\dfrac{\sqrt{2}}{2}$	$\dfrac{\sqrt{2}}{2}$	1
60°	$\dfrac{\sqrt{3}}{2}$	$\dfrac{1}{2}$	$\sqrt{3}$

Let's restate and reconsider a problem we've already solved. However, this time, we'll use these ratios to find the answer.

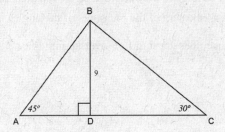

1. In the figure above, what is the length of side $\overline{AC}$?
   (A) 9
   (B) $9\sqrt{3}$
   (C) 18
   (D) $18\sqrt{3}$
   (E) $9 + 9\sqrt{3}$

This figure consists of two triangles that share a common side. Let's first look at the triangle to the right. Here, we can see that the side opposite the 30° angle is of length 9, and we wish to know the length of the side adjacent to the 30° angle. We can find this by using the tangent of the 30° angle, as shown:

$$\tan 30° = \frac{\sqrt{3}}{3} = \frac{\text{Opposite}}{\text{Adjacent}} = \frac{9}{CD}$$

$$\frac{\sqrt{3}}{3} = \frac{9}{CD}$$
$$27 = \sqrt{3} \times CD$$
$$\frac{27}{\sqrt{3}} = CD$$

NOTE: On the GRE and GMAT, answer choices typically do not include radicals in a denominator. Instead, the expression will be rewritten as follows.

$$\frac{27}{\sqrt{3}} \times \frac{\sqrt{3}}{\sqrt{3}} = \frac{27\sqrt{3}}{3} = 9\sqrt{3}$$

This process is called "rationalizing the denominator."

As for the other triangle, it is a 45-45-90 triangle, with one of the 45° sides equal to 9. Using a trigonometric equation yields:

$$\tan 45° = 1 = \frac{\text{Opposite}}{\text{Adjacent}} = \frac{9}{AD}$$

$1 = \dfrac{9}{AD}$, so $AD = 9$

As before, add up the two determined lengths to obtain $9 + 9\sqrt{3}$. **The correct answer is (E).**

Properties of Quadrilaterals

This section summarizes some of the key properties of four-sided figures, called *quadrilaterals*. Note that we have already seen one of the more important properties—the sum of the measures of the angles in any quadrilateral is 360°.

A quadrilateral is a geometric figure whose sides are four non-overlapping line segments. For example, consider the figure shown below.

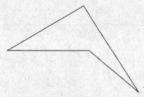

Just as there are a variety of special triangles (e.g., right, isosceles, equilateral), there are also a variety of special quadrilaterals.

A quadrilateral having only one pair of opposite sides that are parallel to each other is called a *trapezoid*. As the figure below shows, the two parallel sides are called the trapezoid's *bases*, and the other two sides are called its *legs*.

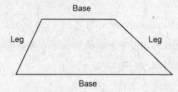

If both pairs of opposite sides are parallel, we obtain a figure called a *parallelogram*.

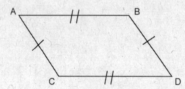

In this parallelogram, $\overline{AB} \parallel \overline{CD}$ and $\overline{AC} \parallel \overline{BD}$. There are some other special properties of parallelograms that you should know for the GRE and GMAT. Specifically:

- The parallel sides are congruent, that is, they have the same length. In the figure above, $AB = CD$, and $AC = BD$.

- The opposite angles are congruent, that is, they have the same measures. In the figure above, $\angle A \cong \angle D$ and $\angle B \cong \angle C$.

This second property is particularly important, because it tells you that, if you know the measure of one of the angles of a parallelogram, you can find the measures of the other three. In the figure above, for example, if the measure of $\angle A = 60°$, then the measure of $\angle D$ is also 60°. Recall that there are 360° in a quadrilateral. Since we have already accounted for 60° + 60° = 120°, there are 360° − 120° = 240° left. This 240° must be split up evenly between the other two angles, so each of them must be 120°.

The figure below illustrates what is known as a *rhombus*, i.e., a parallelogram in which all four sides have the same length.

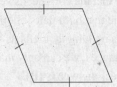

Note that, while in a parallelogram only the pairs of opposite sides may be congruent, in a rhombus all four sides are congruent. In addition, in a rhombus, pairs of opposite angles are congruent. Note also that every rhombus is also a parallelogram, but not every parallelogram is also a rhombus.

The two remaining quadrilaterals are likely very familiar to you. A parallelogram with four equal angles is called a *rectangle*. Because all four angles are equal, they all must measure 90°, since $4 \times 90° = 360°$. Also note that if you draw a diagonal from one vertex to the vertex opposite, you form two right triangles. This means that you can use the Pythagorean theorem to find the length of the diagonal of a rectangle. Finally, note that the two diagonals of a rectangle are the same length.

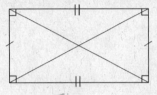

A *square* is a parallelogram with four equal sides and four right angles. A square has all of the properties of both the rhombus and the rectangle.

The problems below will help you familiarize yourself with the properties of quadrilaterals.

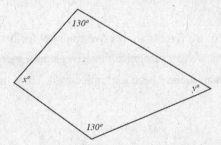

1. Based on the figure above, which of the following must be true?

   I. $x = y$

   II. $x + y = 100$

   III. $x = 50$

   (A) I only
   (B) II only
   (C) III only
   (D) I and III only
   (E) I, II, and III

A common mistake is to assume that, since the two 130° angles are congruent, the other two angles must be congruent as well. This would mean that $x = y = 50$, and indicate that the correct answer would be choice (E). However, as we saw above, there is only one circumstance under which it is true that both pairs of opposite angles are congruent and that is if the quadrilateral is a parallelogram. In this problem, there is nothing that tells us that the quadrilateral is a parallelogram, so there is no reason that x must equal y. Under these circumstances, we can only make one conclusion: $x + y = 100$, which is necessary to make all of the angles add up to 360°. **The correct answer is (B).**

2. In the rectangle above, the length of the diagonal is 20. What is the length of side $\overline{AD}$?

   (A) 8
   (B) 12
   (C) 16
   (D) 20
   (E) 24

Perhaps the most efficient strategy for solving this problem is to first draw the diagonal $\overline{AC}$ and label its length as 20. **The correct answer is (C).**

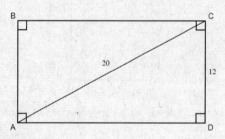

Notice that we have cut the rectangle into two right triangles. We can now focus on the triangle formed by the corners C, D, and A. Using the Pythagorean theorem, we can recognize this triangle as a member of the 3-4-5 family of Pythagorean triples. In this case, one leg and the hypotenuse have been multiplied by 4. Thus, the other leg must be $4 \times 4 = 16$.

Properties of Circles

The *circle* is another basic shape that occurs in GRE and GMAT geometry questions. Recall that a circle is defined as consisting of the set of points that are the same distance from a fixed point, called the "center."

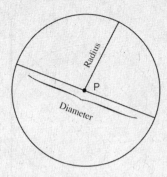

Often, the circle is identified by naming the point at the center. Thus, for example, the circle above might be called circle *P*.

As the above figure shows, the distance from the center of the circle to any point on the circle is called the *radius* of the circle. Any line segment, drawn from one point on the circle, through the center of the circle, to another point on the circle is called a *diameter*. From the picture, you can visualize the most fundamental fact about a circle—the length of the radius is half of the diameter. Using standard notation, we write $2r = d$, where r = the radius and d = the diameter.

Any line segment that has both of its endpoints on the circle is called a *chord*. Unlike the radius and the diameter, chords are not required to pass through the center point. Thus, chords can have different lengths, with the longest possible chord being a diameter. In fact, you can think of a diameter as a chord that goes through the center of a circle. In the figure below, there are three chords drawn, $\overline{AB}$, $\overline{CD}$, and $\overline{EF}$. Note that $\overline{CD}$ is also a diameter.

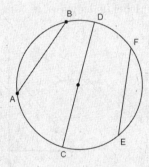

A line that is outside of a circle and only touches the circle in one point is called a *tangent* line. Perhaps the most important thing to know about tangent lines on the GRE and GMAT is the fact that the radius of a circle drawn to the point of intersection of the circle and a tangent line is perpendicular to the tangent line.

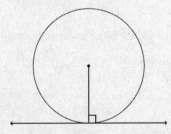

Knowing this property allows you to take advantage of the Pythagorean theorem in a "circle" problem.

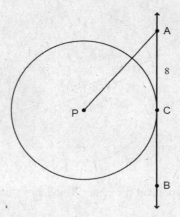

1. Point *P* is at the center of the circle with radius 6 shown in the figure above. If line $\overleftrightarrow{AB}$ is tangent to the circle at point *C*, what is the length of line segment $\overline{AP}$?

   (A) 6

   (B) 8

   (C) 10

   (D) 12

   (E) It cannot be determined.

Begin by drawing radius $\overline{PC}$ in the figure and label its length as 6. Note that $\angle PCA$ must have a measure of 90°. **The correct answer is (C).**

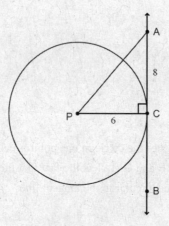

Thus, triangle *APC* is a right triangle, and, based on the fact that the legs are of lengths 6 and 8, the hypotenuse must be 10. Therefore, the length of line segment $\overline{AP}$ must be 10.

EXERCISES: PROPERTIES OF GEOMETRIC FIGURES

Directions: Select the answer choice that best answers the question.

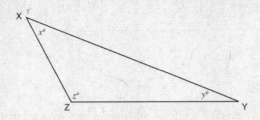

1. In the figure above, $z > x + y$. Which of the following *must* be true?

    (A) $XY > XZ + YZ$

    (B) $XZ > XY + YZ$

    (C) $(XY)^2 > (XZ)^2 + (YZ)^2$

    (D) $(XY)^2 = (XZ)^2 + (YZ)^2$

    (E) $(XY)^2 < (XZ)^2 + (YZ)^2$

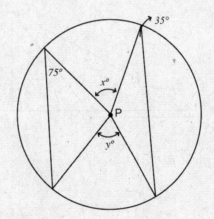

2. The center of the circle above is at point P. What is the value of $x + y$?

    (A) $40°$

    (B) $110°$

    (C) $140°$

    (D) $220°$

    (E) $250°$

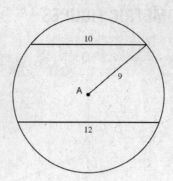

3. The circle above has center *A*. What is the length of the longest line segment that can be drawn from one point on the circle to another point on the circle?

   (A) 10
   (B) 12
   (C) 14
   (D) 16
   (E) 18

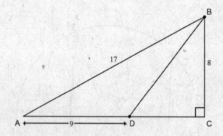

4. In the figure above, what is the length of $\overline{BD}$?

   (A) 6
   (B) 8
   (C) 10
   (D) 15
   (E) 17

ANSWER KEY AND EXPLANATIONS

| 1. C | 2. D | 3. E | 4. C |

1. **The correct answer is (C).** This problem requires a good understanding of the Pythagorean theorem. To begin this problem, consider what it means to say that $z > x + y$. Since the three angles added up must total 180°, the only way the measure of one of the angles can possibly be more than the sum of the measures of the other two angles is if the largest angle is more than half of the total of 180°. In other words, it must be more than 90°. Thus, we know that the angle labeled z is more than 90°.

   Note that neither choice (A) nor choice (B) can be correct, since in any triangle the lengths of two sides added together must be greater than the length of the third side.

2. **The correct answer is (D).** The first step in solving this problem is to fill in the missing angle measurements for both of the triangles in the picture. The key is to notice that both triangles are isosceles, since two sides of both triangles are radii of the circle. Remember that all radii of the same circle are the same length. In the triangle with the 75° angle, then, the measure of the other angle that touches the circle must also be 75°, and the measure of the angle that touches the center must be $180° - 75° - 75° = 30°$. As for the other triangle, it must have two 35° angles, and the third angle therefore, must be $180° - 70° = 110°$. The next thing to remember is that a full circle must contain 360°. Looking at the figure, we can see that $x° + y° + 30° + 110° = 360°$. Therefore, $x° + y° + 140° = 360°$, which means that $x° + y° = 220°$.

3. **The correct answer is (E).** Only one of the line segments shown in the figure is relevant to the problem, and that is the line segment that goes from the center of the circle to the circle itself. This segment is a radius of the circle, and its length is 9. If a radius of the circle is 9, then the diameter must be 18. The diameter is the longest line segment that can be drawn from one point on the circle to another.

4. **The correct answer is (C).** In order to find the solution, the Pythagorean theorem must be used twice. Consider triangle ABC. It is a right triangle with hypotenuse of 17 and one side of 8. This means that the missing side, $\overline{AC}$, must be of length 15. Since $\overline{AD}$ has length of 9, the length of $\overline{DC}$ must be $15 - 9 = 6$.

   Now, consider triangle BCD. It is a right triangle with legs of 6 and 8. This means that the hypotenuse $\overline{BD}$ must have length 10.

PERIMETER, AREA, AND VOLUME

Another major category of GRE and GMAT geometry problems relates to finding the perimeter, the area, or the volume of various geometric figures.

The *perimeter* of a figure is the length of its boundary. The *area* of a figure is the amount of surface contained within its boundary. And, finally, the *volume* of a three-dimensional geometric figure is the amount of space contained within its surfaces.

Sometimes, the answer choices on multiple-choice GRE and GMAT questions may refer to the area of a figure when the problem asks for the perimeter. To be certain that you can answer such questions correctly, it is very important to make certain that you understand the differences between the concepts of perimeter, area, and volume.

For example, suppose that you had a summer landscaping job. If you needed to put a fence up around a garden, you would need to know the perimeter of the garden. If you wanted to buy fertilizer to spread over the garden, you would need to know the area of the garden. Finally, if you wanted to buy water clarifier for the garden's pond, you would need to know the volume of the pond, that is, the amount of water that it holds.

Perimeter Formulas

In order to find the perimeter of any figure whose sides are straight line segments, all you need to do is add together the lengths of all of the sides. For example, consider the six-sided figure below.

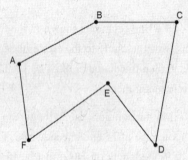

The perimeter of this figure is $AB + BC + CD + DE + EF + FA$.

A few geometric figures have special perimeter formulas.

Recall that in a rectangle, the pairs of opposite sides are of the same length. Typically, the letter L (for "length") is used to symbolize the length of one pair of sides and the letter W (for "width") is used to stand for the other pair of sides. Then, if we let P stand for the perimeter, the formula for the perimeter of a rectangle can be expressed as $P = L + L + W + W$. This formula can also be rewritten as $P = 2L + 2W$, or as $P = 2(L + W)$.

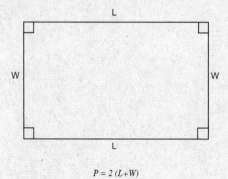

$P = 2 (L+W)$

A square is a rectangle that has all four sides of the same length. Thus, if we let s (for "side") represent the length of the side of the square, the perimeter of a square can be expressed by the formula $P = s + s + s + s$, or, more simply, $P = 4s$.

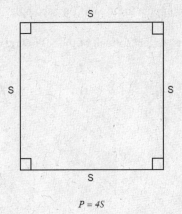

$P = 4S$

Let's look at some sample questions dealing with perimeter.

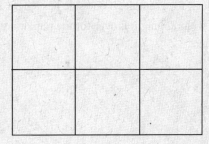

1. The figure above is a rectangle that has been partitioned into six congruent squares. If the perimeter of one of the squares is 12, what is the perimeter of the entire rectangle?

    (A) 30
    (B) 51
    (C) 54
    (D) 60
    (E) 72

In order to solve this problem, we can use the fact that the perimeter of each of the squares is 12. This means that the length of a side of each square is $12 \div 4 = 3$. Note also that the length of the rectangle is equal to the combined length of three square sides. Thus, the length of the rectangle is $3 \times 3 = 9$. Similarly, the width of the rectangle is equal to the combined length of two square sides, or $3 \times 2 = 6$. Therefore, the perimeter of the rectangle must be $P = 2(9) + 2(6) = 18 + 12 = 30$. **The correct answer is (A).**

One very common error is to assume that, since the perimeter of each of the six squares is 12, the perimeter of the rectangle would be $6 \times 12 = 72$. But the problem asks us to find the distance around the rectangle, not the perimeters of six little squares. Also, be careful not to accidentally compute the area of the rectangle.

2. The perimeter of a rectangular garden is 40 feet. Which of the following could be the length of one of its sides?
   I. 10 feet
   II. 15 feet
   III. 20 feet

   (A) I only
   (B) II only
   (C) III only
   (D) I and II only
   (E) I, II, and III

Remember that the opposite sides of a rectangle are the same length. This means that no side can possibly be greater than or equal to half of the perimeter. In this problem, for example, if one side has length 20, then so does its opposite side. But this means we already have a perimeter of 40, with nothing left over for the remaining two side lengths. **The correct answer is (D).**

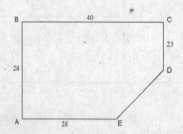

3. What is the perimeter of figure *ABCDE* above?
   (A) 119
   (B) 124
   (C) 131
   (D) 132
   (E) 136

The figure has five sides, and, to find the perimeter we simply need to add together the lengths of the five sides. The difficulty is that we are given the lengths of only four of the sides. We need to find the length of side $\overline{DE}$.

NOTE: When solving geometry problems, it is sometimes helpful to add some line segments to the figures that you are given. Consider the figure with the additional segments drawn in as shown below:

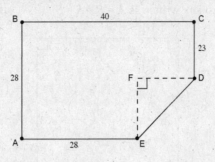

Note that, by adding these extra line segments, we have created the right triangle *DEF*. The unlabeled line segment $\overline{DE}$ is the hypotenuse of this right triangle.

If we can we find the lengths *EF* and *DF*, then we can use the Pythagorean theorem to find the length of the hypotenuse. Notice that, at the top of the figure, we have a horizontal length of 40. At the bottom, the horizontal length is only 28. The difference between these two lengths is 40 − 28 = 12, so this must be the length of the segment $\overline{DF}$. In the same way, the length of $\overline{AB}$ is 28, and the length of segment $\overline{CD}$ is 23. The difference, 28 − 23 = 5, will be the length of segment $\overline{EF}$.

This means that the legs of the right triangle are 5 and 12. So, not only is this a Pythagorean theorem problem, but it uses a common Pythagorean triple, namely 5–12–13. Thus, *DE* = 13, which means that the perimeter is 119 + 13 = 132. **The correct answer is (D).**

Area Formulas

As stated earlier, the area of a figure is the amount of surface contained within its boundary. Area is measured in square units, such as square yards, square feet, or square centimeters.

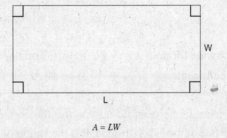

$$A = LW$$

To find the area of a rectangle, we simply multiply the length by the width. For example, if a rectangle measures 7 inches by 2 inches, its area would be 7 inches × 2 inches = 14 square inches.

NOTE: Since a square is really just a special type of rectangle, you can find the area of a square by using the same formula that we used for the area of a rectangle. Namely, since all four sides of the square have the same length, the formula for the area of the square is usually written as $A = S \times S = S^2$.

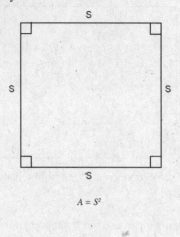

$$A = S^2$$

Let's consider how to find the area of a triangle:

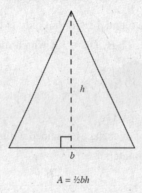

$$A = \frac{1}{2}bh$$

The area of a triangle can be expressed by the formula $A = \dfrac{1}{2}\,bh$. In this formula, b stands for the length of the base of the triangle, and h stands for the height of the triangle.

NOTE: When finding the area of a triangle, be careful that you use the correct value for the height. Typically, the height is *not* the same as the length of one of the sides. Instead, it is the length of the line segment drawn from a vertex of the triangle, perpendicularly down to the base, or the line containing the base.

The figure below shows some triangles and indicates their bases and heights.

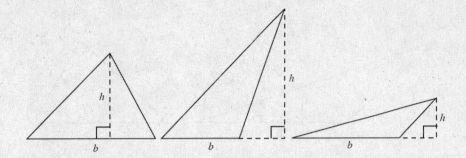

If you need to find the area of a *right* triangle, use one of the legs as the base. In this case only, the other leg *will* be the height since this leg is the same as the line segment drawn from the vertex perpendicularly to the base.

As an example, the area of the *right* triangle below, where b equals 20 and h equals 12, is $A = \dfrac{1}{2}(20)(12) = 120$.

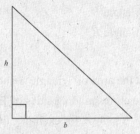

There is one other area formula that you should be familiar with. The formula for the area of a parallelogram is $A = bh$. Once again, b represents the length of the base. And, just as with the triangle, h is not the length of one of the sides, but the height of the parallelogram, that is, the length of the line segment drawn from the top of the parallelogram perpendicularly down to the base.

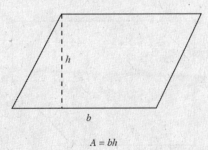

$A = bh$

Let's take a look at some typical GRE and GMAT area problems.

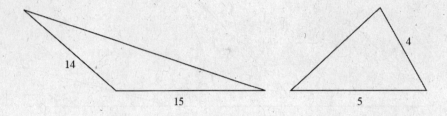

Note: Figures not drawn to scale

1. Which of the following statements about the areas of Triangle *A,* above left, and Triangle *B,* above right, must be true?

    (A) The area of Triangle *A* = the area of Triangle *B*

    (B) The area of Triangle *A* > the area of Triangle *B*

    (C) The area of Triangle *A* < the area of Triangle *B*

    (D) The area of Triangle *A* ≥ the area of Triangle *B*

    (E) It cannot be determined.

Be careful. We might be tempted to assume that the area of Triangle *A* should be bigger than that of Triangle *B*. After all, two of the sides of Triangle *A* are longer than the corresponding sides of Triangle *B*. The problem is that we know nothing about the length of the third side of each triangle. Suppose, for example, that the third side of Triangle *A* is very short, e.g., suppose the length equals 1. This means that Triangle *A* is not going to enclose very much area. On the other hand, perhaps the length of the third side of Triangle *B* is large, e.g., suppose the length equals 6. Then, this triangle would have more "room on the inside" than the other triangle. So, the area of Triangle *A* could actually be very tiny, and the area of Triangle *B* could then be bigger. Thus, there really is no way to tell which area is bigger, without any knowledge of the lengths of the third sides. **The correct answer is (E).**

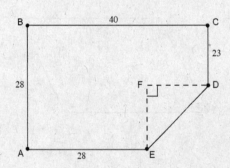

2. What is the area of the figure above?

    (A) 1,120

    (B) 1,103

    (C) 1,090

    (D) 920

    (E) 784

In the previous section, we were asked to determine the perimeter of this figure. An efficient way to find the area is to add some line segments to the figure. As the drawing below indicates, it is helpful to view the figure as if it were a rectangle with its corner torn off.

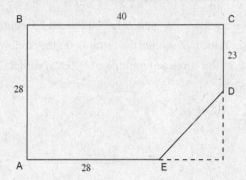

In order to find the area of the figure, all we really need to do is find the area of the entire rectangle, and then subtract the area of the torn-off corner, which is a right triangle.

The area of the entire rectangle, had the corner not been cut off, would be $40 \times 28 = 1,120$. We can now find the area of the right triangle if we use one of the legs as the base and the other leg as the height. Thus, since the area of a triangle is $\frac{1}{2} bh$, we have that the area is $\frac{1}{2} (12)(5) = 30$. Therefore, the area of the original figure is $1,120 - 30 = 1,090$. **The correct answer is (C).**

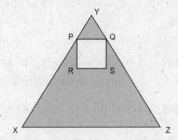

3. In the figure above, the area of triangle XYZ is 21. If the area of the grey region is 12, what is the length of the diagonal of square $PQRS$?

    (A) 3

    (B) $3\sqrt{2}$

    (C) 6

    (D) $6\sqrt{2}$

    (E) 9

Sometimes, area problems are designed to test several geometry facts all at once. The first concept that is needed for this problem is the idea that we can find the area of the square by subtracting the area of the white region from the area of the triangle. The area of the square must be $21 - 12 = 9$. From this fact, we can determine that each side of the square must be 3, since $3^2 = 9$. Note that if you draw in the diagonal from P to S, you can see that triangle PSR is a 45-45-90 triangle. Now, at this point, you could use the Pythagorean theorem to find the length of the diagonal. You can also use the property that states that the hypotenuse of a 45-45-90 triangle is equal to the length of the side times $\sqrt{2}$ to see that the diagonal must be $3\sqrt{2}$. **The correct answer is (B).**

The Circumference and the Area of a Circle

The formulas for the area and the circumference of a circle both involve the Greek letter π, pronounced "pi." This symbol stands for the value of the ratio of the circumference to the diameter of a circle. The value of π is approximately 3.14.

When dealing with a circle, instead of using the word "perimeter," the word "circumference" is used. If the letter C is used to stand for circumference, and r represents the radius, then the formula for the circumference of a circle is given by $C = 2\pi r$. This formula tells you to take the radius of the circle and multiply it by 2π to compute the circumference.

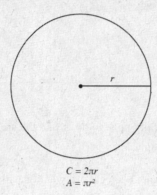

$C = 2\pi r$
$A = \pi r^2$

> **NOTE:** When you are working on a multiple-choice question that involves the circumference of a circle, take a quick look at the multiple-choice answers before you begin. Frequently, the circumference of a circle can be left in terms of π. In some problems, however, it is necessary to approximate the value of π using 3.14. Once you look at the choices, you will know how to express your answer.

The formula for the area of the circle once again involves the number π. The area of a circle is given by the formula $A = \pi r^2$. This means that, in order to find the area of a circle, you need to square the radius and multiply the result by the number π.

Let's look at some typical GRE and GMAT problems that involve the area or the perimeter of a circle.

1. The wheel of a truck has a radius of 3 feet. In driving across a parking lot, the wheel makes 20 complete rotations. What is the distance that the center of the wheel has traveled?
   (A) 30π
   (B) 36π
   (C) 60π
   (D) 120π
   (E) 180π

Note that every time the wheel rotates, the center of the wheel travels a distance that is equal to the circumference of the wheel. In making 20 rotations, thus, the center of the wheel travels a distance equal to 20 circumferences.

Note also that each answer choice contains π, so we must express our answer in terms of π. The formula for the circumference of a circle is $C = 2\pi r$, where r is the radius of the circle. With a radius of 3, the circumference would be $2\pi(3) = 6\pi$. In making 20 rotations, then, the distance traveled by the center of the wheel would be $20 \times 6\pi = 120\pi$. **The correct answer is (D).**

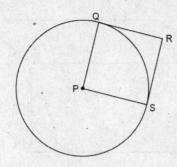

2. In the figure above, if the length of arc QS is 4π, what is the area of square $PQRS$?

   (A) 8

   (B) 16

   (C) 32

   (D) 64

   (E) 128

This problem combines a variety of geometric concepts. To begin, recall that an arc is a portion of the circumference of a circle, so arc QS is the portion of the circle that runs from point Q to point S. Note that this arc represents $\frac{1}{4}$ of the distance around the circle. Why $\frac{1}{4}$? We know $\angle QPS$ is a right angle since the problem statement tells us that $PQRS$ is a square. Now, if $\frac{1}{4}$ of the distance around the circle is 4π, the entire distance around the circle must be $4 \times 4\pi = 16\pi$.

In order to find the area of the square, we need to know the length of its side. Note that the length of a side of the square is the same as the length of the radius of the circle. We can find the radius of the circle since we know the circumference is 16π. Namely, since the circumference of a circle is given by the formula $C = 2\pi r$, we have $C = 16\pi = 2\pi r$. Solving for r by dividing both sides by 2π, yields $r = 8$. Therefore, the area of the square must be $8^2 = 64$. **The correct answer is (D).**

Volume Formulas

The volume of a three-dimensional figure is the amount of space contained within its surface. Volume is measured in cubic units, e.g., cubic centimeters, or cubic inches, or cubic feet.

> **NOTE:** Sometimes, they are based on formulas that are given within the problems themselves.

There are two volume formulas that you should definitely know. The first is the formula for the volume of a *rectangular solid*. A rectangular solid is a six-sided figure, each of whose sides is a rectangle. A shoebox is an example of a rectangular solid. The six sides of a rectangular solid can be thought of as the top, bottom, left, right, front, and back. Note that the top and bottom of a rectangular solid are congruent to each other. Similarly, the left and right sides are congruent to each other, and the front and back are also congruent to each other.

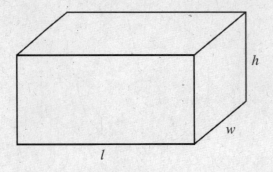

$$V = lwh$$

To find the volume of a rectangular solid, you simply multiply the length times the width times the height.

A *cube* is a rectangular solid with all sides the same length. The formula for the volume of a cube is the same as the formula for the volume of a rectangular solid. However, since in a cube all of the sides are the same length, the volume of a cube is often given by $V = lwh = e \times e \times e = e^3$, where e represents the length of the edge of the cube.

The other volume formula applies to the *right circular cylinder*. Perhaps the most familiar example of this type of solid is a tin can.

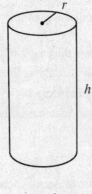

$$V = \pi r^2 h$$

A useful way to think about this formula is to notice that the volume of a cylinder is simply the area of the base (which is a circle) times the height. That is, $V = (\text{Area of Base})(\text{Height}) = \pi r^2 \times h$.

Occasionally, problems will appear on the GRE and GMAT that involve other figures, such as a *cone* or a *sphere,* but when these figures are used, you will be given the formula within the problem itself.

Let's conclude this section by looking at some typical GRE and GMAT volume questions.

1. The edges of a cube are 12 inches in length. If the cube is $\frac{3}{4}$ full of water, what is the volume of the water in the cube?
   (A) 216 cu. in.
   (B) 324 cu. in.
   (C) 729 cu. in.
   (D) 1,296 cu. in.
   (E) 1,728 cu. in.

An effective strategy for solving this problem is to first determine the volume of the cube. Note that the cube's volume is 12 inches × 12 inches × 12 inches = 1,728 cubic inches. Note also that the amount of water required so that the cube is $\frac{3}{4}$ full must be equal to $\frac{3}{4}$ of the volume of the cube: $\frac{3}{4}$ × 1,728 cubic inches = 1,296 cubic inches. **The correct answer is (D).**

BE CAREFUL: Make certain not to find $\frac{3}{4}$ of the length of *each* side initially. If you do this, you will compute a volume of 9 inches × 9 inches × 9 inches = 729 cubic inches, and select choice (C). If you picture the cube $\frac{3}{4}$ full of water, you can see that the dimensions of the water in the cube would actually be 12 inches *(length)* × 12 inches *(width)* × 9 inches *(height)* = 1,296 cubic inches.

2. A cube has a volume of 343 cubic inches. What is the surface area of the cube?
   (A) 49 sq. in.
   (B) 98 sq. in.
   (C) 147 sq. in.
   (D) 294 sq. in.
   (E) 588 sq. in.

Note that the surface area of a figure is the sum of the areas of all of its surfaces. In a cube, all of the surfaces are squares, so if we can find the area of *one* of the squares, we can multiply it by 6 to find the surface area. Since the volume of the cube is 343 cubic inches, we can construct the equation $343 = e^3$, where e = the length of the edge of the cube. Taking the cube root of both sides of this equation yields $\sqrt[3]{343} = \sqrt[3]{e^3}$, which means that $7 = e$. Thus, each square that helps form the cube has the area given by $A = e^2 = 7^2 = 49$. Six such squares taken together have a total area of 6 × 49 = 294 sq. in. Thus, the surface area is 294 square inches. **The correct answer is (D).**

EXERCISES: PERIMETER, AREA, AND VOLUME

Directions: Select the answer choice that best answers the question.

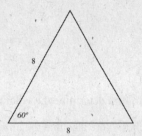

1. What is the perimeter of the triangle shown above?

   (A) 20

   (B) 22

   (C) 24

   (D) 26

   (E) 28

2. How many rectangular boxes with dimensions of 2 cm × 3 cm × 4 cm would fit inside a rectangular box with dimensions 12 cm × 12 cm × 12 cm?

   (A) 18

   (B) 24

   (C) 36

   (D) 72

   (E) 144

3. A cube has a volume of 64. What is the length of the diagonal of one of its square faces?

   (A) 4

   (B) $4\sqrt{2}$

   (C) $4\sqrt{3}$

   (D) 8

   (E) $8\sqrt{2}$

4. What is the volume of a cube whose surface area is $600x^2$?

   (A) $10x^2$

   (B) $10x^3$

   (C) $60x^2$

   (D) $100a^3$

   (E) $1,000x^3$

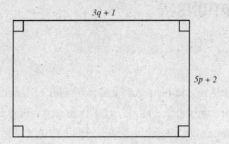

5. What is the perimeter of the figure above?

(A) $3q + 5p + 3$

(B) $15pq + 6q + 5p + 2$

(C) $6q + 10p + 6$

(D) $15pq + 2$

(E) $8pq + 3$

ANSWER KEY AND EXPLANATIONS

1. C	2. D	3. B	4. E	5. C

1. **The correct answer is (C).** The triangle in the figure has two sides of length 8, so it is isosceles. Thus, the two non-labeled angles must be equal. Since the labeled angle is 60°, the remaining angles must add up to 180° − 60° = 120°. Since these two angles are the same size, they must each equal 120° ÷ 2 = 60°. This means that all three angles in the figure must be 60°. Therefore, the triangle is equilateral. In this case, all of the sides must be of length 8, and the perimeter is 8 + 8 + 8 = 24.

2. **The correct answer is (D).** The volume of each of the small boxes is 2 cm × 3 cm × 4 cm = 24 cu. cm. The volume of the big box is 12 cm × 12 cm × 12 cm = 1,728 cu. cm. Now, all we need to do is determine how many times 24 goes into 1,728. Since 1,728 ÷ 24 = 72, we can fit 72 of the smaller boxes inside the larger box.

3. **The correct answer is (B).** Note that if the volume of the cube is 64, then each edge is of length 4, since 4 × 4 × 4 = 64. In other words, each face of the cube is a 4 × 4 square. The problem asks us to find the diagonal of one of these 4 × 4 squares. At this point, you could use the Pythagorean theorem, or simply use the property of 45-45-90 triangles. In either case, you will find that the diagonal is $4\sqrt{2}$.

4. **The correct answer is (E).** Since a cube has 6 surfaces, the area of each surface of this cube must be $600x^2 \div 6 = 100x^2$. Since each surface is a square, the dimensions of each surface must be $10x$ by $10x$. Finally, if an edge of the cube has $10x$, the volume must be $(10x)^3 = 1,000x^3$.

5. **The correct answer is (C).** Since the perimeter of a rectangle is the distance around the boundary, the perimeter must be $(3q + 1) + (3q + 1) + (5p + 2) + (5p + 2) = 6q + 10p + 6$.

COORDINATE GEOMETRY

The GRE and GMAT also include questions that test your knowledge of some basic concepts from coordinate geometry associated with the *rectangular coordinate system*. In particular, you will need to be able to solve problems that deal with *finding the slopes of parallel and perpendicular lines.*

Rectangular Coordinate System

You may recall that *coordinate axes* allow us to construct a reference system designed to give a name to any point in a plane. To use this system, you begin by drawing two number lines, perpendicular to each other, which intersect at the number 0 on each number line. This point of intersection is known as the *origin*.

The horizontal line is called the *x*-axis and is numbered with positive numbers increasing to the right and with negative numbers decreasing to the left. In the same way, the vertical line is called the *y*-axis and is numbered with positive numbers going up and negative numbers going down.

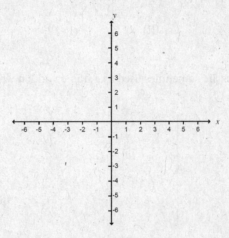

To describe a point on this grid, we begin by identifying the number that represents how far horizontally the point is from the origin. After this, we identify the number that represents how far vertically the point is from the origin. For example, the point (5,2) represents a point that is a horizontal distance of 5 from the origin and a vertical distance of 2 from the origin. The values 5 and 2 are called the *coordinates* of the point. The number that indicates horizontal distance, 5 in this case, is called the *x*-coordinate, and the number that indicates the vertical distance is called the *y*-coordinate. This point, along with a number of others, is illustrated in the following graphic.

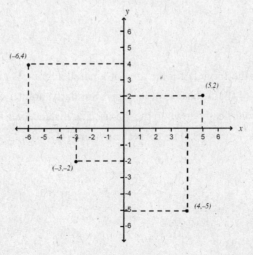

Note that the two number lines partition the plane into four regions, called *quadrants*. The quadrant in the top right is called the first quadrant. Similarly, the quadrant in the top left is called the second quadrant, the quadrant in the lower left is called the third quadrant, and the quadrant in the lower right is called the fourth quadrant. As the figure below shows, for any point in the first quadrant, the coordinates are both positive. In the second quadrant, the *x*-coordinate is negative, but the *y*-coordinate is positive. In the third quadrant, both coordinates are negative, and in the fourth quadrant, the *x*-coordinate is positive and the *y*-coordinate is negative.

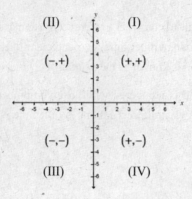

On the GRE and GMAT, coordinate axes are sometimes used as a framework on which to ask perimeter and area problems.

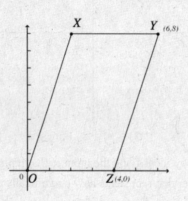

1. In the figure above, what is the area of parallelogram *OXYZ*?

   (A) 16
   (B) 24
   (C) 32
   (D) 64
   (E) It cannot be determined.

Recall from the previous section that the formula for the area of a parallelogram is given by $A = bh$. Since the base of the given quadrilateral runs from (0,0) to (4,0), the base is of length 7. Similarly, point *Y* is located at a distance of 6 units from the *y*-axis and at a distance of 8 units vertically down to the *x*-axis. The distance vertically down to the *x*-axis is the height of the parallelogram. Thus, the area is $4 \times 8 = 32$. **The correct answer is (C).**

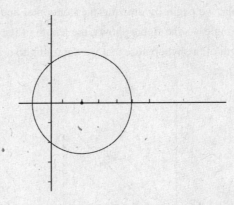

2. The circle above has its center at (2,0). What is the circumference of the circle?

    (A) 3π

    (B) 6π

    (C) 9π

    (D) 12π

    (E) 18π

Recall the formula for the circumference of a circle: $C = 2\pi r$. Note that the given circle goes through the point (5,0). Since the distance from (2,0) to (5,0) is 3, this means that the radius of the circle is 3. Thus, the circumference is $2 \times \pi \times 3 = 6\pi$. **The correct answer is (B).**

The Distance and Midpoint Formulas

In the previous problem, we needed to find the distance between the points (2,0) and (5,0). This wasn't too difficult to do since the two points lie on a horizontal line. However, in some problems, you will need to find the distance between two points that do not lie on a horizontal line, e.g., (2,2) and (5,6).

Note that the *Distance Formula* enables you to determine the distance between any pair of points, as long as you know their x- and y-coordinates. In order to develop the formula, let's see how to find the distance between two generic points, (x_1, y_1) and (x_2, y_2).

The figure below depicts these two points using the rectangular coordinate system. Also shown is the line segment that connects the two points. The length of this line segment is the distance between the two points.

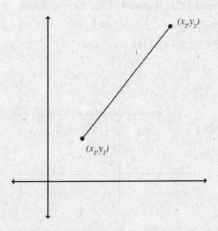

In order to develop the distance formula, we begin by drawing the horizontal and vertical lines shown in the following picture. We have thus formed a right triangle. As the figure shows, the length of the horizontal leg is $x_2 - x_1$, and the length of the vertical leg is $y_2 - y_1$. It is the length of the hypotenuse that we are trying to determine.

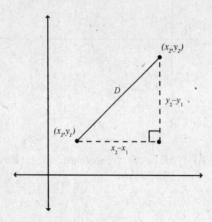

The length of the hypotenuse can be found by applying the Pythagorean theorem to the triangle, as shown below.

$$\left(\text{length of hypotenuse}\right)^2 = \left(\text{length of horizontal leg}\right)^2 + \left(\text{length of vertical leg}\right)^2$$

Using the side lengths as labeled in the figure yields the equation $D^2 = \left(x_2 - x_1\right)^2 + \left(y_2 - y_1\right)^2$.

By taking the square root of both sides of the equation, we solve the equation for D and develop the distance formula: $D = \sqrt{\left(x_2 - x_1\right)^2 + \left(y_2 - y_1\right)^2}$.

For example, to find the distance between the points (2,2) and (5,6), we apply the distance formula. Note that $(x_2 - x_1) = 5 - 2 = 3$. Similarly, $(y_2 - y_1) = 6 - 2 = 4$. Thus, $D = \sqrt{3^2 + 4^2} = \sqrt{9 + 16} = \sqrt{25} = 5$.

Therefore, the distance between the two points is 5.

> **NOTE:** The Distance Formula is really just another way of writing the Pythagorean theorem. Thus, if you forget the Distance Formula, you can reconstruct it by making a quick sketch of the line segment connecting the two points, as in the figure above. After you do this, form a right triangle, determine the lengths of the legs, and use the Pythagorean theorem to find the desired distance.

The *midpoint* of a line segment is the point in the middle of the line segment. For example, as the following figure shows, the midpoint of the line segment with endpoints (−2,3) and (4,3) is (1,3). Once again, this was relatively easy to determine since the line segment that connects (−2,3) and (4,3) is horizontal.

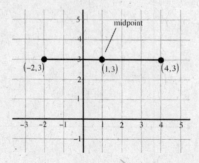

However, some questions will require you to find the midpoint for two arbitrary points, e.g., the points (6,4) and (2,8).

In general, we can determine the midpoint for a given pair of points as long as we know the coordinates of both points.

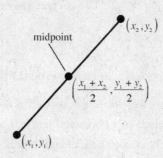

Specifically, if we let (x_1,y_1) and (x_2,y_2) represent two generic points, the coordinates of the midpoint are given by the *Midpoint Formula:*

$$\text{Coordinates of Midpoint} = \left(\frac{x_1 + x_2}{2}, \frac{y_1 + y_2}{2} \right)$$

For example, the midpoint for the points (6,4) and (2,8) is given by $\left(\frac{x_1 + x_2}{2}, \frac{y_1 + y_2}{2} \right) = \left(\frac{6+2}{2}, \frac{4+8}{2} \right) = \left(\frac{8}{2}, \frac{12}{2} \right) = (4,6)$.

> **NOTE:** You do not have to memorize the Midpoint Formula. All you need to do is remember that the *x*-coordinate of the midpoint is the *average* of the *x*-coordinates of the two endpoints, and the *y*-coordinate of the midpoint is the *average* of the *y*-coordinates of the two endpoints.

Let's take a look at a couple of sample GRE and GMAT questions using these formulas.

1. What is the area of the circle whose center is at the point (3,2), and which passes through the point (8,14)?
    (A) 13π
    (B) 26π
    (C) 54π
    (D) 169π
    (E) 676π

Note that the distance between the two points (3,2) and (8,14) tells us the radius of the circle. Once we know the radius, we can use the formula $A = \pi r^2$ to find the area. To begin, then, note that $(x_2 - x_1) = 8 - 3 = 5$. Similarly, $(y_2 - y_1) = 14 - 2 = 12$. Using the distance formula yields $D = \sqrt{5^2 + 12^2} = \sqrt{25 + 144} = \sqrt{169} = 13$. Therefore, the radius of the circle is 13. The area, then, is $A = \pi r^2 = \pi (13)^2 = 169\pi$. **The correct answer is (D).**

2. The circle with center at point P has a diameter whose endpoints are at (–5,7) and (9,–3). What are the coordinates of point P?
    (A) (2,2)
    (B) (7,2)
    (C) (6,5)
    (D) (7,5)
    (E) (2,5)

Note that the midpoint of a diameter will be the center of the circle. Thus, the coordinates of point P are given by $\left(\dfrac{x_1+x_2}{2}, \dfrac{y_1+y_2}{2}\right) = \left(\dfrac{-5+9}{2}, \dfrac{7+(-3)}{2}\right) = \left(\dfrac{4}{2}, \dfrac{4}{2}\right) = (2,2)$. **The correct answer is (A).**

Parallel and Perpendicular Lines

In order to be able to work with *parallel* and *perpendicular* lines, you must first understand the concept of the *slope* of a line.

The slope of a line is a number that tells us *how steep the line is*, as well as *whether the line is rising or falling as we travel along the line from left to right*. Note that the slope of a horizontal line is 0, since a horizontal line is flat. A vertical line is said to have an infinite slope since it is infinitely steep. The standard terminology used when describing the slope of a vertical line is *no slope*, or *undefined slope*. A line that rises as we travel along the line from the left to the right is said to have a positive slope, and a line that falls as we travel along the line from the left to the right is said to have a negative slope.

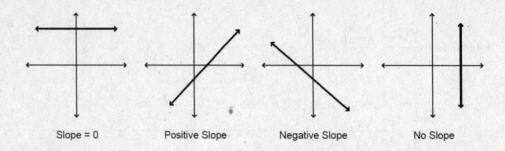

Slope = 0   Positive Slope   Negative Slope   No Slope

Traditionally, the slope of a line is represented by the letter m. If you know the coordinates of any two points on a line, you can compute the slope of the line by using the *Slope Formula*. In general, if we let the points (x_1,y_1) and (x_2,y_2) represent two generic points on a line, the slope of the line is given by the following formula:

$$\text{Slope} = m = \frac{y_2 - y_1}{x_2 - x_1}$$

For example, the slope of the line that contains the points $(5,6)$ and $(4,2)$ is $m = \dfrac{y_2 - y_1}{x_2 - x_1} = \dfrac{6-2}{5-4} = \dfrac{4}{1} = 4$. This means that as x increases by 1 unit, y increases by 4 units. Equivalently, we could have calculated the slope by $m = \dfrac{y_2 - y_1}{x_2 - x_1} = \dfrac{2-6}{4-5} = \dfrac{-4}{-1} = 4$.

In this case, as x decreases by 1 unit, y decreases by 4 units. Either way we calculate the slope, we get the same number.

Therefore, to draw the line with a slope of 4, we can start with either of the given points. If we start with $(5,6)$ and then either increase x by 1 and increase y by 4—equivalently, from $(5,6)$ move 1 unit right and 4 units up—or decrease x by 1 and decrease y by 4—equivalently, from $(5,6)$ move 1 unit left and 4 units down.

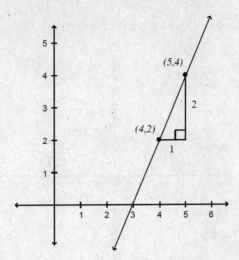

In Chapter 3: Algebra Review, we introduced the idea of *first-degree equations in two unknowns*. These equations, which contain two variables raised to the first but no higher power, have an infinite number of solutions. For example, some of the solutions of the equation $y = 2x + 5$ are (0,5), (1,7), (2,9), (–1,3), (–2,1), and so on. On the coordinate axes below, we have graphed some of the solutions to the equation $y = x + 5$.

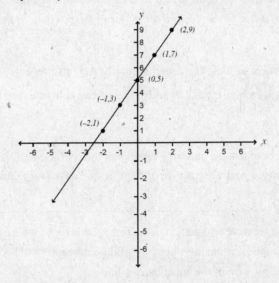

Note that all of the points lie on the same line. This is not an accident. Whenever a group of points that solve a first-degree equation in two unknowns are graphed using coordinate axes, the points will always lie on the same line. For this reason, this type of equation is called a *linear equation*.

There are many different ways that a linear equation can be written. For example, the equation can be written with both variables on the left and a constant on the right, e.g., $2x - y = -5$. The equation could be "solved for x," e.g., $x = \frac{1}{2}y - \frac{5}{2}$. Or it could be "solved for y," e.g., $y = 2x + 5$. Of all of the different ways to write a linear equation, the "solved for y" format is perhaps the most useful.

For example, consider the equation $y = 2x + 5$, whose graph is shown next:

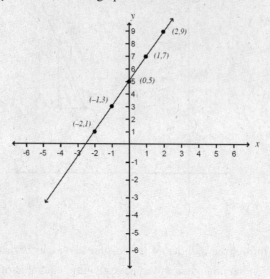

Note that the graph crosses the y-axis at the point (0,5). The value $y = 5$ is called the *y-intercept* of the given equation. Note also that the number 5 appears as the constant being added to the x-term in the equation $y = 2x + 5$. This is not an accident. *Whenever you write the equation of a line in the "solved for y" form, the constant at the end will always be the y-intercept of the line.*

Furthermore, provided we know where to look, the equation $y = 2x + 5$ also reveals the slope of the line that graphs the equation. Using two points on the given line, e.g., (2,9) and (1,7), we can compute the slope as:

$$m = \frac{y_2 - y_1}{x_2 - x_1} = \frac{9 - 7}{2 - 1} = \frac{2}{1} = 2$$

Therefore, the slope of the line is 2. Note that the number 2 appears as the coefficient of the x-term in the equation $y = 2x + 5$. This is also not an accident. *Whenever you write the equation of a line in the "solved for y" form, the coefficient of the x will always be the slope of the line.*

> **IMPORTANT FACT:** Any time we have an equation in the form $y = mx + b$, where a and b represent real numbers, it means that we are working with the line having slope $= m$, and y-intercept $= b$. This form of the equation of a line is, therefore, called the *slope–intercept form* of the equation of a line.

For example, suppose you need to find the slope of the equation of the line given by the formula $6x + 2y = 13$. A very quick way to do this is to rewrite the equation in the slope–intercept form:

$$6x + 2y = 13$$
$$2y = -6x + 13$$
$$y = -3x + \frac{13}{2}$$

Therefore, the slope of the line is –3. This means that for every horizontal unit moved to the right, the line goes *down* three units. Note also that the y-intercept of this line is $\frac{13}{2}$.

There are two especially important facts that you need to know about slopes and lines for the GRE and GMAT.

Important Fact #1: *Parallel* lines have the *same steepness and direction,* which means that they never intersect one another. The way to express this mathematically is to say that *parallel lines have the same slope.* For example, we can conclude that the lines expressed by the equations $y = 5x - 7$ and $y = 5x + 2$ are parallel since they both have a slope of 5. On the other hand, the lines $y = 5x - 7$ and $y = 2x + 5$ are not parallel, since they have different slopes.

Important Fact #2: *Perpendicular* lines intersect to form a right angle. *The slopes of any two non-horizontal perpendicular lines are negative reciprocals of each other.* For example, if a line has a slope of $\frac{2}{3}$, the slope of any perpendicular line must be $-\frac{3}{2}$. A line perpendicular to the line with slope -2 must have slope $\frac{1}{2}$.

SPECIAL NOTE: The only time the "negative reciprocal rule" doesn't apply to perpendicular lines is when one of the lines is horizontal. This is because a horizontal line has slope = 0. Thus, if we try to compute the negative reciprocal we get $-\frac{1}{0}$, which is not a valid computation due to the zero in the denominator. In fact, the only lines that can be perpendicular to a given horizontal line must be vertical.

NOTE: The most important facts about lines that you should remember for the GRE and GMAT can be quickly summarized. First, if you write the equation of a line in the form $y = mx + b$, the value of m represents the slope of the line, and the value of b represents the y-intercept of the line. Also, know that parallel lines have the same slopes, and non-horizontal perpendicular lines have slopes that are negative reciprocals of each other. Armed with these facts, you should be able to answer any slope questions that you are asked.

Here are some examples of slope questions that might appear on the GRE and GMAT.

1. Which of the following equations represents a line with a slope of -4?
   I. $y + 4x = 16$
   II. $3y - 12x = 11$
   III. $3y + 12x = 13$

   (A) I only
   (B) I and II only
   (C) II and III only
   (D) I and III only
   (E) I, II, and III

The quickest way to determine the slope of a line is to write the equation in slope–intercept form. For the first equation, the slope–intercept form is $y = -4x + 16$, so the slope is -4. For the second equation, we need to do a small amount of manipulation to express it in slope–intercept form.

$$3y - 12x = 11$$
$$3y = 12x + 11$$
$$y = 4x + \frac{11}{3}$$

Thus, the slope of this line is 4. Going through the same procedure with the third line reveals that its slope is -4. Therefore, the first and third lines have slopes of -4. **The correct answer is (D).**

2. Which of the following equations represents a line that is perpendicular to the line $y = -\frac{1}{5}x + 17$?

    (A) $y = \frac{1}{5}x - 11$

    (B) $y = -5x + 11$

    (C) $y = -\frac{1}{5}x - 17$

    (D) $y = 5x + 12$

    (E) $y = \frac{1}{5}x - \frac{1}{17}$

The line that is given in the problem statement, $y = -\frac{1}{5}x + 17$, has a slope of $-\frac{1}{5}$. The slope of the line perpendicular to this will have a slope equal to the "negative reciprocal" of $-\frac{1}{5}$. Since the negative reciprocal of $-\frac{1}{5}$ is 5, the line we are looking for must have a slope of 5. The equation $y = 5x + 12$ is the only answer choice that has this property. **The correct answer is (D).**

3. Which of the following equations is parallel to the line $y = -\frac{1}{3}x + 4$ and passes through the point (3,1)?

    (A) $y = -\frac{1}{3}x + 2$

    (B) $y = 3x - 8$

    (C) $y = -\frac{1}{3}x$

    (D) $y = 3x$

    (E) $y = 3x + 8$

To begin, the line parallel to the given line must have a slope of $-\frac{1}{3}$. Of the five answer choices, only choices (A) and (C) have $-\frac{1}{3}$ as their slope. In order to determine the correct answer, we need to find out which of these two lines passes through the point (3,1). We can determine this by substituting $x = 3$ into both equations and see which equation yields $y = 1$. For choice (C) we have $y = \left(-\frac{1}{3}\right)(3) = -1$. Thus, choice (C) is not correct. **The correct answer is (A).**

GEOMETRY PRACTICE TEST

GRE Multiple-Choice Questions—Select One Answer Choice

Directions: For Questions 1–4, select a single answer choice.

1. Which of the following triples *does not* represent the lengths of the sides of a right triangle?

   (A) 9 feet, 12 feet, 15 feet

   (B) 5 inches, 12 inches, 13 inches

   (C) 8 meters, 15 meters, 17 meters

   (D) 7 yards, 9 yards, 11 yards

   (E) 12 miles, 16 miles, 20 miles

2. A rectangle has a length of 8 yards and a width of 6 yards. What is the ratio of the perimeter of the rectangle to the length of its diagonal?

   (A) 7 to 5

   (B) 7 to $5\sqrt{2}$

   (C) 14 to 5

   (D) 14 to $5\sqrt{2}$

   (E) 4 to 3

3. A circle has a circumference of 12π feet. If the diameter of the circle is doubled, what is the area of the new circle formed?

   (A) 12π square feet

   (B) 24π square feet

   (C) 48p square feet

   (D) 72p square feet

   (E) 144p square feet

4. A circular cylinder has a volume of 176π cubic inches and a height of 11 inches. What is the diameter of its circular base?

   (A) 4 inches

   (B) 6 inches

   (C) 8 inches

   (D) 11 inches

   (E) 16 inches

GRE Multiple-Choice Questions—Select One or More Answer Choices

Directions: For Questions 5–7, select one or more answer choices according to the specific question directions. If the question does not specify how many answer choices to select, select all that apply.

- The correct answer may be just one of the choices or may be as many as all of the choices, depending on the question.
- No credit is given unless you select all of the correct choices and no others.
- If the question specifies how many answer choices to select, select exactly that number of choices.

5. Which of the following lines is perpendicular to the line $y = \dfrac{3}{4}x + 1$?

   (A) $y = \dfrac{4}{3}x + 2$

   (B) $y = -\dfrac{4}{3}x + 2$

   (C) $4x + 3y = 9$

   (D) $1 - 9y = 12x$

6. In the figure above, which are pairs of vertical angles?

   (A) 1 and 3

   (B) 2 and 4

   (C) $1 + 2$ and $3 + 4$

   (D) $1 + 2 + 3$ and 4

   (E) None

7. Which of the following points lie on the circle with center point (2,–1) and radius 3?

   (A) (2,–5)

   (B) (5,–1)

   (C) (2,3)

   (D) (2,1)

   (E) (–1,–1)

   (F) (0, 1)

GRE Quantitative Comparison Questions

Directions: For Questions 8–10, compare Quantity A and Quantity B, using additional information centered above the two quantities if such information is given, and select one of the following four answer choices:

(A) Quantity A is greater.

(B) Quantity B is greater.

(C) The two quantities are equal.

(D) The relationship cannot be determined from the information given.

A symbol that appears more than once in a question has the same meaning throughout the question.

Given the circle shown below.

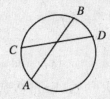

8.   Quantity A   Quantity B

The circle's circumference   The length of chord AB plus twice the length of chord BC

(A) Quantity A is greater.

(B) Quantity B is greater.

(C) The two quantities are equal.

(D) The relationship cannot be determined from the information given.

In the given figure, $x + y = 122$.

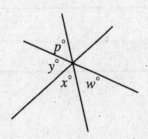

9.   Quantity A   Quantity B

$y + w$ $x + p$

(A) Quantity A is greater.

(B) Quantity B is greater.

(C) The two quantities are equal.

(D) The relationship cannot be determined from the information given.

10.

Quantity A	Quantity B
Number of cubic meters in a cylindrical tank with height 4 meters and radius 3 meters	Number of square meters in a circular garden with diameter 12 meters

(A) Quantity A is greater.

(B) Quantity B is greater.

(C) The two quantities are equal.

(D) The relationship cannot be determined from the information given.

GRE Numeric Entry Questions

Directions: For Questions 11–16, enter your answer as an integer or as a decimal if there is a single answer box OR as a fraction if there are two separate boxes—one for the numerator and one for the denominator.

To enter an integer or a decimal, write the number in the answer box provided. On the computer-based test you can either type the number in the answer box using the keyboard or use the Transfer Display button on the calculator. Also, note the following directions for the computer-based test:

- You can click on the answer box and then type the number. You can use the backspace key to erase a number.
- Type a hyphen for a negative sign. Type a hyphen again, and it will disappear. For a decimal point, type a period.
- The Transfer Display button on the calculator will move the calculator display to the answer box.
- Equivalent forms of the correct answer, such as 2.5 and 2.50, are all correct.
- Enter the exact answer unless the question asks you to round your answer.

11. Two cars leave town at the same time. If one of the cars travels due south at 30 miles per hour, and the other travels due west at 40 miles per hour, how many miles apart will they be after 4 hours?

☐ miles

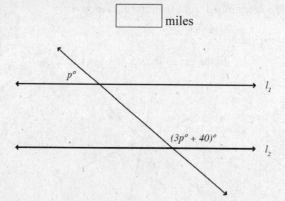

12. In the figure above, lines l_1 and l_2 are parallel. What is the value of p?

☐

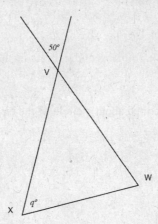

13. In the figure above, if $XV = WV$, what is the value of q?

14. What is the slope of the line that is parallel to the line represented by the equation $4y - 20x = 17$?

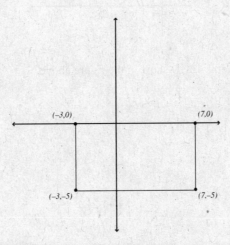

15. What is the area of the quadrilateral shown in the figure above?

16. A right triangle is drawn on a coordinate axis. The coordinates of the endpoints of the hypotenuse are $(-7,3)$ and $(9,-2)$. What is the x-coordinate of the midpoint of the hypotenuse?

GMAT Problem-Solving Questions

Directions: For Questions 17–19, solve the problems and indicate the best of the answer choices given.

17. A square with side length 8 is circumscribed about a circle. If the circumference of the circle is $k\pi$, what is the value of k^2?

    (A) 8

    (B) 16

    (C) 64

    (D) $16\pi^2$

    (E) $64\pi^2$

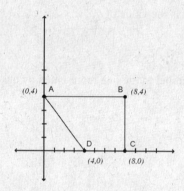

18. What is the perimeter of quadrilateral *ABCD* show in the figure above?

    (A) $8 + \sqrt{2}$

    (B) 20

    (C) $16 + 4\sqrt{2}$

    (D) 24

    (E) $20\sqrt{2}$

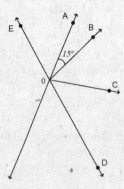

19. In the figure above, if rays $\overrightarrow{OB}$ and $\overrightarrow{OC}$ trisect $\angle AOD$, what is the measure of $\angle AOE$?

    (A) 45°

    (B) 75°

    (C) 135°

    (D) 145°

    (E) 165°

GMAT Data Sufficiency Questions

Directions: Questions 20–22 consist of a question and two statements, labeled (1) and (2), in which certain data is given. You have to decide whether the data given in the statements is sufficient for answering the question. Using the data given in the statements plus your knowledge of mathematics and everyday facts (such as the number of days in July and the meaning of "counterclockwise"), you must indicate whether

(A) Statement (1) ALONE is sufficient, but statement (2) is not sufficient.

(B) Statement (2) ALONE is sufficient, but statement (1) is not sufficient.

(C) BOTH statements TOGETHER are sufficient, but NEITHER statement ALONE is sufficient.

(D) EACH statement ALONE is sufficient.

(E) Statements (1) and (2) TOGETHER are NOT sufficient.

20. What is the area of the square?

    (1) The perimeter of a square is 81 cm.

    (2) The diagonal of a square is $5\sqrt{2}$ in.

    (A) Statement (1) ALONE is sufficient, but statement (2) is not sufficient.
    (B) Statement (2) ALONE is sufficient, but statement (1) is not sufficient.
    (C) BOTH statements TOGETHER are sufficient, but NEITHER statement ALONE is sufficient.
    (D) EACH statement ALONE is sufficient.
    (E) Statements (1) and (2) TOGETHER are NOT sufficient.

21. Triangle ABC is given such that p and q are angles opposite sides $\overline{AC}$ and $\overline{AB}$, respectively. Is triangle ABC isosceles?

    (1) $3AB = BC$
    (2) $p \neq q$

    (A) Statement (1) ALONE is sufficient, but statement (2) is not sufficient.
    (B) Statement (2) ALONE is sufficient, but statement (1) is not sufficient.
    (C) BOTH statements TOGETHER are sufficient, but NEITHER statement ALONE is sufficient.
    (D) EACH statement ALONE is sufficient.
    (E) Statements (1) and (2) TOGETHER are NOT sufficient.

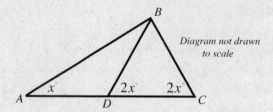

Diagram not drawn
to scale

22. In triangle *ABC* above, what is the length of segment $\overline{BC}$?

(1) Segment $\overline{AD}$ has length 3

(2) $x = 41$

(A) Statement (1) ALONE is sufficient, but statement (2) is not sufficient.

(B) Statement (2) ALONE is sufficient, but statement (1) is not sufficient.

(C) BOTH statements TOGETHER are sufficient, but NEITHER statement ALONE is sufficient.

(D) EACH statement ALONE is sufficient.

(E) Statements (1) and (2) TOGETHER are NOT sufficient.

ANSWER KEY AND EXPLANATIONS

1. D	6. E	11. 200	15. 50	19. C
2. C	7. B, E	12. 35	16. 1	20. D
3. E	8. A	13. 65	17. C	21. E
4. C	9. D	14. 5	18. C	22. A
5. B, C, D	10. C			

1. **The correct answer is (D).** Perhaps the quickest way to solve this problem is to determine which of the answer choices is not a Pythagorean triple. Note that choice (A) is the 9-12-15 triple, which is a part of the 3-4-5 family. Choice (B) is the 5-12-13 triple, and choice (C) is the 8-15-17 triple. Choice (E) is the 12-16-20 triple, which is also in the 3-4-5 family. Therefore, the correct answer must be choice (D).

2. **The correct answer is (C).** This problem is essentially a Pythagorean theorem problem. To begin, the perimeter of the rectangle is 2(8 yards) + 2(6 yards) = 16 yards + 12 yards = 28 yards. Two consecutive sides of the rectangle, along with its diagonal, form a 6-8-10 right triangle, so the diagonal must be 10. Thus, the required ratio is $\frac{28}{10} = \frac{14}{5}$.

3. **The correct answer is (E).** Recall that the formula for the circumference of a circle is $C = 2\pi r$. Thus, if the circumference is 12π, we have $2\pi r = 12\pi$, which means that $r = 6$ and $d = 12$. If the diameter is doubled, it becomes 24, and the new radius is 12. Therefore, the new area is $A = \pi r^2 = \pi(12)^2 = 144\pi$ square feet.

4. **The correct answer is (C).** You need to know the formula for the volume of a cylinder in order to solve this problem: $V = \pi r^2 h$. Be careful. This problem does not ask for the volume, but rather the diameter of the base. We must use the formula to find the radius, and then double the radius to get the diameter.

$$V = \pi r^2 h$$
$$176\pi = 11\pi r^2$$
$$16 = r^2$$
$$\pm 4 = r$$

Since the radius must be a positive number, we have $r = 4$, which means that $d = 8$.

5. **The correct answers are (B), (C), and (D).** The given line is in slope-intercept form, which means its slope is the coefficient of the x term, i.e., $\frac{3}{4}$. Every line that is perpendicular to the given line must have slope $-\frac{4}{3}$. Rewriting each answer choice in slope-intercept form reveals the following. Choice (A) is a line with slope $\frac{4}{3}$. Choice (B) is a line with slope $-\frac{4}{3}$. Choice (C) yields the equation $y = -\frac{4}{3}x + 3$, which is a line with slope $-\frac{4}{3}$. Choice (D) yields the equation $y = -\frac{4}{3}x + \frac{1}{9}$, which is a line with slope $-\frac{4}{3}$.

6. **The correct answer is (E).** Recall that vertical angles are formed when two lines cross each other. But this does not happen in the given figure.

7. **The correct answers are (B) and (E).** Note that every point on the circle with center point (2,−1) and radius 3 must be a distance of 3 units from the center point. Perhaps the quickest way to solve this problem is to make a sketch and plot the given points.

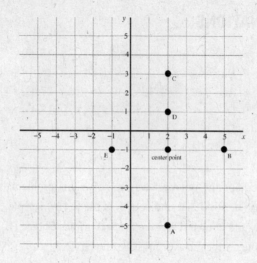

We can now see that (5,–1) and (–1,–1) are the only answer choices that lie a distance of 3 units from the center point (2,–1).

8. **The correct answer is (A).** Note that Quantity A equals πd, where d equals the circle's diameter. If chords AB and CD each were as large as possible, they would each be diameters of the circle. Thus, Quantity B $= 2d + d = 3d$. Since $\pi > 3$, we can conclude that Quantity A is greater.

9. **The correct answer is (D).** Angles w and p are vertical, since they are opposite each other across the intersection of two lines. Vertical angles are always equal in size; thus, $w = p$. Thus, the problem hinges on comparing x and y. The centered information tells us that $x + y = 122$. However, this equation can be true for $x > y$ (e.g., $x = 62$, $y = 60$), for $y > x$ (e.g., $y = 62$, $x = 60$), and for $x = y$ (i.e., $x = y = 61$). Thus, the relationship cannot be determined from the given information.

10. **The correct answer is (C).** This problem tests your ability to use the formulas for the volume of a cylinder and the area of a circle. For Quantity A, we have: Volume $= \pi r^2 h = \pi (3)^2 (4) = 36\pi$ cubic meters. For Quantity B, note that a circle with diameter 12 has radius 6. So we have: Area $= \pi r^2 = \pi (6)^2 = 36\pi$ square meters. Thus, Quantity A equals Quantity B.

11. **The correct answer is 200 miles.** This problem can be solved using the Pythagorean theorem. Note that, in 4 hours, one car will travel 4 hours × 30 miles per hour = 120 miles, and the other will travel 4 hours × 40 miles per hour = 160 miles per hour. So this problem requires you to find the hypotenuse of a right triangle whose legs are 120 and 160.

    Recall that 12-16-20 is a Pythagorean triple. If we multiply all of the sides by 10, we get another triple, 120-160-200. This means the hypotenuse in our problem is 200. Thus, the cars will be 200 miles apart.

12. **The correct answer is 35.** By the properties of parallel lines, the two labeled angles must be supplementary. Therefore, $p + 3p + 40 = 180$. Solving for p yields $4p + 40 = 180$, which means that $4p = 140$. Thus, $p = 35$.

13. **The correct answer is 65.** This problem tests your knowledge of the basic properties of angles. By the properties of vertical angles, we have that the measure of $\angle XVW = 50°$. Then, since $XV = WV$, we have that $\angle VXW$ and $\angle VWX$ are congruent. Since a triangle has angles whose sum is 180°, $\angle VXW$ and $\angle VWX$ must total 130°, making each angle 65°.

14. **The correct answer is 5.** We can find the slope of the line given by the equation $4y + 20x = 17$ by rewriting the equation in slope–intercept form.

$$4y - 20x = 17$$
$$4y = 20x + 17$$
$$y = 5x + \frac{17}{4}$$

The coefficient of x is the slope of the line. Thus, the slope is 5.

15. **The correct answer is 50.** The quadrilateral is a rectangle of length 10 and width 5. Thus, the area is $5 \times 10 = 50$.

16. **The correct answer is 1.** Using the midpoint formula, the x-coordinate of the midpoint can be computed as $\frac{-7+9}{2} = \frac{2}{2} = 1$.

17. **The correct answer is (C).** This problem is more manageable if we draw and label a figure. Note that in order for the square to circumscribe the circle, they must have the same center point, and the circle's diameter must equal the square's side length.

Thus, we can conclude that the radius of the circle is 4 units. Since we are given that the circle has circumference $k\pi$, we can use the formula for the circumference of a circle as follows.

$$C = 2\pi r$$
$$k\pi = 2\pi(4)$$
$$k\pi = 8\pi$$
$$k = 8$$

Thus, $k^2 = 8^2 = 64$.

18. **The correct answer is (C).** Using the coordinates given in the figure, we can find the lengths of three of the sides of the quadrilateral. The "top" runs between (0,4) and (8,4), and so is of length 8. The bottom runs from (4,0) to (8,0), and so is of length 4. The right side runs from (8,4) and (8,0) and so is of length 4. Thus, we only need to find the length represented by AD in order to determine the perimeter.

The easiest way to do this is to note that triangle AOD is an isosceles right triangle, that is to say, a 45-45-90 triangle. The legs, line segments $\overline{OD}$ and $\overline{OA}$, both are of length 4, and so, by the properties of 45-45-90 triangles, the hypotenuse $\overline{AD}$ is of length $4\sqrt{2}$. Note that the hypotenuse could also be found using the Pythagorean theorem, the Distance Formula, or a Trigonometric Equation, but we have found it in the easiest way. The perimeter, then, is $8 + 4 + 4 + 4\sqrt{2} = 16 + 4\sqrt{2}$.

19. **The correct answer is (C).** To trisect something means to cut it into three congruent pieces. Since $\angle AOB$ measures 15°, the other two angles $\angle BOC$ and $\angle COD$ are also 15°, and overall, the measure of $\angle AOD$ would be 45°. Since $\angle AOE$ is supplementary to this angle, its measure must be $180° - 45° = 135°$.

20. **The correct answer is (D).** If statement (1) is true, we know that the square must have side length $\frac{81}{4}$ cm. Thus, we can conclude that the square has area $\left(\frac{81}{4}\right)^2$ square cm. Thus, statement (1) ALONE is sufficient. If statement (2) is true, we know that the square must have side length $\frac{5\sqrt{2}}{\sqrt{2}} = 5$ in. Recall that the diagonal of a square is always the hypotenuse of a 45-45-90 triangle whose legs are 2 sides of the square. So, we know that the length of the hypotenuse equals $\sqrt{2} \times \left(\text{length of a leg}\right)$, which means that the length of the leg $= \frac{\text{hypotenuse length}}{\sqrt{2}}$. Thus, we can conclude that the square has area 5^2 square in. Thus, statement (2) ALONE is sufficient. Therefore, EACH statement ALONE is sufficient.

21. **The correct answer is (E).** Once again, drawing and labeling a figure is very helpful in solving the problem.

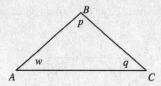

If statement (1) is true, our figure becomes:

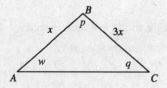

We know that $w = 180 - (p + q)$. Also, since $AB \neq BC$, we know that $q \neq w$. So, the only way the triangle can be isosceles is if $q = p$ or $p = w$. However, the given information is only sufficient to conclude that $p + q < 180$. Thus, statement (1) ALONE is not sufficient. If statement (2) is true, we still don't have enough information to determine whether $w = p$ or $w = q$. Thus, statement (2) ALONE is not sufficient.

Taken together, statements (1) and (2) imply that $AB \neq BC$ and $AB \neq AC$. However, we cannot determine whether or not $AC = BC$. Therefore, statements (1) and (2) TOGETHER are NOT sufficient.

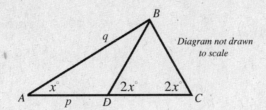

Diagram not drawn to scale

22. **The correct answer is (A).** Note that labeling the figure helps us organize our solution strategy. We know from the figure that triangle DBC is isosceles, with $BD = BC$. We also know that $2x + p = 180$. Similarly, we know that $x + p + q = 180$. Thus, $x + p + q = 2x + p$. Subtracting p from both sides yields $x + q = 2x$, which means that $q = x$. Thus, triangle ABD is isosceles, with $AD = BD$. Therefore, we know that $BC = AD$ even before we examine statements (1) and (2).

If statement (1) is true, we can immediately conclude that $BC = 3$. Thus, statement (1) ALONE is sufficient. If statement (2) is true, we can find the measures of the angles in the figure, but we do not have enough information to determine any of the side lengths without using topics from Trigonometry that are not covered on the GRE and GMAT. Thus, statement (2) ALONE is not sufficient.

CHAPTER 5

Data Interpretation Review

The data interpretation questions on the GRE and GMAT are designed to test your knowledge of the following basic concepts:

- Basic concepts of statistics involving arithmetic mean, median, mode, and weighted average

- Correlation, scatterplots, and line of best fit for a data set

- Data tables

- Circle graphs

- Bar graphs

- Time plots

- Basic counting formulas involving permutations, combinations, and inclusion-exclusion

- Using factorial notation

- Basic probability problems, including geometric probability problems

- Graphs of functions, including domain and range of a function

- Graphs of linear functions, including finding the slope of a line

- Graphs of quadratic functions, including finding extreme values

- Exponential functions and geometric sequences

Each GRE and GMAT test always contains a number of questions that ask you to analyze and interpret numerical information. For example, you might be given a set of data and asked to compute the average value. You might be asked to work with data contained in a table or in a graph. You might be given a situation and asked to compute the probability that a certain outcome happens. In these *data interpretation* problems, you will need to use your knowledge of arithmetic, algebra, and geometry to find the correct answers.

In this chapter, we will examine all of the types of questions that ask you to interpret or examine numerical data. We will begin with some topics from statistics, and then move to tables and graphs. After this, we will look at topics involving probability and functions.

STATISTICS

Average Problems

Typically, the GRE and GMAT will have a variety of problems involving averages. Recall that, in order to compute an average of a list of values, we add up all of the values, and then divide the total by the number of values.

IMPORTANT NOTE: There are actually several different "types" of averages. The most common type of average is technically known as the "arithmetic mean." To avoid any possible confusion on the GRE and GMAT, whenever you are asked to find this type of average, the phrase "arithmetic mean" will appear in parentheses next to it. Thus, if you see a problem that says, "What is the average (arithmetic mean) of 8 and 10," you are just being asked to add 8 and 10 and divide by 2.

In practical terms, the *arithmetic mean* tells us the average size of all the numbers in the list.

Some data interpretation problems on the GRE and GMAT refer to the *median* of a set of values. If a group of numbers is arranged in numerical order, the median is simply the number in the middle. For example, to find the median of 7, 4, 9, 10, and 15, put the numbers in order: 4, 7, 9, 10, and 15. The number in the middle is 9, since there are two numbers to the left of 9 and two numbers to the right of 9.

In practical terms, the *median* tells us the size of the number in the middle of the list.

BE CAREFUL: When finding the median of a set with an even number of values, you need to find the *arithmetic mean of the middle two numbers*. For example, given the values, 5, 6, 8, 12, 14, and 21, the middle two numbers are 8 and 12. Thus, the median is $\frac{8+12}{2} = \frac{20}{2} = 10$.

Other data interpretation problems on the GRE and GMAT refer to the *mode* of a list of values. The mode identifies the number that appears most often in the list. For example, for the list, 1, 2, 3, 3, 6, 7, 8, 8, 8, 8, 12, 13, 13, 13, 16, the mode is 8, since 8 appears four times, which is more than any other number appears.

Here are some sample problems similar to those that appear on the GRE and GMAT.

1. The Nichols School Junior Varsity basketball team scored 64, 48, 76, and 52 points in their final four games of the season. What was the average (arithmetic mean) number of points that they scored in these four games?

    (A) 48
    (B) 58
    (C) 60
    (D) 62
    (E) 80

We add the values in the list, then divide by the number of values in the list. Thus, the arithmetic mean is $\frac{64+48+76+52}{4} = \frac{240}{4} = 60$. **The correct answer is (C).**

2. If the average (arithmetic mean) of 82, 74, and p is 76, what is the value of p?

(A) 71

(B) 72

(C) 73

(D) 74

(E) 75

Here you have a very common variation on the usual average problem. Instead of giving you three numbers and asking you to compute the average, this problem gives you *two* numbers and the average and asks you to find the missing third number. By the definition of average, it follows that $\dfrac{82 + 74 + p}{3} = 76$. Multiplying both sides by 3 yields $156 + p = 228$, which means that $p = 228 - 156 = 72$. **The correct answer is (B).**

3. At a neighborhood grocery store, the three stock workers earn $28,000 a year, the two department managers earn $31,000 a year, and the store manager earns $34,000 a year. What is the average (arithmetic mean) salary of these employees?

(A) $29,000

(B) $30,000

(C) $31,000

(D) $32,000

(E) $33,000

This problem exhibits another common variation of the average problem. This type of problem is called a *weighted average* problem. It is called a weighted average because, while there are only three numbers mentioned in the problem, they are "weighted" differently. Namely, there are *three* salaries of $28,000, *two* salaries of $31,000, and *one* salary of $34,000. The mistake to avoid is to simply compute the average of $28,000, $31,000, and, $34,000. This will give you choice (C), $31,000, which is incorrect. **The correct answer is (B).**

BE CAREFUL: When you are given a weighted average problem, do not simply use one of each of the numbers that you are given. Be sure to take the weights into account.

You need to average six numbers to solve this problem, not three. There are three $28,000's, two $31,000's, and one $34,000 in the problem. So we need to add up the six salaries and divide by 6:

$$\frac{3(28,000) + 2(31,000) + 1(34,000)}{6} = \frac{84,000 + 62,000 + 34,000}{6} = \frac{180,000}{6} = 30,000$$

Thus, the weighted average salary is $30,000.

4. Consider the eight numbers 1, 1, 2, 3, 5, 8, 8, and 8. What is the product of the average (arithmetic mean), the median, and the mode of these numbers?

(A) 108

(B) 128

(C) 144

(D) 160

(E) 180

This problem tests your knowledge of the definitions of arithmetic mean, median, and mode. We find the mean by adding up the numbers and dividing by 8. Thus, the mean is 4.5.

Since we have an even number of numbers, the median is the average (arithmetic mean) of the two numbers in the middle when the numbers are arranged in numerical order. Since the numbers are already in numerical order, the median is the average of 3 and 5, which is 4. The mode is the most frequently occurring number, which is 8. The product of the three is $4.5 \times 4 \times 8 = 144$. **The correct answer is (C).**

5. If 13 is the average (arithmetic mean) of *a, a,* 6, and 22, then *a* =

   (A) 10
   (B) 11
   (C) 12
   (D) 13
   (E) 14

This is a variation of problem 2. In that problem, you were given the average and one number was missing. In this problem, two numbers (which are both the same) are missing. We can construct the equation $\frac{a+a+6+22}{4} = 13$. Solving for *a* yields $a + a + 6 + 22 = 52$, which means that $2a + 28 = 52$. Thus, $a = 12$. **The correct answer is (C).**

The Concept of Correlation

Some of the data interpretation problems that appear on the GRE and GMAT require you to analyze the *correlation between two variables*. Two variables are said to be *correlated* whenever a change in one of the variables causes a predictable change in the other variable. For example, there is a correlation between the number of hours a painter works and the number of walls he is able to paint. In particular, the *more* hours the painter works, the *more* walls he can paint. Similarly, there is likely a correlation between the price that a computer store charges for a printer and the number of printers it sells. In this case, the *more* they charge for a printer, the *fewer* printers they will sell.

As the painting example above illustrates, sometimes when one variable (the number of hours worked) gets larger, the second variable (the number of walls painted) gets larger as well. In such a case, the variables are said to be *positively correlated*. On the other hand, sometimes when one variable (the price of a printer) gets larger, the second variable (the number of printers sold) gets smaller. In this case, the variables are said to be *negatively correlated*. Finally, sometimes two variables simply are not correlated, that is, a change in one variable does not relate to a change in the other in any predictable way. For example, student grade point average is not correlated with student height.

One way of determining whether two variables are correlated or not is to draw what is known as a *scatterplot*. A scatterplot is a graph on which the *x*-axis represents the possible values of one of the variables and the *y*-axis represents the possible values of the other variable. To make a scatterplot, we measure a value of one of the variables and the corresponding value of the other variable, and plot the result as a point on the graph. The scatterplot is the graph obtained by plotting all pairs of corresponding values in the given data set.

NOTE: If the points on the scatterplot appear to lie on a straight line, or are relatively close to lying on a straight line, then it is likely that the variables are correlated. If the slope of the line is positive, then the variables are said to be *positively correlated*. This means that as one of the variables increases, so does the other. If the slope of the line is negative, then the variables are said to be *negatively correlated*. This means that as one of the variables increases, the other decreases.

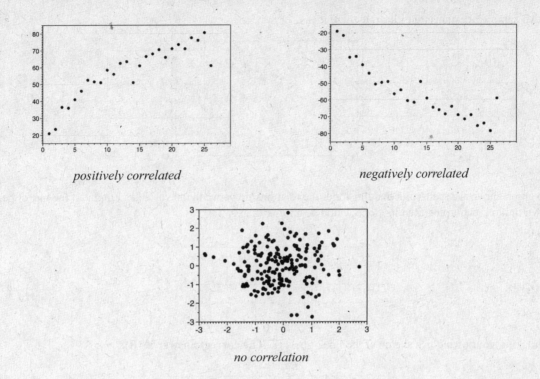

positively correlated   *negatively correlated*

no correlation

When drawing a scatterplot, it is unusual, even for variables that are strongly correlated, for all of the points to lie exactly on the same line. However, if the variables are strongly correlated, it is likely that a line exists that is fairly close to all of the points on the scatterplot. Statisticians refer to the line that comes the closest to all of the points on a scatterplot as the *line of best fit*. Note that you can visualize the line of best fit on a scatterplot without making any specific calculations. The following two graphs below show the line of best fit for two different scatterplots.

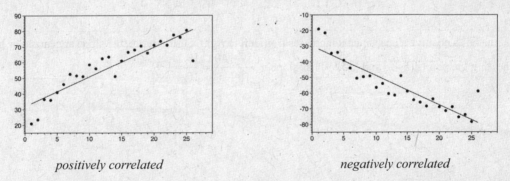

positively correlated   *negatively correlated*

Although you will not be asked to draw a scatterplot on the GRE and GMAT, you might be given a scatterplot and asked whether the variables appear to be correlated or not. Similarly, you might be given a scatterplot and asked a question about the line of best fit, such as the approximate value of its slope.

Here are two sample questions that illustrate these ideas.

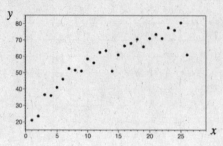

1. The graph above is a scatterplot that illustrates the relationship between the variables x and y. If the line of best fit were drawn on this scatterplot, then its slope would be approximately

   (A) 0

   (B) 1

   (C) 2

   (D) −2

   (E) −1

Begin by making your own quick sketch of the line of best fit. **The correct answer is (B).**

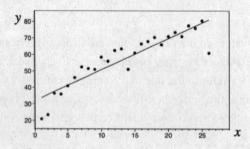

Note that the line has a positive slope, since it increases from left to right. Furthermore, the slope appears to be about 2, since the line connecting the points (5,40) and (15,59) has slope $= \dfrac{59-40}{15-5} = \dfrac{19}{10} = 1.9$.

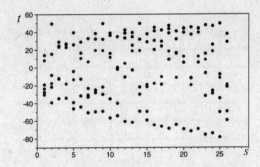

2. Above is a scatterplot depicting the relationship between *s* and *t*. Which of the following best describes the relationship between *s* and *t* depicted in the graph?

(A) There is a strong negative correlation between the two variables in the graph.

(B) There is a strong positive correlation between the two variables in the graph.

(C) The two variables appear to be uncorrelated.

(D) As the value of *s* increases, the value of *t* increases.

(E) As the value of *s* decreases, the value of *t* decreases.

The points appear to be randomly distributed on the graph. In other words, there is no line that comes close to all of the points on the graph. This indicates that the variables are *not* correlated. **The correct answer is (C).**

EXERCISES: STATISTICS

> **Directions:** Select the answer choice that best answers the question.

1. What is the average (arithmetic mean) of $5y + 7$, $3y - 3$, 0, 7, and $2y + 9$?

   (A) $2y + 20$

   (B) $10y + 4$

   (C) $2y + 4$

   (D) $5y + 5$

   (E) $\dfrac{5y + 10}{2}$

2. If A is the average (arithmetic mean) of 8 and q, and a is the average (arithmetic mean) of 10 and p, what is the average of A and a?

   (A) 6

   (B) 18

   (C) $18 + p + q$

   (D) $\dfrac{18 + p + q}{2}$

   (E) $\dfrac{18 + p + q}{4}$

3. If $AB = (x + y)C$, what is the average (arithmetic mean) of x and y in terms of A, B, and C?

   (A) ABC

   (B) $\dfrac{AB}{C}$

   (C) $\dfrac{AB}{2C}$

   (D) $\dfrac{AB}{4C}$

   (E) $\dfrac{2C}{AB}$

4. If the average of $12h$ and $16h$ is 84, then the value of h is

   (A) 5

   (B) 6

   (C) 7

   (D) 8

   (E) 9

5. If $a > 0$ and $b > 0$, then which of the following is true?

   (A) The average (arithmetic mean) of a^3 and b^3 is greater than the average of a^2 and b^2.

   (B) The average (arithmetic mean) of a^3 and b^3 is less than the average of a^2 and b^2.

   (C) The average (arithmetic mean) of a^3 and b^3 is equal to the average of a^2 and b^2.

   (D) The average (arithmetic mean) of a^3 and b^3 is greater than or equal to the average of a^2 and b^2.

   (E) The relationship between the averages (arithmetic means) of a^3 and b^3 and a^2 and b^2 cannot be determined.

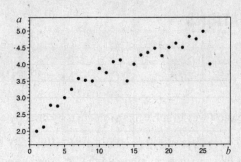

6. The scatterplot above illustrates the relationship between two variables, *a* and *b*. Which of the following best describes the line that best fits the data in the scatterplot?

(A) The slope of the line of best fit is 1.

(B) The slope of the line of best fit is −10.

(C) The slope of the line of best fit is $-\dfrac{1}{10}$.

(D) The slope of the line of best fit is 10.

(E) The slope of the line of best fit is $\dfrac{1}{10}$.

ANSWER KEY AND EXPLANATIONS

1. C	3. C	5. E
2. E	4. B	6. E

1. **The correct answer is (C).** The easiest way to solve this problem is by directly computing the average. Begin by adding together the five quantities: $(5y + 7) + (3y - 3) + 0 + 7 + (2y + 9) = 10y + 20$. Next, divide by 5: $\frac{10y + 20}{5} = 2y + 4$ Be careful. Zero is a number just like any other number. So the list contains a total of five values.

2. **The correct answer is (E).** If A is the average of 8 and q, then $A = \frac{8+q}{2}$. Similarly, if a is the average of 10 and p, then $a = \frac{10+p}{2}$. We are asked to find the average of A and a. So we need to calculate $\frac{A+a}{2}$.

   Using the given information, we have: $A + a = \frac{8+q}{2} + \frac{10+p}{2} = \frac{8+q+10+p}{2} = \frac{18+p+q}{2}$.

   To find $\frac{A+a}{2}$, we need to divide the above expression by 2: $\frac{\frac{18+p+q}{2}}{2} = \frac{18+p+q}{4}$.

3. **The correct answer is (C).** In order to find the average of x and y, we need to compute $\frac{x+y}{2}$. Note that the right-hand side of the given equation, $AB = (x + y)C$, looks almost exactly like what you want, except for the presence of the C. Recall that one of the themes of Chapter 3: Algebra Review was the importance of being able to quickly manipulate equations. This skill is very useful here. Dividing both sides by C yields:

   $\frac{AB}{C} = x + y$. Dividing both sides by 2 gives us $\frac{AB}{2C} = \frac{x+y}{2}$.

4. **The correct answer is (B).** We can use the average formula, and solve it for h. Namely, we have $\frac{12h + 16h}{2} = 84$, which tells us that $12h + 16h = 168$. Therefore, $h = 6$.

5. **The correct answer is (E).** This question asks us to determine whether $a^2 + b^2$ is larger or smaller than $a^3 + b^3$. Be careful. It is tempting to conclude that $a^3 + b^3$ is larger. However, remember that squaring or cubing a number only makes it bigger when that number is greater than 1. We are told that the numbers are positive, but we don't know how big they are. For example, a and b could both be 1. In this case $a^2 + b^2 = 2$, and $a^3 + b^3 = 2$, so the averages would be the same. If, on the other hand, a and b are fractions between 0 and 1, $a^2 + b^2$ would be bigger than $a^3 + b^3$, and the average of $a^2 + b^2$ would be bigger. This ambiguity means that the correct answer is choice (E).

6. **The correct answer is (E).** The figure below shows the scatterplot with the approximate line of best fit sketched in.

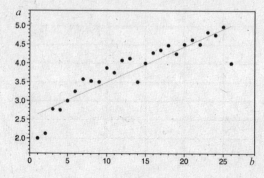

Note that the line has a positive slope, since it increases from left to right. Furthermore, the slope appears to be about $\frac{1}{10}$, since the line connecting the points (5,3) and (15,4) has slope $= \frac{4-3}{15-5} = \frac{1}{10}$.

INTERPRETING DATA IN TABLES AND GRAPHS

Some questions on the GRE and GMAT will ask you to solve mathematical problems using data contained in tables or in graphs. All such problems are based on problem-solving techniques that we have already reviewed in this book. The key to answering table and graph questions is to be able to correctly read and interpret the table or the graph so that you know what is being asked and can recognize the data needed to answer the question. Remember, since the GRE and GMAT is a multiple-choice and grid-in test, you will never be asked to create a table or sketch a graph.

Working with Tables

When you see a problem involving a table, carefully examine the table. Read the title and any subtitles. Make certain that you understand the meaning of the data contained in the table. Then, after you read the question, carefully select the row and the column that contains the data that you need to answer the question. Be particularly careful with problems that contain more than one table.

Questions 1–3 are based on the following two tables.

NUMBER OF HOURS WORKED							
Employee	Mon	Tues	Wed	Thurs	Fri	Sat	Sun
Janet	3	2	0	4	0	3	3
Hazel	2	2	5	3	4	4	4

HOURLY SALARY		
Employee	Weekdays	Weekends
Janet	$5.50	$7.00
Hazel	$6.25	$7.75

1. Janet and Hazel have part-time summer jobs at the Boys and Girls Club. The two tables show their hourly salaries and the number of hours worked during a particular week. How much money did Janet earn during the week shown in the table?

    (A) $82.50
    (B) $91.50
    (C) $96.00
    (D) $105.00
    (E) $111.75

The key to solving this problem correctly is being able to interpret what the tables tell you. Note that the first table indicates the number of hours a day that Janet and Hazel worked. The second table gives you their hourly salaries, but also indicates something very important—both Janet and Hazel get paid more when they work on the weekend than when they work on weekdays.

This problem relates to Janet, so we only need to consider her data. Note that Janet earns $5.50 when working on weekdays and $7.00 when working on weekends. The number of weekday hours she works is $3 + 2 + 0 + 4 + 0 = 9$. On the weekend, she worked $3 + 3 = 6$ hours. Her total pay is given by $9 \times \$5.50 + 6 \times \$7.00 = \$49.50 + \$42.00 = \$91.50$. **The correct answer is (B).**

2. How much more money did Hazel earn on Saturday than on Thursday?

   (A) $1.00

   (B) $6.25

   (C) $7.00

   (D) $7.75

   (E) $12.25

On Saturday, Hazel worked 4 hours and, at $7.75 an hour, earned a total of 4 × $7.75 = $31.00. On Thursday, she worked 3 hours and, at $6.25 an hour, earned 3 × $6.25 = $18.75. Thus, she earned $31.00 – $18.75 = $12.25 more on Saturday than on Thursday. **The correct answer is (E).**

3. What is the total amount that Janet and Hazel earned on Monday?

   (A) $27.50

   (B) $29.00

   (C) $32.00

   (D) $33.50

   (E) $36.50

On Monday, Janet worked 3 hours at $5.50, and Hazel worked 2 hours at $6.25. The total amount they earned was 3 × $5.50 + 2 × $6.25 = $16.50 + $12.50 = $29.00. **The correct answer is (B).**

In some GRE and GMAT problems, tables are used as a way of asking percent or ratio questions. The three following problems demonstrate how this is done.

	Votes for Sonia	Votes for Mike
Freshman Class	43	50
Sophomore Class	65	30
Junior Class	72	24
Senior Class	20	80

1. All of the students at Rozelle High School must vote once for either Sonia or Mike for president of the student council. The results of the vote are given in the table above. What percent of the Junior class voted for Sonia?

   (A) 25%

   (B) 30%

   (C) 33.3%

   (D) 66.7%

   (E) 75%

We are told that 72 students in the Junior class voted for Sonia, and 24 voted for Mike. Since each student in the Junior class voted once, there must be 72 + 24 = 96 students in the Junior class. Thus, 72 out of 96 voted for Sonia, which is 72 ÷ 96 = 0.75 = 75% of the Junior class. **The correct answer is (E).**

2. What is the ratio of the total number of votes received by Sonia to the total number of votes received by Mike?

   (A) 25:23

   (B) 23:25

   (C) 4:5

   (D) 5:4

   (E) 25:22

Sonia received 43 + 65 + 72 + 20 = 200 votes in total, and Mike received 50 + 30 + 24 + 80 = 184. Therefore, the ratio of votes received by Sonia to votes received by Mike is $\frac{200}{184} = \frac{100}{92} = \frac{50}{46} = \frac{25}{23}$, i.e., 25:23. **The correct answer is (A).**

3. The number of votes cast by the Freshman class accounted for what percent of the total number of votes cast by the entire high school? Round off the answer to the nearest whole number percent.

   (A) 20%

   (B) 23%

   (C) 24%

   (D) 25%

   (E) 26%

The freshman class cast 43 + 50 = 93 votes. Recall from the previous problem that Sonia received 200 votes and Mike received 184 votes, so that the total number of votes received was 384. Then, 93 ÷ 384 = 0.242 ≈ 24%. **The correct answer is (C).**

Working with Graphs

Interpreting data contained in graphs becomes much easier when you realize that, fundamentally speaking, there are only three basic relationships that a graph can display. The first is a "component breakdown," that is, the breakdown of a *whole* into its individual *parts,* showing their relative sizes as percents. A component breakdown is most frequently displayed by a *circle graph.*

Recall that every percent problem involves three quantities—the whole, the part, and the percent. Further, in each percent problem, you will be given the values for two of the three quantities and will be asked to find the third.

In a circle graph, the entire circle is used to represent the whole. The circle is partitioned into a number of *sectors,* each of which represents a part. You might be given the whole and a part and be asked to find a percent. Or, some percents might be labeled on the graph, and you might be asked to find the part or the whole.

NOTE: Whenever you see a circle graph on a GRE or GMAT question, the problem that you need to solve is almost always a basic percent problem. In particular, you will be given two of the three quantities—*percent, part,* and *whole*—and will be asked to find the third component.

The following problems illustrate the ways in which circle graphs can be used to solve percent problems.

Distribution of Workforce by Occupation

Total Workforce: 60,000

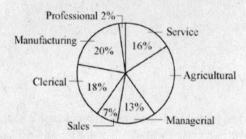

1. How many employees are in the agricultural sector?
   (A) 16,400
   (B) 24,000
   (C) 14,400
   (D) 26,000
   (E) 20,600

Note that the percent associated with every sector is labeled, with the exception of the sector you are being asked about. In order to answer the question, you need to remember that the sector percentages must total 100%. Thus, the agricultural sector percentage is given by $100 - (16 + 2 + 20 + 18 + 7 + 13) = 24$. Be careful to answer the question being asked. You need to compute 24% of the total workforce, i.e., $0.24 \times 60,000 = 14,400$ employees. **The correct answer is (C).**

Consider the following sample problem.

UNITED STATES PRODUCTION OF PHOTOGRAPHIC
EQUIPMENT AND SUPPLIES IN 1979

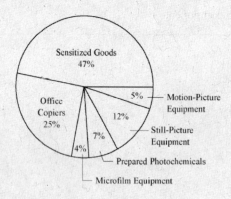

2. Using the given chart, if $3 million was spent on Still-Picture Equipment, how much was spent on all categories combined?
   (A) $30 million
   (B) $45 million
   (C) $20 million
   (D) $35 million
   (E) $25 million

This is a percent problem in which we are given the amount of the part and the percent and asked to determine the whole. Thus, we can use the formula $whole = \dfrac{part}{\%}$. So, we have $whole = \dfrac{part}{\%} = \dfrac{3\text{ million}}{0.12} = 25\text{ million}$. **The correct answer is (E).**

Let's look at one other variation of the circle graph problem.

3. In an employee bonus program, $27,000 is distributed to six different employees as shown in the circle graph above. Which of the employees received the amount nearest to $11,000?

    (A) Peter

    (B) Jane

    (C) Greg

    (D) Marcia

    (E) Robert

This problem begins by giving us the whole and the part. Instead of simply asking you to find the percent, however, the problem asks you to identify the sector in the circle graph that corresponds to the percent. Note that $\dfrac{11,000}{27,000} \approx 0.407 \approx 41\%$. In order to answer the question, all you need to do is find the sector that represents about 41% of the circle. Note that Robert's sector is the second largest and is about $\dfrac{1}{4} = 25\%$ of the circle. The only sector larger is Jane's. So, her sector must be the sector that is 41% of the circle. **The correct answer is (B).**

At the start of this section, we learned that there were only three fundamental relationships that could be depicted in a graph. The first was the component breakdown, typically depicted by the circle graph. The second relationship is what is known as a *time series*. A time series depicts the way in which a particular variable changes over a period of time. Time series relationships are typically illustrated by means of either a bar graph or a line graph. The following three problems illustrate the types of questions that you can be asked based on time series graphs.

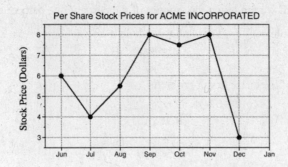

Per Share Stock Prices for ACME INCORPORATED

4. According to the graph above, the increase in stock price was the greatest from

    (A) July to August.

    (B) November to December.

    (C) June to July.

    (D) October to November.

    (E) August to September.

Note that the greatest *change* in net sales occurs between November and December, when price dropped by $8 – $3 = $5. However, the problem does not ask for the greatest *change,* it asks for the greatest *increase.* This happens from August to September, when stock price increased by $8 – $5.50 = $2.50. **The correct answer is (E).**

NOTE: In problems involving the interpretation of graphs, read every word very carefully. In particular, look for words such as *increase, decrease, change, largest,* and *smallest.* These words can alter the meaning of a problem.

Consider this variation of the previous problem.

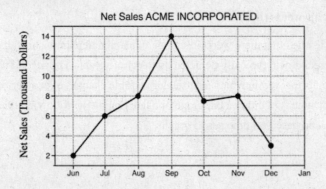

Net Sales ACME INCORPORATED

5. According to the graph above, the percent of increase in net sales was the greatest from

    (A) July to August.

    (B) August to September.

    (C) June to July.

    (D) October to November.

    (E) November to December.

This is another problem that is easy to answer incorrectly if you read it too quickly. We can see that the increase in net sales was the greatest from August to September, when it went up $6 thousand. However, this is not what the problem asks for. It wants to know when the *percent of increase* was the greatest. Note that the percent of increase from August to September is given by percent of increase $= \dfrac{change}{original} = \dfrac{14-8}{8} = \dfrac{6}{8} = 75\%$. However, the percent of increase from June to July is given

by percent of increase $= \dfrac{change}{original} = \dfrac{6-2}{2} = \dfrac{4}{2} = 200\%$. **The correct answer is (C).**

Let's consider another version of the time series problem.

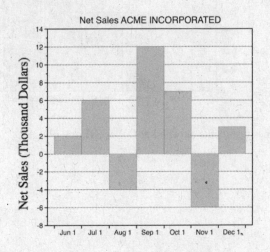

6. According to the graph above, the change in net sales was the greatest from

  (A) Jul 1 to Aug 1.

  (B) Aug 1 to Sep 1.

  (C) Jun 1 to Jul 1.

  (D) Oct 1 to Nov 1.

  (E) Nov 1 to Dec 1.

The graph associated with this problem is slightly different from the ones that we saw previously. Note that the Aug 1 bar and the Nov 1 bar each go below the *x*-axis, which indicates that there were negative net sales during these months. This is another way of saying that they lost money. These negative values must be taken into account when determining the change in net sales from one month to the next. Note that the change from Jul 1 to Aug 1 is $6 – ($–4) = $10 thousand. Similarly, the change from Aug 1 to Sep 1 is $12 – ($–4) = $16 thousand. The change from Jun 1 to Jul 1 is only $6 – $2 = $4 thousand. The change from Oct 1 to Nov 1 is $7 – ($–6) = $13 thousand. The change from Nov 1 to Dec 1 is $3 – ($–6) = $9 thousand. Thus, the greatest change is from Aug 1 to Sep 1. **The correct answer is (B).**

The final relationship that can be displayed in a graph is the simplest. It is what is called an *item comparison*. An item comparison is typically displayed in a bar graph. In such a graph, the lengths of the bars indicate the sizes of various quantities and you are simply asked to compare the sizes of the quantities.

When examining these graphs, remember to read the problem statement carefully and analyze the graph carefully. The following two problems are based on the same bar graph to illustrate the sort of item comparison questions that appear on the GRE and GMAT.

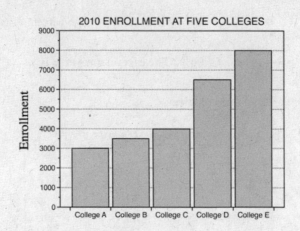

7. Using the above chart, how many students enrolled at College B or College D?

   (A) 10,000
   (B) 6,500
   (C) 3,500
   (D) 9,000
   (E) 8,500

Note that the graph contains five bars. The second bar represents the enrollment for College B, and the fourth bar represents the enrollment for College D. These two bars taken together represent the number of students enrolled at College B or College D, i.e., $3,500 + 6,500 = 10,000$. **The correct answer is (A).**

8. Which of the following represents the percent of the students enrolled at the five colleges who are enrolled at College B or College D?

   (A) 14%
   (B) 26%
   (C) 30%
   (D) 40%
   (E) 44%

The total number of students enrolled at the five colleges is given by $3,000 + 3,500 + 4,000 + 6,500 + 8,000 = 25,000$.

In the previous problem, we calculated that 10,000 students are enrolled at College B or College D. Thus, we calculate $\% = \dfrac{10,000}{25,000} = 0.4 = 40\%$. **The correct answer is (D).**

EXERCISES: INTERPRETING DATA IN TABLES AND GRAPHS

Directions: Select the answer choice that best answers the question.

Questions 1–3 are based on the tables below.

TOTAL SALES					
	Monday	**Tuesday**	**Wednesday**	**Thursday**	**Friday**
Mr. Tretola	$1,250	$750	$520	$1,375	$650
Mr. Scalici	$1,075	$600	$650	$1,400	$500

COMMISSION PERCENTS	
Associate	16%
Manager	20%

1. Mr. Tretola and Mr. Scalici are salespeople who are paid a commission that is a percent of their total sales. If Mr. Tretola is an associate and Mr. Scalici is a manager, on which day did Mr. Tretola and Mr. Scalici earn the same amount in commissions?

   (A) Monday
   (B) Tuesday
   (C) Wednesday
   (D) Thursday
   (E) Friday

2. On which day did Mr. Tretola earn more in commissions than Mr. Scalici?

   (A) Monday
   (B) Tuesday
   (C) Wednesday
   (D) Thursday
   (E) Friday

3. What is the total commission amount earned by Mr. Tretola and Mr. Scalici together on Wednesday?

   (A) $187.20
   (B) $208.00
   (C) $213.20
   (D) $223.20
   (E) $234.00

# of cupcakes purchased	1	3	6	12
# of customers	7	5	2	6

4. Gus sells cupcakes at a high school football game. Customers can either purchase single cupcakes or buy cupcakes in packages of 3, 6, or 12. The table above summarizes the purchases of the first 20 customers. If Gus started the day with 424 cupcakes, what percent of his cupcakes has he sold so far?

   (A) 19%
   (B) 20%
   (C) 25%
   (D) 28%
   (E) 30%

Number of Hours Worked in July	
Linda	60
Bob	160
Michael	40
Joe	60
Kristina	80

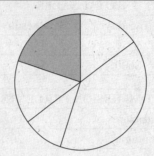

5. The information contained in the table is displayed in the circle graph above. Which person is represented by the shaded sector?

   (A) Linda

   (B) Bob

   (C) Michael

   (D) Joe

   (E) Kristina

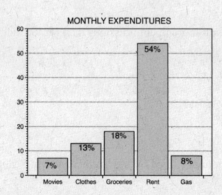

6. The chart above represents Marcy's monthly expenditures. If Marcy spent $432 on groceries during the month, what was the total of her monthly expenditures?

   (A) $2,600

   (B) $2,400

   (C) $1,800

   (D) $3,200

   (E) $2,800

ANSWER KEY AND EXPLANATIONS

1. B	3. C	5. E
2. E	4. C	6. B

1. **The correct answer is (B).** Note that, since Mr. Scalici is a manager, he earns a higher commission percent than Mr. Tretola. This means that the only way the two men can earn the same amount in commission is if Mr. Tretola earned more in Total Sales. Since this happens on only Monday, Tuesday, and Friday, those are the only days that need to be checked.

   On Monday, Mr. Scalici earns $1,075 \times 0.20 = \$215$, while Mr. Tretola earns $\$1,250 \times 0.16 = \$200$.

   On Tuesday, Mr. Scalici earns $\$600 \times 0.20 = \$120$, while Mr. Tretola earns $\$750 \times 0.16 = \$120$.

2. **The correct answer is (E).** Again, since Mr. Scalici is a manager, he earns a higher commission percent than Mr. Tretola. Thus, the only way Mr. Tretola can earn more in commission is if he earns more in salary. This happens on Monday, Tuesday, and Friday, and, if you look at the numbers in the explanation to problem 1, you can see that he didn't earn more on Monday or Tuesday. Let's check Friday. On Friday, Mr. Scalici earns $\$500 \times 0.20 = \$100$, while Mr. Tretola earns $\$650 \times 0.16 = \$104$.

3. **The correct answer is (C).** The total commission on Wednesday is the sum of the commissions earned by Mr. Tretola and Mr. Scalici, i.e., $\$650 \times 0.20 + \$520 \times 0.16 = \$130 + \$83.20 = \$213.20$.

4. **The correct answer is (C).** So far, Gus has sold $1 \times 7 + 3 \times 5 + 6 \times 2 + 12 \times 6 = 7 + 15 + 12 + 72 = 106$ cupcakes. Therefore, he has sold $106 \div 424 = 0.25 = 25\%$ of his cupcakes.

5. **The correct answer is (E).** The shaded sector is the second largest of the five sectors in the graph, so it must refer to the person who worked the second largest number of hours. This is Kristina.

6. **The correct answer is (B).** The graph shows us that $432 represents 18% of her expenditures. Thus, we know the part and the percent, and we need the whole. Therefore, $\text{whole} = \dfrac{\text{part}}{\%} = \dfrac{\$432}{0.18} = \$2400$.

COUNTING AND PROBABILITY

Some GRE and GMAT questions describe a situation and ask you to determine the number of possible outcomes.

For example, suppose you are ordering dinner in a restaurant and need to choose an entree and a dessert from the menu. The menu offers 8 different entrees and 4 different desserts. If you order both an entree and a dessert, how many different meal choices do you have?

One strategy for solving this problem is to list all of the possible combinations of entrees and desserts. Let's represent the entrees by E1, E2, E3, ..., E8, and the desserts by D1, D2, D3, and D4. Thus, the possible meal choices include E1D1, E1D2, E1D3, E1D4, and so on. Note that this strategy can be very time-consuming if the number of choices is large. Therefore, it would be very helpful if there were a way to construct a general formula that can tell us the total number of combinations, no matter how big the numbers get.

The Fundamental Counting Principle

Whenever we have a collection of choices, each of which has a number of options, we can count the total number of possible choices by using a general formula called the *Fundamental Counting Principle*.

The Fundamental Counting Principle: If C_1 can be made in any of n_1 possible ways, C_2 can be made in any of n_2 possible ways, C_3 can be made in any of n_3 possible ways, ..., C_m can be made in any of n_m possible ways, then there are $n_1 \times n_2 \times n_3 \times \cdots n_m$ possible choices.

In the above example, we have C_1 = entree, which has 8 options, and C_2 = dessert, which has 4 options. So we have a total of $8 \times 4 = 32$ meal choices.

Consider the following examples.

1. Brian is getting dressed to go to a party and needs to select a shirt, a pair of pants, and a pair of shoes. If he owns 5 pairs of pants, 4 shirts, and 2 pairs of shoes, in how many different ways can he make his selection?

Solution: In this problem we have three choices: C_1 = pants, which has 5 options, C_2 = shirts, which has 4 options, and C_3 = shoes, which has 2 options. Thus, the total number of ways Brian can dress for the party is $5 \times 4 \times 2 = 40$.

2. How many different three-digit numbers can be formed from the digits 2, 4, and 6, if each digit can only be used once?

Solution: In this problem we have three choices: C_1 = 1st digit, which has 3 options, C_2 = 2nd digit, which has 2 options, and C_3 = 3rd digit, which has 1 option. Note that the number of digit options decreases by one at each stage since repeated digits are not allowed. Thus, the total number of possibilities is given by the product $3 \times 2 \times 1 = 6$.

NOTE: When you need to determine the number of ways that a specific task can be done, try to visualize the task as consisting of a series of steps, one following the other. Count the number of ways that each step can be performed, and multiply these numbers to obtain the total number of possible ways to perform the task.

Factorial Notation

The second sample problem above introduces a type of computation that frequently occurs as part of a counting problem. Specifically, the expression $3 \times 2 \times 1$ is often represented using what's known as *factorial notation*, i.e., $3 \times 2 \times 1 = 6!$. The exclamation point denotes a special kind of multiplication.

In general, given any non-negative integer n, the notation $n!$ represents the product $n! = n \times (n-1) \times (n-2) \times (n-3) \cdots \times 1$.

For example, $1! = 1 \times 1 = 1$, $2! = 2 \times 1 = 2$, $3! = 3 \times 2 \times 1 = 6$, $4! = 4 \times 3 \times 2 \times 1 = 24$, and so on.

SPECIAL NOTE: It is mathematically convenient to define $0! = 1$.

Permutations and Combinations

The Fundamental Counting Principle can be used to solve two special types of counting problems known as *permutations* and *combinations*. The basic difference between these two types of problems is that permutations take into account the *order* of the choices being made, while combinations do not.

For example, there are six different permutations of the letters A, B, and C, i.e., ABC, ACB, BCA, BAC, CBA, and CAB.

However, if we don't care about the order of the letters, we have only one combination.

In general, permutations and combinations can be calculated using two special formulas:

Combinations: The total number of ways to combine (i.e., choose) a total of k different objects from a collection of n different objects is given by the formula: $_nC_k = \dfrac{n!}{k!(n-k)!}$.

Permutations: The total number of ways to permute (i.e., arrange) a total of k different objects from a collection of n different objects is given by the formula: $_nP_k = \dfrac{n!}{(n-k)!}$.

Note that $_nP_n = n!$ counts the number of ways to arrange n objects.

The following examples demonstrate how to use these formulas:

$$_8C_3 = \frac{8!}{3!(8-3)!} = \frac{8!}{(3!)(5!)} = \frac{40,320}{(6)(120)} = 56 \qquad _8P_3 = \frac{8!}{(8-3)!} = \frac{8!}{5!} = \frac{40,320}{120} = 336$$

Note that $_8C_3 = 56$ counts the number of ways to select 3 different objects from a collection of 8 different objects, irrespective of the selection order. On the other hand, $_8P_3 = 336$ counts the number of such selections with respect to selection order. Thus, $_8P_3 = 336$ must be greater than $_8C_3 = 56$.

Consider the following examples.

1. Bob is going on vacation and plans to bring 3 books with him. If he has 5 books to choose from, in how many ways can he make his selection?

Solution: In this problem, Bob is choosing 3 books from a collection of 5 books. Since the order in which he chooses the books does not make a difference in which of the books he takes with him, we compute $_5C_3 = \dfrac{5!}{3!(5-3)!} = \dfrac{5!}{(3!)(2!)} = \dfrac{120}{(6)(2)} = 10$. Thus, there are 10 different ways he can make his selection.

2. In how many ways can Bob arrange 3 books on his bookcase if he has 5 books to choose from?

Solution: In this problem, Bob is choosing 3 books from a collection of 5 books. Moreover, he is arranging the selected books on the bookshelf. Since order matters, we compute $_5P_3 = \dfrac{5!}{(5-3)!} = \dfrac{5!}{2!} = \dfrac{120}{2} = 60$. This means that Bob can arrange the selected books in 60 different ways.

Permutations and Combinations with Repeated Elements

We can modify the above counting formulas to solve counting problems that allow for the repeated selection of individual elements from a set.

Consider the following example.

1. How many different three-digit numbers can be formed from the digits 2, 4, and 6 if each digit can be used more than once?

Solution: In this problem we have three choices. C_1 = first digit, which has 3 options, C_2 = second digit, which has 3 options, and C_3 = third digit, which has 3 options. Using the Fundamental Counting Principle yields a total of $3 \times 3 \times 3 = 27$ possibilities.

Inclusion-Exclusion Formula

Counting problems can often be solved by examining the ways in which elements from different sets can be combined. This solution strategy requires that you be able to use an important formula called the *Inclusion-Exclusion Formula*.

Inclusion-Exclusion Formula: Given sets A and B, each containing a finite number of elements, we have the following formula:

# of elements in A or B = # of elements in A + # of elements in B − # of elements in A and B

This formula is often written as $|A \cup B| = |A| + |B| - |A \cap B|$, where the absolute value bars denote the size of the set.

The basic idea is that in order to count the total number of elements after combining sets A and B, we need to subtract the number of shared elements so that we don't over-count.

Consider the following example.

1. Using only the letters V, W, X, Y, and Z, how many 5-letter combinations can be formed that begin with V or end with Z, without using any repeated letters?

Solution: Note that we can consider the following two sets: S = {all valid "combinations" that begin with V}, and T = {all valid combinations that end with Z}. We need to determine how many elements are in the set $|S \cup T|$. Applying the Inclusion-Exclusion Formula, $|S \cup T| = |S| + |T| - |S \cap T|$, we see that we need to determine three different quantities, i.e., $|S|$, $|T|$, and $|S \cap T|$.

For $|S|$, we note that valid words that begin with V have 1 choice for the first letter, then 4 choices for the second letter, then 3 choices for the third letter, then 2 choices for the fourth letter, and then 1 choice for the fifth letter. Thus, $|S| = 4! = 24$.

For $|T|$, we note that valid combinations that end with Z have 1 choice for the fifth letter, then 4 choices for the first letter, then 3 choices for the second letter, then 2 choices for the third letter, and then 1 choice for the fourth letter. Thus, $|T| = 4! = 24$.

For $|S \cap T|$, we note that valid combinations that begin with V *and* end with Z have 1 choice for the first letter, 1 choice for the fifth letter, then 3 choices for the second letter, then 2 choices for the third letter, and then 1 choice for the fourth letter. Thus, $|S \cap T| = 3! = 6$.

Therefore, there are $|S \cup T| = |S| + |T| - |S \cap T| = 24 + 24 - 6 = 42$ possibilities.

Consider the following sample GRE and GMAT problems.

2. If $W = \{2, 4, 6, 8\}$, $X = \{10, 12\}$, $Y = \{14, 16, 18\}$ and $Z = \{20, 22, 24, 26, 28\}$, how many different sets can be formed containing one member from W, one member from X, one member from Y, and one member from Z?

   (A) 14
   (B) 16
   (C) 60
   (D) 120
   (E) 180

This problem tests your ability to use the Fundamental Counting Principle. Since there are 4 ways to select a number from set W, 2 ways to select a number from set X, 3 ways to select a number from set Y, and 5 ways to select a number from set Z, there are $4 \times 2 \times 3 \times 5 = 120$ different sets that could be formed containing one member from W, once member from X, one member from Y, and one member from Z. **The correct answer is (D).**

3. How many *odd* three-digit numbers larger than 400 can be formed from the numbers 5, 3, and 2 if each number can be used more than once?

   (A) 1
   (B) 2
   (C) 4
   (D) 6
   (E) 27

Be careful. Perhaps the most common wrong answer is $3 \times 3 \times 3 = 27$, since there are three different numbers, each of which can be used more than once. However, note that we are told that the number must be larger than 400, which means the hundred's digit has to be 5. We are also told that the number must be odd. Thus, the one's digit must be either 3 or 5. The middle digit can be any of the numbers 5, 3, or 2. Therefore, we have a total of $1 \times 2 \times 3 = 6$ possibilities. **The correct answer is (D).**

NOTE: When applying the Counting Principle, be certain to take into account any restrictions on the number of choices. This idea is illustrated in a different way in Question 4.

---

4. $T = \{-5, 0, 5\}$ $S = \{0, 5, 10\}$

If t is any number from set T, and s is any number from set S, how many different values of $s - t$ are there?

(A) 4

(B) 5

(C) 6

(D) 8

(E) 9

Here is another problem that requires a bit of caution. The most tempting wrong answer is 9, since there are three choices for the value of s, and three choices for the value of t. However, note that it is possible that different choices of s and t might lead to the same value of $s - t$. Perhaps the most efficient way to solve this problem is to write down all of the possibilities for $s - t$. **The correct answer is (B).**

If $s = 0$, then $s - t$ could be $0 - (-5) = 5$, $0 - 0 = 0$, or $0 - 5 = -5$. So far, then, we have three different values for $s - t$, i.e., -5, 0, and 5.

If $s = 5$, the possible values of $s - t$ are $5 - (-5) = 10$, $5 - 0 = 5$, and $5 - 5 = 0$. Of these three values, the only new one is 10. Thus, up to this point, we have four possible values for $s - t$.

If $s = 10$, the possible values for $s - t$ are $10 - (-5) = 15$, $10 - 0 = 10$, and $10 - 5 = 5$. The only new value here is 15. Thus, there are only five possible values for $s - t$, i.e., -5, 0, 5, 10, and 15.

Probability

Probability problems on the GRE and GMAT require you to be able to work with a number of fundamental concepts and vocabulary terms. An *experiment* is a process that results in one of a certain number of possible outcomes. For example, selecting a piece of paper from a bag is an experiment, as is tossing a coin or rolling a die. If the bag contains 27 pieces of paper, each labeled using exactly one number from the set $\{1, 2, 3, ..., 27\}$, we say that the experiment of selecting a piece of paper from the bag has 27 possible *outcomes*. Similarly, tossing a coin has two possible outcomes, and rolling a 6-sided die has 6 possible outcomes.

Probability provides us with a way of assigning a number to the likelihood that a specific outcome will happen. The probability of an outcome is always a number between 0 and 1. If an outcome has a probability of 0; that means that it *cannot possibly* happen. For example, the outcome of reaching into the bag and selecting a piece of paper labeled with the number 500 has probability 0, because 500 has not been written on any of the pieces of paper. If an outcome has a probability of 1; that means it *must* happen. If, for example, a penny is tossed, the outcome that the penny ends up on either heads or tails is an outcome of probability 1. If an outcome has a probability of $\frac{1}{2}$, it is as likely to happen as to not happen. The outcome of obtaining heads when a fair penny is tossed has a probability of $\frac{1}{2}$.

In almost all GRE and GMAT probability questions, the possible outcomes of experiments are *equally likely*. That is, every possible outcome has the same likelihood of happening. For example, if the 27 pieces of paper in the bag are thoroughly mixed, and someone reaches in and picks a piece of paper at random, then each of the 27 outcomes is equally likely.

In general, if an experiment has n possible equally likely outcomes, then the probability of each outcome is defined to be $\frac{1}{n}$.

Thus, in the "27 pieces of paper in the bag" experiment, the probability of each particular outcome is $\frac{1}{27}$.

Let's consider the following example:

Suppose that each one of the 27 possible three-digit numbers containing 2, 4, and 6 is written on a different piece of paper, and all 27 pieces of paper are put in a bag. If someone reaches into the bag and pulls out one piece of paper at random, what is the probability that the piece of paper contains a number that does not repeat any digits?

In order to solve this problem, we need to utilize the counting techniques from the previous section. We also need to know the following definition.

$$\text{The probability of a particular event happening} = \frac{\text{The number of favorable outcomes}}{\text{The number of possible outcomes}}.$$

We have already noted that this experiment has a total of 27 possible outcomes. We now need to count the number of *favorable outcomes*, i.e., the number of different three-digit numbers that can be formed from the digits 2, 4, and 6 if each digit can only be used once. Recall that an example from the previous section shows that there are only 6 such numbers. Therefore, the probability of the desired outcome is $\frac{6}{27} = \frac{2}{9}$.

Computing the probability of an event involves solving two counting problems—counting the number of possible outcomes and counting the number of favorable outcomes. The probability is the ratio of favorable outcomes to possible outcomes.

Consider the following sample problems.

1. A card is selected at random from a standard deck of 52 playing cards. What is the probability that the card is an ace?

Solution: Note that the deck has 52 cards, and 4 of them are aces. Therefore, the probability of selecting an ace is $\frac{4}{52}$, which reduces to $\frac{1}{13}$.

2. Rhonda has 7 coins in her purse: a penny, two nickels, a dime, two quarters, and a half-dollar. If she selects a coin at random from her purse, what is the probability that the value of the coin is at least 25 cents?

Solution: There are 7 possible outcomes, 3 of which are favorable, i.e., 2 quarters and 1 half-dollar. Thus, the probability is $\frac{3}{7}$.

3. There are 8 red balls, 6 yellow balls, and 4 blue balls in a container. If a ball is selected at random, what is the probability that it is *not* red?

Solution: Make sure you read this problem carefully. Note that there are $8 + 6 + 4 = 18$ balls, 8 of which are red. But, the problem asks for the probability that the selection is *not* red. Since 10 of the balls are not red, the desired probability is $\frac{10}{18} = \frac{5}{9}$.

Here are some sample GRE and GMAT probability problems.

4. At a carnival game, Nelson throws a softball into a box with 10 holes of equal size, labeled 1–10. If it is equally likely that the ball falls into any one of the 10 holes, what is the probability that the ball falls into a hole labeled with a multiple of 3?

(A) $\dfrac{1}{5}$

(B) $\dfrac{3}{10}$

(C) $\dfrac{2}{5}$

(D) $\dfrac{1}{2}$

(E) $\dfrac{3}{5}$

In this problem there are 10 equally likely outcomes. Three of these outcomes are favorable, that is, the numbers 3, 6, and 9. Thus, the probability is given by $\dfrac{3}{10}$. **The correct answer is (B).**

5. Roger's four best friends are Alexandra, Beverly, Charles, and Danielle. Roger takes an individual picture of each one of his four friends and decides to randomly place one of the four pictures on each of the first four pages of a photo album. If Alexandra's picture is randomly placed on the first page, what is the probability that Beverly's picture will randomly be put on the second page?

(A) $\dfrac{1}{6}$

(B) $\dfrac{1}{4}$

(C) $\dfrac{1}{3}$

(D) $\dfrac{1}{2}$

(E) $\dfrac{2}{3}$

After Alexandra's picture is placed on the first page, there are three possible outcomes for the second page. Only one of these (Beverly's picture) is favorable. Thus, the probability is $\dfrac{1}{3}$. **The correct answer is (C).**

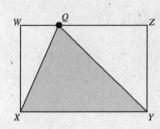

6. In the figure above, *WXYZ* is a rectangle, and point *Q* lies on $\overline{WZ}$. If a point in the interior of the rectangle is selected at random, what is the probability that it will lie within the shaded portion?

(A) $\dfrac{1}{4}$

(B) $\dfrac{1}{3}$

(C) $\dfrac{1}{2}$

(D) $\dfrac{2}{3}$

(E) It cannot be determined.

This is an example of what is called a *geometric probability* problem. We need to find the probability that a randomly selected point will lie within a shaded region. In order to solve this problem, we need to determine what percent of the total area of the rectangle is shaded.

At first, it may appear as if the correct answer is choice (E) since we do not know the specific location of point *Q*. However, note that the area of triangle *XQY* is half of the area of the rectangle, regardless of the specific location of *Q*. This is due to the fact that *XY* is the base of both the rectangle and the triangle, and the rectangle and the triangle also both have the same height. If we let *b* = the length of the base, and *h* = the height, then the area of the rectangle is *A* = *bh*, and the area of the triangle is $\dfrac{1}{2} bh$.

Thus, the problem is asking you to find the probability that a randomly selected point will lie in a region that is equal to half of the area of the rectangle. Since $\dfrac{1}{2}$ of the outcomes are favorable, the probability is $\dfrac{1}{2}$. **The correct answer is (C).**

EXERCISES: COUNTING AND PROBABILITY

Directions: Select the answer choice that best answers the question.

1. How many three-digit positive odd integers are there?
   (A) 1,000
   (B) 750
   (C) 500
   (D) 450
   (E) 360

2. Twenty people enter a race, in which there are prizes for first and second place. In how many different ways can the prizes be awarded?
   (A) 39
   (B) 360
   (C) 361
   (D) 380
   (E) 400

3. Jose selects two unique numbers at random from the set $\{5, 6, 7, 8, 9\}$. What is the probability that the product of the numbers will be greater than 60?
   (A) $\dfrac{1}{20}$
   (B) $\dfrac{1}{10}$
   (C) $\dfrac{2}{20}$
   (D) $\dfrac{1}{5}$
   (E) $\dfrac{2}{5}$

4. Monica is only able to hear the first five digits of a seven-digit phone number that is left on her answering machine. If she guesses the last two digits and dials the number, what is the probability that she will guess the correct phone number?
   (A) $\dfrac{1}{1,000}$
   (B) $\dfrac{1}{100}$
   (C) $\dfrac{1}{99}$
   (D) $\dfrac{1}{90}$
   (E) $\dfrac{1}{10}$

5. A bag contains 50 balls with the letter "A" written on them, and 30 balls with the letter "B" written on them. How many balls containing the letter "B" would need to be added to the bag so that, when a ball is randomly selected from the bag, the probability that the ball has the letter "A" written on it will only be 20%?

   (A) 120
   (B) 140
   (C) 150
   (D) 160
   (E) 170

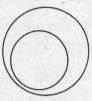

6. In the diagram above, a circle of radius 2 has been drawn inside a circle of radius 3. If a point is selected at random from the interior of the circle of radius 3, what is the probability that the point will also lie within the circle of radius 2?

   (A) $\dfrac{2}{5}$

   (B) $\dfrac{4}{9}$

   (C) $\dfrac{1}{2}$

   (D) $\dfrac{3}{5}$

   (E) $\dfrac{2}{3}$

ANSWER KEY AND EXPLANATIONS

1. D	3. B	5. E
2. D	4. B	6. B

1. **The correct answer is (D).** In order for the number to be odd, there are only 5 possible choices for the unit's digit, i.e., 1, 3, 5, 7, and 9. There are 10 choices for the ten's digit. However—be careful—there are only 9 choices for the hundred's digit, since the hundred's digit cannot be 0. Thus, there are a total of $5 \times 10 \times 9 = 450$ possibilities.

2. **The correct answer is (D).** There are 20 possible first-place winners, after which there are only 19 possible second-place winners. This means that the prizes can be awarded in $20 \times 19 = 380$ different ways.

3. **The correct answer is (B).** Jose has 5 choices for first number, and then 4 choices for second number, so overall there are $5 \times 4 = 20$ possible choices he can make. Of these, the only choices that lead to a product of greater than 60 are 8 and 9 (product is 72), and 9 and 7 (product is 63). Thus, the probability is $\dfrac{2}{20} = \dfrac{1}{10}$.

4. **The correct answer is (B).** There are 10 choices for each of the two missing digits, so there are 100 possible phone numbers she could try. Of these, only 1 is correct, so her chances of guessing the correct phone number are only $\dfrac{1}{100}$.

5. **The correct answer is (E).** One effective solving strategy is to note that, currently, 50 out of 80 balls have "A" on them. Let x represent the number of balls with "B" on them to be added to the bag. After we add the new balls to the bag, the ratio of balls with "A" to balls without "A" will be $\dfrac{50}{80+x}$. We need this ratio to be equal to 20%, that is, we want $\dfrac{50}{80+x} = 0.20$.

   Solving this equation for x yields $50 = 0.20(80 + x)$, which means that $50 = 16 + 0.20x$. Subtracting 16 from both sides, we get $34 = 0.20x$, which means that $170 = x$. Therefore, 170 balls must be added to the bag. Note that when this is done, the ratio becomes $\dfrac{50}{80+x} = \dfrac{50}{80+170} = \dfrac{50}{250}$ which is equal to 20%.

6. **The correct answer is (B).** The area of the circle with radius 3 is $A_1 = \pi r^2 = \pi(3)^2 = 9\pi$. The area of the circle of radius 2 is $A_2 = \pi r^2 = \pi(2)^2 = 4\pi$. The desired probability then, is given by $\dfrac{4\pi}{9\pi} = \dfrac{4}{9}$.

FUNCTIONS AND THEIR GRAPHS

A *function* is simply a rule that tells you how to associate the members of a first set with the members of a second set so that no element from the first set is associated with more than one element from the second set. For example, suppose that we have two sets of numbers, $D = \{1, 3, 5, 7\}$ and $R = \{2, 4, 6, 8\}$. A function would need to tell you which unique element of R is associated with which element of D.

One way to specify a function is to simply list all of the elements in the first set, and next to each element, list the corresponding element of the second set. For example, the diagram below specifies a function from set D to set R.

$$
\begin{array}{ccc}
D & & R \\
1 & \longrightarrow & 2 \\
3 & \longrightarrow & 4 \\
5 & \longrightarrow & 6 \\
7 & \longrightarrow & 8
\end{array}
$$

This diagram indicates that the number 1 from set D is associated with the number 2 from set R. Similarly, 3 is associated with 4, 5 is associated with 6, and 7 is associated with 8.

In order to work with function questions on the GRE and GMAT, you will need to be familiar with a number of vocabulary terms. The first set is called the *domain* of the function. The second set is called the *range* of the function. Typically, functions are named using letters of the alphabet. If we call the function defined above *f*, note that *f* can also be described in words by saying that the function associates each domain value with a range value that is one bigger than the domain value. That is, 1 is associated with $1 + 1 = 2$, and 3 is associated with $3 + 1 = 4$, and so on.

Frequently, the letter x is used to stand for a member of the domain, and the letter y is used to stand for a member of the range. Using this notation, we can write formulas to express the rule of a function. For example, in the function above, the rule can be written as $y = x + 1$. Whenever a domain value x is selected, the rule enables us to determine the associated range value y by performing the computation $x + 1$.

Function notation is often used to express the rule of association for a function. In this notation, the symbol $f(x)$ is used to represent the range value instead of the letter y. Using this notation, the rule for the above function can be written as $f(x) = x + 1$. Symbolically, this notation tells you that the function takes a domain value x and associates it with the range value $x + 1$. Thus, if you wanted to determine which range value was associated with the domain value 7, you would compute $f(7) = 7 + 1 = 8$. Note that the symbol "$f(7)$" is read as "*f* of 7."

> **NOTE:** The letter that is used to stand for the rule of a function doesn't matter. The function $f(x) = x + 1$ can also be written $g(x) = x + 1$ or $h(x) = x + 1$.

Consider the following sample function questions.

1. Use function notation to write a function that associates each domain value to a range value that is 9 more than the square of the domain value.

Solution: According to the problem statement, the domain value x is associated with the range value $x^2 + 9$. Using function notation, this can be written $f(x) = x^2 + 9$.

2. In the function from problem 1, what range value is associated with the domain value –5?

Solution: Here, we are asked to compute $f(-5)$. Using the rule earlier, we get $f(-5) = (-5)^2 + 9 = 25 + 9 = 34$.

3. If $g(x) = \dfrac{2x}{3}$, what are the values of $f(9), f(0), f(w), f(z+2)$, and $f(k^2)$?

Solution: In each case we need to substitute the value given for x into the expression $\dfrac{2x}{3}$.

$$f(9) = \frac{2(9)}{3} = \frac{18}{3} = 6 \qquad f(0) = \frac{2(0)}{3} = \frac{0}{3} = 0 \qquad f(w) = \frac{2w}{3}$$

$$f(z+2) = \frac{2(z+2)}{3} = \frac{2z+4}{3} \qquad f(k^2) = \frac{2k^2}{3}$$

Determining the Domain and Range of a Function

Look back at the very first function that we discussed in this section. Note that you were told that the domain was the set {1, 3, 5, 7} and the range was the set {2, 4, 6, 8}. Often, however, you may just be given the rule for a function, without anything specifically being said about the domain and the range. When this happens, there are some strategies that enable you to determine what numbers are in the domain and the range.

To begin, if you are told nothing about the domain of a function, it is assumed that the domain is all of the real numbers, unless there are any numbers for which the rule of the function is undefined (i.e., doesn't make sense.) Any such numbers must be excluded from the domain. On the GRE and GMAT, a function is typically undefined for any values that either lead to a division by 0 or to the square root of a negative number.

Consider the following functions:

$$f(x) = 21x^5 - 3x^2 + 17$$

$$g(x) = \frac{5}{x^2 + 2x - 3}$$

$$h(x) = \sqrt{7x - 14}$$

Since the function $f(x)$ contains no divisions and no radicals, its domain is all of the real numbers. In the function $g(x)$, however, there is a division, and we must exclude any numbers that make the denominator equal to 0. In order to determine which values of x make this denominator 0, we need to solve the quadratic equation $x^2 + 2x - 3 = 0$.

$$x^2 + 2x - 3 = 0$$
$$(x+3)(x-1) = 0$$
$$x = -3, x = 1$$

Therefore, we need to exclude $x = 1$ and $x = -3$ from the domain. This means that the domain is all real numbers except 1 and –3.

For the function $h(x) = h(x) = \sqrt{7x - 14}$, we need to exclude any values of x for which $7x - 14$ is negative. To determine what these values are, we need to solve the inequality $7x - 14 < 0$.

$$7x - 14 < 0$$
$$7x < 14$$
$$x < 2$$

We must therefore exclude any values of x that are less than 2 from the domain. In other words, the domain is all values of x greater than or equal to 2.

> **NOTE:** When working with functions on the GRE and GMAT, if the domain is not specified, it is assumed to be all of the real numbers except for any real numbers that lead to either division by 0 or the square root of a negative number.

Determining the range of a function is typically a bit more difficult. The range of a function can be thought of as the set of all possible outputs yielded by using all possible inputs for the function.

Since the domain may contain infinitely many numbers, it isn't practical to try to substitute all possible domain values separately. Thus, we need to examine the fundamental structure of the formula that is producing the range values. Consider the following examples.

$$j(x) = 3x - 7$$

$$k(x) = 5x^2$$

$$m(x) = 4 + \sqrt{3x - 9}$$

The range of the function $j(x) = 3x - 7$ is the set of all real numbers since $3x - 7$ can yield every possible real number as long as we input an appropriate x-value. For example, let's prove that the number 9 is in the range. In order to do this, we need to find a specific domain value that is associated with the range value of 9. We can find the appropriate domain value by solving the equation $3x - 7 = 9$.

$$3x - 7 = 9$$
$$3x = 16$$
$$x = \frac{16}{3}$$

Note that $j\left(\frac{16}{3}\right) = 3\left(\frac{16}{3}\right) - 7 = 16 - 7 = 9$.

In general for this function, given any real number, call it n, choosing $x = \frac{n + 7}{3}$ will yield $j(x) = n$.

The range of the function $k(x) = 5x^2$ is the set of all real numbers greater than or equal to 0. Note that, since x^2 is never negative, there are no negative numbers in the range. The number 0 is in the range, however, since $k(0) = 5(0)^2$. All positive numbers are also in the range, and so the range contains all real numbers bigger than or equal to 0.

Finally, let's look at $m(x) = 4 + \sqrt{3x - 9}$. Begin by noting that the smallest possible value of $\sqrt{3x - 9}$ is 0. Therefore, the smallest possible value of $4 + \sqrt{3x - 9}$ is $4 + 0 = 4$. Any larger value can be obtained, so the range is all numbers greater than or equal to 4.

Consider the following sample GRE and GMAT function questions.

1. If $f(x) = -3x^2 + 2x + 7$, what is the value of $f(x+1)$?
   (A) $-3x^2 + 8x + 6$
   (B) $-3x^2 + 8x + 12$
   (C) $-3x^2 - 4x + 5$
   (D) $-3x^2 + 2x + 8$
   (E) $-3x^2 - 4x + 6$

In order to find the solution, we need to substitute $x + 1$ for every appearance of x in the expression $-3x^2 + 2x + 7$. Pay careful attention to minus signs.

$$f(x+1) = -3(x+1)^2 + 2(x+1) + 7 = -3(x^2 + 2x + 1) + 2x + 2 + 7 = -3x^2 - 6x - 3 + 2x + 2 + 7 = -3x^2 - 4x + 6$$

The correct answer is (E).

2. If $p(x) = \dfrac{5}{(x-9)^2}$ and $q(x) = 2x + 7$, what is the value of $p(10) - q(10)$?
   (A) -33
   (B) -22
   (C) 0
   (D) 22
   (E) 33

Note that $p(10) = \dfrac{5}{(10-9)^2} = \dfrac{5}{1} = 5$. Also, $q(10) = 2(10) + 7 = 20 + 7 = 27$. Therefore, $p(10) - q(10) = 5 - 27 = -22$.

The correct answer is (B).

3. What is the domain of the function $g(x) = \dfrac{5x+10}{x^2+x-6}$?
   (A) All real numbers except 3 and –2
   (B) All real numbers except 2 and –3
   (C) All real numbers except –2, 2, and –3
   (D) All real numbers except –2, 2, and 3
   (E) All real numbers

Remember that, in general, the domain of a function, when not specified, is all real numbers except those that lead to division by 0 or the square root of a negative number. Since there are no radicals in this expression, we only need to concern ourselves with division by 0. This will happen whenever $x^2 + x - 6 = 0$. We can solve this equation by factoring. **The correct answer is (B).**

$$x^2 + x - 6 = 0$$
$$(x+3)(x-2) = 0$$
$$x = -3, x = 2$$

Thus, the domain is all real numbers except 2 and –3.

Note that the numerator of the fraction is $5x + 10$, and this is equal to 0 when $x = -2$. However, there is no need to exclude this value from the domain. A value of 0 in the numerator is fine; we cannot have values of 0 in the denominator.

4. What is the range of the function $s(x) = 17 + \sqrt{4x + 12}$?

   (A) All real numbers
   (B) All real numbers greater than or equal to –3
   (C) All real numbers greater than or equal to 17
   (D) All real numbers less than or equal to 17
   (E) All positive real numbers

Begin by noting that the smallest value that $\sqrt{4x + 12}$ can possibly have is 0. This means that the smallest value that $17 + \sqrt{4x + 12}$ can have is 17. Any larger values, however, are possible, so the range is all real numbers greater than or equal to 17. **The correct answer is (C).**

Special Functions and Their Graphs

There are three special types of functions that you may be asked specific questions about on the GRE and GMAT:

1. A *linear function* is a function of the form $f(x) = mx + b$, where m and b are real numbers. Some examples of linear functions are $f(x) = 5x + 7$, $g(x) = 100x - 32$, and $h(x) = \pi x + \sqrt{3}$.

2. A *quadratic function* is a function of the form $f(x) = ax^2 + bx + c$, where a, b, and c are any real numbers, and $a \neq 0$. Examples of quadratic functions are $f(x) = 4x^2 - 7x + 4$, $p(x) = \frac{1}{3}x^2 + 9$, and $g(x) = -12x^2 + 14x - 12$.

3. An *exponential function* is a function of the form $f(x) = ar^x$, where a and r are constants. Examples of exponential functions are $f(x) = 5(2)^x$, $p(x) = -10(\pi)^x$, and $g(x) = 3\left(\frac{1}{2}\right)^x$.

Linear Functions and Their Graphs

Consider the following example. A limousine company charges $15.00 for a trip, plus an extra 60 cents a mile. In this case, we can write a *cost function* that relates the cost of a limousine trip to the number of miles traveled in the following way: $C(x) = \$15 + \$0.60x$, where x represents the number of miles traveled (which is the domain), and $C(x)$ represents the cost (in dollars) for the trip (the range values).

Using this function, we can compute the cost associated with a trip of a particular length. Suppose, for example, you wished to determine the cost of a 30-mile ride. In this case, $x = 30$, and we need to compute the value of $C(30) = \$15 + \$0.60(30) = \$15 + \$18 = \$33$. Thus, a 30-mile ride would cost $33.

SPECIAL NOTE: Since the formula contains no radicals and no divisions, you might be inclined to conclude that the domain of the function $C(x) = \$15 + \$0.60x$ consists of all real numbers. However, there are some real numbers that do not make sense as members of the domain of $C(x)$. Remember that x represents the number of miles traveled in the limousine. The shortest distance that you can possibly travel is 0 miles. It does not make sense to include negative numbers as a part of the domain, since it is not possible to travel a negative number of miles.

Therefore, there is one additional rule when it comes to determining the domain of a function. If there are certain values that do not make sense in the context of the problem for which the function was developed, then they must be excluded from the domain as well.

NOTE: When determining the domain of a function, be certain to exclude any values that do not make sense in the context of the problem. If it does not make sense for a domain value to be a negative number, for example, the negative numbers must be eliminated from the domain.

One variation on this problem involves being given the range value and asked to determine the corresponding domain value. Suppose that you wanted to determine the maximum distance you could travel if you only had $45 to spend. In this case, you know that $C(x) = \$45$, that is, the range value is $45, and you are looking for the associated domain value. We can determine this by manipulating the function algebraically.

$$C(x) = 15 + 0.60x$$
$$45 = 15 + 0.60x$$
$$30 = 0.60x$$
$$\frac{30}{0.60} = x$$
$$50 = x$$

Thus, for $45, you could travel 50 miles.

Suppose the company determines that it costs them $0.25 for every mile that it takes a passenger. We can now create a *profit function* for the limousine company by subtracting their $0.25 per mile expense from the $15 plus $0.60 per mile that they collect. Their profit function would be given by $P(x) = \$15 + \$0.60x - \$0.25x = \$15 + \$0.35x$. Thus, we can determine the company's profit for a specified trip provided we know the mileage for the trip. For example, a 60-mile trip yields a profit determined by $P(60)$. In practical terms, we substitute $x = 60$ into the formula for $P(x)$ as follows:

$$P(60) = \$15 + \$0.35(60) = \$15 + \$21 = \$36$$

Therefore, the company makes a $36 profit on a 60-mile trip.

Consider the following examples.

Questions 1–3 refer to the following information.

In order to raise money so that the football team can travel to the city for a tournament, Brian sells t-shirts. Brian spends $120 to purchase the supply of t-shirts and sells them for $8 each.

1. Write a function that represents the profit that Brian makes from the sale of t-shirts, using x to represent the number of t-shirts sold.

Solution: Note that the number of dollars Brian makes from selling t-shirts would be $\$8x$, where x represents the number of t-shirts sold. In order to determine Brian's profit, we need to subtract his $120 cost from the $8x. If we name the profit function P, then $P(x) = 8x - 120$.

2. Use Brian's profit function to determine the profit Brian would make if he sold 48 t-shirts at the game.

Solution: Note that if Brian sells 48 t-shirts, then his profit is $P(48) = 8(48) - 120 = \$264$.

3. Brian hopes to make a $304 profit selling t-shirts at the game. How many t-shirts does he need to sell in order to make this profit?

Solution: In order to make a $304 profit, $P(x)$ must be equal to 304. Therefore, we need to solve the equation $8x - 120 = 304$.

$$8x - 120 = 304$$
$$8x = 424$$
$$x = \frac{424}{8} = 53$$

Therefore, Brian must sell 53 shirts in order to make a $304 profit.

Graphing Linear Functions

Functions can be graphed in much the same way that we graphed equations in Chapter 3: Algebra Review. Typically, the domain values are graphed along the horizontal, x-axis, and the corresponding range values are graphed along the vertical, y-axis.

Consider the cost function for the limousine ride, $C(x) = 15 + 0.60x$. Remember that we have determined that the domain consists of all non-negative numbers. Let's compute a few pairs of numbers, x and $C(x)$, which satisfy the rule for the function.

x	$C(x)$
0	$15
1	$15.60
2	$16.20
3	$16.80
5	$18
8	$19.80

When you graph all of these points on a coordinate axis, you will see that they all lie on the same line.

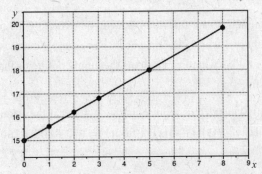

In general, the graph of any linear function is a straight line or, depending upon the domain, a part of a straight line. Remember that initially we stated that the general form for a linear function is $f(x) = mx + b$. In this form, the value of m represents the slope of the line and the value of b represents the y-intercept.

Let's look once more at the limousine cost function: $C(x) = 15 + 0.60x$. Based on the information in the paragraph above, we can see that the graph of this function is a straight line with y-intercept $15 and a slope of $0.60. The interpretation of these numbers is that it costs $15 to use the limousine plus an extra $0.60 for each mile traveled.

Consider the following two questions regarding the graph of the limousine cost function.

1. If the limousine company changed the basic cost for a trip from $15 to $20, how would this affect the graph of the cost function?

In this case, since the cost per mile remains the same, the slope of the graph remains the same. However, the y-intercept increases from $15 to $20, which has the effect of raising the entire graph 5 units vertically upwards.

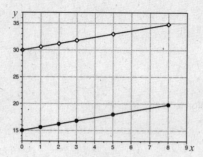

2. If the basic cost remained at $15 but the charge per mile was raised to $0.80, how would the graph of the function be affected?

This time, we are keeping the y-intercept the same, but increasing the slope of the line. Both the original graph and the graph of this function begin at the same point, but the new graph is steeper.

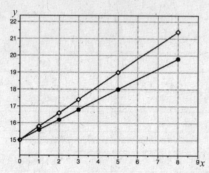

Quadratic Functions and Their Graphs

As we have already seen, quadratic functions are functions that can be written in the form $f(x) = ax^2 + bx + c$. These functions can also be used to model many real-world circumstances. For example, suppose that a particular manufacturer has a revenue function of $R(x) = -40x^2 + 800x$, where x represents the number of items that they produce each month. Let's take a look at some of the values of this function.

If $x = 0$, then $R(0) = -40(0)^2 + 800(0) = 0$. This represents the fact that if they don't manufacture any of the items, then they do not make any money. Similarly, $R(1) = -40(1)^2 + 800(1) = -40 + 800 = 760$ indicates that the revenue from one item is $760.

Note that as they manufacture more and more items, the revenue goes up. For example, $R(5) = -40(5)^2 + 800(5) = 3,000$. Similarly, $R(10) = -40(10)^2 + 800(10) = 4,000$. Thus, the revenue from 5 items is $3,000, and the revenue from 10 items is $4,000.

However, notice that the revenue from 11 items is $R(11) = -40(11)^2 + 800(11) = 3,960$. Thus, the revenue from 11 items is *less than* the revenue from 10 items. How could this be? There might be many reasons. Perhaps, when they make 11 items, they are making more than they can sell and the extra items must be stored at a certain expense. On the other hand, perhaps the extra items cannot be sold and must be destroyed.

Note that value $R(20) = -40(20)^2 + 800(20) = 0$. This means that by the time the company manufactures 20 items, they have overproduced to such an extent that they end up with no revenue at all. Thus, if they make more than 20 items in a month, they will end up losing money.

What would the graph of this quadratic function look like? Note that it cannot be a straight line, since it begins by increasing and then starts to decrease. In order to develop the graph, let's create another table of values.

Begin by noting that the smallest amount of items that they can manufacture is 0. Thus, the domain is all of the non-negative numbers. Choosing a few of the possible values for x and then substituting into the formula for $R(x)$ leads to the following table of values.

x	$R(x)$
0	0
1	760
3	2,040
5	3,000
8	3,840
9	3,960
10	4,000
11	3,960
15	3,000
20	0

Knowing these points, we can begin to draw the graph of the function.

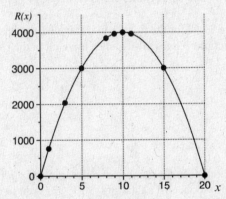

Note that the graph starts at (0,0), and reaches its highest point at (10,4000). It then begins to decrease until it reaches 0 again at (20,0). After this, the graph crosses the x-axis and continues downward.

The above graph is known as a *parabola*. This particular parabola is said to *open down*, and the coordinates of its *maximum point* are (10,4000). In general, the graph of *any* quadratic function is a parabola.

As we have seen, the general form for a quadratic function is $f(x) = ax^2 + bx + c$. If the value of a is positive, the parabola will open up, and if the value of a is negative, the parabola will open down. The highest or lowest point on a parabola is known as the *extreme point* or *turning point* or *vertex* of the function. Specifically, if the parabola opens up, its extreme point is the minimum value of the function. If the parabola opens down, its extreme point is the maximum value of the function.

SPECIAL NOTE: There is a quick way to determine the coordinates of the extreme point of a quadratic function. The x-coordinate of the extreme point is equal to $-\dfrac{b}{2a}$. To determine the y-coordinate of the extreme point, we compute the value of $f\left(-\dfrac{b}{2a}\right)$.

Let's verify that this formula works for our revenue function $R(x) = -40x^2 + 800x$. In this formula, the value of a is -40, and the value of b is 800. Therefore, the x-coordinate of the extreme point is $-\dfrac{b}{2a} = -\dfrac{800}{2(-40)} = \dfrac{-800}{-80} = 10$. This is the same result that we obtained when we plotted the previous graph. Furthermore, $R(10) = 4000$ means that the extreme point is (10,4000).

> **NOTE:** Since all of the math questions on the GRE and GMAT are either multiple-choice or grid-in questions, you will never be asked to draw a graph on the test. However, you may be asked about the properties of graphs, and in order to do this, you may need to make quick sketches of graphs in the margin of your test booklet.

Below are some problems that illustrate the way linear and quadratic functions are dealt with on the GRE and GMAT.

1. The Beta Corporation makes digital cameras. Their cost function for a particular type of camera is $C(x) = 12x^2 - 135x - 21$, where x represents the number of cameras made and the cost is in dollars. How much does it cost the Beta Corporation to make 14 cameras?

   (A) $141

   (B) $263

   (C) $441

   (D) $1,407

   (E) $2,631

This question tests your understanding of function notation. The cost of 14 cameras is given by the value of $C(14) = 12(14)^2 - 135(14) - 21 = \$441$. **The correct answer is (C).**

2. The Union Cab Company charges $3.50 for the first 2 miles traveled and an extra $0.30 for each mile after the second mile. Which of the following functions relates the distance traveled to the cost of the trip?

   (A) $C(x) = 3.50 + 0.30x$

   (B) $C(x) = 3.50 + 0.30(x - 2)$

   (C) $C(x) = 3.50x + 0.30(x - 2)$

   (D) $C(x) = 3.50 + 0.30(2 - x)$

   (E) $C(x) = 3.50 + 0.30(x + 2)$

If x represents the number of miles traveled, then the number of miles traveled *after the first 2* can be expressed algebraically as $x - 2$. At $0.30 each, these $x - 2$ miles would cost a total of $0.30(x - 2)$. Add to this the $3.50 for the first 2 miles and we have a cost function given by $C(x) = 3.50 + 0.30(x - 2)$. **The correct answer is (B).**

3. The function $h(x) = -34x^2 + 39x + 16$ is graphed on a coordinate axis. Which of the following best describes the appearance of the graph?

   (A) A line that increases as it moves from left to right

   (B) A horizontal line

   (C) A line that decreases as it moves from left to right

   (D) A parabola that opens up

   (E) A parabola that opens down

This is an example of a problem that requires knowledge of graphs without actually asking you to draw a graph. It is not necessary to spend time determining points and sketching this function. Simply note that it is a quadratic function, which means the graph is a parabola. Further, since the value of a is negative, the parabola opens down. **The correct answer is (E).**

4. What is the x-coordinate of the point where the function $f(x) = 15x + 7$ crosses the x-axis?

(A) $-\dfrac{15}{7}$

(B) $-\dfrac{7}{15}$

(C) $\dfrac{7}{15}$

(D) $\dfrac{15}{7}$

(E) 7

The graph of the function $f(x)$ crosses the x-axis when $f(x) = 0$. Thus, you need to solve the equation $15x + 7 = 0$ to determine the x-coordinate of the point where the graph crosses the x-axis. **The correct answer is (B).**

$$15x + 7 = 0$$
$$15x = -7$$
$$x = -\frac{7}{15}$$

Exponential Functions

We previously defined an exponential function as a function of the form $f(x) = ar^x$, where a and r are constants. While such functions can be defined for all real numbers, let's begin by restricting the domain to the set of non-negative integers and look at the sequence of range values. Consider, for example, the exponential function $f(x) = 3(2)^x$:

$$f(0) = 3(2)^0 = 3 \times 1 = 3$$

$$f(1) = 3(2)^1 = 3 \times 2 = 6$$

$$f(2) = 3(2)^2 = 3 \times 4 = 12$$

$$f(3) = 3(2)^3 = 3 \times 8 = 24$$

$$f(4) = 3(2)^4 = 3 \times 16 = 48$$

Let's take a look at the range values of this function: 3, 6, 12, 24, 48, and so on. This sequence of values is called a *geometric sequence*. This means that each successive term is formed by multiplying the previous term by the same number. Here, starting with the number 3, we obtain the successive terms of the sequence by multiplying each previous term by 2.

In this geometric sequence of numbers, the number 3 is called the *first* term, and the number 2 is called the *common ratio*. Typically, in any geometric sequence, the first term is symbolized by the letter a, and the common ratio is symbolized by r. Thus, starting with the first term of a, each following term is obtained by multiplying the previous term by r. That is to say, the terms of a geometric sequence can be computed as follows.

First term: a

Second term: $a \times r = ar$

Third term: $ar \times r = ar^2$

Fourth term: $ar^2 \times r = ar^3$

In other words, the terms of a geometric sequence with first term a and common ratio r, are a, ar, ar^2, ar^3, ar^4, and so on.

Note carefully that in the fifth term of the sequence, the common ratio is raised to the 4th power.

NOTE: In general, the nth term of any geometric sequence is expressed as ar^{n-1}.

Consider these sample problems.

1. Find the first four terms of a geometric sequence whose first term is 5 and whose common ratio is 3.

Solution: The first term of the sequence is 5. To find the subsequent terms, we need to multiply each preceding term by the common ratio of 3.

5

$5 \times 3 = 15$

$15 \times 3 = 45$

$45 \times 3 = 135$

Therefore, the first four terms are 5, 15, 45, 135. Note that these four terms can be generated from the function $f(n) = 5 \times 3^{n-1}$ by letting $n = 1, 2, 3$ and 4.

2. What is the seventh term of a geometric sequence whose first term is 2 and whose common ratio is 5?

Solution: Here, you need to use the formula for the nth term of a sequence, ar^{n-1}, with $n = 7$, $a = 2$, and $r = 5$. Thus, compute, $ar^{n-1} = 2(5)^{7-1} = 2(5)^6 = 2(15,625) = 31,250$.

3. What is the fourth term of a geometric sequence whose first term is 4 and whose common ratio is 7?

Solution: Here, you need to use the formula for the nth term of a sequence, ar^{n-1}, with $n = 4$, $a = 4$, and $r = 7$. Thus, compute, $ar^{n-1} = 4(7)^{4-1} = 4(7)^3 = 4(343) = 1,372$.

NOTE: The key fact to remember about geometric sequences is that if a is the first term and r is the common ratio, then the nth term is given by the expression ar^{n-1}.

Let's look at a couple of word problems that involve exponential growth and geometric sequences.

4. The population of Tonawanda is 3,750 in its first year. If the population doubles every year after the first year, what is the population of Tonawanda after 6 years?

Solution: The yearly populations of the city form a geometric sequence with first term $a = 3,750$ and common ratio $r = 2$. To find the population after $n = 6$ years, we compute $ar^{n-1} = 3,750(2)^{6-1} = 3,750(2)^5 = 3,750(32) = 120,000$.

5. Katy buys a boat for \$35,000. If the boat loses 15% of its value each year, what is the value of the boat after 5 years?

Solution: The first term is $a = 35,000$ and the number of terms is $n = 5$. We need to determine the value of r, the common ratio. Note that, since the boat loses 15% of its value each year, then each year the boat is worth $100\% - 15\% = 85\%$ of its value from the year before. Thus, the common ratio is $85\% = 0.85$. Knowing this, we can compute as follows: $ar^{n-1} = 35,000(0.85)^{5-1} = 35,000(0.85)^4 = 18,270$, rounded to the nearest dollar.

Here are some examples of GRE- and GMAT-type geometric sequence questions.

6. In a town lottery, the first person whose name is chosen wins $2,000. Each following person selected wins half as much as the previous winner. How much money will be won by the person whose name is selected fifth?

   (A) $31.25
   (B) $62.50
   (C) $125.00
   (D) $250.00
   (E) $500.00

Solution: The amount of money received by the winners forms a geometric sequence with first term 2,000 and common ratio 0.5. We need to find the fifth term, so that $n = 5$.

$$ar^{n-1} = 2,000(0.5)^{5-1} = 2,000(0.5)^4 = 125$$

The correct answer is (C).

7. The number of bacteria in a colony starts at 25 and doubles every 6 hours. The formula for the number of bacteria in the colony is given by $25 \times 2^{t/6}$, where t is the number of hours that have elapsed. How many bacteria will there be in the colony after 30 hours?

   (A) 400
   (B) 800
   (C) 1,200
   (D) 1,600
   (E) 3,200

This is a geometric sequence problem, but instead of requiring you to write the formula for the nth term, as in the previous problem, we are given the formula and simply need to substitute the value $t = 30$ into the formula.

$$25 \times 2^{30/6} = 25 \times 2^5 = 25 \times 32 = 800$$

The correct answer is (B).

EXERCISES: FUNCTIONS AND THEIR GRAPHS

Directions: Select the answer choice that best answers the question.

1. What is the domain of the function $r(x) = \dfrac{6x-3}{x^2+1}$?
   - **(A)** All real numbers except –1
   - **(B)** All real numbers except 1 and –1
   - **(C)** All real numbers except $\dfrac{1}{2}$
   - **(D)** All real numbers except $\dfrac{1}{2}$, 1, and –1
   - **(E)** All real numbers

2. Which domain values of the function $s(x) = x^2 + 4x - 21$ are associated with the range value of 0?
   - **(A)** –7
   - **(B)** 3
   - **(C)** –3 and 7
   - **(D)** 3 and –7
   - **(E)** 3 and 7

3. June rents a stand at a local flea market on Saturday to sell the decorative ornaments that she has made. If her profit function is $P(x) = \$3.50x - \$32.50$, how many ornaments does she need to sell to make a profit of $132?
   - **(A)** 47
   - **(B)** 49
   - **(C)** 50
   - **(D)** 52
   - **(E)** 53

4. What is the y-coordinate of the point at which the function $d(x) = -36x + 18$ crosses the y-axis?
   - **(A)** –2
   - **(B)** $-\dfrac{1}{2}$
   - **(C)** $\dfrac{1}{2}$
   - **(D)** 2
   - **(E)** 18

5. On Friday nights, a video game parlor charges a $5.00 admission fee and then an additional 75 cents for each video game played. Which of the following functions relates the number of games played, x, to the total cost *in dollars*?
   - **(A)** $f(x) = 5.75x$
   - **(B)** $f(x) = 5 + 75x$
   - **(C)** $f(x) = 5x + 0.75$
   - **(D)** $f(x) = 5 + 0.75x$
   - **(E)** $f(x) = 0.75x - 5$

6. If the functions $q(x) = -x + 12$ and $r(x) = x - 14$ are both graphed on the same coordinate axis, which of the following best describes what the graph will look like?

    (A) Two parallel lines, one with a y-intercept of 12 and the other with a y-intercept of -14.

    (B) Two parallel lines, one with a y-intercept of -12 and the other with a y-intercept of 14.

    (C) Two perpendicular lines, one with a y-intercept of 12 and the other with a y-intercept of -14.

    (D) Two perpendicular lines, one with a y-intercept of -12 and the other with a y-intercept of 14.

    (E) Two parabolas, one with a y-intercept of 12 and the other with a y-intercept of -14.

ANSWER KEY AND EXPLANATIONS

1. E	3. A	5. D
2. D	4. E	6. C

1. **The correct answer is (E).** There are no radicals in this function, so all we need to worry about is the possibility of a division by 0. Note, however, that the denominator is *never* 0, since the value of x^2 can never be -1 for any real number. Thus, there are no values that need to be excluded, and the domain is all real numbers.

2. **The correct answer is (D).** In order to answer this question, we need to determine the values for which $x^2 + 4x - 21 = 0$. Solving the quadratic equation by factoring yields:

$$x^2 + 4x - 21 = 0$$
$$(x+7)(x-3) = 0$$
$$x = -7, x = 3$$

3. **The correct answer is (A).** We need to find the value of x for which $3.50x - 32.50 = 132$.

$$3.50x - 32.50 = 132$$
$$3.50x = 164.50$$
$$x = \frac{164.50}{3.50} = 47$$

Therefore, she must sell 47 ornaments to make a profit of $132.

4. **The correct answer is (E).** The question is using alternate vocabulary to ask for the y-intercept of a linear function. If a linear function is written in the form $f(x) = mx + b$, then the y-intercept is b. In this function, then, the y-intercept is 18.

5. **The correct answer is (D).** Note that the cost of x games at 75 cents each would be $0.75x$. Add to this the $5.00 admission fee, and you obtain a function of $f(x) = 5 + 0.75x$.

   In this problem, you must watch the units very carefully to avoid an extremely common error. Remember, you are asked to find the total cost in dollars. Thus, the charge of 75 cents per game must be expressed as $0.75. Do not select choice (B), which indicates a charge of $75 per game.

6. **The correct answer is (C).** This problem tests your ability to interpret linear function formulas. First of all, both functions are linear, so their graphs will be straight lines. Next, the slope of the function $q(x) = -x + 12$ is the coefficient of the x-term, which is -1. Similarly, the slope of $r(x) = x - 14$ is 1. Therefore, the slopes of the two lines are negative reciprocals of each other, which means that their graphs represent perpendicular lines. Finally, $q(x) = -x + 12$ has a y-intercept of 12 and $r(x) = x - 14$ has a y-intercept of -14.

DATA INTERPRETATION PRACTICE TEST

GRE Multiple-Choice Questions—Select One Answer Choice

Directions: For Questions 1–7, select a single answer choice.

1. If the average (arithmetic mean) of q, $3q$, and $5q$ is 105, what is the value of $2q$?

   (A) 20
   (B) 23
   (C) 35
   (D) 40
   (E) 70

2. In how many different orders can 5 students get on a bus?

   (A) 10
   (B) 30
   (C) 60
   (D) 120
   (E) 240

Questions 3–4 are based on the table shown below.

Price of Printer	Number Sold
$150	25,000
$175	22,000
$200	18,000
$225	16,000
$250	13,000

The AMPEX Company has just designed a new printer and now needs to determine the selling price. The table above shows the results of the research into how many printers it will be able to sell at various prices.

3. At which price will the AMPEX Company receive the greatest amount of money?

   (A) $150
   (B) $175
   (C) $200
   (D) $225
   (E) $250

4. How much more money will AMPEX receive if the company sells the printer for $150 instead of for $200?

   (A) $75,000
   (B) $100,000
   (C) $125,000
   (D) $150,000
   (E) $350,000

5. At the Wardlaw Hartridge School, there are two different sections of Physics. Section *A* has 12 students, and Section *B* has 18 students. On the final exam, the average (arithmetic mean) grade for Section *A* was 70, and the average (arithmetic mean) grade for Section *B* was 85. What was the average score on the final exam for all 30 students?

    (A) 76

    (B) 77.5

    (C) 78

    (D) 79

    (E) It cannot be determined.

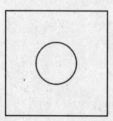

6. If a point is selected at random from the interior of the 16-by-16 square shown in the diagram above, which of the following is the closest to the probability that the point is also within the interior of the circle with radius 4?

    (A) 0.256

    (B) 0.196

    (C) 0.314

    (D) 0.201

    (E) 0.422

7. A password of length 4 is formed using each of the characters *M*, *N*, 2, 7 exactly once. What is the probability that the password begins with *M*?

    (A) 0.40

    (B) 0.50

    (C) 0.25

    (D) 0.45

    (E) 0.35

GRE Multiple-Choice Questions—Select One or More Answer Choices

Directions: For Questions 8–11, select one or more answer choices according to the specific question directions. If the question does not specify how many answer choices to select, select all that apply.

- The correct answer may be just one of the choices or may be as many as all of the choices, depending on the question.
- No credit is given unless you select all of the correct choices and no others.
- If the question specifies how many answer choices to select, select exactly that number of choices.

Questions 8–9 are based on the table shown below.

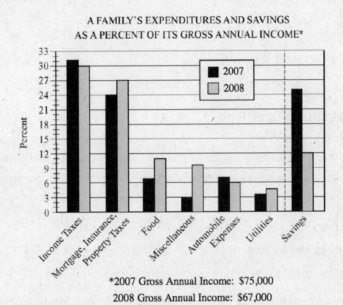

A FAMILY'S EXPENDITURES AND SAVINGS
AS A PERCENT OF ITS GROSS ANNUAL INCOME*

*2007 Gross Annual Income: $75,000
2008 Gross Annual Income: $67,000

8. In 2007, the family used a total of 49 percent of its gross annual income for two of the categories listed. What was the total dollar amount of the family's income used for those same two categories in 2008?

 (A) $19,430
 (B) $23,450
 (C) $32,830
 (D) $30,150
 (E) $26,130

9. Of the seven categories listed, which category of expenditure had greater than a 2% increase from 2007 to 2008?

 (A) Savings
 (B) Food
 (C) Miscellaneous
 (D) Utilities
 (E) Mortgage, Insurance, Property Taxes
 (F) Automobile Expenses
 (G) Income Taxes

10. Which real numbers must be excluded from the domain of the function $f(x) = \dfrac{x^2 - 1}{2x^2 + 13x + 21}$?

(A) 1

(B) −1

(C) 3

(D) −3

(E) −3.5

(F) 4

11. Which of the following equals 10?

(A) $_5C_3$

(B) $_5P_3$

(C) $_5C_2$

(D) $\dfrac{_5P_5}{12}$

(E) $_5P_2$

GRE Quantitative Comparison Questions

Directions: For Questions 12–14, compare Quantity A and Quantity B, using additional information centered above the two quantities if such information is given, and select one of the following four answer choices:

(A) Quantity A is greater.

(B) Quantity B is greater.

(C) The two quantities are equal.

(D) The relationship cannot be determined from the information given.

A symbol that appears more than once in a question has the same meaning throughout the question.

Given the four numbers $p, q, p+q, q-p$, such that $0 < q < p$.

12.

Quantity A	Quantity B
The median of the list	The arithmetic mean of the list

(A) Quantity A is greater.

(B) Quantity B is greater.

(C) The two quantities are equal.

(D) The relationship cannot be determined from the information given.

13.

Quantity A	Quantity B
The sum of five consecutive integers whose median is zero (0)	The sum of six consecutive odd integers whose median is zero (0)

(A) Quantity A is greater.

(B) Quantity B is greater.

(C) The two quantities are equal.

(D) The relationship cannot be determined from the information given.

14.

Quantity A	Quantity B

The maximum value of the function $f(x) = -2x^2 + 8x + 7$

The total number of ways to choose two different letters from the set $\{P, Q, R, S, T, U\}$, discounting the order in which the letters are chosen

(A) Quantity A is greater.

(B) Quantity B is greater.

(C) The two quantities are equal.

(D) The relationship cannot be determined from the information given.

GRE Numeric Entry Questions

Directions: For Questions 15–21, enter your answer as an integer or as a decimal if there is a single answer box OR as a fraction if there are two separate boxes—one for the numerator and one for the denominator.

To enter an integer or a decimal, write the number in the answer box provided. On the computer-based test you can either type the number in the answer box using the keyboard or use the Transfer Display button on the calculator. Also, note the following directions for the computer-based test:

- You can click on the answer box and then type the number. You can use the backspace key to erase a number.

- Type a hyphen for a negative sign. Type a hyphen again, and it will disappear. For a decimal point, type a period.

- The Transfer Display button on the calculator will move the calculator display to the answer box.

- Equivalent forms of the correct answer, such as 2.5 and 2.50, are all correct.

- Enter the exact answer unless the question asks you to round your answer.

15. If a is a number from set $A = \{-1, 0, 1\}$ and b is a number from set $B = \{-4, 0, 4\}$, how many different possible values are there for ab?

16. If 83 is the average (arithmetic mean) of $a, a, a, a,$ 14, and 106, what is the value of a?

Questions 17–19 refer to the given diagram.

Travelers Surveyed: 575

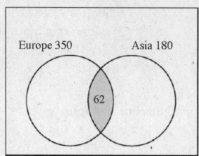

In a survey of a total of 575 American travelers, 350 have traveled to Europe, 180 have traveled to Asia, and 62 have traveled to both Europe and Asia.

17. How many of the travelers surveyed have traveled to Europe but *not* Asia?

18. How many of the travelers surveyed have traveled to *at least one of* Europe or Asia?

19. How many of the travelers surveyed have traveled *neither* to Europe *nor to* Asia?

DISTRIBUTION OF WORKFORCE BY OCCUPATION
FOR RIVER CITY IN 2010 AND PROJECTED FOR 2025

Total Workforce: 45,000   Total Workforce: 60,000

2010   2025 (Projected)

20. Using the above diagram, what is the ratio of the number of workers in the Manufacturing category in 2010 to the projected number of such workers in 2025?

21. What is the slope of the graph of the function $p(w) = \frac{3}{2}w - 7$?

Give your answer as a fraction.

GMAT Problem-Solving Questions

Directions: For Questions 22–28, solve the problems and indicate the best of the answer choices given.

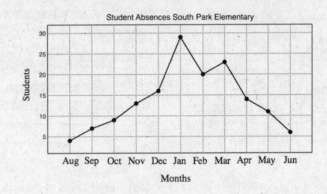

22. Based on the above graph, between which two months was the greatest change in absences?

    (A) March to April

    (B) October to November

    (C) May to June

    (D) December to January

    (E) January to February

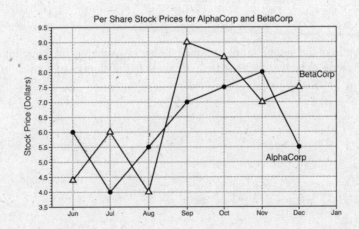

The chart above plots the per-share price of stock in two corporations—AlphaCorp and BetaCorp—for the first day of each month from June through December.

23. On September 1, by approximately what percent did BetaCorp's stock price exceed AlphaCorp's stock price?

(A) 149%

(B) 129%

(C) 258%

(D) 200%

(E) 150%

Questions 24–25 refer to the given diagram.

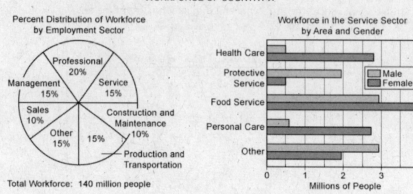

24. Approximately what fraction of the workforce in the Protective Service area of the service sector is female?

(A) $\dfrac{2}{5}$

(B) $\dfrac{1}{10}$

(C) $\dfrac{3}{5}$

(D) $\dfrac{1}{5}$

(E) $\dfrac{3}{10}$

25. In the workforce, the ratio of the number of men to the number of women is the same for the Sales sector as it is for the Protective Service sector. Which of the following is closest to the number of women in the Sales sector?

(A) 2.8 million

(B) 3.5 million

(C) 10.4 million

(D) 11.1 million

(E) 14.0 million

26. The formula for the size (in grams) of a sample of a radioactive substance is given by $A \times \left(\frac{1}{3}\right)^{t/4}$, where t is the number of hours that have elapsed, and A is the initial sample size. How long will it take for $\frac{8}{9}$ of the sample to decay?

    (A) 4 hours

    (B) 6 hours

    (C) 8 hours

    (D) 3 hours

    (E) 9 hours

Relative Humidity	Apparent Temperature
x	y
20	67
60	72

27. The data listed in the table above represents the relative humidity versus the apparent temperature in a room whose actual temperature is 72 degrees Fahrenheit. Construct a formula for a linear function that demonstrates the relationship between the apparent temperature and relative humidity for this data.

    (A) $f(x) = \frac{1}{8}y + 64.5$

    (B) $f(y) = \frac{1}{8}x + 64.5$

    (C) $f(x) = 8x - 93$

    (D) $f(y) = 8y - 93$

    (E) $f(x) = \frac{1}{8}x + 60$

28. A ball is thrown vertically upward from the top of a building 96 feet tall with an initial velocity of 80 feet per second. The height in feet of the ball above the ground is given by the function $h(t) = 96 + 80t - 16t^2$, where t is measured in seconds. What is the maximum height reached by the ball?

    (A) 96 feet

    (B) 396 feet

    (C) 296 feet

    (D) 176 feet

    (E) 196 feet

GMAT Data Sufficiency Questions

Directions: Questions 29–31 consist of a question and two statements, labeled (1) and (2), in which certain data is given. You have to decide whether the data given in the statements is sufficient for answering the question. Using the data given in the statements plus your knowledge of mathematics and everyday facts (such as the number of days in July and the meaning of "counterclockwise"), you must indicate whether

(A) Statement (1) ALONE is sufficient, but statement (2) is not sufficient.

(B) Statement (2) ALONE is sufficient, but statement (1) is not sufficient.

(C) BOTH statements TOGETHER are sufficient, but NEITHER statement ALONE is sufficient.

(D) EACH statement ALONE is sufficient.

(E) Statements (1) and (2) TOGETHER are NOT sufficient.

29. What is the value of m?

(1) $y = mx + 6$ and $4y + 2x = 1$ are parallel lines.
(2) The graph of $y = mx^2 + 5x + 1$ opens up.

(A) Statement (1) ALONE is sufficient, but statement (2) is not sufficient.
(B) Statement (2) ALONE is sufficient, but statement (1) is not sufficient.
(C) BOTH statements TOGETHER are sufficient, but NEITHER statement ALONE is sufficient.
(D) EACH statement ALONE is sufficient.
(E) Statements (1) and (2) TOGETHER are NOT sufficient.

30. What is the maximum value of $f(x) = ax^2 + bx + 3$?

(1) $a + b = 8$
(2) $a + 2b = 18$

(A) Statement (1) ALONE is sufficient, but statement (2) is not sufficient.
(B) Statement (2) ALONE is sufficient, but statement (1) is not sufficient.
(C) BOTH statements TOGETHER are sufficient, but NEITHER statement ALONE is sufficient.
(D) EACH statement ALONE is sufficient.
(E) Statements (1) and (2) TOGETHER are NOT sufficient.

31. How many elements are in the set $A \cup B$?

(1) A contains 8 elements.
(2) B contains 5 elements.

(A) Statement (1) ALONE is sufficient, but statement (2) is not sufficient.
(B) Statement (2) ALONE is sufficient, but statement (1) is not sufficient.
(C) BOTH statements TOGETHER are sufficient, but NEITHER statement ALONE is sufficient.
(D) EACH statement ALONE is sufficient.
(E) Statements (1) and (2) TOGETHER are NOT sufficient.

ANSWER KEY AND EXPLANATIONS

1. E	8. E	14. C	20. 21:20	26. C
2. D	9. B, C, E	15. 3	21. $\frac{3}{2}$	27. B
3. B	10. D, E	16. 94.5		28. E
4. D	11. A, C, D	17. 288	22. D	29. A
5. D	12. A	18. 468	23. B	30. C
6. B	13. C	19. 107	24. D	31. E
7. C			25. A	

1. **The correct answer is (E).** This problem can be solved algebraically by solving the following equation.

$$\frac{q+3q+5q}{3}=105$$
$$9q=315$$
$$q=\frac{315}{9}=35$$

The question asks for the value of $2q$, so the correct answer is 70.

2. **The correct answer is (D).** Using the Fundamental Counting Principle, there would be 5 choices for the student who gets on the bus first, 4 choices for second, 3 choices for third, 2 choices for fourth, and 1 choice for fifth. Overall, then, there are $5 \times 4 \times 3 \times 2 \times 1 = 120$ ways for the students to get on the bus.

3. **The correct answer is (B).** In order to answer this question, you need to multiply each possible price by the number of printers that would be sold at that price.

$150 \times 25,000 = \$3,750,000$

$175 \times 22,000 = \$3,850,000$

$200 \times 18,000 = \$3,600,000$

$225 \times 16,000 = \$3,600,000$

$250 \times 13,000 = \$3,250,000$

Thus, they will make the most money of they sell the printers for $175.

4. **The correct answer is (D).** If the company sells the printer for $150, it will receive $3,750,000. If it sells the printer for $200, it will receive $3,600,000. Note that $3,750,000 – $3,600,000 = $150,000.

5. **The correct answer is (D).** Perhaps the quickest way to solve this problem is to assume that the 12 students in section *A* who had an average of 70 *all* got a 70 on the test, and the 18 students in section *B* all got scores of 85 on the test. Then, using the weighted average formula, you can compute:

$$\frac{12(70)+18(85)}{30}=\frac{840+1,530}{30}=\frac{2,370}{30}=79$$

6. **The correct answer is (B).** The area of the square is $16 \times 16 = 256$. The area of the circle is $A = \pi r^2 = \pi (4)^2 = 16\pi$. The probability you are looking for can be expressed as $\frac{16\pi}{256} = \frac{\pi}{16}$. Performing the indicated division, you obtain a probability of 0.196.

7. **The correct answer is (C).** The total number of passwords that begin with *M* is given by $3! = 6$. The total number of passwords is given by $4! = 24$. Thus, the desired probability is $\frac{6}{24} = 0.25$.

8. **The correct answer is (E).** Note that in 2007, the combined total percentage of the Mortgage, Insurance, Property Taxes category and the Savings category is 24% + 25% = 49%. The 2008 total for these same two categories is 27% + 12% = 39%. Therefore, we compute 39% of the 2008 income, as follows: $0.39 \times \$67,000 = \$26,130$.

9. **The correct answers are (B), (C), and (E).** From the table, we can see that the Food category increased from 7% to 10%. The Miscellaneous category increased from 3% to 10%. The Mortgage, Insurance, Property Taxes category increased from 24% to 27%.

10. **The correct answers are (D) and (E).** We need to exclude all x-values that cause the denominator to equal 0.

$$2x^2 + 13x + 21 = 0$$
$$(2x+7)(x+3) = 0$$
$$2x+7 = 0 \qquad x+3 = 0$$
$$x = -3.5 \qquad x = -3$$

11. **The correct answers are (A), (C), and (D).** We can calculate each answer choice by using combination and permutation formulas as follows.

$$_5C_3 = \frac{5!}{(3!)(2!)} = \frac{120}{(6)(2)} = 10$$

$$_5P_3 = \frac{5!}{2!} = \frac{120}{2} = 60$$

$$_5C_2 = \frac{5!}{(2!)(3!)} = \frac{120}{(2)(6)} = 10$$

$$\frac{_5P_5}{12} = \frac{5!}{12} = \frac{120}{12} = 10$$

$$_5P_2 = \frac{5!}{3!} = \frac{120}{6} = 20$$

12. **The correct answer is (A).** Since $0 < q < p$, we know that $q-p$ must be negative, which means that $q-p$ is the smallest number in the list. Therefore, the ordered list is $q-p, p, q, p+q$. The median of the list is given by the average of the two middle terms, i.e., $\frac{p+q}{2}$. The arithmetic mean is given by: $\frac{q-p+p+q+p+q}{4} = \frac{q+q+p+q}{4} = \frac{3q+p}{4}$. We want to compare $\frac{p+q}{2}$ with $\frac{3q+p}{4}$.

That is, we need to determine whether $\boxed{?}$ in the following expression should be $<, >,$ or $=$:

$$\frac{p+q}{2} \;\boxed{?}\; \frac{3q+p}{4}.$$

Note that we can multiply both sides by 4 to clear out the denominators without changing the value of $\boxed{?}$. So we have

$2p + 2q \boxed{?} 3q + p$. Rearranging the terms yields $p \boxed{?} q$. The given information tells us that $0 < q < p$. So we have

$p > q$, which means that $\boxed{?}$ must be replaced by >. Therefore, Quantity A is greater.

13. **The correct answer is (C).** For Quantity A, consider the five consecutive integers $n, n+1, n+2, n+3, n+4$ The

median is given by $n + 2$, which must equal 0. Thus, $n = -2$. Therefore, the list is $-2, -1, 0, 1, 2$, which yields the sum

$-2 + (-1) + 0 + 1 + 2 = 0$. For Quantity B, consider the six consecutive odd integers $m, m+2, m+4, m+6, m+8, m+10$.

The median is given by the average of the middle two numbers, i.e., $\dfrac{m+4+m+6}{2} = \dfrac{2m+10}{2}$, which must equal 0.

Thus, $2m + 10 = 0$, which means that $m = -5$. Therefore, the list is $-5, -3, -1, 1, 3, 5$, which yields the sum

$-5 + (-3) + (-1) + 1 + 3 + 5 = 0$. Therefore, the two quantities are equal.

14. **The correct answer is (C).** For Quantity A, we know that the maximum value of the quadratic function occurs

when $x = -\dfrac{b}{2a} = -\dfrac{8}{(2)(-2)} = 2$, which yields the maximum value $f(2) = -2(2)^2 + 8(2) + 7 = -8 + 16 + 7 = 15$. For

Quantity B, $_6C_2 = \dfrac{6!}{(2!)(4!)} = \dfrac{720}{(2)(24)} = 15$. Therefore, the two quantities are equal.

15. **The correct answer is 3.** As we have already seen, it is a mistake to conclude that the correct answer is $3 \times 3 = 9$, since some products may occur more than once. In order to obtain the answer, you need to compute all 9 possible products and see how many different results there are:

If $a = -1$, we can obtain three different values for ab: $-1 \times -4 = 4$, $-1 \times 0 = 0$, and $-1 \times 4 = -4$.

If $a = 0$, all values of ab will be 0. Since 0 has already turned up as a value, we still have a total of three possible different values.

If $a = 1$, we get the values $1 \times -4 = -4$, $1 \times 0 = 0$, and $1 \times 4 = 4$. None of these are new, either. Thus, there are only three possible values.

16. **The correct answer is 94.5.** Set up and solve the following equation:

$$\frac{a+a+a+a+14+106}{6} = 83$$

$$\frac{4a+120}{6} = 83$$

$$4a + 120 = 498$$

$$4a = 378$$

$$a = \frac{378}{4} = 94.5$$

17. **The correct answer is 288.** We need to find the total number of travelers who visited Europe and subtract the number of those travelers who also visited Asia. Letting E = {travelers who visited Europe}, and A = {travelers who visited Asia}, we need to compute $|E| - |E \cap A| = 350 - 62 = 288$.

18. **The correct answer is 468.** We need to compute $|E \cup A|$. Using the Inclusion-Exclusion Formula yields

$|E \cup A| = |E| + |A| - |E \cap A| = 350 + 180 - 62 = 468$.

19. **The correct answer is 107.** We know that the total number of travelers surveyed is 575, of which 468 traveled either to Europe or Asia. Therefore, the number of people who traveled neither to Europe nor Asia is given by 575 − 468 = 107.

20. **The correct answer is 21:20.** The number of workers in the Manufacturing category in 2010 is given by 28% of 45,000, which equals $0.28 \times 45,000 = 12,600$. Similarly, the projected number of workers in the Manufacturing category in 2025 is given by 20% of 60,000, which equals $0.20 \times 60,000 = 12,000$. Thus, the desired ratio is 12,600:12,000, which reduces to 21:20.

21. **The correct answer is $\dfrac{3}{2}$.** This is a linear function. So the slope is simply the coefficient of the *x*-term. Therefore, the slope is $\dfrac{3}{2}$.

22. **The correct answer is (D).** This question asks us to identify the segment of the graph that has the steepest positive slope. Therefore, we choose the segment from December to January.

23. **The correct answer is (B).** The difference in stock prices on Sep 1 is given by $9 − $7 = $2, which means the percentage difference is $\dfrac{\$2}{\$7} \approx 0.2857 \approx 29\%$. Therefore, BetaCorp's stock price was 129% greater than AlphaCorp's stock price.

24. **The correct answer is (D).** The chart on the right shows that there are approximately 0.5 million women in the Protective Service sector. Similarly, the chart shows that there are approximately 2 + 0.5 = 2.5 million workers in this sector. Thus, we compute $\dfrac{0.5}{2.5} = \dfrac{5}{25} = \dfrac{1}{5}$.

25. **The correct answer is (A).** In the Protective Service sector, the ratio of men to women is approximately $\dfrac{2}{0.5} = \dfrac{20}{5} = \dfrac{4}{1}$, i.e., 4:1. Using the chart on the left, we see that 10% of the total workforce is in Sales, which means there are $0.10 \times 140 = 14$ million workers in Sales. Therefore, there are approximately $\dfrac{14}{5} = 2.8$ million women in Sales.

26. **The correct answer is (C).** Note that when $\dfrac{8}{9}$ of the sample has decayed, $\dfrac{1}{9}$ of the sample remains. Using the given formula for the amount present after *t* hours, we have the equation $A \times \left(\dfrac{1}{3}\right)^{t/4} = \dfrac{1}{9}A$.

We need to solve this equation for *t*. Dividing both sides by *A* yields $\left(\dfrac{1}{3}\right)^{t/4} = \dfrac{1}{9}$. Note that the right-hand side can be rewritten using the fact that $\dfrac{1}{9} = \left(\dfrac{1}{3}\right)^2$. So, our equation becomes $\left(\dfrac{1}{3}\right)^{t/4} = \left(\dfrac{1}{3}\right)^2$. The only way this equation can be true is if the exponents are equal, i.e., $\dfrac{t}{4} = 2$. Therefore, $t = 8$ hours.

27. **The correct answer is (B).** The key thing to note here is that we need to build a *linear function*. This means we need to determine the slope of the line. Letting x = relative humidity and y = apparent temperature, the table gives us two points on the desired line, i.e., $(20, 67)$ and $(60, 72)$. Therefore, the slope is $m = \dfrac{72 - 67}{60 - 20} = \dfrac{5}{40} = \dfrac{1}{8}$. Recall that a linear function with slope m can be written as $f(x) = mx + b$, where b = the y-intercept. One way to find the value of b is to plug the coordinates of one of the given points into the equation. Choosing the point $(20, 67)$ yields $67 = \dfrac{1}{8}(20) + b$. Thus, $67 = 2.5 + b$, which means that $64.5 = b$. Therefore, we have the equation $f(x) = \dfrac{1}{8}x + 64.5$.

28. **The correct answer is (E).** We know that $h(t) = 96 + 80t - 16t^2$. Since the coefficient on the t^2-term is -16, we know that the maximum value occurs when $t = -\dfrac{b}{2a} = -\dfrac{80}{2(-16)} = 2.5$. The maximum value of the function is given by $h(2.5) = 96 + 80(2.5) - 16(2.5)^2 = 96 + 200 - 100 = 196$ feet.

29. **The correct answer is (A).** If statement (1) is true, we know that the lines $y = mx + 6$ and $4y + 2x = 1$ must have equal slopes. The slope of $y = mx + 6$ is m. We can determine the slope of $4y + 2x = 1$ by solving the equation for y to get $y = -\dfrac{1}{2}x + \dfrac{1}{4}$. Therefore, we can conclude that $m = -\dfrac{1}{2}$. Thus, statement (1) ALONE is sufficient. If statement (2) is true, we know that the graph of $y = mx^2 + 5x + 1$, which means that $m > 0$. However, we have no way of knowing which positive number m equals. Thus, statement (2) ALONE is not sufficient.

30. **The correct answer is (C).** In order to determine the maximum value of $f(x) = ax^2 + bx + 3$, we need to determine the value of $x = -\dfrac{b}{2a}$. Moreover, a must be a negative number. If statement (1) is true, we have $a + b = 8$. However, there are infinitely pairs of a- and b-values for which this equation is true. Thus, statement (1) ALONE is not sufficient. If statement (2) is true, we have $a + 2b = 18$. However, there are infinitely pairs of a- and b-values for which this equation is true. Thus, statement (2) ALONE is not sufficient. Note that if statements (1) and (2) are both true, then we have the system of equations:

$a + b = 8$
$a + 2b = 18$

Subtracting the second equation from the first yields:

$\begin{aligned} a + b &= 8 \\ \underline{a + 2b} &= \underline{18} \\ -b &= -10 \end{aligned}$

Thus, $b = 10$. Substituting into the first equation yields $a + 10 = 8$, which means that $a = -2$. Since we now have specific values for a and b, we can determine $x = -\dfrac{b}{2a}$, which means we can determine the maximum value for

$f(x) = ax^2 + bx + 3$. Therefore, BOTH statements TOGETHER are sufficient, but NEITHER statement ALONE is sufficient.

31. **The correct answer is (E).** In order to determine how many elements are in the set $A \cup B$, we must know how many elements are in sets A, B, and $A \cap B$, respectively. Since neither statement (1) nor statement (2) includes information about the number of elements in $A \cap B$, statements (1) and (2) TOGETHER are NOT sufficient.

PART III

Three Math Practice Tests

PRACTICE TEST 1 ANSWER SHEET

1. Ⓐ Ⓑ Ⓒ Ⓓ Ⓔ
2. Ⓐ Ⓑ Ⓒ Ⓓ Ⓔ
3. ☐
4. Ⓐ Ⓑ Ⓒ Ⓓ Ⓔ
5. Ⓐ Ⓑ Ⓒ Ⓓ Ⓔ
6. Ⓐ Ⓑ Ⓒ Ⓓ Ⓔ
7. Ⓐ Ⓑ Ⓒ Ⓓ Ⓔ
8. Ⓐ Ⓑ Ⓒ Ⓓ Ⓔ

9. ☐
10. Ⓐ Ⓑ Ⓒ Ⓓ Ⓔ
11. Ⓐ Ⓑ Ⓒ Ⓓ Ⓔ
12. Ⓐ Ⓑ Ⓒ Ⓓ Ⓔ
13. Ⓐ Ⓑ Ⓒ Ⓓ Ⓔ
14. Ⓐ Ⓑ Ⓒ Ⓓ Ⓔ
15. Ⓐ Ⓑ Ⓒ Ⓓ Ⓔ Ⓕ Ⓖ
16. Ⓐ Ⓑ Ⓒ Ⓓ Ⓔ

17. Ⓐ Ⓑ Ⓒ Ⓓ
18. Ⓐ Ⓑ Ⓒ Ⓓ
19. Ⓐ Ⓑ Ⓒ Ⓓ
20. Ⓐ Ⓑ Ⓒ Ⓓ
21. Ⓐ Ⓑ Ⓒ Ⓓ
22. Ⓐ Ⓑ Ⓒ Ⓓ
23. Ⓐ Ⓑ Ⓒ Ⓓ
24. Ⓐ Ⓑ Ⓒ Ⓓ Ⓔ

25. Ⓐ Ⓑ Ⓒ Ⓓ Ⓔ
26. Ⓐ Ⓑ Ⓒ Ⓓ Ⓔ
27. Ⓐ Ⓑ Ⓒ Ⓓ Ⓔ
28. Ⓐ Ⓑ Ⓒ Ⓓ Ⓔ
29. Ⓐ Ⓑ Ⓒ Ⓓ Ⓔ
30. Ⓐ Ⓑ Ⓒ Ⓓ Ⓔ
31. ☐
32. Ⓐ Ⓑ Ⓒ Ⓓ Ⓔ

33. Ⓐ Ⓑ Ⓒ Ⓓ Ⓔ Ⓕ Ⓖ
34. Ⓐ Ⓑ Ⓒ Ⓓ Ⓔ
35. ☐
36. Ⓐ Ⓑ Ⓒ Ⓓ Ⓔ
37. Ⓐ Ⓑ Ⓒ Ⓓ Ⓔ
38. Ⓐ Ⓑ Ⓒ Ⓓ Ⓔ
39. ☐
40. ☐

Practice Test 1

Directions: For Question 1, select a single answer choice.

1. How many 6-inch by 6-inch square tiles would be needed to cover a floor 2.5 feet by 2.5 feet?

    (A) 2 tiles

    (B) 2.4 tiles

    (C) 5 tiles

    (D) 17 tiles

    (E) 25 tiles

Directions: For Question 2, solve the problem and indicate the best of the answer choices given.

2. Which must be true, given $a > b, c > d, b > 0, c < 0,$ and $b > d$?

    I. $d < 0$

    II. $cd > 0$

    III. $bc > 0$

    (A) I and II

    (B) I and III

    (C) II only

    (D) III only

    (E) I, II, and III

Directions: For Question 3, enter your answer as an integer or as a decimal if there is a single answer box OR as a fraction if there are two separate boxes—one for the numerator and one for the denominator.

To enter an integer or a decimal, write the number in the answer box provided. On the computer-based test you can either type the number in the answer box using the keyboard or use the Transfer Display button on the calculator. Also, note the following directions for the computer-based test:

- You can click on the answer box and then type the number. You can use the backspace key to erase a number.
- Type a hyphen for a negative sign. Type a hyphen again, and it will disappear. For a decimal point, type a period.
- The Transfer Display button on the calculator will move the calculator display to the answer box.
- Equivalent forms of the correct answer, such as 2.5 and 2.50, are all correct.
- Enter the exact answer unless the question asks you to round your answer.

3. If $7x - y = k$ and $(x,y) = (1,-3)$, then what is y when $x = -4$?

Directions: For Question 4, solve the problem and indicate the best of the answer choices given.

4. Given that x is a negative integer such that $xy > 6$, which of the following must be true?

I. $y \leq 0$

II. $y < 0$

III. $x > \dfrac{6}{y}$

IV. $x < \dfrac{6}{y}$

(A) I, II, and IV
(B) I, III, and IV
(C) II, III, and IV
(D) II and IV
(E) IV only

Questions 5–9 are based on the following data.

PRECIPITATION AMOUNTS IN TWO MAJOR CITIES

OKLAHOMA CITY	
Month	**Average Precipitation**
January	1.10 inches
February	1.60 inches
March	2.70 inches
April	2.80 inches
May	5.20 inches
June	4.30 inches
July	2.60 inches
August	2.60 inches
September	3.80 inches
October	3.20 inches
November	2.00 inches
December	1.40 inches

SEATTLE	
Month	**Average Precipitation**
January	5.13 inches
February	4.18 inches
March	3.75 inches
April	2.59 inches
May	1.78 inches
June	1.49 inches
July	0.79 inches
August	1.02 inches
September	1.63 inches
October	3.19 inches
November	5.90 inches
December	5.62 inches

Directions: For Questions 5–8, select a single answer choice.

5. During how many months did Oklahoma City average more precipitation than Seattle?

   (A) None

   (B) Two

   (C) Three

   (D) Four

   (E) Seven

6. During how many months did Seattle's average precipitation increase over the previous month?

   (A) None

   (B) Two

   (C) Four

   (D) Five

   (E) Ten

7. What month showed the greatest percentage increase in Oklahoma City's average precipitation over the previous month?

   (A) February

   (B) March

   (C) April

   (D) May

   (E) November

8. What is the approximate average of the average precipitation amounts for Seattle?

   (A) 1.14

   (B) 2.23

   (C) 3.09

   (D) 4.10

   (E) 5.20

Directions: For Question 9, enter your answer as an integer or as a decimal if there is a single answer box OR as a fraction if there are two separate boxes—one for the numerator and one for the denominator.

To enter an integer or a decimal, write the number in the answer box provided. On the computer-based test you can either type the number in the answer box using the keyboard or use the Transfer Display button on the calculator. Also, note the following directions for the computer-based test:

- You can click on the answer box and then type the number. You can use the backspace key to erase a number.
- Type a hyphen for a negative sign. Type a hyphen again, and it will disappear. For a decimal point, type a period.
- The Transfer Display button on the calculator will move the calculator display to the answer box.
- Equivalent forms of the correct answer, such as 2.5 and 2.50, are all correct.
- Enter the exact answer unless the question asks you to round your answer.

9. What was the approximate, to the nearest percent, decrease in average precipitation from September to October in Oklahoma City?

Directions: Question 10 consists of a question and two statements, labeled (1) and (2), in which certain data is given. You have to decide whether the data given in the statements is sufficient for answering the question. Using the data given in the statements plus your knowledge of mathematics and everyday facts (such as the number of days in July and the meaning of "counterclockwise"), you must indicate whether

   (A) Statement (1) ALONE is sufficient, but statement (2) is not sufficient.

   (B) Statement (2) ALONE is sufficient, but statement (1) is not sufficient.

   (C) BOTH statements TOGETHER are sufficient, but NEITHER statement ALONE is sufficient.

   (D) EACH statement ALONE is sufficient.

   (E) Statements (1) and (2) TOGETHER are NOT sufficient.

10. X and Y are two points on the x-axis at $(-2,0)$ and $(4,0)$, respectively. Another point, Z, is at an equal distance from both X and Y. Where is point Z?

   (1) Z is above the x-axis.
   (2) Z's y-coordinate is 7.

   (A) Statement (1) ALONE is sufficient, but statement (2) alone is not sufficient.
   (B) Statement (2) ALONE is sufficient, but statement (1) alone is not sufficient.
   (C) BOTH statements TOGETHER are sufficient, but NEITHER statement ALONE is sufficient.
   (D) EACH statement ALONE is sufficient.
   (E) Statements (1) and (2) TOGETHER are NOT sufficient.

Directions: For Questions 11–12, solve the problems and indicate the best of the answer choices given.

11. A trio of students wanted to determine the need for a coffee shop on the west end of campus. They surveyed fifty people. Nineteen of these fifty people declared that a coffee shop on the west end of campus was unnecessary. Five people neglected to answer. The rest were in favor of such a coffee shop. What percent of the students surveyed wanted a coffee shop on the west end of campus?

    (A) 26%
    (B) 38%
    (C) 48%
    (D) 52%
    (E) 95%

12. A receptionist greeted the following numbers of people during one workweek: 4, 19, 21, 18, 23. What is the mean of the number of people she greeted?

    (A) 17
    (B) 19
    (C) 20
    (D) 21
    (E) 85

Directions: Question 13 consists of a question and two statements, labeled (1) and (2), in which certain data is given. You have to decide whether the data given in the statements is sufficient for answering the question. Using the data given in the statements plus your knowledge of mathematics and everyday facts (such as the number of days in July and the meaning of "counterclockwise"), you must indicate whether

    (A) Statement (1) ALONE is sufficient, but statement (2) is not sufficient.
    (B) Statement (2) ALONE is sufficient, but statement (1) is not sufficient.
    (C) BOTH statements TOGETHER are sufficient, but NEITHER statement ALONE is sufficient.
    (D) EACH statement ALONE is sufficient.
    (E) Statements (1) and (2) TOGETHER are NOT sufficient.

13. If $A \geq B$, is B negative?

    (1) $A > 1$
    (2) $AB < 0$

    (A) Statement (1) ALONE is sufficient, but statement (2) alone is not sufficient.
    (B) Statement (2) ALONE is sufficient, but statement (1) alone is not sufficient.
    (C) BOTH statements TOGETHER are sufficient, but NEITHER statement ALONE is sufficient.
    (D) EACH statement ALONE is sufficient.
    (E) Statements (1) and (2) TOGETHER are NOT sufficient.

14. What is $f(-1)$, given $f(x) = -3x^{57} - x^5$?

    (A) −4
    (B) −2
    (C) 0
    (D) 2
    (E) 4

15. Which of the following integers are prime?

    Indicate all such integers.

    (A) 7
    (B) 19
    (C) 23
    (D) 51
    (E) 123
    (F) 124
    (G) 125

16. How many games would a team have to win from now on to have won 80% of the games they played this season? Their current record is five wins, three losses, and two ties. (Assume that the rest of the games they play will be wins.)

    (A) 3
    (B) 5
    (C) 13
    (D) 15
    (E) 25

Directions: For Questions 17–23, compare Quantity A and Quantity B, using additional information centered above the two quantities if such information is given, and select one of the following four answer choices:

(A) Quantity A is greater.

(B) Quantity B is greater.

(C) The two quantities are equal.

(D) The relationship cannot be determined from the information given.

A symbol that appears more than once in a question has the same meaning throughout the question.

17.

Quantity A	Quantity B
$5 - x^2$	$5 - x$

(A) Quantity A is greater.
(B) Quantity B is greater.
(C) The two quantities are equal.
(D) The relationship cannot be determined from the information given.

18.

Quantity A	Quantity B
Number of degrees in each angle of a regular pentagon	Number of degrees in one exterior angle of a regular decagon

(A) Quantity A is greater.
(B) Quantity B is greater.
(C) The two quantities are equal.
(D) The relationship cannot be determined from the information given.

19.

Quantity A	Quantity B
Possible number of ways that five people can line up to get into a movie	Possible number of ways that four people can be picked to serve on a committee out of a group of eight people

(A) Quantity A is greater.
(B) Quantity B is greater.
(C) The two quantities are equal.
(D) The relationship cannot be determined from the information given.

20.

Quantity A	Quantity B
$4x^2 - 16 = 0$	$x^3 = 8$
$x =$	$x =$

(A) Quantity A is greater.
(B) Quantity B is greater.
(C) The two quantities are equal.
(D) The relationship cannot be determined from the information given.

21.   Quantity A   Quantity B

     Third leg of a triangle with sides of 3 and 4   Third leg of a triangle with sides of 12 and 13

   (A) Quantity A is greater.
   (B) Quantity B is greater.
   (C) The two quantities are equal.
   (D) The relationship cannot be determined from the information given.

22.   Quantity A   Quantity B

                       $16 + x$ $(4 - \sqrt{x})^2$

   (A) Quantity A is greater.
   (B) Quantity B is greater.
   (C) The two quantities are equal.
   (D) The relationship cannot be determined from the information given.

                         12 more than twice x is y.

23.   Quantity A   Quantity B

               x when $y = 10$ y when $x = -7$

   (A) Quantity A is greater.
   (B) Quantity B is greater.
   (C) The two quantities are equal.
   (D) The relationship cannot be determined from the information given.

Directions: Question 24 consists of a question and two statements, labeled (1) and (2), in which certain data is given. You have to decide whether the data given in the statements is sufficient for answering the question. Using the data given in the statements plus your knowledge of mathematics and everyday facts (such as the number of days in July and the meaning of "counterclockwise"), you must indicate whether

   (A) Statement (1) ALONE is sufficient, but statement (2) is not sufficient.
   (B) Statement (2) ALONE is sufficient, but statement (1) is not sufficient.
   (C) BOTH statements TOGETHER are sufficient, but NEITHER statement ALONE is sufficient.
   (D) EACH statement ALONE is sufficient.
   (E) Statements (1) and (2) TOGETHER are NOT sufficient.

24. Which is the smaller quantity: x^y or y^x?

   (1) $y = 2$
   (2) $x > y$

   (A) Statement (1) ALONE is sufficient, but statement (2) alone is not sufficient.
   (B) Statement (2) ALONE is sufficient, but statement (1) alone is not sufficient.
   (C) BOTH statements TOGETHER are sufficient, but NEITHER statement ALONE is sufficient.
   (D) EACH statement ALONE is sufficient.
   (E) Statements (1) and (2) TOGETHER are NOT sufficient.

Directions: For Questions 25–26, solve the problems and indicate the best of the answer choices given.

25. Approximately 2.54 cm make an inch. Approximately how many cm make a foot?

 (A) 4.8
 (B) 6
 (C) 24
 (D) 30.5
 (E) 36

26. What is the quotient of 72! and 69!?

 (A) 1.1
 (B) 4
 (C) 4!
 (D) 213
 (E) 357,840

Directions: Question 27 consists of a question and two statements, labeled (1) and (2), in which certain data is given. You have to decide whether the data given in the statements is sufficient for answering the question. Using the data given in the statements plus your knowledge of mathematics and everyday facts (such as the number of days in July and the meaning of "counterclockwise"), you must indicate whether

 (A) Statement (1) ALONE is sufficient, but statement (2) is not sufficient.

 (B) Statement (2) ALONE is sufficient, but statement (1) is not sufficient.

 (C) BOTH statements TOGETHER are sufficient, but NEITHER statement ALONE is sufficient.

 (D) EACH statement ALONE is sufficient.

 (E) Statements (1) and (2) TOGETHER are NOT sufficient.

27. What is the perimeter of rectangle *ABCS*?

 (1) The length of the rectangle is 4 inches longer than the width.
 (2) The area of the rectangle is 45 square inches.

 (A) Statement (1) ALONE is sufficient, but statement (2) alone is not sufficient.
 (B) Statement (2) ALONE is sufficient, but statement (1) alone is not sufficient.
 (C) BOTH statements TOGETHER are sufficient, but NEITHER statement ALONE is sufficient.
 (D) EACH statement ALONE is sufficient.
 (E) Statements (1) and (2) TOGETHER are NOT sufficient.

Directions: For Questions 28–29, solve the problems and indicate the best of the answer choices given.

28. The ratio of mums to roses to tulips in a garden is 4 to 6 to 9. If there are thirty roses in the garden, how many tulips are in the garden?

    (A) 20
    (B) 30
    (C) 38
    (D) 45
    (E) 95

29. If $5x - 2y = -12$ and $-10x + y = -3$, what does x equal?

    (A) $\dfrac{-6}{5}$

    (B) $\dfrac{-5}{6}$

    (C) $\dfrac{5}{6}$

    (D) $\dfrac{6}{5}$

    (E) 9

Directions: Question 30 consists of a question and two statements, labeled (1) and (2), in which certain data is given. You have to decide whether the data given in the statements is sufficient for answering the question. Using the data given in the statements plus your knowledge of mathematics and everyday facts (such as the number of days in July and the meaning of "counterclockwise"), you must indicate whether

   (A) Statement (1) ALONE is sufficient, but statement (2) is not sufficient.
   (B) Statement (2) ALONE is sufficient, but statement (1) is not sufficient.
   (C) BOTH statements TOGETHER are sufficient, but NEITHER statement ALONE is sufficient.
   (D) EACH statement ALONE is sufficient.
   (E) Statements (1) and (2) TOGETHER are NOT sufficient.

30. What is the next consecutive integer greater than n?

   (1) Let n be the positive even integer formed by multiplying the smallest positive even integer by the next positive integer larger than the smallest positive even integer.
   (2) Let n be the product of the smallest positive integer and the only even prime number.

   (A) Statement (1) ALONE is sufficient, but statement (2) alone is not sufficient.
   (B) Statement (2) ALONE is sufficient, but statement (1) alone is not sufficient.
   (C) BOTH statements TOGETHER are sufficient, but NEITHER statement ALONE is sufficient.
   (D) EACH statement ALONE is sufficient.
   (E) Statements (1) and (2) TOGETHER are NOT sufficient.

Directions: For Question 31, enter your answer as an integer or as a decimal if there is a single answer box OR as a fraction if there are two separate boxes—one for the numerator and one for the denominator.

To enter an integer or a decimal, write the number in the answer box provided. On the computer-based test you can either type the number in the answer box using the keyboard or use the Transfer Display button on the calculator. Also, note the following directions for the computer-based test:

- You can click on the answer box and then type the number. You can use the backspace key to erase a number.
- Type a hyphen for a negative sign. Type a hyphen again, and it will disappear. For a decimal point, type a period.
- The Transfer Display button on the calculator will move the calculator display to the answer box.
- Equivalent forms of the correct answer, such as 2.5 and 2.50, are all correct.
- Enter the exact answer unless the question asks you to round your answer.

31. The number of square feet in a rectangle's area is 11 more than the number of feet in its perimeter. If the length measures 2 feet more than its width, what is the area of this rectangle, in square feet?

    ☐ square feet

Directions: For Question 32, solve the problem and indicate the best of the answer choices given.

32. What is the product of the solutions to $x^2 - 2x = 3$?
    - **(A)** -4
    - **(B)** -3
    - **(C)** -2
    - **(D)** 1
    - **(E)** 2

Directions: For Question 33, select one or more answer choices according to the specific question directions. If the question does not specify how many answer choices to select, select all that apply.

- The correct answer may be just one of the choices or may be as many as all of the choices, depending on the question.
- No credit is given unless you select all of the correct choices and no others.
- If the question specifies how many answer choices to select, select exactly that number of choices.

33. Which three of the following numbers are the product of two distinct prime numbers?
    - **(A)** 6
    - **(B)** 11
    - **(C)** 21
    - **(D)** 35
    - **(E)** 49
    - **(F)** 50
    - **(G)** 56

Directions: For Question 34, solve the problem and indicate the best of the answer choices given.

34. How many degrees is an inscribed angle intercepting a semicircle?

(A) 0°

(B) 45°

(C) 90°

(D) 180°

(E) 360°

Directions: For Question 35, enter your answer as an integer or as a decimal if there is a single answer box OR as a fraction if there are two separate boxes—one for the numerator and one for the denominator.

To enter an integer or a decimal, write the number in the answer box provided. On the computer-based test you can either type the number in the answer box using the keyboard or use the Transfer Display button on the calculator. Also, note the following directions for the computer-based test:

- You can click on the answer box and then type the number. You can use the backspace key to erase a number.
- Type a hyphen for a negative sign. Type a hyphen again, and it will disappear. For a decimal point, type a period.
- The Transfer Display button on the calculator will move the calculator display to the answer box.
- Equivalent forms of the correct answer, such as 2.5 and 2.50, are all correct.
- Enter the exact answer unless the question asks you to round your answer.

35. An apprentice completes a job in ten hours. Her mentor can complete the job in six hours. How many hours does it take them to complete the job when working together?

[ ] hours

Directions: Question 36 consists of a question and two statements, labeled (1) and (2), in which certain data is given. You have to decide whether the data given in the statements is sufficient for answering the question. Using the data given in the statements plus your knowledge of mathematics and everyday facts (such as the number of days in July, and the meaning of "counterclockwise"), you must indicate whether

(A) Statement (1) ALONE is sufficient, but statement (2) is not sufficient.

(B) Statement (2) ALONE is sufficient, but statement (1) is not sufficient.

(C) BOTH statements TOGETHER are sufficient, but NEITHER statement ALONE is sufficient.

(D) EACH statement ALONE is sufficient.

(E) Statements (1) and (2) TOGETHER are NOT sufficient.

36. Let AB be a two-digit number, with a unit's digit of B and a ten's digit of A. Also, let $AB = -1$ be an odd number and AB be divisible by 3. Is AB divisible by 4?

 (1) B is divisible by 10.
 (2) A is divisible by 9.

 (A) Statement (1) ALONE is sufficient, but statement (2) alone is not sufficient.
 (B) Statement (2) ALONE is sufficient, but statement (1) alone is not sufficient.
 (C) BOTH statements TOGETHER are sufficient, but NEITHER statement ALONE is sufficient.
 (D) EACH statement ALONE is sufficient.
 (E) Statements (1) and (2) TOGETHER are NOT sufficient.

Directions: For Question 37, select a single answer choice.

37. What is the probability that a letter chosen randomly from the word *ONOMATOPOEIA* is an O?

 (A) $\dfrac{1}{12}$

 (B) $\dfrac{1}{3}$

 (C) $\dfrac{1}{2}$

 (D) $\dfrac{2}{3}$

 (E) 4

Directions: For Question 38, solve the problem and indicate the best of the answer choices given.

38. What is the area of a square inscribed in a circle with a radius of 10 cm?
    (A) 25 cm²
    (B) 25π cm²
    (C) 50 cm²
    (D) 100 cm²
    (E) 200 cm²

Directions: For Questions 39–40, enter your answer as an integer or as a decimal if there is a single answer box OR as a fraction if there are two separate boxes—one for the numerator and one for the denominator.

To enter an integer or a decimal, write the number in the answer box provided. On the computer-based test you can either type the number in the answer box using the keyboard or use the Transfer Display button on the calculator. Also, note the following directions for the computer-based test:

- You can click on the answer box and then type the number. You can use the backspace key to erase a number.
- Type a hyphen for a negative sign. Type a hyphen again, and it will disappear. For a decimal point, type a period.
- The Transfer Display button on the calculator will move the calculator display to the answer box.
- Equivalent forms of the correct answer, such as 2.5 and 2.50, are all correct.
- Enter the exact answer unless the question asks you to round your answer.

Questions 39–40 are based on the following trapezoid.

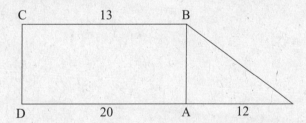

39. The rectangle and right triangle share a side. The base of the rectangle measures 20 cm, while the base of the right triangle measures 12 cm. If the hypotenuse of the right triangle measures 13 cm, how long is the perimeter of ABCD?

 cm

40. What is the area of trapezoid ABCD (combined rectangle and right triangle)?

ANSWER KEY AND EXPLANATIONS

1. E	9. 15.79%	17. D	25. D	33. A, C, D
2. A	10. B	18. A	26. E	34. C
3. −38	11. D	19. A	27. C	35. 3.75
4. D	12. A	20. D	28. D	36. C
5. E	13. C	21. D	29. D	37. B
6. C	14. E	22. A	30. D	38. E
7. D	15. A, B, C	23. A	31. 35	39. 70
8. C	16. D	24. E	32. B	40. 130

1. **The correct answer is (E).**

$$2\frac{1}{2} \text{ feet} = 30 \text{ inches}$$

Floor area = 30 inches by 30 inches = 900 square inches

Tile area = 6 inches by 6 inches = 36 square inches

$$\frac{\text{Floor area}}{\text{Tile area}} = \frac{900}{36} = 25 \text{ tiles}$$

2. **The correct answer is (A).** $a > b > 0 > c > d$. Option I is true. Since c and d are both negative, cd is positive. Hence option II is true. b is positive, and c is negative. So, bc is negative, and choice (D) is incorrect. Since both options I and II are correct the answer is choice (A).

3. **The correct answer is −38.**

$$7x - y = k$$
$$7(1) - (-3) = k$$
$$7 + 3 = k = 10$$
$$7x - y = 10$$
$$7(-4) - y = 10$$
$$-28 - y = 10$$
$$-28 - 10 = y$$
$$-38 = y$$

4. **The correct answer is (D).** Since $xy > 6$, either x or y are both negative or they are both positive. Because x is negative, y is also negative. So, option I is false, and option II is true. Hence, the correct answer is either choice (C) or choice (D). Dividing both sides of $xy > 6$ by y, which is negative, results in $x < \frac{6}{y}$, since dividing by a negative require that the sign be flipped. Therefore, option III is false, and option IV is true. Since options II and IV are true, the correct answer is choice (D).

5. **The correct answer is (E).** Oklahoma City received more precipitation in seven months: April, May, June, July, August, September, and October.

6. **The correct answer is (C).** Seattle's average precipitation increased over the previous month in August, September, October, and November.

7. **The correct answer is (D).** Percentage increase is found by taking the amount of increase divided by the original amount. Comparing those quantities, May is the largest.

OKLAHOMA CITY		
Month	Average Precipitation	Percent Increase Over Previous Month
January	1.10 inches	
February	1.60 inches	45.45
March	2.70 inches	68.75
April	2.80 inches	3.70
May	5.20 inches	85.71
June	4.30 inches	−17.31
July	2.60 inches	−39.53
August	2.60 inches	0.00
September	3.80 inches	46.15
October	3.20 inches	−15.79
November	2.00 inches	−37.50
December	1.40 inches	−30.00

8. **The correct answer is (C).** The approximate sum of the precipitation amounts is 38. Dividing this by 12 months gives a bit more than 3.

9. **The correct answer is 18.75.** The change was from 3.80 to 3.20. So, the percent change is:

$$\frac{\text{Percent}}{100} = \frac{\text{Amount of change}}{\text{Original amount}}$$

$$\frac{p}{100} = \frac{3.80 - 3.20}{3.20}$$

$$\frac{p}{100} = \frac{0.6}{3.8}$$

$$3.8p = 60$$

$$p = \frac{60}{3.8} = \frac{6000}{328} = \frac{600}{38} = \frac{300}{19} \approx 15.79\%$$

10. **The correct answer is (B).** Knowing that the point Z is equidistant from both X and Y leads to an x-coordinate of 1. This, along with a y-coordinate of 7, indicates the point (1,7).

11. **The correct answer is (D).** Twenty-six people were in favor of this coffee shop. This is 26 out of 50, which is 52 out of 100, which is 52 percent.

12. **The correct answer is (A).** The mean is the average. The sum of the numbers is eighty-five. There are five data points. Dividing the sum by the number of data points results in seventeen.

13. **The correct answer is (C).** Knowing that A is positive from statement (1) and that the product is negative from statement (2) leads us to know that B would have to be negative.

14. **The correct answer is (E).** Just do the work: $f(-1) = -3(-1)^{57} - (-1)^5 = -3(-1) - (-1) = 3 + 1 = 4$.

15. **The correct answers are (A), (B), and (C).** Prime numbers have only two factors: 1 and the number itself. Both 51 and 123 are divisible by 3. 124 is divisible by 2. 125 is divisible by 5.

16. **The correct answer is (D).**

$$\frac{Percent}{100} = \frac{Part}{Whole}$$

$$\frac{80}{100} = \frac{5+x}{10+x}$$

$$80(10+x) = 100(5+x)$$

$$800 + 80x = 500 + 100x$$

$$300 = 20x$$

$$15 = x$$

17. **The correct answer is (D).** A good approach on quantitative comparison exercises is to consider if the two quantities could ever be equal. If x were 0 or 1 on this one, the two quantities would be equal. Otherwise, the two quantities are not equal.

18. **The correct answer is (A).** The number of degrees in an angle of a pentagon of s sides is found by the following:

$\frac{180(s-2)}{s}$. So, each angle of a regular pentagon has $\frac{180(5-2)}{5} = \frac{180(3)}{5} = \frac{540}{5} = 108$ degrees. Any polygon's exterior angles total $360°$. Each exterior angle of a regular decagon measures $\frac{360}{10} = 36$ degrees. Quantity A is bigger.

19. **The correct answer is (A).** Quantity A: $5 \times 4 \times 3 \times 2 \times 1 = 120$; Quantity B: $\frac{8 \times 7 \times 6 \times 5}{4 \times 3 \times 2 \times 1} = 70$. As you can see, Quantity A is greater.

20. **The correct answer is (D).** The x in Quantity A could be either ± 2; the x in Quantity B is 2.

21. **The correct answer is (D).** The third leg in Quantity A must be greater than 1 and less than 7. (The sum of the lengths of a triangle must be greater than the length of the third leg.) The third leg in Quantity B must be greater than 1 and less than 25. Hence, the correct answer is choice (D).

22. **The correct answer is (A).** A good approach on quantitative comparison exercises is to consider if the two quantities could ever be equal.

$$16 + x = (4 - \sqrt{x})^2$$
$$16 + x = 16 - 8\sqrt{x} + x$$
$$x = -8\sqrt{x} + x$$

Since x is on both sides, we know the equations are not equal. $-8\sqrt{x}$ is going to cause Quantity B to be less than Quantity A. So, the correct answer is choice (A).

23. The correct answer is (A). The equation "12 more than twice x is y" translates to $12 + 2x = y$.

Quantity A: $\quad 12 + 2x = y$

$\qquad\qquad 12 + 2x = 10$

$\qquad\qquad\qquad 2x = -2$

$\qquad\qquad\qquad\quad x = -1$

Quantity B: $\quad 12 + 2x = y$

$\qquad\qquad 12 + 2(-7) = y$

$\qquad\qquad\quad 12 - 14 = y$

$\qquad\qquad\qquad\quad -2 = y$

Because -1 is greater than -2, choice (A) is correct.

24. The correct answer is (E). Statement (1) would give us x^2 or $2x$. If x were equal to 2, the quantities would be equal. Otherwise, they would not be equal. That statement does not give us a definitive answer. Statement (2) does not give us a definitive answer:

$3^2 > 2^3$
$\quad$ but
$4^3 < 3^4$

What if both statements (1) and (2) are used?

$x^2 ? 2^x$
$3^2 > 2^3$
$4^2 = 2^4$

Both statements together do not give us enough information, and so the correct answer is choice (E).

25. The correct answer is (D).

$$\frac{1 \text{ ft.}}{1} \times \frac{12 \text{ in.}}{1 \text{ ft.}} \times \frac{2.54 \text{ cm}}{1 \text{ in.}} = (12 \times 2.54) \text{ cm} = 30.48 \text{ cm}$$

26. The correct answer is (E).

$$\frac{72!}{69!} = \frac{72 \times 71 \times 70 \times 69!}{69!} = 72 \times 71 \times 70 = ?$$

You don't need to do any calculations, if you think about this. The only reasonable answer is choice (E).

27. The correct answer is (C).

$$l = 4 + w$$
$$A = l \times w = (4 + w) \times w = 45$$

That would provide a solution for w. A simple substitution would provide the solution for l. The perimeter could be found by adding up the four sides of the rectangle: two widths plus two lengths. Remember that you do not need to find the perimeter; you just need to know if you could find the perimeter!

28. The correct answer is (D).

Flowers	Mums	Roses	Tulips	Total
Ratio	4	6	9	19
Times		5	5	
Actual		30	45	

This chart organizes the information. Since we know how many roses are in the garden and want the number of tulips, those are the only sections we complete.

29. The correct answer is (D).

$$5x - 2y = -12$$
$$-10x + y = -3$$

In order to solve this system, let's multiply the bottom equation by 2, so that the y's will cancel when we add the two equations.

$$5x - 2y = -12$$
$$-20x + 2y = -6$$

$$-15x = -18$$
$$x = \frac{-18}{-15} = \frac{6}{5}$$

30. The correct answer is (D). Statement (1) alone works. So, the correct answer is either choice (A) or choice (D). Statement (2) alone would also work. Hence, the correct answer is choice (D).

31. The correct answer is 35 square feet.

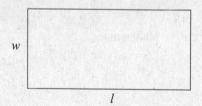

$$A = 11 + P$$
$$A = lw$$
$$P = 2l + 2w$$
$$lw = 11 + 2l + 2w$$
$$l = 2 + w$$
$$(2 + w)w = 11 + 2(2 + w) + 2w$$
$$2w + w^2 = 11 + 4 + 2w + 2w$$
$$2w + w^2 = 15 + 4w$$
$$w^2 - 2w - 15 = 0$$
$$(w - 5)(w + 3) = 0$$
$$w = 5 \qquad w = -3$$

A negative width makes no sense, so the width is 5 feet. The length is 7 feet, and the area is 35 square feet.

32. The correct answer is (B).

$$x^2 - 2x = 3$$
$$x^2 - 2x - 3 = 0$$
$$(x+1)(x-3) = 0$$
$$x = -1. \qquad x = 3$$

The product of the solutions is $(-1)(3) = -3$.

33. The correct answers are (A), (C), and (D).

$$6 = (2)(3)$$
$$21 = (3)(7)$$
$$35 = (5)(7)$$

34. The correct answer is (C). The number of degrees in an inscribed angle in a circle measures half of its intercepted arc. A semicircle contains $180°$. Taking half of $180°$ gives $90°$.

35. The correct answer is 3.75 hours.

Worker	Rate	Time	Fraction of Job Completed
Apprentice	1/10	t	t/10
Mentor	1/6	t	t/6
			1

$$\frac{t}{10} + \frac{t}{6} = 1$$

Multiply by 30.

$$3t + 5t = 30$$

$$8t = 30$$

$$t = \frac{30}{8} = \frac{15}{4} = 3.75 \text{ hours}$$

36. The correct answer is (C). If $AB - 1$ is odd, then AB is even. That means that B must be an even digit. If AB is divisible by 3, the sum of the digits is divisible by 3: $A + B$ is divisible by 3. Statement (1) indicates that B is 0 in order for AB to be divisible by 10. A could be 3, 6, or 9 in order for the sum of the digits of AB to be divisible by 3. Some of those two-digit numbers, 30 and 90, are not divisible by 4. The other one, 60, is divisible by 4. Statement (1) alone does not provide enough information. Statement (2) indicates that AB is a number between 90 and 99. Some of those are divisible by 4; some are not. Together, the only possibility would be 90. That would give us the answer! Therefore, it takes statement (1) and statement (2) together to determine the answer.

37. The correct answer is (B). Four of the twelve letters in the word are the letter O. So, the probability that an O is chosen is $\frac{4}{12} = \frac{1}{3}$.

38. The correct answer is (E).

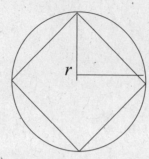

The radius of the circle is 10 cm. The right triangle formed by the two radii as legs has a hypotenuse of $10\sqrt{2}$ cm. That hypotenuse is the length of the side of the square. The area of a square is the side squared. Hence, the area of the square is $(10\sqrt{2})^2 = 10^2(\sqrt{2})^2 = 100(2) = 200$ cm^2.

39. The correct answer is 70. By the Pythagorean theorem, the height of the right triangle is 5:

$a^2 + b^2 = c^2 \rightarrow a^2 + 12^2 = 13^2 \rightarrow a^2 + 144 = 169 \rightarrow a^2 = 25 \rightarrow a = \pm5$. Of course, the length of a side of a triangle would be a positive number. The perimeter of the shape is found by summing all of the sides:

20 + 12 + 13 + 20 + 5 = 70 cm.

40. The correct answer is 130. The area of the figure will be the area of the rectangle plus the area of the right triangle.

Area of rectangle + area of right triangle

$$(\text{base})(\text{height}) + (\frac{1}{2})(\text{base})(\text{height})$$

$$(20)(5) + (\frac{1}{2})(12)(5)$$

$$100 + 30 = 130$$

PRACTICE TEST 2 ANSWER SHEET

1. Ⓐ Ⓑ Ⓒ Ⓓ Ⓔ
2. Ⓐ Ⓑ Ⓒ Ⓓ Ⓔ
3. Ⓐ Ⓑ Ⓒ Ⓓ Ⓔ
4. Ⓐ Ⓑ Ⓒ Ⓓ
5. Ⓐ Ⓑ Ⓒ Ⓓ
6. Ⓐ Ⓑ Ⓒ Ⓓ
7. Ⓐ Ⓑ Ⓒ Ⓓ
8. Ⓐ Ⓑ Ⓒ Ⓓ

9. Ⓐ Ⓑ Ⓒ Ⓓ Ⓔ
10. Ⓐ Ⓑ Ⓒ Ⓓ Ⓔ
11. Ⓐ Ⓑ Ⓒ Ⓓ Ⓔ
12. Ⓐ Ⓑ Ⓒ Ⓓ Ⓔ
13. Ⓐ Ⓑ Ⓒ Ⓓ Ⓔ
14. Ⓐ Ⓑ Ⓒ Ⓓ Ⓔ
15. Ⓐ Ⓑ Ⓒ Ⓓ Ⓔ
16. ☐

17. Ⓐ Ⓑ Ⓒ Ⓓ Ⓔ
18. Ⓐ Ⓑ Ⓒ Ⓓ Ⓔ
19. Ⓐ Ⓑ Ⓒ Ⓓ Ⓔ
20. ☐
21. Ⓐ Ⓑ Ⓒ Ⓓ Ⓔ
22. Ⓐ Ⓑ Ⓒ Ⓓ
23. Ⓐ Ⓑ Ⓒ Ⓓ
24. Ⓐ Ⓑ Ⓒ Ⓓ

25. Ⓐ Ⓑ Ⓒ Ⓓ
26. Ⓐ Ⓑ Ⓒ Ⓓ Ⓔ
27. Ⓐ Ⓑ Ⓒ Ⓓ Ⓔ
28. Ⓐ Ⓑ Ⓒ Ⓓ Ⓔ
29. Ⓐ Ⓑ Ⓒ Ⓓ Ⓔ
30. Ⓐ Ⓑ Ⓒ Ⓓ Ⓔ
31. ☐
☐

32. Ⓐ Ⓑ Ⓒ Ⓓ Ⓔ
33. Ⓐ Ⓑ Ⓒ Ⓓ Ⓔ
34. Ⓐ Ⓑ Ⓒ Ⓓ Ⓔ
35. Ⓐ Ⓑ Ⓒ Ⓓ Ⓔ
36. Ⓐ Ⓑ Ⓒ Ⓓ Ⓔ
37. ☐
38. Ⓐ Ⓑ Ⓒ Ⓓ Ⓔ
39. Ⓐ Ⓑ Ⓒ Ⓓ Ⓔ
40. Ⓐ Ⓑ Ⓒ Ⓓ Ⓔ

Practice Test 2

Directions: For Question 1, solve the problem and indicate the best of the answer choices given.

1. Given $x = (-2)^3 - (-1)$, which of the following has the largest value?

   (A) x

   (B) x^2

   (C) x^3

   (D) $\dfrac{1}{x}$

   (E) $\dfrac{1}{x^2}$

Directions: For Question 2, select a single answer choice.

2. How much material is required to make a cube that has an edge of length 9 cm?

   (A) 27 square centimeters

   (B) 27 cubic centimeters

   (C) 243 cubic centimeters

   (D) 486 square centimeters

   (E) 729 cubic centimeters

Directions: Question 3 consists of a question and two statements, labeled (1) and (2), in which certain data is given. You have to decide whether the data given in the statements is sufficient for answering the question. Using the data given in the statements plus your knowledge of mathematics and everyday facts (such as the number of days in July and the meaning of "counterclockwise"), you must indicate whether

(A) Statement (1) ALONE is sufficient, but statement (2) is not sufficient.

(B) Statement (2) ALONE is sufficient, but statement (1) is not sufficient.

(C) BOTH statements TOGETHER are sufficient, but NEITHER statement ALONE is sufficient.

(D) EACH statement ALONE is sufficient.

(E) Statements (1) and (2) TOGETHER are NOT sufficient.

3. Is this answer positive or negative: $x^3y + xy$?

   (1) $x < 0$
   (2) $xy > 0$

   (A) Statement (1) ALONE is sufficient, but statement (2) alone is not sufficient.
   (B) Statement (2) ALONE is sufficient, but statement (1) alone is not sufficient.
   (C) BOTH statements TOGETHER are sufficient, but NEITHER statement ALONE is sufficient.
   (D) EACH statement ALONE is sufficient.
   (E) Statements (1) and (2) TOGETHER are NOT sufficient.

Directions: For Questions 4–8, compare Quantity A and Quantity B, using additional information centered above the two quantities if such information is given, and select one of the following four answer choices:

    (A) Quantity A is greater.

    (B) Quantity B is greater.

    (C) The two quantities are equal.

    (D) The relationship cannot be determined from the information given.

A symbol that appears more than once in a question has the same meaning throughout the question.

4.

Quantity A	Quantity B
15% of 19% of 20	38% of 75% of 2

    (A) Quantity A is greater.

    (B) Quantity B is greater.

    (C) The two quantities are equal.

    (D) The relationship cannot be determined from the information given.

5.

Quantity A	Quantity B
25 ounces	Number of ounces in $1\frac{1}{2}$ pounds

    (A) Quantity A is greater.

    (B) Quantity B is greater.

    (C) The two quantities are equal.

    (D) The relationship cannot be determined from the information given.

Questions 6–8 are based on the following data.

Scores on recent test: 59%, 81%, 15%, 100%, 68%, 90%, 81%

6.

Quantity A	Quantity B
Median test score	Mode test score

    (A) Quantity A is greater.

    (B) Quantity B is greater.

    (C) The two quantities are equal.

    (D) The relationship cannot be determined from the information given.

7.

Quantity A	Quantity B
Range of test scores	Mean test score

    (A) Quantity A is greater.

    (B) Quantity B is greater.

    (C) The two quantities are equal.

    (D) The relationship cannot be determined from the information given.

8.

Quantity A	Quantity B
Difference between median and mode	Twice lowest score

(A) Quantity A is greater.

(B) Quantity B is greater.

(C) The two quantities are equal.

(D) The relationship cannot be determined from the information given.

Directions: For Questions 9–10, solve the problems and indicate the best of the answer choices given.

9. Claudette bought a new parka for $215. If she had waited one week, she would have saved $25.80 on it. What percent discount would she have received?

   (A) 1.2%

   (B) 8.3%

   (C) 12%

   (D) 83%

   (E) 88%

10. Completely factor: $4x^2 - 28x + 24$.

    (A) $4(x^2 - 7x + 6)$

    (B) $4(x - 1)(x + 7)$

    (C) $4(x - 7)(x + 1)$

    (D) $4(x + 1)(x + 6)$

    (E) $4(x - 6)(x - 1)$

Directions: Question 11 consists of a question and two statements, labeled (1) and (2), in which certain data is given. You have to decide whether the data given in the statements is sufficient for answering the question. Using the data given in the statements plus your knowledge of mathematics and everyday facts (such as the number of days in July and the meaning of "counterclockwise"), you must indicate whether

(A) Statement (1) ALONE is sufficient, but statement (2) is not sufficient.

(B) Statement (2) ALONE is sufficient, but statement (1) is not sufficient.

(C) BOTH statements TOGETHER are sufficient, but NEITHER statement ALONE is sufficient.

(D) EACH statement ALONE is sufficient.

(E) Statements (1) and (2) TOGETHER are NOT sufficient.

11. Daphne and Clem had a lovely dinner. How much did they pay, including tip, for their scrumptious feast?

(1) Daphne's meal cost $3.25 less than Clem's.
(2) They paid a tip of $12.50, which was 15% of their meal cost.

(A) Statement (1) ALONE is sufficient, but statement (2) alone is not sufficient.

(B) Statement (2) ALONE is sufficient, but statement (1) alone is not sufficient.

(C) BOTH statements TOGETHER are sufficient, but NEITHER statement ALONE is sufficient.

(D) EACH statement ALONE is sufficient.

(E) Statements (1) and (2) TOGETHER are NOT sufficient.

Directions: For Questions 12–13, select a single answer choice.

12. A recipe calls for one part cornstarch, three parts butter, two parts oil, and four parts sugar. If two batches require one cup of sugar, how much cornstarch should be used for one batch?

(A) $\frac{1}{8}$ cup

(B) $\frac{1}{4}$ cup

(C) 1 cup

(D) 2 cups

(E) 8 cups

13. Which of the following is a possible length of the third side of a triangle with sides of lengths 4 and 8?

(A) 2

(B) 3

(C) 4

(D) 7

(E) 14

Directions: For Question 14, solve the problem and indicate the best of the answer choices given.

14. Martina can paint a room in 6 hours. It takes Jasmine 9 hours to paint the same room. How long would it take them, if they worked together?

   (A) 1 hour
   (B) 3.6 hours
   (C) 4.5 hours
   (D) 5.5 hours
   (E) 11 hours

Directions: Question 15 consists of a question and two statements, labeled (1) and (2), in which certain data is given. You have to decide whether the data given in the statements is sufficient for answering the question. Using the data given in the statements plus your knowledge of mathematics and everyday facts (such as the number of days in July and the meaning of "counterclockwise"), you must indicate whether

   (A) Statement (1) ALONE is sufficient, but statement (2) is not sufficient.
   (B) Statement (2) ALONE is sufficient, but statement (1) is not sufficient.
   (C) BOTH statements TOGETHER are sufficient, but NEITHER statement ALONE is sufficient.
   (D) EACH statement ALONE is sufficient.
   (E) Statements (1) and (2) TOGETHER are NOT sufficient.

15. What is x?

   (1) $x^2 - 4 = -3x$
   (2) $x < 0$

   (A) Statement (1) ALONE is sufficient, but statement (2) alone is not sufficient.
   (B) Statement (2) ALONE is sufficient, but statement (1) alone is not sufficient.
   (C) BOTH statements TOGETHER are sufficient, but NEITHER statement ALONE is sufficient.
   (D) EACH statement ALONE is sufficient.
   (E) Statements (1) and (2) TOGETHER are NOT sufficient.

Directions: For Question 16, enter your answer as an integer or as a decimal if there is a single answer box OR as a fraction if there are two separate boxes—one for the numerator and one for the denominator.

To enter an integer or a decimal, write the number in the answer box provided. On the computer-based test you can either type the number in the answer box using the keyboard or use the Transfer Display button on the calculator. Also, note the following directions for the computer-based test:

- You can click on the answer box and then type the number. You can use the backspace key to erase a number.
- Type a hyphen for a negative sign. Type a hyphen again, and it will disappear. For a decimal point, type a period.
- The Transfer Display button on the calculator will move the calculator display to the answer box.
- Equivalent forms of the correct answer, such as 2.5 and 2.50, are all correct.
- Enter the exact answer unless the question asks you to round your answer.

16. Dusty's timecard follows. Dusty makes $7.60 per hour on weekdays, Monday through Friday. If he earns time and a half on the weekend, how much will he earn for his weekend hours for the week indicated on this timecard?

Day	Hour(s) of Work
Monday	7.5
Tuesday	6
Wednesday	10.25
Thursday	8.75
Friday	0
Saturday	1.5
Sunday	4.25

$

Directions: For Questions 17–18, solve the problems and indicate the best of the answer choices given.

17. Sydney travels at 55 miles per hour to get to her vacation getaway. Taking a much more scenic route, which happens to be the same number of miles, it takes her 10 hours to get there. If she travels 22 miles per hour slower on the scenic route, how many miles does she travel to get to her vacation getaway?

    (A) 14
    (B) 33
    (C) 330
    (D) 550
    (E) 770

18. $\dfrac{8^3 2^7 4^6}{4^{10}} =$

 (A) 2^{-6}

 (B) 2^6

 (C) 2^8

 (D) 4^9

 (E) 16^3

Directions: Question 19 consist of a question and two statements, labeled (1) and (2), in which certain data is given. You have to decide whether the data given in the statements is sufficient for answering the question. Using the data given in the statements plus your knowledge of mathematics and everyday facts (such as the number of days in July and the meaning of "counterclockwise"), you must indicate whether

 (A) Statement (1) ALONE is sufficient, but statement (2) is not sufficient.

 (B) Statement (2) ALONE is sufficient, but statement (1) is not sufficient.

 (C) BOTH statements TOGETHER are sufficient, but NEITHER statement ALONE is sufficient.

 (D) EACH statement ALONE is sufficient.

 (E) Statements (1) and (2) TOGETHER are NOT sufficient.

19. Is $x < 0$?

 (1) $x^4 \geq 0$

 (2) $\dfrac{x^3}{x} > 0$

 (A) Statement (1) ALONE is sufficient, but statement (2) alone is not sufficient.

 (B) Statement (2) ALONE is sufficient, but statement (1) alone is not sufficient.

 (C) BOTH statements TOGETHER are sufficient, but NEITHER statement ALONE is sufficient.

 (D) EACH statement ALONE is sufficient.

 (E) Statements (1) and (2) TOGETHER are NOT sufficient.

Directions: For Question 20, enter your answer as an integer or as a decimal if there is a single answer box OR as a fraction if there are two separate boxes—one for the numerator and one for the denominator.

To enter an integer or a decimal, write the number in the answer box provided. On the computer-based test you can either type the number in the answer box using the keyboard or use the Transfer Display button on the calculator. Also, note the following directions for the computer-based test:

- You can click on the answer box and then type the number. You can use the backspace key to erase a number.

- Type a hyphen for a negative sign. Type a hyphen again, and it will disappear. For a decimal point, type a period.

- The Transfer Display button on the calculator will move the calculator display to the answer box.

- Equivalent forms of the correct answer, such as 2.5 and 2.50, are all correct.

- Enter the exact answer unless the question asks you to round your answer.

20. How many ways can three officers, (president, vice president, and treasurer), be chosen from a group of five people?

$$\boxed{}$$

Directions: For Question 21, solve the problem and indicate the best of the answer choices given.

21. $\dfrac{2(3-2^3)-3(5-7)}{(3-5)^2(4-5)} =$

(A) $\dfrac{-23}{2}$

(B) -1

(C) 0

(D) 1

(E) 2

$$x2 - 4x = 21$$

22.

Quantity A	Quantity B
Larger x minus smaller x	4

(A) Quantity A is greater.

(B) Quantity B is greater.

(C) The two quantities are equal.

(D) The relationship cannot be determined from the information given.

Questions 23–25 are based on the following data.

An urn contains 7 green and 5 red marbles.

23.

Quantity A	Quantity B
Probability of choosing a red marble from the urn	Probability of choosing a green marble from the urn

(A) Quantity A is greater.

(B) Quantity B is greater.

(C) The two quantities are equal.

(D) The relationship cannot be determined from the information given.

24.

Quantity A	Quantity B
Probability of choosing a green marble followed by a red marble from the urn, without replacement	Probability of choosing a green marble followed by another green marble from the urn, without replacement

(A) Quantity A is greater.

(B) Quantity B is greater.

(C) The two quantities are equal.

(D) The relationship cannot be determined from the information given.

25.

Quantity A	Quantity B
Probability of choosing a red marble followed by another red marble from the urn, without replacement	Probability of choosing consecutively two marbles of the same color from the urn, without replacement

(A) Quantity A is greater.

(B) Quantity B is greater.

(C) The two quantities are equal.

(D) The relationship cannot be determined from the information given.

Directions: For Questions 26–27, solve the problems and indicate the best of the answer choices given.

26. How many prime numbers are between, but not including, 21 and 45?

(A) 2

(B) 4

(C) 6

(D) 7

(E) 9

27. If n is the largest two-digit prime number, which of the following is the correct representation of the next odd integer larger than n?

(A) $n+1$

(B) $n+2$

(C) $2n-1$

(D) $2n+1$

(E) $3n-1$

Directions: Question 28 consists of a question and two statements, labeled (1) and (2), in which certain data is given. You have to decide whether the data given in the statements is sufficient for answering the question. Using the data given in the statements plus your knowledge of mathematics and everyday facts (such as the number of days in July and the meaning of "counterclockwise"), you must indicate whether

(A) Statement (1) ALONE is sufficient, but statement (2) is not sufficient.

(B) Statement (2) ALONE is sufficient, but statement (1) is not sufficient.

(C) BOTH statements TOGETHER are sufficient, but NEITHER statement ALONE is sufficient.

(D) EACH statement ALONE is sufficient.

(E) Statements (1) and (2) TOGETHER are NOT sufficient.

28. Is $x > y$?

(1) $x^4 \geq y^2$
(2) $y > 0$

(A) Statement (1) ALONE is sufficient, but statement (2) alone is not sufficient.
(B) Statement (2) ALONE is sufficient, but statement (1) alone is not sufficient.
(C) BOTH statements TOGETHER are sufficient, but NEITHER statement ALONE is sufficient.
(D) EACH statement ALONE is sufficient.
(E) Statements (1) and (2) TOGETHER are NOT sufficient.

Directions: For Questions 29–30, select a single answer choice.

29. A triangle contains angles such that the largest angle is four times the smallest angle and the smallest angle is six degrees less than the medium-sized angle. How large is the medium-sized angle?
(A) 29°
(B) 31°
(C) 35°
(D) 37°
(E) 60°

30. How many distinct, real solutions are there to this equation: $5x^3 + 625 = 0$?
(A) None
(B) One
(C) Two
(D) Three
(E) It cannot be determined.

Directions: For Question 31, enter your answer as an integer or as a decimal if there is a single answer box OR as a fraction if there are two separate boxes—one for the numerator and one for the denominator.

To enter an integer or a decimal, write the number in the answer box provided. On the computer-based test you can either type the number in the answer box using the keyboard or use the Transfer Display button on the calculator. Also, note the following directions for the computer-based test:

- You can click on the answer box and then type the number. You can use the backspace key to erase a number.
- Type a hyphen for a negative sign. Type a hyphen again, and it will disappear. For a decimal point, type a period.
- The Transfer Display button on the calculator will move the calculator display to the answer box.
- Equivalent forms of the correct answer, such as 2.5 and 2.50, are all correct.
- Enter the exact answer unless the question asks you to round your answer.

31. What is the y-intercept of a line that passes through $(-4, 2)$ and $(3, -1)$?

    Give your answer as a fraction.

Directions: For Questions 32–33, solve the problems and indicate the best of the answer choices given.

32. How many squares measuring 4 inches on a side are needed to cover a rectangular area measuring 16 inches by 4 feet?
    - (A) 4
    - (B) 5
    - (C) 8
    - (D) 16
    - (E) 48

33. The ratio of blue cars to red cars in a parking lot is 7 to 11. Which of the following could be the total number of cars in this parking lot?
    - (A) 21
    - (B) 25
    - (C) 33
    - (D) 40
    - (E) 54

Directions: Question 34 consists of a question and two statements, labeled (1) and (2), in which certain data is given. You have to decide whether the data given in the statements is sufficient for answering the question. Using the data given in the statements plus your knowledge of mathematics and everyday facts (such as the number of days in July and the meaning of "counterclockwise"), you must indicate whether

    (A) Statement (1) ALONE is sufficient, but statement (2) is not sufficient.

    (B) Statement (2) ALONE is sufficient, but statement (1) is not sufficient.

    (C) BOTH statements TOGETHER are sufficient, but NEITHER statement ALONE is sufficient.

    (D) EACH statement ALONE is sufficient.

    (E) Statements (1) and (2) TOGETHER are NOT sufficient.

34. Is x an improper fraction?

    (1) $|x| < 1$

    (2) $x^2 < x$

    (A) Statement (1) ALONE is sufficient, but statement (2) alone is not sufficient.

    (B) Statement (2) ALONE is sufficient, but statement (1) alone is not sufficient.

    (C) BOTH statements TOGETHER are sufficient, but NEITHER statement ALONE is sufficient.

    (D) EACH statement ALONE is sufficient.

    (E) Statements (1) and (2) TOGETHER are NOT sufficient.

Directions: For Questions 35–36, select a single answer choice.

35. What is the area of the "doughnut" created between two concentric circles, one with a radius of 5 cm, the other with a radius of 7 cm?

    (A) 4 cm^2

    (B) 4π cm^2

    (C) 24π cm^2

    (D) 51π cm^2

    (E) 74π cm^2

Questions 36–39 are based on the following function.

$$x \nabla y = \frac{x^2 y}{x - y}$$

36. What is $2 \nabla 3$?

   (A) -12

   (B) -6

   (C) 2

   (D) 6

   (E) 12

Directions: For Question 37, enter your answer as an integer or as a decimal if there is a single answer box OR as a fraction if there are two separate boxes—one for the numerator and one for the denominator.

To enter an integer or a decimal, write the number in the answer box provided. On the computer-based test you can either type the number in the answer box using the keyboard or use the Transfer Display button on the calculator. Also, note the following directions for the computer-based test:

- You can click on the answer box and then type the number. You can use the backspace key to erase a number.

- Type a hyphen for a negative sign. Type a hyphen again, and it will disappear. For a decimal point, type a period.

- The Transfer Display button on the calculator will move the calculator display to the answer box.

- Equivalent forms of the correct answer, such as 2.5 and 2.50, are all correct.

- Enter the exact answer unless the question asks you to round your answer.

37. How much more is $3 \nabla 2$ than $2 \nabla 3$?

Directions: For Questions 38–39, select a single answer choice.

38. Which of these results in the largest value?

   (A) $-1 \nabla 2$

   (B) $-1 \nabla 3$

   (C) $2 \nabla 3$

   (D) $3 \nabla 2$

   (E) $3 \nabla 4$

39. What is the value of $(2\nabla3)(3\nabla2)$?

    (A) -216

    (B) -144

    (C) 1

    (D) 144

    (E) 216

Directions: Question 40 consists of a question and two statements, labeled (1) and (2), in which certain data is given. You have to decide whether the data given in the statements is sufficient for answering the question. Using the data given in the statements plus your knowledge of mathematics and everyday facts (such as the number of days in July and the meaning of "counterclockwise"), you must indicate whether

    (A) Statement (1) ALONE is sufficient, but statement (2) is not sufficient.

    (B) Statement (2) ALONE is sufficient, but statement (1) is not sufficient.

    (C) BOTH statements TOGETHER are sufficient, but NEITHER statement ALONE is sufficient.

    (D) EACH statement ALONE is sufficient.

    (E) Statements (1) and (2) TOGETHER are NOT sufficient.

40. Did Pablo earn a raise of at least 6% on his gross pay?

    (1) Pablo's latest paycheck showed that his gross pay is now $50 more than it was on his previous paycheck.

    (2) His latest paycheck showed that his gross pay is now $2,400.

    (A) Statement (1) ALONE is sufficient, but statement (2) alone is not sufficient.

    (B) Statement (2) ALONE is sufficient, but statement (1) alone is not sufficient.

    (C) BOTH statements TOGETHER are sufficient, but NEITHER statement ALONE is sufficient.

    (D) EACH statement ALONE is sufficient.

    (E) Statements (1) and (2) TOGETHER are NOT sufficient.

ANSWER KEY AND EXPLANATIONS

1. B	9. C	17. C	25. B	33. E
2. D	10. E	18. C	26. C	34. B
3. B	11. B	19. E	27. B	35. C
4. C	12. A	20. 60	28. E	36. A
5. A	13. D	21. D	29. C	37. 30
6. C	14. B	22. A	30. B	38. D
7. A	15. C	23. B	31. $\frac{2}{7}$	39. A
8. B	16. 65.55	24. B		40. C
			32. E	

1. **The correct answer is (B).** Since $x = (-2)^3 - (-1) = -8 + 1 = -7$, substitute -7 into each expression. Since x is negative, the only possible largest values are choice (B), 49, or choice (E), $\frac{1}{49}$. Choice (B) is the greater value of the two.

2. **The correct answer is (D).** Each face of a cube is a square. The area of one face is $(\text{edge})^2 = 9^2 = 81$. A cube has six congruent faces. The total surface area of the cube is $6(81) = 486$ square centimeters.

3. **The correct answer is (B).** Statement (1) indicates that x is negative. However, without knowing the sign of y, the sign of the expression is unknown. Statement (2) indicates that x and y have the same sign. This is sufficient information to indicate the sign of the expression.

4. **The correct answer is (C).**

15% of 19% of 20   38% of 75% of 2

$\frac{15}{100} \times \frac{19}{100} \times \frac{20}{1}$ $\frac{38}{100} \times \frac{75}{100} \times \frac{2}{1}$

Ignoring the two 100's in the denominators of each quantity, the quantities become:
$15 \times 19 \times 20$ $38 \times 75 \times 2$

By partially factoring, you get:
$15 \times 19 \times 2 \times 10$ $2 \times 19 \times 5 \times 15 \times 2$

Look! A 15, 19, and 2 are in each quantity. When you ignore these numbers, you are left with:
10   5×2

As you can see, the two quantities are equal.

5. **The correct answer is (A).** Column B is $16(1\frac{1}{2}) = 16(\frac{3}{2}) = 24$ ounces.

6. **The correct answer is (C).** Put the values in order first: 15%, 59%, 68%, 81%, 81%, 90%, 100%. The median is the middle score, 81%. The mode is the score occurring most frequently, 81%.

7. **The correct answer is (A).** The range is the difference between the largest and the smallest values: $100\% - 15\%$
= 85%. The mean is the average of all of the scores: $\dfrac{15+59+68+81+81+90+100}{7} = \dfrac{492}{7} = 70\dfrac{2}{7}$. Quantity A is
larger.

8. **The correct answer is (B).** The median, as found in Question 6, is 81%. The mode, also found in Question 6, is
81%. So, the difference between them is 0%. The lowest score is 15%; twice that is 30%.

9. **The correct answer is (C).**

$$\dfrac{\text{Percent}}{100} = \dfrac{\text{Part (amount of discount)}}{\text{Whole (original price)}}$$

$$\dfrac{P}{100} = \dfrac{25.80}{215}$$

$$215P = 2{,}580$$

$$P = \dfrac{2{,}580}{215} = 12$$

10. **The correct answer is (E).** $4x^2 - 28x + 24 = 4(x^2 - 7x + 6) = 4(x - 6)(x - 1)$. Always take out the greatest common
factor first. Be sure that each final factor cannot be factored any further. Be careful of the signs!

11. **The correct answer is (B).** Statement (1) is not enough to determine the answer. Statement (2) alone can be used to
determine the total cost. The percents help determine the meal cost. Add the meal cost and the tip to receive the total
cost. Thus, statement (2) alone is sufficient.

12. **The correct answer is (A).**

Ingredients	Cornstarch	Butter	Oil	Sugar
Ratio	1	3	2	4
Times	¼			¼
Actual for Two Batches	¼			1
Actual for One Batch	½(¼) = 1/8			½

13. **The correct answer is (D).** Any two sides of a triangle need to add up to be more than the third side. The third side
must be greater than 4 and less than 12. The only possible answer is choice (D).

14. **The correct answer is (B).**

Worker	Rate	Time	Fraction of Job Completed
Martina	1/6	t	$t/6$
Jasmine	1/9	t	$t/9$
			1

$$\frac{t}{6} + \frac{t}{9} = 1$$

Multiply every term by 18.

$$3t + 2t = 18$$

$$5t = 18$$

$$t = \frac{18}{5} = 3.6$$

15. **The correct answer is (C).** Statement (1) would give two possible solutions for x, one negative and one positive, since $x^2 + 3x - 4 = 0$, and thus $(x + 4)(x - 1) = 0$, and thus $x = -4$ and $x = 1$. Statement (2) indicates that x is negative. These statements together provide enough information to determine the value of x.

16. **The correct answer is $65.55.** Dusty works a total of 5.75 hours on Saturday and Sunday. Earning time and half means that he earns $7.60(1.5) = $11.40 per hour. Thus, Dusty earns $65.55 for his weekend work: 5.75 hours times $11.40 per hour.

17. **The correct answer is (C).**

Trip	Rate	Time	Distance
Less Scenic Route	55	t	$55t$
Much More Scenic Route	$(55 - 22) = 33$	10	330

As you can see, the mileage to get to her vacation getaway is 330 miles.

18. **The correct answer is (C).** Convert all factors into factors of base 2: $\dfrac{8^3 2^7 4^6}{4^{10}} = \dfrac{(2^3)^3 2^7 (2^2)^6}{(2^2)^{10}}$. Next, use the rules of exponents to simplify the expression: $\dfrac{(2^3)^3 2^7 (2^2)^6}{(2^2)^{10}} = \dfrac{(2^9) 2^7 (2^{12})}{(2^{20})} = \dfrac{2^{28}}{2^{20}} = 2^8$. Multiply exponents when a base raised to a power is raised to a power. Add exponents when factors with the same base are multiplied. (That base does not change.) Subtract exponents when dividing factors with the same base. (Again, the base does not change.)

19. **The correct answer is (E).** Statement (1) is not enough to determine the answer. Statement (2) can be simplified to $x^2 > 0$. That is not enough to determine the answer either. Also, the two statements together are not enough to determine the answer.

20. **The correct answer is 60.** This is a permutation, since the order matters. Hence, the solution, since there are three positions to be filled, is $5 \times 4 \times 3 = 60$. The president can be chosen from five people. Once that position is filled, the vice president position can be filled by any one of the four remaining people. After that position is filled, the treasurer position can be filled from the three remaining people.

21. **The correct answer is (D).** To help you remember the order of operations, think of the mnemonic *Please excuse my dear Aunt Sally:* parentheses, exponents and radicals, multiplication and division, and addition and subtraction.

$$\frac{2(3-2^3)-3(5-7)}{(3-5)^2(4-5)}=\frac{2(3-8)-3(5-7)}{(3-5)^2(4-5)}=\frac{2(-5)-3(-2)}{(-2)^2(-1)}=\frac{2(-5)-3(-2)}{4(-1)}=$$

$$\frac{-10-(-6)}{-4}=\frac{-10+6}{-4}=\frac{-4}{-4}=1$$

22. **The correct answer is (A).** $x^2-4x=21 \rightarrow x^2-4x-21=0 \rightarrow (x+3)(x-7)=0 \rightarrow x=-3$ and $x=7$

    Quantity A: $7-(-3)=7+3=10$

23. **The correct answer is (B).**

    Quantity A: $\dfrac{5}{12}$

    Quantity B: $\dfrac{7}{12}$

24. **The correct answer is (B).**

    Quantity A: $\dfrac{7}{12} \times \dfrac{5}{11}$

    Quantity B: $\dfrac{7}{12} \times \dfrac{6}{11}$

    No need to do the arithmetic. The denominators will be the same. Multiplying the numerators for Quantity B results in a larger quantity than does multiplying the numerators for Quantity A.

25. **The correct answer is (B).**

    Quantity A: $\dfrac{5}{12} \times \dfrac{4}{11}$

    Quantity B: $\dfrac{12}{12} \times \dfrac{6}{11} + \dfrac{5}{12} \times \dfrac{4}{11}$ (This shows picking the first marble, followed by picking another green, if the first one picked had been green or picking another red, if the first one picked had been red.)

    No need to do the arithmetic. Quantity B is larger.

26. **The correct answer is (C).** Prime numbers have only two factors: 1 and the number itself. List the prime numbers in this set: 23, 29, 31, 37, 41, and 43. There are 6 of them, so the correct answer is choice (C).

27. **The correct answer is (B).** The largest two-digit prime is 97. The next odd integer larger than 97 is 99.

28. **The correct answer is (E).** Statement (1) is not enough to determine the answer, since this statement merely informs that $|x| \geq |y|$. The statement means that x and y could both be equal to 0 or that the absolute values of x and y are both greater than or equal to 1. There is not enough information to determine which is the bigger value, x or y. Statement (2) indicates that y is positive. That is not enough to determine the answer either. Putting the two statements together does not help. If, for example, x is -3 and y is 2, one answer is determined. If, on the other hand, x is 3 and y is 2, another answer is determined. There is not enough information.

29. The correct answer is (C).

$$l = \text{measure of largest angle}$$
$$m = \text{measure of medium-sized angle}$$
$$s = \text{measure of smallest angle}$$
$$l = 4s$$
$$s = m - 6 \rightarrow s + 6 = m$$
$$s + m + l = 180$$
$$s + (s+6) + (4s) = 180$$
$$6s + 6 = 180$$
$$6s = 174$$
$$s = 29$$
$$s + 6 = m \rightarrow 29 + 6 = 35$$

30. The correct answer is (B).

$$5x^3 + 625 = 0$$
$$5x^3 = -625$$
$$x^3 = -125$$
$$x = -5$$

31. The correct answer is $\dfrac{2}{7}$.

$$\text{slope } m = \frac{\Delta y}{\Delta x} = \frac{-1-2}{3-(-4)} = \frac{-1-2}{3+4} = \frac{-3}{7}$$
$$y = mix + b$$
$$2 = (\frac{-3}{7})(-4) + b$$
$$2 = \frac{12}{7} + b$$
$$2 - \frac{12}{7} = b$$
$$\frac{2}{7} = b$$

32. The correct answer is (E). The area of the rectangle is 16 inches times 4 feet or 16 inches by 48 inches. The total number of square inches is 768 square inches. The area of each square is 4 inches by 4 inches, which is 16 square inches. How many of those 16 square inch squares can fit into the 768 square inch rectangle? The answer is found by division: $\dfrac{768}{16} = 48$.

33. The correct answer is (E).

Cars	Blue	Red	Total
Ratio	7	11	18
Times			3
Actual Number of Cars			54

The total number of cars in the parking lot must be a positive multiple of 18. The only choice that is such a number is the one given in choice (E).

34. **The correct answer is (B).** An improper fraction has a numerator that is less than the denominator, and both the numerator and denominator are greater than 0. Statement (1) indicates that x is between -1 and 1, not including the endpoints of -1 and 1. A proper fraction must be positive, so statement (1) is not enough. Statement (2) indicates that squaring x creates a value smaller than x itself. This happens with a fraction strictly between 0 and positive 1. Hence, statement (2) alone is sufficient to determine whether x is a proper fraction.

35. **The correct answer is (C).** The area of the larger circle is $\pi r^2 = \pi(7)^2 = 49\pi$. The area of the smaller circle is $\pi r^2 = \pi(5)^2 = 25\pi$. The doughnut is the difference between those two areas: $49\pi - 25\pi = 24\pi$.

36. **The correct answer is (A).**

$$x \nabla y = \frac{x^2 y}{x - y}$$

$$2 \nabla 3 = \frac{2^2(3)}{2-3} = \frac{4(3)}{2-3} = \frac{12}{2-3} = \frac{12}{-1} = -12$$

37. **The correct answer is 30.**

$$x \nabla y = \frac{x^2 y}{x - y}$$

$$3 \nabla 2 = \frac{3^2(2)}{3-2} = \frac{9(2)}{3-2} = \frac{18}{3-2} = \frac{18}{1} = 18$$

$$3 \nabla 2 - 2 \nabla 3 = 18 - (-12) = 18 + 12 = 30$$

38. **The correct answer is (D).**

$$x \nabla y = \frac{x^2 y}{x - y}$$

Choice (A): $-1 \nabla 2 = \frac{(-1)^2 (2)}{-1 - 2} = \frac{1(2)}{-1 - 2} = \frac{2}{-1 - 2} = \frac{2}{-3} = \frac{-2}{3}$

Choice (B): $-1 \nabla 3 = \frac{(-1)^2 (3)}{-1 - 3} = \frac{1(3)}{-1 - 3} = \frac{3}{-1 - 3} = \frac{3}{-4} = \frac{-3}{4}$

Choice (C): $2 \nabla 3 = -12$

Choice (D): $3 \nabla 2 = 18$

Choice (E): $3 \nabla 4 = \frac{3^2 (4)}{3 - 4} = \frac{9(4)}{3 - 4} = \frac{36}{3 - 4} = \frac{36}{-1} = -36$

39. **The correct answer is (A).** $(2 \nabla 3)(3 \nabla 2) = (-12)(18) = -216$

40. **The correct answer is (C).** Statement (1) does not give enough information to answer the question. Statement (2) alone does not give enough information. However, those two statements together indicate that Pablo's previous gross pay was $2,350. Computing $50/$2,350 gives the percent raise. That is enough to answer the question. There is no need to do any more computing.

PRACTICE TEST 3 ANSWER SHEET

1. Ⓐ Ⓑ Ⓒ Ⓓ Ⓔ　　9. Ⓐ Ⓑ Ⓒ Ⓓ Ⓔ　　17. Ⓐ Ⓑ Ⓒ Ⓓ Ⓔ　　25. ☐　　33. Ⓐ Ⓑ Ⓒ Ⓓ Ⓔ

2. Ⓐ Ⓑ Ⓒ Ⓓ Ⓔ　　10. Ⓐ Ⓑ Ⓒ Ⓓ Ⓔ　　18. Ⓐ Ⓑ Ⓒ Ⓓ Ⓔ Ⓕ Ⓖ　　26. Ⓐ Ⓑ Ⓒ Ⓓ Ⓔ　　34. Ⓐ Ⓑ Ⓒ Ⓓ

3. ☐　　11. Ⓐ Ⓑ Ⓒ Ⓓ Ⓔ　　19. Ⓐ Ⓑ Ⓒ Ⓓ Ⓔ　　27. Ⓐ Ⓑ Ⓒ Ⓓ Ⓔ　　35. Ⓐ Ⓑ Ⓒ Ⓓ

　☐　　12. Ⓐ Ⓑ Ⓒ Ⓓ Ⓔ　　20. Ⓐ Ⓑ Ⓒ Ⓓ Ⓔ　　28. Ⓐ Ⓑ Ⓒ Ⓓ Ⓔ　　36. Ⓐ Ⓑ Ⓒ Ⓓ Ⓔ

4. Ⓐ Ⓑ Ⓒ Ⓓ Ⓔ　　13. Ⓐ Ⓑ Ⓒ Ⓓ Ⓔ　　21. Ⓐ Ⓑ Ⓒ Ⓓ Ⓔ　　29. Ⓐ Ⓑ Ⓒ Ⓓ Ⓔ　　37. Ⓐ Ⓑ Ⓒ Ⓓ Ⓔ

5. Ⓐ Ⓑ Ⓒ Ⓓ Ⓔ　　14. Ⓐ Ⓑ Ⓒ Ⓓ Ⓔ　　22. Ⓐ Ⓑ Ⓒ Ⓓ Ⓔ　　30. Ⓐ Ⓑ Ⓒ Ⓓ　　38. Ⓐ Ⓑ Ⓒ Ⓓ Ⓔ

6. Ⓐ Ⓑ Ⓒ Ⓓ Ⓔ　　15. Ⓐ Ⓑ Ⓒ Ⓓ Ⓔ　　23. Ⓐ Ⓑ Ⓒ Ⓓ Ⓔ　　31. Ⓐ Ⓑ Ⓒ Ⓓ　　39. Ⓐ Ⓑ Ⓒ Ⓓ Ⓔ

7. Ⓐ Ⓑ Ⓒ Ⓓ Ⓔ　　16. Ⓐ Ⓑ Ⓒ Ⓓ Ⓔ　　24. Ⓐ Ⓑ Ⓒ Ⓓ Ⓔ　　32. Ⓐ Ⓑ Ⓒ Ⓓ Ⓔ　　40. Ⓐ Ⓑ Ⓒ Ⓓ Ⓔ

8. ☐

Practice Test 3

Directions: For Question 1, select a single answer choice.

1. What is the volume of a cylinder with a base radius of 10 cm and a height of 7 cm?
   (A) 24π cm³
   (B) 490 cm³
   (C) 490π cm³
   (D) 700 cm³
   (E) 700π cm³

Directions: Question 2 consists of a question and two statements, labeled (1) and (2), in which certain data is given. You have to decide whether the data given in the statements is sufficient for answering the question. Using the data given in the statements plus your knowledge of mathematics and everyday facts (such as the number of days in July and the meaning of "counterclockwise"), you must indicate whether

   (A) Statement (1) ALONE is sufficient, but statement (2) is not sufficient.

   (B) Statement (2) ALONE is sufficient, but statement (1) is not sufficient.

   (C) BOTH statements TOGETHER are sufficient, but NEITHER statement ALONE is sufficient.

   (D) EACH statement ALONE is sufficient.

   (E) Statements (1) and (2) TOGETHER are NOT sufficient.

2. How much money does Sam have in his piggy bank?
   (1) Same has 4 more dimes than nickels in his piggy bank.
   (2) Sam has only dimes and nickels in his piggy bank.

   (A) Statement (1) ALONE is sufficient, but statement (2) alone is not sufficient.
   (B) Statement (2) ALONE is sufficient, but statement (1) alone is not sufficient.
   (C) BOTH statements TOGETHER are sufficient, but NEITHER statement ALONE is sufficient.
   (D) EACH statement ALONE is sufficient.
   (E) Statements (1) and (2) TOGETHER are NOT sufficient.

Directions: For Question 3, enter your answer as an integer or as a decimal if there is a single answer box OR as a fraction if there are two separate boxes—one for the numerator and one for the denominator.

To enter an integer or a decimal, write the number in the answer box provided. On the computer-based test you can either type the number in the answer box using the keyboard or use the Transfer Display button on the calculator. Also, note the following directions for the computer-based test:

- You can click on the answer box and then type the number. You can use the backspace key to erase a number.
- Type a hyphen for a negative sign. Type a hyphen again, and it will disappear. For a decimal point, type a period.
- The Transfer Display button on the calculator will move the calculator display to the answer box.
- Equivalent forms of the correct answer, such as 2.5 and 2.50, are all correct.
- Enter the exact answer unless the question asks you to round your answer.

3. $\frac{1}{2} + \frac{3}{4} + \frac{5}{6} + \frac{7}{8} =$

   Give your answer as a fraction.

Directions: For Question 4, select a single answer choice.

4. The perimeter of a square is 100 decimeters. What is its area?
   - **(A)** 40 square decimeters
   - **(B)** 100 square decimeters
   - **(C)** 400 square decimeters
   - **(D)** 625 square decimeters
   - **(E)** 6,250 square decimeters

Directions: For Question 5, solve the problem and indicate the best of the answer choices given.

5. Simplify: $\dfrac{x^2 - 4}{x^2 - x - 2}$.

   (A) -2

   (B) $\dfrac{x - 2}{x - 1}$

   (C) $\dfrac{x + 2}{x + 1}$

   (D) $\dfrac{4}{3}$

   (E) 2

Directions: Question 6 consists of a question and two statements, labeled (1) and (2), in which certain data is given. You have to decide whether the data given in the statements is sufficient for answering the question. Using the data given in the statements plus your knowledge of mathematics and everyday facts (such as the number of days in July and the meaning of "counterclockwise"), you must indicate whether

   (A) Statement (1) ALONE is sufficient, but statement (2) is not sufficient.

   (B) Statement (2) ALONE is sufficient, but statement (1) is not sufficient.

   (C) BOTH statements TOGETHER are sufficient, but NEITHER statement ALONE is sufficient.

   (D) EACH statement ALONE is sufficient.

   (E) Statements (1) and (2) TOGETHER are NOT sufficient.

6. What was the average daily temperature in Las Vegas in January?

   (1) The difference between the highest and lowest temperatures in Las Vegas in January was 14°F.

   (2) Las Vegas' highest temperature in January was 58°F.

   (A) Statement (1) ALONE is sufficient, but statement (2) alone is not sufficient.

   (B) Statement (2) ALONE is sufficient, but statement (1) alone is not sufficient.

   (C) BOTH statements TOGETHER are sufficient, but NEITHER statement ALONE is sufficient.

   (D) EACH statement ALONE is sufficient.

   (E) Statements (1) and (2) TOGETHER are NOT sufficient.

Directions: For Question 7, solve the problem and indicate the best of the answer choices given.

7. Last week, Dot saw a pair of pants that she wanted to buy. They were priced at $56. Yesterday, she saw that they were priced at $50.40. By what percent had they been discounted?

   (A) 10%

   (B) 11%

   (C) 56%

   (D) 60%

   (E) 90%

Directions: For Question 8, enter your answer as an integer or as a decimal if there is a single answer box OR as a fraction if there are two separate boxes—one for the numerator and one for the denominator.

To enter an integer or a decimal, write the number in the answer box provided. On the computer-based test you can either type the number in the answer box using the keyboard or use the Transfer Display button on the calculator. Also, note the following directions for the computer-based test:

- You can click on the answer box and then type the number. You can use the backspace key to erase a number.

- Type a hyphen for a negative sign. Type a hyphen again, and it will disappear. For a decimal point, type a period.

- The Transfer Display button on the calculator will move the calculator display to the answer box.

- Equivalent forms of the correct answer, such as 2.5 and 2.50, are all correct.

- Enter the exact answer unless the question asks you to round your answer.

8. Mindy earned an average of 83% on three tests. What would she need to earn on her fourth test in order for her average to be 84%?

Questions 9−11 are based on the following isosceles right triangle, with right angle at C and with hypotenuse $12\sqrt{2}$ **cm.**

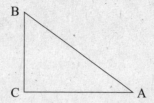

Directions: For Questions 9–12, select a single answer choice.

9. What is the length of each congruent leg of this triangle?

(A) $4\sqrt{6}$

(B) 6

(C) $6\sqrt{2}$

(D) $6\sqrt{2}$

(E) 12

10. What is the area of this right triangle?

(A) $\dfrac{25}{2}\sqrt{3}$ cm²

(B) 25 cm²

(C) 72 cm²

(D) 100 cm²

(E) 200 cm²

11. What is the perimeter of this isosceles right triangle?

(A) $24+12\sqrt{2}$ cm

(B) $36\sqrt{2}$ cm

(C) 50 cm²

(D) 100 cm²

(E) $36\sqrt{2}$ cm

12. The diameter of a circle measures 24 inches. What is the exact circumference of this circle?

   (A) 24 inches

   (B) 24π inches

   (C) 36 inches

   (D) 36π inches

   (E) 144π inches

Directions: Question 13 consists of a question and two statements, labeled (1) and (2), in which certain data is given. You have to decide whether the data given in the statements is sufficient for answering the question. Using the data given in the statements plus your knowledge of mathematics and everyday facts (such as the number of days in July and the meaning of "counterclockwise"), you must indicate whether

   (A) Statement (1) ALONE is sufficient, but statement (2) is not sufficient.

   (B) Statement (2) ALONE is sufficient, but statement (1) is not sufficient.

   (C) BOTH statements TOGETHER are sufficient, but NEITHER statement ALONE is sufficient.

   (D) EACH statement ALONE is sufficient.

   (E) Statements (1) and (2) TOGETHER are NOT sufficient.

---

13. How old is Duke?

   (1) Duke is 11 years older than Bud.

   (2) Bud is half as old as Duke.

   (A) Statement (1) ALONE is sufficient, but statement (2) alone is not sufficient.

   (B) Statement (2) ALONE is sufficient, but statement (1) alone is not sufficient.

   (C) BOTH statements TOGETHER are sufficient, but NEITHER statement ALONE is sufficient.

   (D) EACH statement ALONE is sufficient.

   (E) Statements (1) and (2) TOGETHER are NOT sufficient.

Directions: For Questions 14–17, solve the problems and indicate the best of the answer choices given.

---

14. Denise saved 12% on a lamp. The sale price was $70.40. What was the original price of the lamp?

   (A) $58.40

   (B) $78.84

   (C) $78.85

   (D) $80.00

   (E) $82.40

15. Given $(-2, 3)$ is a solution to $x + 3y = -k$, what y-value would correspond to an x-value of -1 for a solution to this equation?

    (A) -7

    (B) $\dfrac{-8}{3}$

    (C) $\dfrac{8}{3}$

    (D) 4

    (E) 7

16. Myrtle just filled her gas tank. She spent $59.22 to do so. If her tank holds 20 gallons and she knows she had 2 gallons left, how much does gas cost her per gallon?

    (A) $0.30

    (B) $0.34

    (C) $2.96

    (D) $3.29

    (E) $3.37

17. Juan earned grades of 70%, 72%, 91%, 32%, 97%, and 86% on his first 6 history tests. What is his median score on these 6 tests?

    (A) 10%

    (B) 59%

    (C) 78%

    (D) 79%

    (E) 94%

Directions: For Question 18, select one or more answer choices according to the specific question directions. If the question does not specify how many answer choices to select, select all that apply.

- The correct answer may be just one of the choices or may be as many as all of the choices, depending on the question.
- No credit is given unless you select all of the correct choices and no others.
- If the question specifies how many answer choices to select, select exactly that number of choices.

18. Which of the following numbers are one more than a prime number?

    Indicate <u>all</u> such numbers.

    (A) 18
    (B) 22
    (C) 34
    (D) 58
    (E) 62
    (F) 64
    (G) 73

Directions: For Questions 19–20, select a single answer choice.

19. What is the product of the square root of the largest solution to $x^2 - 5x + 4 = 0$ and the square of the smallest solution to $x^2 - 5x + 4 = 0$?

    (A) −2
    (B) −1
    (C) 0
    (D) 1
    (E) 2

20. How many distinct positive factors does 16 have?

    (A) 2
    (B) 3
    (C) 4
    (D) 5
    (E) 6

Directions: Question 21 consists of a question and two statements, labeled (1) and (2), in which certain data is given. You have to decide whether the data given in the statements is sufficient for answering the question. Using the data given in the statements plus your knowledge of mathematics and everyday facts (such as the number of days in July and the meaning of "counterclockwise"), you must indicate whether

(A) Statement (1) ALONE is sufficient, but statement (2) is not sufficient.

(B) Statement (2) ALONE is sufficient, but statement (1) is not sufficient.

(C) BOTH statements TOGETHER are sufficient, but NEITHER statement ALONE is sufficient.

(D) EACH statement ALONE is sufficient.

(E) Statements (1) and (2) TOGETHER are NOT sufficient.

21. How many more points would Dexter need to earn to have as many points as Shelba?
    (1) If Shelba earns 6 more points, she will double the number of points she already has.
    (2) Dexter has half as many points as Shelba has right now.

    (A) Statement (1) ALONE is sufficient, but statement (2) alone is not sufficient.
    (B) Statement (2) ALONE is sufficient, but statement (1) alone is not sufficient.
    (C) BOTH statements TOGETHER are sufficient, but NEITHER statement ALONE is sufficient.
    (D) EACH statement ALONE is sufficient.
    (E) Statements (1) and (2) TOGETHER are NOT sufficient.

Directions: For Questions 22–23, solve the problems and indicate the best of the answer choices given.

22. Bella mowed half of her lawn. After having a glass of iced tea, she mowed half of the unmowed lawn. How much of her lawn does she still need to mow?

    (A) 0

    (B) $\frac{1}{6}$

    (C) $\frac{1}{4}$

    (D) $\frac{3}{4}$

    (E) $\frac{5}{6}$

23. Della owes Fawn $1,250. Fawn is charging Della 6% per week simple interest on that $1,250. If Della finally pays Fawn after having the money for three weeks, how much interest will she pay?

    (A) $7.50
    (B) $22.50
    (C) $75.00
    (D) $225.00
    (E) $750.00

Directions: For Question 24, select a single answer choice.

24. How much change would Madden receive from $30.00, if he bought four notebooks and five pens? All of the merchandise is on sale at a 10% discount. The notebooks regularly sell for $3.50 each, while the pens regularly sell for $2.20 each. The tax on all items is 4%, based upon the sale price of each item.

    (A) $4.40
    (B) $5.00
    (C) $6.00
    (D) $6.60
    (E) $6.72

Directions: For Question 25, enter your answer as an integer or as a decimal if there is a single answer box OR as a fraction if there are two separate boxes—one for the numerator and one for the denominator.

To enter an integer or a decimal, write the number in the answer box provided. On the computer-based test you can either type the number in the answer box using the keyboard or use the Transfer Display button on the calculator. Also, note the following directions for the computer-based test:

- You can click on the answer box and then type the number. You can use the backspace key to erase a number.
- Type a hyphen for a negative sign. Type a hyphen again, and it will disappear. For a decimal point, type a period.
- The Transfer Display button on the calculator will move the calculator display to the answer box.
- Equivalent forms of the correct answer, such as 2.5 and 2.50, are all correct.
- Enter the exact answer unless the question asks you to round your answer.

25. What is the sum of the greatest integer less than −5 and the smallest integer greater than −10?

    [   ]

Directions: For Question 26, solve the problem and indicate the best of the answer choices given.

26. Simplify: $(4x^3 - x - 2) - (5x^3 + 6x^2 + x - 7)$.

    (A) $-x^3 + 6x^2 - 9$
    (B) $-x^3 - 6x^2 - 2x + 5$
    (C) $9x^3 + 6x^2 - 2x - 9$
    (D) $4x^3 - 6x^2 - 2x + 5$
    (E) $4x^3 - 6x^2 - 2x - 5$

Directions: Question 27 consists of a question and two statements, labeled (1) and (2), in which certain data is given. You have to decide whether the data given in the statements is sufficient for answering the question. Using the data given in the statements plus your knowledge of mathematics and everyday facts (such as the number of days in July and the meaning of "counterclockwise"), you must indicate whether

(A) Statement (1) ALONE is sufficient, but statement (2) is not sufficient.

(B) Statement (2) ALONE is sufficient, but statement (1) is not sufficient.

(C) BOTH statements TOGETHER are sufficient, but NEITHER statement ALONE is sufficient.

(D) EACH statement ALONE is sufficient.

(E) Statements (1) and (2) TOGETHER are NOT sufficient.

27. Lola earns $25 per week. How many more weeks than Jasper has to work does Lola have to work to make the same amount of money per year?

    (1) Jasper earns $30 per week and works for 20 weeks of the year.

    (2) Lola needs to make $100 more dollars in order to match what Jasper earns per year.

    (A) Statement (1) ALONE is sufficient, but statement (2) alone is not sufficient.

    (B) Statement (2) ALONE is sufficient, but statement (1) alone is not sufficient.

    (C) BOTH statements TOGETHER are sufficient, but NEITHER statement ALONE is sufficient.

    (D) EACH statement ALONE is sufficient.

    (E) Statements (1) and (2) TOGETHER are NOT sufficient.

Directions: For Questions 28–29, solve the problems and indicate the best of the answer choices given.

28. Butch is ordering pizza. He has a choice of 6 different toppings. If he can order as few as 1 topping and as many as 3 different toppings, how many different pizzas can he order?

    (A) 15

    (B) 20

    (C) 41

    (D) 120

    (E) 156

29. Given a = –1, b = 2, c = –3, what is $\dfrac{a^2b - a^3}{c - b}$?

    (A) $\dfrac{-7}{5}$

    (B) $\dfrac{-3}{5}$

    (C) $\dfrac{7}{5}$

    (D) 3

    (E) 7

Directions: For Questions 30–31, compare Quantity A and Quantity B, using additional information centered above the two quantities if such information is given, and select one of the following four answer choices:

(A) Quantity A is greater.

(B) Quantity B is greater.

(C) The two quantities are equal.

(D) The relationship cannot be determined from the information given.

A symbol that appears more than once in a question has the same meaning throughout the question.

Questions 30–31 are based on this information.

$$x + 2y = -4$$
$$4x - 2y = -11$$

30.

Quantity A	Quantity B
x	y

(A) Quantity A is greater.

(B) Quantity B is greater.

(C) The two quantities are equal.

(D) The relationship cannot be determined from the information given.

31.

Quantity A	Quantity B
$2y$	$\dfrac{1}{3}x$

(A) Quantity A is greater.

(B) Quantity B is greater.

(C) The two quantities are equal.

(D) The relationship cannot be determined from the information given.

Directions: For Question 32, solve the problem and indicate the best of the answer choices given.

32. Milly travels 16 miles from her house to work each day. Her car gets 10 miles per gallon. If gas costs $3.35 per gallon, how much does she spend on her five round-trip journeys to work and back home each week?

(A) $26.80

(B) $33.50

(C) $53.60

(D) $67.00

(E) $536.00

Directions: Question 33 consists of a question and two statements, labeled (1) and (2), in which certain data is given. You have to decide whether the data given in the statements is sufficient for answering the question. Using the data given in the statements plus your knowledge of mathematics and everyday facts (such as the number of days in July and the meaning of "counterclockwise"), you must indicate whether

    (A) Statement (1) ALONE is sufficient, but statement (2) is not sufficient.

    (B) Statement (2) ALONE is sufficient, but statement (1) is not sufficient.

    (C) BOTH statements TOGETHER are sufficient, but NEITHER statement ALONE is sufficient.

    (D) EACH statement ALONE is sufficient.

    (E) Statements (1) and (2) TOGETHER are NOT sufficient.

33. Fabian is getting ready for his annual fiesta. He always invites an odd number of people. How many people has he invited this year?

    (1) Fabian invites twice as many males as females to his fiesta.

    (2) Fabian invites an even number of males to his fiesta.

    (A) Statement (1) ALONE is sufficient, but statement (2) alone is not sufficient.

    (B) Statement (2) ALONE is sufficient, but statement (1) alone is not sufficient.

    (C) BOTH statements TOGETHER are sufficient, but NEITHER statement ALONE is sufficient.

    (D) EACH statement ALONE is sufficient.

    (E) Statements (1) and (2) TOGETHER are NOT sufficient.

Directions: For Questions 34–35, compare Quantity A and Quantity B, using additional information centered above the two quantities if such information is given, and select one of the following four answer choices:

    (A) Quantity A is greater.

    (B) Quantity B is greater.

    (C) The two quantities are equal.

    (D) The relationship cannot be determined from the information given.

A symbol that appears more than once in a question has the same meaning throughout the question.

34.

Quantity A	Quantity B
$\frac{2}{3}$ of 15	66% of 15

    (A) Quantity A is greater.
    (B) Quantity B is greater.
    (C) The two quantities are equal.
    (D) The relationship cannot be determined from the information given.

35.

Quantity A	Quantity B
Difference in the number of degrees in a regular pentagon and a regular quadrilateral	Difference between the number of degrees in one interior angle of a regular decagon and an exterior angle of that same decagon

(A) Quantity A is greater.

(B) Quantity B is greater.

(C) The two quantities are equal.

(D) The relationship cannot be determined from the information given.

Directions: For Questions 36–39, solve the problems and indicate the best of the answer choices given.

36. Zip travels by train to work. He is one of 40% of the employees at his firm who does so. Matilda, like the others in the firm, drives to work. If Matilda is one of 114 employees who drive to work, how many people does this firm employ?

(A) 158

(B) 190

(C) 228

(D) 268

(E) 285

37. Buffy has dogs, canaries, and fish. She has three times as many dogs as canaries. She has two fewer fish than dogs. If she has a total of 26 pets, how many fish does she have?

(A) 3

(B) 5

(C) 7

(D) 10

(E) 15

38. One angle of a triangle measures 4 degrees more than twice the smallest angle. The largest angle measures 4 degrees less than three times the smallest angle. How many degrees is the largest angle?

(A) 30°

(B) 56°

(C) 64°

(D) 86°

(E) 94°

39. A store had a 10% off sale. After a week, the shopkeeper raised the sale prices 10%. How much would a customer now pay for an item that originally (before the sale) cost $50?

(A) $49.00

(B) $49.50

(C) $50.00

(D) $54.50

(E) $55.00

Directions: Question 40 consists of a question and two statements, labeled (1) and (2), in which certain data is given. You have to decide whether the data given in the statements is sufficient for answering the question. Using the data given in the statements plus your knowledge of mathematics and everyday facts (such as the number of days in July and the meaning of "counterclockwise"), you must indicate whether

(A) Statement (1) ALONE is sufficient, but statement (2) is not sufficient.

(B) Statement (2) ALONE is sufficient, but statement (1) is not sufficient.

(C) BOTH statements TOGETHER are sufficient, but NEITHER statement ALONE is sufficient.

(D) EACH statement ALONE is sufficient.

(E) Statements (1) and (2) TOGETHER are NOT sufficient.

40. What is the difference between the median and the mode of a data set containing five elements? (Some of the elements are 5, 10, and 21.)

    (1) The data set's range is 26.

    (2) The data set has a mode of 15.

    (A) Statement (1) ALONE is sufficient, but statement (2) alone is not sufficient.

    (B) Statement (2) ALONE is sufficient, but statement (1) alone is not sufficient.

    (C) BOTH statements TOGETHER are sufficient, but NEITHER statement ALONE is sufficient.

    (D) EACH statement ALONE is sufficient.

    (E) Statements (1) and (2) TOGETHER are NOT sufficient.

ANSWER KEY AND EXPLANATIONS

1. E	9. E	17. D	25. −15	33. E
2. E	10. C	18. A, E	26. B	34. A
3. $\frac{71}{24}$	11. A	19. E	27. D	35. A
4. D	12. B	20. D	28. C	36. B
5. C	13. C	21. C	29. B	37. D
6. E	14. D	22. C	30. B	38. D
7. A	15. C	23. D	31. C	39. B
8. 87	16. D	24. D	32. C	40. B

1. **The correct answer is (E).**

$$V = \pi r^2 h$$
$$V = \pi (10)^2 (7) = \pi (100)(7) = 700\pi$$

2. **The correct answer is (E).** Statement (1) is not enough to determine the answer. Statement (2) alone cannot determine the answer. Statements (1) and (2) together do not provide enough information to answer the question. Hence, the correct answer is choice (E).

3. **The correct answer is $\frac{71}{24}$.** Solve: $\frac{1}{2} + \frac{3}{4} + \frac{5}{6} + \frac{7}{8} = \frac{12}{24} + \frac{18}{24} + \frac{20}{24} + \frac{21}{24} = \frac{71}{24}$

4. **The correct answer is (D).** A square's perimeter is found by multiplying the length of a side of the square by 4. The area of a square is found by squaring the length of a side of the square.

$$\text{Perimeter} = 4s$$
$$\text{Perimeter} = 4s = 100$$
$$s = 25$$
$$\text{Area} = s^2 = 25^2 = 625$$

5. **The correct answer is (C).**

$$\frac{x^2 - 4}{x^2 - x - 2} = \frac{(x-2)(x+2)}{(x-2)(x+1)} = \frac{(x+2)}{(x+1)}$$

6. **The correct answer is (E).** Statement (1) is not enough to determine the answer. Statement (2) alone cannot determine the answer. Statements (1) and (2) together do not provide enough information to answer the question. The lowest temperature in January in Las Vegas could be determined. That's it, though. Hence, the correct answer is choice (E).

7. **The correct answer is (A).** The discount in price is $56 − $50.40 = $5.60.

$$\frac{\text{Percent}}{100} = \frac{\text{Amount of discount}}{\text{Original price}}$$

$$\frac{p}{100} = \frac{5.60}{56}$$

$$56p = 560$$

$$p = \frac{560}{56} = 10\%$$

8. **The correct answer is 87.** The average is found by adding all the scores and dividing that sum by the number of scores added.

$$\text{Average} = \frac{\text{Total of scores}}{\text{Number of scores}}$$

$$83 = \frac{T}{3}$$

$$83(3) = T$$

$$T = 249$$

$$\text{New Average} = \frac{\text{Total of first three tests } + \text{ score on fourth test}}{4}$$

$$84 = \frac{249 + f}{4}$$

$$84(4) = 249 + f$$

$$336 = 249 + f$$

$$87\% = f$$

9. **The correct answer is (E).** An isosceles right triangle has two congruent legs that form the right angle and a hypotenuse that measures $\sqrt{2}$ times the length of a congruent leg. So, if the hypotenuse measures $12\sqrt{2}$, the length of a congruent leg measures $\frac{12\sqrt{2}}{\sqrt{2}} = 12$.

10. **The correct answer is (C).**

$$\text{Area} = \frac{1}{2}(\text{base})(\text{height})$$

$$\text{Area} = \frac{1}{2}(12)(12)$$

$$\text{Area} = 72$$

11. **The correct answer is (A).**

Perimeter = the sum of the lengths of the three legs of the triangle

$$\text{Perimeter} = 12 + 12 + 12\sqrt{2}$$

$$\text{Perimeter} = 24 + 12\sqrt{2}$$

12. **The correct answer is (B).** The circumference of a circle is found by multiplying π times the diameter.

circumference = π(diameter)

circumference = $\pi(24) = 24\pi$

13. **The correct answer is (C).** Statement (1) is not enough to determine the answer. Statement (2) alone cannot determine the answer. Statements (1) and (2) together work!

$$\text{Duke} = 11 + \text{Bud}$$

$$\text{Bud} = (\frac{1}{2})(\text{Duke})$$

$$\text{Duke} = 11 + (\frac{1}{2})(\text{Duke})$$

That's it! Duke's age can be found, using both statements.

14. **The correct answer is (D).** The sale price is 88% (100% − 12%) of the original price.

$$\frac{\text{Percent}}{100} = \frac{\text{Sale price}}{\text{Original price}}$$

$$\frac{88}{100} = \frac{70.40}{x}$$

$$88x = 7,040$$

$$x = \frac{7,040}{88} = 80$$

15. **The correct answer is (C).**

$$x + 3y = -k$$
$$-2 + 3(3) = -k$$
$$-2 + 9 = -k$$
$$7 = -k$$
$$-7 = k$$

$$x + 3y = -k$$
$$x + 3y = -(-7)$$
$$x + 3y = 7$$
$$-1 + 3y = 7$$
$$3y = 8$$
$$y = \frac{8}{3}$$

16. **The correct answer is (D).** Myrtle needed to purchase 18 (20 − 2) gallons of gas to fill her tank. Dividing the amount she pays by the number of gallons she purchases gives the cost per gallon.

$$\frac{59.22}{18} = 3.29$$

The only answer that starts that way is choice (D), and it is the correct answer.

17. **The correct answer is (D).** The median is the middle score, once the values are arranged from smallest to largest: 32%, 70%, 72%, 86%, 91%, and 97%. There is no middle score, so the median is found by averaging the two middle scores:

$$\frac{72+86}{2} = \frac{158}{2} = 79$$

18. **The correct answers are (A) and (E).** 17 is prime. 21 is not prime because it is 3 times 7. 33 is not prime because it equals 3 times 11. 57 is not prime because it equals 3 times 19. 61 is prime. 63 is not prime because it equals 3 times 21. 72 is not prime because it equals 2 times 36.

19. **The correct answer is (E).**

$$x^2 - 5x + 4 = 0$$
$$(x-1)(x-4) = 0$$
$$x = 1 \qquad x = 4$$

The largest solution to $x^2 - 5x + 4 = 0$ is 4. The smallest solution to $x^2 - 5x + 4 = 0$ is 1. The square root of 4 is 2. The square of 1 is 1. The product of the square root of the largest solution to $x^2 - 5x + 4 = 0$ and the square of the smallest solution to $x^2 - 5x + 4 = 0$ is 2 times 1, which is 2.

20. **The correct answer is (D).**

Distinct factors are factors that do not repeat. So, factors of 16 are 1, 16, 2, 8, 4, 4. Since 4 repeats there are five distinct factors that are positive: 1, 2, 4, 8, 16.

21. **The correct answer is (C).** Statement (1) is enough to indicate that Shelba has 6 points currently. That is not enough to determine the answer. Statement (2) alone cannot determine the answer. All that gives is that Dexter has half the number of points Shelba has. That is not enough to determine the answer. Statements (1) and (2) together work! Knowing that Shelba has 6 points and Dexter has half as many as Shelba has, that indicates that Dexter has 3 points. That is enough to determine how many points Dexter would need to have as many as Shelba has.

22. **The correct answer is (C).** Bella mowed half of the lawn. At that point, she had one half left to mow. After her tea, she mowed half of the half, which is one quarter. The total lawn mowed is one half plus one quarter, which is three quarters. She needs to mow the rest: $1 - \frac{3}{4} = \frac{1}{4}$.

23. **The correct answer is (D).** Fawn charges Della 6% interest per week on the $1,250. Six percent of $1,250 = 0.06(1,250) = $75. Three times this, for the three weeks, totals $225.

24. **The correct answer is (D).** Madden bought 4 notebooks at $3.50 each for a total of $14. He bought 5 pens at $2.20 each, which total $11.00. The total of the merchandise is $14 + $11 = $25. Saving 10% is a savings of 0.10($25) = $2.50. The total charge for the merchandise, with the discount, is $25 − $2.50 = $22.50. The tax is 4%. Taking 4% of $22.50 is 0.04($22.50) = $.90. Adding the tax to the discounted merchandise total is $0.90 + $22.50 = $23.40. The amount of money Madden would get back from $30 is $30.00 − $23.40 = $6.60.

25. **The correct answer is −15.** The greatest integer less than −5 is −6. The smallest integer greater than −10 is −9. The sum of these is −6 plus −9, which is −15.

26. The correct answer is (B).

$$(4x^3 - x - 2) - (5x^3 + 6x^2 + x - 7) =$$
$$4x^3 - x - 2 - 5x^3 - 6x^2 - x + 7 =$$
$$4x^3 - 5x^3 - 6x^2 - x - x - 2 + 7 = -x^3 - 6x^2 - 2x + 5$$

27. The correct answer is (D). EACH statement ALONE is sufficient. Statement (1) is enough to indicate the total that Jasper earns per year. Statement (2) alone is enough to determine the answer. Knowing how much more Lola needs to earn and her weekly pay is enough to figure out the additional number of weeks she needs to work to match Jasper's yearly pay.

28. The correct answer is (C). Butch can order a pizza with 1 topping. He could have 6 different pizzas. Butch can order a pizza with 2 toppings: $\frac{6 \times 5}{2 \times 1} = \frac{30}{2} = 15$ pizzas. The division by 2 is necessary because the order in which the toppings are chosen does not matter. Butch can order a pizza with 3 toppings: $\frac{6 \times 5 \times 4}{3 \times 2 \times 1} = \frac{120}{6} = 20$ pizzas. The division by 6 is necessary because the order in which the toppings are chosen does not matter. The grand total number of pizzas that Butch can order is $6 + 15 + 20 = 41$ pizzas.

29. The correct answer is (B). $\dfrac{a^2 bc - a^3}{c - b} = \dfrac{(-1)^2(2) - (-1)^3}{-3 - 2} = \dfrac{2 - (-1)}{-3 - 2} = -\dfrac{3}{5}$

30. The correct answer is (B).

$$x + 2y = -4$$
$$4x - 2y = -11$$

Add the two equations:

$$5x = -15$$
$$x = -3$$

Substitute into the first equation:

$$x + 2y = -4$$
$$-3 + 2y = -4$$
$$2y = -1$$
$$y = \frac{-1}{2}$$

31. The correct answer is (C).

Quantity A: $2y = 2\left(\dfrac{-1}{2}\right) = -1$

Quantity B: $\dfrac{1}{3}x = \dfrac{1}{3}(-3) = -1$

32. The correct answer is (C). Each day, Milly travels 32 miles. Each week, she makes this round-trip five times, for a total of 160 miles. Her car gets 10 miles per gallon, so she uses 16 gallons per week. Paying $3.35 per gallon for 16 gallons costs $53.60.

33. The correct answer is (E). Statement (1) is not enough information to answer the question. Statement (2) alone is not enough to determine the answer. Even statements (1) and (2) together are not enough to answer the question.

34. The correct answer is (A).

Quantity A: $\frac{2}{3}$ of $15 = \frac{2}{3}(\frac{15}{1}) = \frac{30}{3} = 10$

Quantity B: 66% of $15 = 0.66(15) = 9.9$

35. The correct answer is (A). The number of degrees in an n-sided regular polygon is $180(n-2)$. There are 180 degrees in any triangle. There are $n-2$ triangles formed by an n-sided regular polygon. A regular pentagon has five sides, so the number of degrees in a regular pentagon is $180(5-2) = 180(3) = 540$. A regular quadrilateral has four sides, so the number of degrees in a regular quadrilateral is $180(4-2) = 180(2) = 360$. The difference is $540 - 360 = 180$.

The number of degrees in one interior angle of an n-sided regular polygon is $\frac{180(n-2)}{n}$. The number of degrees in one interior angle of a regular decagon is $\frac{180(10-2)}{10} = \frac{180(8)}{10} = 18(8) = 144$. The sum of the exterior angles of a polygon is 360. Each exterior angle of a regular decagon measures $\frac{360}{10} = 36$ degrees. The difference is $144 - 36 = 108$. The correct answer is choice (A).

36. The correct answer is (B). Zip is one of the 40% who travel by train to work. The others, 60%, drive to work.

$$\frac{\text{Percent}}{100} = \frac{\text{Part}}{\text{Whole}}$$

$$\frac{60}{100} = \frac{114}{x}$$

$$60x = 11,400$$

$$x = \frac{11,400}{60} = 190$$

37. The correct answer is (D).

$$\text{dogs} = d = 3c$$
$$\text{canaries} = c$$
$$\text{fish} = f = d - 2$$
$$\text{dogs + canaries + fish} = 26$$
$$d + c + f = 26$$
$$3c + c + (d-2) = 26$$
$$3c + c + (3c-2) = 26$$
$$7c - 2 = 26$$
$$7c = 28$$
$$c = 4$$
$$f = d - 2 = 3c - 2 = 3(4) - 2 = 12 - 2 = 10$$

38. The correct answer is (D).

$$1 \text{ angle} = m = 4 + 2s$$
$$\text{largest angle } = l = 3s - 4$$
$$\text{smallest angle } = s$$
$$m + l + s = 180$$
$$(4 + 2s) + (3s - 4) + s = 180$$
$$6s = 180$$
$$s = 30$$
$$l = 3s - 4 = 3(30) - 4 = 90 - 4 = 86$$

39. The correct answer is (B).

$$\frac{\text{Percent}}{100} = \frac{\text{Part}}{\text{Whole}}$$
$$\frac{10}{100} = \frac{x}{50}$$
$$100x = 500$$
$$x = 5$$

After the sale, the item cost \$45, because \$50 − \$5 = \$45.

$$\frac{\text{Percent}}{100} = \frac{\text{Part}}{\text{Whole}}$$
$$\frac{10}{100} = \frac{x}{45}$$
$$100x = 450$$
$$x = 4.50$$

The price was raised \$4.50 after a week, putting the price at \$45 + \$4.50, for a new price of \$49.50.

40. The correct answer is (B). Statement (1) is not enough information to answer the question. Statement (2) alone is enough to determine the answer. Since there are five elements, the two missing elements must each be 15. The set is complete. Knowing all five elements, the median can each be determined. Thus, the answer to the question can be determined.

AMIT SOOD | sports business major

BE A BILLIKEN

Find out how the breadth and depth of the fully accredited undergraduate and graduate programs at Saint Louis University's **JOHN COOK SCHOOL OF BUSINESS** will give you the knowledge and tools necessary for success in today's global and highly technical business world.

— + Visit **BeABilliken.com** for more information on our undergraduate business programs and to see what life is like as a Billiken.

To learn about our graduate business programs, attend an open house or visit **gradbiz.slu.edu.** + ————

SAINT LOUIS UNIVERSITY

CONCENTRATIONS IN THE JOHN COOK SCHOOL OF BUSINESS

Accounting

Economics

Entrepreneurship

Finance

Information Technology Management

International Business

Leadership and Change Management

Marketing

Sports Business

GRADUATE PROGRAMS IN THE JOHN COOK SCHOOL OF BUSINESS

One-Year MBA

Part-Time MBA

Master of Supply Chain Management

Master of Accounting

Executive Master of International Business

Post-MBA Certificate

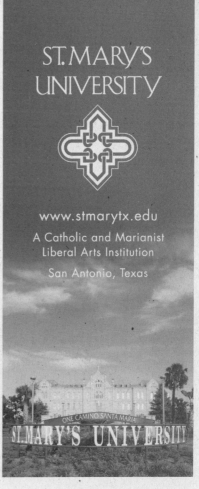

Learn from a National Leader in
Population Health

Jefferson School of Population Health

- **Master of Public Health (MPH); CEPH accredited**

- **PhD in Population Health Sciences**

Online programs

- **Master of Science in Health Policy (MS-HP)**

- **Master of Science in Healthcare Quality and Safety (MS-HQS)**

- **Master of Science in Chronic Care Management (MS-CCM)**

- **Certificates in Public Health, Health Policy, Healthcare Quality and Safety, Chronic Care Management**

Population health – putting health and health care together

215-503-0174
www.jefferson.edu/population_health/ads.cfm

Jefferson®
School of Population Health

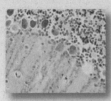

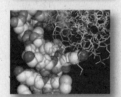
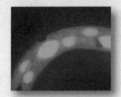
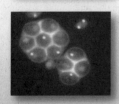

NOTES

NOTES

NOTES

NOTES

NOTES

NOTES